RACE IN CONTEMPORARY BRAZIL

From Indifference to Inequality

RACE IN CONTEMPORARY
BRAZIL

Edited by

Rebecca Reichmann

The Pennsylvania State University Press
University Park, Pennsylvania

Library of Congress Cataloging-in-Publication Data

Race in contemporary Brazil : from indifference to inequality / edited
   by Rebecca Reichmann.
         p.   cm.
      Includes bibliographical references (p.   –   ) and index.
      ISBN 0-271-01905-0 (cloth : alk. paper)
      1. Blacks—Brazil—Social conditions.   2. Women, Black—Brazil
   —Social conditions.   3. Brazil—Race relations.   4. Racism—Brazil.
   I. Reichmann, Rebecca Lynn.
   F2659.N4R245   1999
   305.896'081—dc21   98-37292
                                                              CIP

It is the policy of The Pennsylvania State University Press to use acid-free paper for
the first printing of all clothbound books. Publications on uncoated stock satisfy the
minimum requirements of American National Standard for Information Sciences—
Permanence of Paper for Printed Library Materials, ANSI Z39.48-1992.

CONTENTS

Tables and Figures   vii
Acknowledgments   xi
Acronyms   xiii
Introduction   1
   Rebecca Reichmann

1   Color in the Brazilian Census   37
   Edith Piza and Fúlvia Rosemberg

2   Race and Educational Opportunity in Brazil   53
   Nelson do Valle Silva and Carlos A. Hasenbalg

3   Racial Differences in Income: Brazil, 1988   67
   Nelson do Valle Silva

4   Racial Inequalities in the Labor Market and the Workplace   83
   Nadya Araújo Castro and Antonio Sérgio Alfredo Guimarães

5   Silent Conflict: Discriminatory Practices and Black Responses
in the Workplace   109
   Maria Aparecida Silva Bento

6   Racial Discrimination and Criminal Justice in São Paulo   123
   Sérgio Adorno

7   Measures to Combat Discrimination and Racial Inequality
in Brazil   139
   Antonio Sérgio Alfredo Guimarães

8 Struggling in Paradise: Racial Mobilization and the Contemporary Black Movement in Brazil   155
   Luiz Claudio Barcelos

9 Struggling for a Place: Race, Gender, and Class in Political Elections in Brazil   167
   Cloves Luiz Pereira Oliveira

10 Racial Inequality in the Lives of Brazilian Women   179
   Ana Maria Goldani

11 The Soda Cracker Dilemma: Reproductive Rights and Racism in Brazil   195
   Edna Roland

12 Sterilization and Race in São Paulo   207
   Elza Berquó

13 Black Women's Identity in Brazil   217
   Sueli Carneiro

14 Women Workers of Rio: Laborious Interpretations of the Racial Condition   229
   Caetana Maria Damasceno

   References   251
   About the Authors   273
   Index   277

TABLES AND FIGURES

Tables

2.1 Years of Schooling Completed for Individuals Ages 7 to 24, by Color (Brazil, 1982) 56

2.2 Individuals Ages 7 to 14 Who Never Attended School, by Per Capita Family Income and Race (Brazil, 1982) 59

2.3 Individuals Ages 7 to 24 Who Attended the First Three Years of Primary School, by Race and Per Capita Median Family Income (Brazil, 1982) 60

2.4 Delayed Progress in Schooling for Individuals, Ages 7 to 14 Who Have Attended School, by Race (Brazil, 1982) 62

3.1 Decomposition of Average Income Differentials, by Color 71

3.2 Distribution of Color Groups, by Metropolitan Area 72

4.1 Migration and Whitening in Industry Overall and in Petrochemicals in Metropolitan Salvador, Bahia, from December 1987 to September 1989 87

4.2 Education, Gender, and Color in Industry Overall and Petrochemicals in Metropolitan Salvador, Bahia 91

4.3 Composition of Employees by Sex and Color in Two Petrochemical Plants in Camaçari 94

4.4   Percentage of Employees, Women, and Whites in Two Petro-
      chemical Plants   95

4.5   Distribution of Employees, by Occupation and Color, in the
      Private Plant   97

4.6   Distribution of Employees, by Occupation and Color, in the
      State-Owned Plant   98

4.7   Index of Disparities Among Color Groups in Access to Occu-
      pational Groups in the Two Plants   99

4.8   Average Time in Years Between Promotions for Process Op-
      erators and Office Workers in the Private Company, by Place
      of Origin   103

4.9   Average Length of Interval between Promotions, Number of
      Promotions, and Number of High-Level Positions Occupied
      by High-Level Personnel, by Color   104

6.1   Status of Defendants Tried for Aggravated Robbery, by Race,
      According to Incarceration, Municipality of São Paulo (1990)   132

6.2   Defendants Tried For Aggravated Robbery, by Race, Accord-
      ing to Confession, Municipality of São Paulo (1990)   132

6.3   Defendants Tried for Aggravated Robbery, by Race, Accord-
      ing to Type of Defense Representation, Municipality of São
      Paulo (1990)   136

7.1   The Brazilian Debate About Affirmative Action   151

10.1 Demographic Profile of Brazilian Women, by Color (1980–
      1984)   183

10.2 Distribution of Brazilian Women Ages 15 to 54, by Marital
      Status and Color (1980–1984)   183

10.3 Distribution of Women by Age upon Reaching Motherhood
      (Brazil, 1984)   186

10.4 Marital Status of Brazilian Women, According to Color and
      Cohort   189

11.1 Brazilian Population in Absolute and Percentage Figures, by
      Color/Race (1980 and 1990)   199

11.2 Growth Rate of the Brazilian Population Between 1980 and
      1990, by Color/Race   200

12.1   Prevalence of Contraceptive Use by Women of Reproductive
       Age, by Color (1986)   209

12.2   Prevalence of Contraceptive Use by Women of Reproductive
       Age, by Education and Color (Greater Metropolitan São
       Paulo, 1986)   210

12.3   Women Ages 15 to 50 Using a Contraceptive Method, by
       Color (São Paulo, 1992)   212

12.4   Percentage of Women Sterilized, by Education and Color (São
       Paulo, 1992)   212

12.5   Percentage of Women Sterilized, by Income Level and Color
       (São Paulo, 1992)   213

Figure

8.1   Map of Racial Mobilization in Brazil, 1920s–1980s   162

ACKNOWLEDGMENTS

I am grateful to Lynn Walker Huntley and Bradford Smith for their support for this project through an initial grant from the Ford Foundation. Lynn Huntley has also become an inspiring counselor, mentor, and cherished friend. I wish also to thank, for their aid and advice, Janice Rocha, Dr. Ruth Simms Hamilton, Maria Aparecida Bento, Dr. Sonia Alvarez, Stuart Burden, Dr. Antônio Sérgio Guimarães, and Dr. Melissa Nobles. I wish also to thank for their support, the staff of the Centro de Estudos Afro-Asiáticos (Center of Afro-Asian Studies) of the Candido Mendes University Institute in Rio de Janeiro. Tana Van Dyke Silva deserves my special appreciation for her generous assistance with translating and editing. Dr. Peter Smith of the Center for Iberian and Latin American Studies (CILAS) of the University of California, San Diego, graciously invited me to join CILAS as a Visiting Scholar in 1995, offering me spectacular office space and intellectual inspiration over several years as this volume developed. CILAS staff Shelley Marquez, Julia Adame, Wendy Nicodemus, and Florencia Quintanar were invariably helpful to me and loving *tias* to my son Frank. I am especially indebted to Patricia Rosas, whose meticulous editing enabled the project to come to fruition, and to Sandy Thatcher at Pennsylvania State University Press who guided the manuscript through its final stages. Each of the authors merits special thanks for their patience and flexibility through the many drafts and revisions of their chapters.

Finally, Ricardo Tavares shares my life project and is equally responsible for the small victory this volume represents for all Brazilians.

ACRONYMS

CEERT   Center for the Study of Labor Relations and Inequality (Centro de Estudos das Relações do Trabalho e Desigualdades)

CGT   General Confederation of Workers (Confederação Geral de Trabalhadores)

CNPq   National Council of Scientific and Technological Development (Conselho Nacional de Desenvolvimento Científico e Tecnológico)

CUT   Central Union of Workers (Central Única dos Trabalhadores)

DIEESE   State Intersindical Department for Socioeconomic Studies (Departamento Intersindical de Estudos Sócio-econômicos)

FNB   Brazilian Black Front (Frente Negra Brasileira)

IBGE   Brazilian Institute of Geography and Statistics (Instituto Brasileiro de Geografia e Estatística)

ILO   International Labour Organisation

IUPERJ   University Institute for Research of Rio de Janeiro

LNCC   National Laboratory of Scientific Computation (Laboratório Nacional de Computacão Científica)

MNU   United Black Movement (Movimento Negro Unificado)

NGO   Nongovernmental Organization

PAISM   Program of Integral Assistance to Women's Health (Programa de Assistência Integral de Saúde da Mulher)

PCB   Brazilian Communist Party (Partido Comunista Brasileiro)

PDT   Democratic Workers Party (Partido Democrático Trabalhista)

PED   Research on Employment and Unemployment (Pesquisa de Emprego e Desemprego)

PMDB   Brazilian Democratic Movement Party (Partido do Movimento Democrático Brasileiro)

PNAD   National Household Survey (Pesquisa Nacional por Amostragem de Domicílios)

PPB   Brazilian Popular Party (Partido Popular Brasileiro)

PSP   Social Progressive Party (Partido Social Progressista)

PT   Workers Party (Partido dos Trabalhadores)

PTB   Brazilian Workers' Party (Partido Trabalhista Brasileiro)

SEADE   State Foundation for Data Analysis (Fundação Sistema Estadual de Análise de Dados)

TEN   Black Experimental Theatre (Teatro Experimental do Negro)

TRE   Bahian Regional Electoral Tribunal (Tribunal Regional Eleitoral da Bahia)

UNESCO   United Nations Economic and Social Council

INTRODUCTION

Rebecca Reichmann

In 1992, when this volume was first conceived, almost nothing written by Brazilians themselves had been published in English to explain why Brazil had achieved longstanding fame as a "racial democracy."[1] Brazilians, as well as the thousands of foreigners fascinated with all things Brazilian, have tenaciously hailed the country as a haven of racial reconciliation and affinity. Today in Brazil, the press and academics are only beginning to debate diversity, affirmative action, reverse discrimination, color-blind equal opportunity, and difference. But in the international debates raging over equality and difference, Brazilian voices, particularly Afro-Brazilian voices, have not registered. This has occurred partly because their work has been available only in Portuguese. But there is another cause: the Brazilian myth of racial democracy has denied the existence of difference and stifled racial debates and mobilization in Brazil.[2]

1. Fontaine (1985) contains three chapters written by Brazilian authors, and a Brazilian and an American co-authored a 1988 review of demographic indicators of racial inequality (Wood and Carvalho 1988). Since 1992 Brazilians gradually have been adding to the English language literature on race in Brazil, including Carneiro, "Defining Black Feminism" (1995); Hasenbalg and Silva, "Racial Inequalities in Brazil and Throughout Latin America: Timid Responses to Disguised Racism" (1996); Ribeiro, "Diversity and Assimilation in Brazil" (in James 1996); Vieira, "Brazil" (1995); and Guimarães, "Racism and Anti-Racism in Brazil: A Postmodern Perspective"; Heringer, "Introduction to the Analysis of Racism"; and Vieira, "Black Resistance in Brazil: A Matter of Necessity" (all in Bowser 1995).

2. As Anne Phillips has observed with regard to gender, difference must be recognized before equality can be achieved, but "difference" is constantly reconstructed and renegotiated with other social actors, in ways that can erase "essential" identities, risking an erosion of solidarity.

This volume brings an array of Brazilian voices to the international debate on racial difference and equality. These voices are not driven by a single theoretical concern; instead, the volume is meant to inform the worldwide dialogue on multiracial (and now in South Africa, "nonracial") polities by introducing greater nuance and cultural sensitivity to interpretations of the unique construction and functions of "race" in Brazil.[3] The contributors focus on policy-relevant areas: color-classification systems; access to education, employment, and health; inequality in the judiciary and politics; and black women's status and roles.

Color Perceptions:
Colonization, Consciousness, and Contradiction

Over the last two centuries, dozens of North American and European travelers, scholars, and artists have discovered apparently harmonious relationships among Brazilians: the descendants of African slaves, indigenous peoples, and European immigrants. Seeking if not a utopian unity among races, at least relief from the anguished state of race relations in their own milieux, these visitors recorded their interpretations of the singular character of racial identity, color consciousness, and interracial relationships in Brazil.

Theodore Roosevelt, for example, toured Latin America in 1913, just twenty-five years after abolition, and joined the throngs who touted Brazil's national ideology: "Brazil is absorbing the Negro race; there is no color bar to advancement, there is no social bar to advancement" (Roosevelt 1914). Black North Americans emphasized Brazil's model of equality almost as if they had found a promised land.[4] In 1942 E.

Nevertheless, difference is the basis for identity and thus for solidarity and mobilization: "It is important . . . that this . . . dynamic sense of differences as changing, recomposing, even dissolving, should not lead us to a new version of the older myths of homogeneity. Particular differences can and do go away; solidarities can and are forged across what looked like formidable barriers" (Phillips 1993, 161).

3. The following classifications are the three color denominations used by the Brazilian national census bureau and, as a result, by most social scientists: *branco* (white), *preto* (black) and *pardo* (brown). *Moreno* (swarthy complexioned, from "moor") is a popular term, considered more tactful than *preto*, *pardo*, or *mulato*. *Negro* is the Brazilian term negotiated by activists as the signifier/signified of a race-conscious subject (equivalent to "African-American" in the United States).

4. Hellwig 1992, 44–50. In the early part of the century, black North Americans marveled at what appeared to be equal opportunity for all. L. H. Stinson, an African-American physician, wrote after a trip to Brazil: "There is absolutely no color line. The native Brazilians are mixed Spanish, Portuguese, and Indians. Therefore some are dark, some bright and some very fair. . . .

Franklin Frazier became an important African-American advocate of Brazil's racial "solution" of miscegenation and social integration: "Color distinctions and prejudices against the blacks are seemingly absent . . . from the mind of the masses. . . . In Brazil there is no stigma attached to Negro blood. *One drop of Negro blood* does not make a person a Negro and condemn him to become a member of a lower caste. . . . The Brazilian Negro . . . first of all is a Brazilian. . . . He has faith in the justice of the courts, and he is convinced that his abilities and achievements will be recognized" (Hellwig 1992, 133, 123, 125).

If the North Americans revealed their obsessions by interpreting Brazil's model of appropriation as "equality," the French praised Brazil's cultural and physical convergences, framed in language reflecting their own fascination with the erotic fetish they imagined to be Africa. Anthropologist Roger Bastide's 1960 analysis stressed that Brazil's syncretic values and religious practices, even a common identity, had emerged from the constant close proximity of blacks and whites over generations:·

> [T]he propinquity of the races within the regime of slavery . . . enabled African culture to leave its stamp on the Luso-Brazilian civilization. The little white boy . . . had been suckled by a black nurse, who sang African lullabies as she rocked him. . . . At the age when the mind is most malleable, most susceptible to outside impressions and influences, he was impregnated with totally African values. . . . Later, when his sexual awakening began, he would watch the Negro women bathing naked in the river and wear himself out in enervating, more or less erotic games with the little black girls, finally "proving his manhood" with some black girl he happened to meet in the fields. He would have an endless series of black mistresses and father an infinite number of mulatto babies. . . . And the influence of Africa did not end when he passed from childhood to adolescence but maintained its insidious, subtle hold throughout his life, chiefly through this eroticism, this worship of the black Venus." (Bastide 1978, 69)

In the last twenty years, visitors' interpretations of the construction of race and racial dynamics have been dutifully imbued with postmodern emic sensibilities, but at the same time, they frequently (and incongru-

---

All attend the same churches and schools" (cited in Hellwig 1992, 44–46). Another African-American, E. R. James, wrote an article entitled "Brazil as I Found It," in the *Chicago Defender*, 4 June 1921: "I did my best to find some trace of prejudice among the Brazilian people, kept my eyes and ears open for it and went out of my way to look for it. But I failed to find it. It is not there" (Hellwig 1992, 47–50).

ously) assume an ironic distance. A white U.S. law professor, Joseph Page, for example, clings to the possibility of harmonious assimilation, lamenting "something unmistakably tragic in manifestations of the beginnings of racial polarization in Brazil" (1995, 83). But other observers cannot romanticize Brazil's racial "democracy." U.S. African-American political scientist Melissa Nobles, for example, deconstructs race altogether, arguing that the social functions of the officially reified color categories advance the state's interest in portraying Brazil as a country whose skin color is "lightening" (1995).

Brazil's racial self-consciousness is exquisite, especially in reflecting the gaze of these outsiders. During the 1994 carnival, for example, the Viradouro samba school sang and danced to its own image—one that had been created in the eyes of the French painter Jean-Baptiste Debret when he discovered Brazil in 1815. The contemporary samba lyric proclaimed, "Surprised was I to discover an enchanted paradise where Indians, Whites, and Blacks live in perfect racial harmony, living proof of the true nature of this tropical land" (see Glèlè-Ahanhanzo 1995, 11).

Being known to the world only through the other's eyes, whether as an ideal (as in the carnival song) or a travesty, mirrors Brazil's colonial experience: the outsider seizes power to interpret reality. While visitors' observations were initially shaped by the rhetoric of "racial democracy," Brazilians' own interpretations of racial dynamics in their nation have gradually come to reflect back the impressions recorded by foreigners. In other words, while Brazilian elites' discourse on racial democracy initially influenced visitors' impressions of the country, the Brazilian public has now come to defend that narrative by citing the outsiders as authorities!

Most Brazilians, regardless of appearance, admonish visitors that *all* Brazilians share an African racial heritage. Oddly, they may make this claim even while refusing to share an elevator with a darker-skinned person. Constant informal shifting of boundaries based on color circumscribes all aspects of social life. Daily, difference is both denied and affirmed, as Roberto Da Matta explains: "In a society whose daily life is founded on inequality, the experience of different ethnicities does not spill out of the personal and quotidian sphere and thus allows for the creation of a fable that treats the three races as complementary and, at this level equivalent. The result is the 'equal but different' principle that Otávio Velho (1985) suggests might be the touchstone of an *individualist* socio-logic."[5]

---

5. Da Matta 1985, 274. Da Matta diverges slightly from Velho's formula, proposing instead a *relational* logic in which people are "together and differentiated in a complementary fashion" (274, italics mine).

Like shifting sand, individuals may change identities, foregrounding different selves depending on contextual demands. Anthropologist Livio Sansone (1992, 165) found among Bahians he interviewed that

> the same person could use different (color) terms during the same interview, generally using the term *negro* only at the end of the interview after the antiracist framework of the research and the type of language preferred by the interviewer had become clear. . . . [T]he same dark-skinned person could be seen and feel different ways at different times. A man could be a "worker" in the factory, *preto* on his birth certificate, *moreno* or *escuro* [dark] with friends on the street and *negro* during carnival or in the *bloco afro.*

The metaphor of shifting sands applies equally to Brazil's racial identity and to its self-understanding with regard to racial discrimination. In a 1995 national survey conducted by Datafolha, a national polling institute, 89 percent of those self-identifying as white agreed that whites harbor racial prejudice against blacks, but only 11 percent of the whites admitted to being prejudiced themselves. The contradiction, stated in the Datafolha report's subtitle, "Brazilians Deny Racism That They Know Exists" ("Brasileiro não assume racismo que afirma existir") is a perfect statement about how the Brazilian public privately draws the color line while affirming the ideal of racial democracy (Datafolha 1995, 2).

Earlier in this century, Brazil's explicit "whitening" policy was intended to erase blacks through absorption (Skidmore 1974, 200–18), but blacks have refused to disappear and are painfully present among Brazil's poorest citizens. In 1990, 36 percent of all *pretos* earned less than US$100 per month, and the average wage for black males was 40 percent of the average wage for white males. Black women's wages were even lower—25 percent of white males' wages (Boletim Estatístico 1996). When confronted with the fact of black poverty, however, Brazilian elites turn to denial and disguise, appropriating Afro-Brazilian experience (i.e., "culture") as their own. This device, designed to avoid social polarization, requires whites to engage in ritualized roles that gush with Brazil's traditional cordiality and emphasize a mediating common ground—a role filled nicely by the pervasive color term, *moreno.* Roberto Da Matta has described this phenomenon as an *encompassing* approach to conflict, intrinsic to the national character.[6] I experienced this in my first visits

6. Da Matta draws attention to the "hidden motive" of relationships among political parties, social categories, or interest groups; he identifies affective loyalties among elites as a "third party" that can "if not encompass the other two, at least postpone conflicts and their resolution or make ideological disputes secondary" (1995, 284). I propose that this approach to conflict

with Brazilians. In 1988, while meeting with a progressive organization engaged in a women's rights campaign in Rio de Janeiro, I asked if there were any black women involved in the project. The surprised response from a woman who looked just like me (I am of Irish/German background) was "But we are all black!"

Yet race remains one of the most contested territories in contemporary Brazil. Elites and the state portray racial dynamics in reference to what they are not. By drawing comparisons with bipolar or tripolar polities divided by crisp color lines—such as in the tormented United States or South Africa—Brazilian elites have made extensive use of the media to point out exactly what Brazilians have tried to avoid and why they have always insisted on official color blindness. The Rodney King incident in Los Angeles, for example, had extensive coverage in the Brazilian press, which lectured on the need for North Americans to draw "lessons" from Brazil's approach to race relations. Paradoxically, however, embedded in the righteousness of the Brazilian "solution" is a racially charged anxiety. In an analysis of the so-called *arrastões* (dragnets) of black youth that allegedly terrorized Rio beach-goers during Afro-Brazilian Benedita da Silva's 1992 campaign for mayor, a popular columnist compared Rio to post–Rodney King Los Angeles: "Is Rio turning into a species of Los Angeles, where things are run by thousands of gangs that dominate the streets?" (A. Silva 1992, 29).[7]

Interpretations of Brazil's complex racial dynamics, offered here by Brazilians themselves, assume basic categories of analysis that may be unfamiliar to the outsider. This introduction explores them in four sections—The Shifting Color Line and the Myth of Racial Democracy, The Political Construction of the Negro, Black Movement Politics and the State's Response, and To Target or Not to Target: Off the Policy Hook?—which begin a translation process by providing background to debates in Brazil. Brazilian analysts have been unavoidably influenced by observing other polities as well as by the reflections of foreign writers; therefore, the framework for internal dialogue is responsive to what has now become transnational discourse. We will see how the mirroring experience has elicited a defense against imposed terminologies and cate-

---

mediates potential confrontations between non-elite blacks and white elites as well. Following Gilberto Freyre, the image of "one big happy family" is summoned to reproduce the affective loyalties present among elites.

7. During Benedita da Silva's 1992 campaign, the media coverage insinuated that if an Afro-Brazilian woman—a *favelada* (slum dweller) herself—took charge of the city, the *favelados* would descend from their confines on Rio's hilltops and take over the city. This imagery was so vivid in the popular imagination that the epithet *"arrastão"* was hurled at me as I jogged on the beach wearing a T-shirt bearing Benedita da Silva's name.

gories, inevitably framed by those very terms, beginning with the biological notion of race.

The Shifting Color Line and the Myth of Racial Democracy

The color line is perhaps the zone of greatest contention dividing those who believe that Brazil is a racial democracy from those who perceive discrimination based on color. In Brazil, color is the dominant category, while the idea of "racial" or biological ancestry is underplayed, at least by elites.[8] In the past, Brazil has had its share of scientific racists,[9] but in this century a conscious national project has proposed skin color, rather than race, as the marker of difference and has sought in the endless gradations of skin color the key to national identity.

In official accounts, the fluid color line flows directly from miscegenation. Whereas in other polities segregation was the rule, in Brazil intermarriage was actively encouraged. The idea of a miscegenized Brazilian identity as an alternative to "racial" identities is even found in pre-abolition public discourse. Historian Thomas Skidmore cites abolitionists who lauded miscegenation as early as 1887 (1974, 24). José do Patrocínio was among them: "We have been able to fuse all races into a single native population because Portuguese colonization assimilated the savage races instead of trying to destroy them" (do Patrocínio 1887).

By the 1920s, theories of scientific racism had become official ideology. The Brazilian state endorsed miscegenation as a means of "bettering" the race when it published, along with the 1920 census data, an analysis by Oliveira Vianna that concluded that the population was indeed "whitening." Vianna suggested that "pure" black and indigenous racial elements had to be diluted through intermarriage with whites in order to "strengthen" the race. Anthropologist Gilberto Freyre and others opposed this view, suggesting that African and indigenous "blood" gave Brazilian hybridity its resilience (Skidmore 1974, 201–3).

---

8. *Raça* (race) or ethnic identity is now being resuscitated by activists who are connecting to their African identity (Maggie 1996, 225–34; Maggie 1989a, 1–28).

9. Scientific racism was popular in Brazil from the early 1900s to as late as the 1980s, when state officials in São Paulo proposed a campaign to limit the fertility of black women. Over the course of the twentieth century, significant intellectual resources were devoted to proving the hypothesis that the "superior" white race would suffer degenerative effects as a result of miscegenation with Africans (see Skidmore 1974; R. N. Rodriguez 1945; Vianna 1934; N. L. Stepan 1991).

In the following decades, Freyre formalized the peculiarly Brazilian notion that miscegenation would create a unique *moreno* "meta-race," which would unify the country. Freyre's proposition of a noble, elevated meta-race may be understood as a search for his own identity in the mirror of European culture. As a product of the decadent Northeastern plantation economy, Freyre portrayed Brazilian plantation communities as extended families in which slaves and masters were interdependent and even interrelated—a system much more benign, according to Freyre, than other slave societies.[10] The notion of a racial democracy rooted in this agrarian culture captured the national imagination and still prevails today, as the 1995 Datafolha survey results demonstrate.

For generations the appropriation of Africanness by all of Brazil has effectively denied racial difference, enabling elites to maintain an official discourse of racial harmony and equality. Today classroom texts portray African culture, along with indigenous and colonial Portuguese legacies, as consolidated within a single common national identity. Even Fernando Henrique Cardoso, in his 1994 presidential campaign, claimed to be a *mulatinho* (a little mulatto) with "one foot in the kitchen" (*Folha de São Paulo,* 31 May 1994).

But paradoxically, this embracing of African identity is sustained by taking refuge in infinitely variegated color classifications, which amounts to a denial of racial difference. The spectrum of classifications distances individuals from Africanness. Sueli Carneiro (1996), among others, has noted this irony: "A national study in 1976 found 135 different terms by which blacks identified themselves. Each of these terms reflected a desire to be identified as 'not totally black,' or 'almost white,' thus diminishing the social negativity that their African blood conferred in the country with the largest black population outside of Africa."[11] UN Rapporteur Maurice Glèlè-Ahanhanzo also observed that when subjects were asked to identify their color in the 1991 national census, more than a hundred shades of color were "used to describe themselves, out of a desire to distance themselves as far as possible from the colour black" (1995, 12).

---

10. Published in 1933, Freyre's *Casa Grande e Senzala: Formação da Família Brasileira sob o Regime Econômico Patriarcal* (The Masters and Slaves) countered the scientific racism of the period.

11. Carneiro 1996, 221. Carneiro refers to the 1976 PNAD conducted by the Brazilian Institute of Geography and Statistics, in which a sample of 50,000 respondents was asked to self-identify their "color or race" using no predetermined categories. The 1976 PNAD played a critical role in the development of social science research on race in Brazil because it was the first major official survey that tabulated race (color) data so that it could be analyzed by the public. However, distribution of that tabulation was delayed for many years.

As one of the social scientists participating in a series of studies spon-sored by UNESCO on Brazilian race relations, Marvin Harris found over forty different color classifications, which he interpreted as avoid-ance of identification as black. He surmised that "as far as actual behav-ior is concerned, races do not exist for Brazilians" (1952, 47–81). Color identifications are fluid, shifting from one generation to another and even among siblings. A single individual may assume different color clas-sifications over time, as Sansone suggested. "Money whitens" has been a common expression for generations in Brazil, reflecting the belief that, as a darker-skinned person moves up the social ladder by obtaining educa-tion or wealth or by marrying a lighter-skinned person, he or she is treated with more respect and accepted in social spaces reserved for lighter-skinned individuals.

Demographers Wood and Carvalho (1988) suspected that individuals might reclassify themselves as their social status rises. They analyzed Brazilian census data from 1950 to 1980 and found that the number of nonwhites counted in the 1980 census was lower than predicted statisti-cally. Although these results confirmed their "migration" hypothesis, the tendency to "whiten" was not as widespread as expected. Nelson do Valle Silva also tested for individual shifts in color identification, using data from the 1976 Pesquisa Nacional por Amostragem de Domicílios (the National Household Survey, PNAD). In examining those who self-identified as *moreno* in the PNAD's open-ended interviews, Silva found that, when choosing between "white," "*pardo*," and "*preto*" in the closed-item census question, 22 percent claimed they were white, and an-other 8 percent claimed they were *preto* (1996, 91). Based on these find-ings, Silva warns that the move now under way to replace the *"pardo"* category with *"moreno"* in the census would further muddy the already obscure distinctions in census classifications.[12]

Brazil's political system features what Da Matta has described as a cul-tural preference for resolving conflict through "encompassing" accom-modation. In the wake of the authoritarian regime, the Brazilian government encouraged the proliferation of political parties to represent a plurality of interests as a means of diffusing conflict and ensuring that political activity remained within a democratic framework. Today there are twenty-seven registered political parties, and although this fractured party structure serves to represent a plurality of interests, it also pro-duces ineffectual parties and a weakened party system. I suggest that, just

12. See also Harris et al. (1993) and Telles (1993) for a discussion of the pros and cons of re-placing *pardo* with *moreno* in the census.

as a context of multiple parties means political consensus is extremely difficult to negotiate, the official attempt to diffuse racial conflict by allowing racial categories to proliferate has also effectively deterred a consolidated racial identity and racial mobilization.

Elites' support for a fluid color-classification system has been buttressed by rhetoric promoting a color-blind society. Activists claim that the fluid color line is an elitist ploy to reconfigure markers of social relations constantly, thereby impeding race-based policies or measures (da Cunha, 1996). By creating a new census category, official sanction for a shift to the popular and, to use Da Matta's term, "encompassing" *moreno* category could finally put to rest any stirrings toward race-based public policies.

In an attempt to raise consciousness about the significance of identity markers (and improve the accuracy of data on Brazil's racial stratification), activists and researchers organized a mass-media campaign to prevent statistical migration to the white category during the collection of the 1991 census. Thirty thousand posters, flyers, and television advertisements used a clever play on words that urged census respondents: "Don't 'pass' for white! Answer using good sense" (Não deixe sua cor passar em branco: Responda com bom (c)senso). The campaign materials were visually attractive and drew considerable public attention, particularly because a nationally prominent social critic, Herbert de Souza ("Betinho"), endorsed the campaign and called press conferences to explain its purposes.[13] The campaign's central goal was to counter the illusion of black social mobility that has been infused with the rhetoric of racial democracy and the belief in the fluidity of Brazil's color line.

In Brazil no legal segregation or de jure denial of opportunities to Afro-Brazilians has existed to counter the illusion of black mobility. Therefore, proposals for equal-opportunity policies appeared to be missing a political subject. Lacking a legal battleground as a site of struggle, blacks have had to construct a political identity for themselves in order to slice through the clouds obfuscating their true prospects for social mobility. As Luiz Claudio Barcelos explains in his chapter in this volume, political mobilization of Afro-Brazilians has been more about consolidating identity than about ideology.[14]

---

13. See articles in *Jornal do Brasil* 1991. Unfortunately, no evidence is available to evaluate the campaign's impact on self-identification in the 1991 census. For a critical examination of the campaign, see Nobles 1995.

14. See Escobar and Alvarez (1992, 11) for a discussion of processes of negotiation and conflict in the construction of collective identities.

The Political Construction of the *Negro*

Brazilian black movements have reaffirmed racial difference, both to reclaim African culture and to refute the official national myth that black poverty and social exclusion are unrelated to racial discrimination. This has required the construction of a new political subject, the *negro*.[15] In accord with the official version, the *negro* acknowledges and welcomes African identity, embracing Africa's cultural contributions to Brazilian life. In a departure from the received ideology, however, the *negro*'s consciousness is heightened about the significance of ethnicity (rather than color) and, regardless of his or her own status, identifies with the subjugation of black people in Brazil.

The construction of the *negro* as a political subject has required the coupled acts of self-affirmation as citizen (Afro-Brazilian contributions to national culture and religion) and of strategic exit (social exclusion as common ground for solidarity at the margins). To undertake this simultaneous double action requires Herculean effort, for each action demands shifting one's identity much more profoundly than would be the case when assuming any of the innocuous color categories.

To assert citizenship *as* exit is a tall order for anyone and is perhaps unacceptable for those who have lived a life without rights. Frequently, the departure is not only from the interior of the polity but from the narrative of one's own family as well. In Brazil those who take on the *negro* identity must confront deeply private, as well as social, vulnerabilities. Many black movement activists have described their parents' and grandparents' bewilderment when learning that their offspring identifies as *negro*. Yet the transformation is liberating—eliciting both courage and relief comparable perhaps to coming out for gays in a homophobic world.

Melissa Nobles draws that analogy less favorably by comparing the "Don't Pass for White" campaign to "outing" in the U.S. gay community. Nobles suggests that political-identity construction in each setting not only naturalizes group identities but also sacrifices individual sensibilities for political gain:

15. It is interesting to note that in an attempt to be politically correct, the Datafolha survey included *negro* in its three race/color categories—*branco* (white), *mulato*, and *negro*—rather than using the census bureau's official color categories of *branco* (white), *pardo* (brown) and *preto* (black). Datafolha replaced two of the color terms with ethnic categories (that is, *negro* and *mulato*, in place of *preto* and *pardo*), but it ignored the fact that *negro* ("black") is a socially constructed category that encompasses the *mulato*.

In Brazil and the United States, blackness and homosexuality are
highly stigmatized identities, ones that are not easily assumed or
embraced. The Brazilian black and U.S. gay/lesbian movements
have attempted to destigmatize these identities in hopes of advancing an agenda based upon them. . . . In the end, they both attempt to recast the boundaries of group membership in ways
which set the stage for demands of obligation, allegiance and accountability to a group identity. (1995, 200)

The *negro* as political subject has not yet explicitly confronted the problem of essentialism. As Nobles points out, the black movement's tendency to naturalize African origins as a primordial ground for
celebration and solidarity has not been critically appraised, generating a
dangerous precedent for speculation about *negro* life.

A recent study published in Brazil's leading journal of Afro-Brazilian
studies, *Estudos Afro-Asiáticos*, illustrates the risks of constructing the
negro as a political subject. In a long-overdue comprehensive analysis of
black voting patterns in Brazil, sociologist Reginaldo Prandi of the prestigious University of São Paulo studied the *preto* and *pardo* vote in
Brazil's 1994 national elections (Prandi 1996). Undertaking a sophisticated statistical analysis, Prandi discovered that the majority of *pretos*
and *pardos* voted for leftist candidates. He concluded, based on his finding that significant numbers of *pretos* and *pardos* also voted for right-
wing or populist candidates, however, that the strongest determinant of
black voting behavior is not ideology but blacks' identification with the
"excluded":

> *Pardos* and *pretos,* who voted on the left for Lula, were also more
> likely than whites to prefer rightist candidates. It is difficult to
> imagine that Lula's candidacy signifies a leftist choice for the
> blacks who voted for him. Lula didn't only signify an ideological
> position. He represented the choice for something out of the or-
> dinary, . . . coming from the bottom, poor, a Northeasterner, a
> worker and unschooled. Lula was the outsider. . . . It is possible
> that blacks, perpetually marginalized socially, living with preju-
> dice and racial discrimination, found in a vote for Lula the possi-
> bility of expressing a dimension of their identity in which voicing
> of protest has a place. (Prandi 1996, 75)

Prandi's paternalistic reading of the data turns on the idea of a homogenous black identity. He goes so far as to sum up black political be-

havior as that of "orphans" in search of a strong leader (1996, 75).[16] Only one study of *pardos'* and *pretos'* political behavior had appeared prior to the social construction of the *negro* in the 1970s (de Souza 1971), and it reached conclusions similar to Prandi's. With a new political subject, the potential now for deepening these trends in analyses of *"negro"* behavior is a fresh and terrifying terrain.

Another hazard in the act of constructing the *negro* subject is the charge of imitation. The blurred nature of the Brazilian color line has been called into service for decades to lend credence to claims that none of the thinking about race spawned in a bipolar context can contribute to the way Brazilians think about race. Fry (1996) speaks for many Brazilians when he critiques attempts by intellectuals and activists to transfer concepts that emerged in bipolar polities to Brazilian race relations. Among them is the idea of a black "community" encompassing all Brazilians of African descent. In particular, Fry laments that the Cardoso administration's National Human Rights Plan of 1996 caved in to a "politically correct" posture: The government plans to bring the Brazilian system of racial classification in line with that of the United States, "instruct[ing] the IBGE [responsible for collecting census data] to adopt the criterion of considering mulattos, *pardos* and *pretos* as members of the black *(negra)* population." Fry views this stroke of the pen as an exogenous racialization of Brazil's social relations and "radically distinct from the deracializing (actions) of combating racism" (1996, 16).[17]

Both caveats challenging the *negro's* status as an authentic historical subject—the naturalization of race and the subject's derivative nature—are key problems for the design of effective public policies to appraise and address the conditions of Brazil's black population. The challenge implied in these caveats cannot be underestimated, because the need to mobilize politically for targeted public policies is arguably the most important reason for having constructed the *negro* as political subject in the first place.

16. Prandi goes on to say that *"pretos* and *pardos* . . . feel profoundly incapable of organizing their own lives, [they feel] forced to seek leaders and institutions that will do this for them, either as a *dádiva* (gift or favor), with which they were familiar for so long in traditional Brazilian society, or by learning discipline that will train them to improve their lives" (1996, 76).

17. Fry quotes from the National Human Rights Plan, which President Fernando Henrique Cardoso presented in Brasília on May 13, 1996. The text of the speech is available in English from the Brazilian Ministry of Justice.

Black Movement Politics and the State's Response

After decades of organizing and political repression, today's *movimento negro* (black movement) has finally forced the Brazilian state to recognize that *negros* will stand up to be counted. Despite the general insistence that Brazil has no color line, abolition in 1888 gave birth to a robust black movement. During slavery Afro-Brazilians had spun a long tradition of cultural, religious, and recreational organization from which they wove a fabric of social cohesiveness and consciousness after abolition. A number of black newspapers were founded early in this century, and in 1918 a São Paulo paper, *O Alfinete,* was the first to denounce the myth of racial democracy: "[T]he equality and fraternity of peoples . . . which the Republic implanted as a symbol of our democracy, is, as concerns the blacks, a fiction and a lie" (cited in Andrews 1991, 139).

The first Afro-Brazilian political organization, the Frente Negra Brasileira (Brazilian Black Front) was founded in São Paulo in 1931 and expanded to the states of Minas Gerais, Espírito Santo, Bahia, and Rio Grande do Sul. The Front sponsored literacy and vocational courses, health clinics, legal aid, and credit unions for its members, and it lobbied to promote Afro-Brazilian rights. The Front ran candidates for public office but always lost, and when the Estado Novo banned all political parties in 1937, the Front was disbanded.[18]

Afro-Brazilians held important leadership posts in union and party politics in the 1940s and 1950s, although racial issues were never part of elected officials' platform. During this period blacks were actively recruited by Vargas's Brazilian Workers' Party (Partido de Trabalhadores Brasileiros, PTB), the Brazilian Communist Party (PCB), and the Social Progressive Party (PSP). Many blacks supported the PTB because of its statist social security policies and strong anti-immigrant stance, which enhanced employment prospects for blacks. Political scientist Amaury de Souza and others have associated black support for Vargas's PTB with populism because "populism is . . . an ideology of integrating blacks as *equals*" (de Souza 1971, 61–70). Union leaders affiliated with Vargas's National Labor Department, many of whom were black, were offered leadership roles in the new PTB.[19] To this day, the Democratic Workers

18. See George Reid Andrews (1991, 152–54) for the most complete history of the Brazilian Black Front available in English. See also Michael Hanchard (1994) for a comprehensive review of black movement politics.

19. For example, the black president of the Rio de Janeiro Bakers Union, Antonio José da Silva, became president of the PTB's Rio de Janeiro section and treasurer of the PTB's national board of directors. Because of the state of Rio de Janeiro's overwhelming support for Vargas,

Party (PDT), the PTB's breakaway descendent, boasts more black party officials than any other party. It was the first mainstream political party to incorporate an antiracist agenda in its publications. One of the party's leading founders, Leonel Brizola, christened PDT ideology as *"socialismo moreno"* (socialism of color) in an attempt to account for the hybrid and sovereign character of Brazil's socialist agenda (personal communications, Colonel Nazareth Cerqueira, November 1992; Joel Rufino, December 1992; and Anthony Garotinho, January 1995, Rio de Janeiro).

Perhaps because black leaders had access to political office, collective racial mobilization was not strong in the 1940s and 1950s. During the authoritarian period (1964–1985), political organizing of any kind was violently suppressed and the mere discussion of race was explicitly considered subversive and could result in detention and torture. With the beginning of the political opening in the late 1970s, a revitalized black consciousness movement emerged. It first took the form of "study" groups and cultural associations, which were less threatening to the authorities, but then it evolved into a heterogeneous mix of explicitly political organizations. Young blacks were keenly aware of the civil-rights struggles underway in the United States and identified as well with the liberation movements against colonialism in Africa. The first national-level black political organization to form after the 1937 banning of the Brazilian Black Front was the Movimento Negro Unificado (Unified Black Movement, MNU), founded in 1978.

Most black organizations during this period dedicated themselves to consciousness raising, but black movement leaders inevitably came to engage in opposition-party politics, particularly Brizola's *socialismo moreno* in Rio de Janeiro[20] and Franco Montoro's PMDB (Partido do Movimento Democrático Brasileiro) in São Paulo, which each established state-level councils to address Afro-Brazilian affairs.[21] The more

---

under the proportional electoral system, da Silva assumed national office as a federal deputy (see D'Araujo, n.d., 192).

20. Populist Leonel Brizola ostentatiously appointed several blacks to head state secretariats during both his administrations as governor of the state of Rio de Janeiro (1983–86 and 1990–94). Afro-Brazilian activist, educator, and playwright Abdias do Nascimento served as a PDT federal senator, as substitute for Darcy Ribeiro in the late 1980s and again in the mid-1990s, and was Rio's first Extraordinary Secretary for the Defense and Promotion of the Black Population of Rio de Janeiro.

21. Franco Montoro, PMDB governor of the state of São Paulo, created the state-level Council for the Participation and Development of the Black Community in 1983. Similar sections were established in the secretariats of labor and education during Montoro's administration, when many of the Afro-Brazilian cadre who have now assumed national leadership positions cut their teeth.

progressive Partido dos Trabalhadores (PT, Workers Party) established in 1979, paid less attention to racial politics, although significant black leadership emerged within the party. Luisa Erundina, PT mayor of São Paulo between 1989 and 1992, established a Coordenadoria do Negro (Municipal Department of Black Coordination) to combat racial discrimination, but the program was underfunded and fraught with leadership struggles, failing to leave any mark on the populace of São Paulo.

Movement leaders debated whether involvement in party politics compromised their autonomy. In a climate where government had for so long stood for repression and manipulation, many who accepted official positions were considered suspect. Those who maintained their autonomous status, in turn, divided into membership organizations committed to mobilizing the grassroots and groups that joined the legions of new nongovernmental organizations (NGOs) spreading throughout the country.

As the layered processes of democratic transition carried over into the 1990s, civil society gradually consolidated its autonomy, and independent black organizations continued to proliferate. Most groups carried on the tradition of consciousness raising through celebrations of Afro-Brazilian culture. Many of these organizations, such as the program developed by the Afro-Brazilian cultural organization, Olodum, that combined children's drumming instruction with supplemental classroom skills, linked educational programs to cultural strategies.[22] A much smaller number of organizations, primarily based in São Paulo, engaged in explicitly political strategies.[23] For example, the Center for the Study of Labor Relations and Inequality (Centro de Estudos das Relações do Trabalho e Desigualdades, CEERT) organized unionists against racial discrimination and trained teachers to counteract racial stereotypes. The Geledés Black Women's Institute initiated programs to bring discrimination cases to court, to document and denounce institutional racism, and to advocate for black women's health rights.

As racial politics finally began to intensify, both the left and right played more openly to the black vote. One of Brazil's leading labor confederations, the Central Única dos Trabalhadores (CUT), established a National Commission of Blacks in the early 1990s, and the Força Sindi-

---

22. For a critical analysis in English of the movement's cultural strategies, see Hanchard 1994.

23. Sonia E. Alvarez cites the false dualism in most studies of the black movement, which pit "cultural" strategies against "political" strategies. Pervasive biases in the media, the courts, the schools, and political institutions are all cultural phenomena, and actions to combat those biases are both political and cultural actions (personal communication, 1996).

cal and General Confederation of Workers (CGT) followed suit, albeit more symbolically.

The campaign for São Paulo's mayoralty in 1996 represented a significant turning point in debates about black political participation. The right went on the offensive to exploit racial politics unabashedly—which the PT had been afraid to do with Benedita da Silva's 1992 bid for Rio's mayorship. (In both cases, the PT wound up on the defensive.) Despite the fact that Paulo Maluf's Partido Popular Brasileiro (Brazilian Popular Party, PPB) had walked hand in hand with the authoritarian regime, he made a successful preemptive strike, sweeping the São Paulo municipal elections by playing the race card.[24] In the campaign, Maluf and his proxy, candidate Celso Pitta, an Afro-Brazilian economist, banked on the expectation that whites would privilege Pitta's class status over his race and that black voters would privilege race rather than voting according to their class interests. Pitta's campaign slogan was "Don't vote for me because I am black, and don't *not* vote for me because I am black." Afro-Brazilian activist Hédio Silva Jr. published an analysis of Pitta's campaign strategy in the PT newsletter: "Maluf's candidate accelerated the emergence of a phenomenon that even the most optimistic Black Movement activist would not have dared predict: illustrious reactionaries openly defending a racial vote on radio programs; poll workers inciting black voters not to 'pass'; television images of providential black hands stopping pale hands from paralyzing the city" (H. Silva Jr. 1996).

Silva observed that the right had effectively appropriated the moral high ground; the feudal had converted to the modern. Pitta accused Mayor Erundina, the white incumbent PT candidate, of not having appointed a single black to her cabinet during her administration. Erundina desperately accused Pitta of being "an [expletive] Uncle Tom" (*Folha de São Paulo*, 1996, 1, 1–5), generating the eerie scene of Paulo Maluf appearing on national TV to defend the black race.

For the first time in Brazilian history, every election poll analyzed results by race. By the runoff election millions of black votes had migrated to Pitta, and many more black activists had turned to Pitta ("pittaram") than admitted it publicly. Their hopes must have been dashed when the newly elected Pitta stated in a January 1997 press conference, "I have no color."

In the last decade, with the deepening international awareness of the African diaspora, Brazilian blacks have begun to organize transnation-

---

24. Rumors circulated in 1996 that U.S. political consultant James Carville had urged Maluf to select Pitta, predicting that a racial vote lay dormant.

ally as well as nationally. Since 1993 Brazil has collaborated in the organization and leadership of a series of regional Latin American-Caribbean conferences for Afro-Latin organizations and black women's organizations. Coordinating their activities regionally around identity is a relatively new strategy for Brazilian social movements, one that has brought the principles and language of other regions' identity politics to bear on national problems of discrimination.[25] In a clear case, the black movement for reparations in Brazil has borrowed ideology and strategy directly from its U.S. counterparts by presenting a legislative proposal to guarantee financial compensation for all descendants of slaves.[26]

Both internal mobilization strategies and transnational networking have been effective in heightening public awareness of racism in Brazil, and with the advent of revolutionary information technologies, transnational organizing strategies are becoming ever more sophisticated. Brazil-watchers frequently observe that Brazilians avoid confrontation, and Brazil's racial politics follows that pattern. The black movement's networking brings international opinion to bear on Brazil's domestic problems, using it as a "third party" that mediates by appealing to the national concern for maintaining the appearance of the national affective identity (racial democracy) in the eyes of the world (see Hess and Da Matta, eds. 1995, 270–91).

In November 1995 the black movement engaged in international organizing in honor of the 300th commemoration of the death of Zumbi dos Palmares, a black slave who led a successful rebellion against the colonial slaveholders. Scores of international visitors arrived to help bring world attention to racism in Brazil. In response to the black movement's show of strength, a presidential decree was issued on November 20, the date of

25. Transnational strategies are new to this generation of activists, but Skidmore (1974, 18–19) points out that abolitionists applied similar techniques at the end of the nineteenth century to shame their adversaries. Joaquim Nabuco, a leading abolitionist, wrote in one of the first manifestos of the Anti-Slavery Society in 1880: "Brazil does not want to be a nation morally isolated, a leper, expelled from the world community. The esteem and respect of foreign nations are as valuable to us as they are to other peoples" (Braga 1952, 14–22). Skidmore also cites Manoel Vitorino, who, before becoming governor of Bahia and vice president of the Republic, wrote, "My trip to Europe showed me just how far they were slandering us and how our reputation bedeviled us, the fact that we were a country that still had slaves. After returning home [in early 1881] my abolitionist feelings became insistent and uncompromising and on this issue I never again conceded" (Gomes 1953, 161).

26. The proposal was announced on November 21, 1995, sponsored by PT deputy Paulo Paim. The law would provide descendents of slaves $102,000 Reais (about US$100,000) per person; compensatory policies (*políticas compensatórias*) for access to land reserves (*terras remanescentes de quilombos*), employment, and housing assistance; and better access to schools and the media.

Zumbi's death, which created an Interministerial Working Group to Develop Policies Valuing the Black Population. Among its mandates, this executive-level working group collaborated on the government's National Human Rights Plan, announced on May 13, 1996, the anniversary of the abolition of slavery. The Plan marked the government's first official recognition of racial and gender discrimination as human rights violations.

The black movement has sought interlocutors from the international labor movement as well. For example, in November 1994 the CUT and CEERT organized an Inter-American Trade Union Conference for Racial Equality. The conference convened unionists representing Brazil's three labor confederations to meet with a high-level African-American delegation from the AFL-CIO, the A. Philip Randolph Foundation, and South African unionists to exchange strategies for combating racism in the workplace and to debate the labor movement's role in advocating equal-opportunity policies.[27] As a result, a goal for unionists on both sides of the equator is to force U.S. multinationals to implement equal opportunity policies in Brazil that are consistent with their corporate policies toward U.S. workers.

The three Brazilian labor confederations also united in a national Campaign to Enforce the International Labour Organisation (ILO) Convention 111. That campaign convinced President Cardoso to create, in March 1996, a Working Group on the Elimination of Occupational and Employment Discrimination housed within the Ministry of Labor and involving the Ministries of Justice, Health, Education, and Foreign Relations.[28] This working group organized an October 1996 conference on diversity policies, in accord with the strategy developed in 1994 by the labor confederations and CEERT.

Having successfully lobbied the government in favor of ILO Convention 111, the black movement next appealed to other UN instruments to broadcast the hypocrisy of Brazil's racial democracy. Although the Brazilian government ratified the 1969 UN Nondiscrimination Convention, which requires biennial reporting, the government's sole report, submitted in 1970, claimed Brazil had no race problem. However, in 1995 international activists won their campaign to have UNESCO's Commission on Human Rights' Program of Action to Combat Racial

27. This meeting was followed with a conference hosted by the AFL-CIO in Washington, D.C. in 1995.

28. O Grupo de Trabalho para a Eliminação da Discriminação no Emprego was headed by Cardoso's former colleague from the Brazilian Center for Analysis and Planning (CEBRAP), Juarez Brandão Lopes.

Discrimination assign a Special Rapporteur to investigate racism in Brazil (Glèlè-Ahanhanzo 1995).

Following the UNESCO Rapporteur's unfavorable assessment of Brazil's compliance with the nondiscrimination convention (Glèlè-Ahanhanzo 1995), the Ministries of Justice and Foreign Affairs hosted a 1996 international conference on Diversity, Multiculturalism, and Affirmative Action, which broke new ground with the first official recognition of those concepts. The acknowledgment of the existence of Brazilian multiculturalism is remarkable in that it breaks with the official "multiracial" national identity. President Cardoso, in his speech opening the conference, exhorted the audience to promote equal rights, which he acknowledged had been obscured by a false ideal of racial democracy, but he also asked for recognition of the *good* side of Brazil's racial system and for "original" and "creative" solutions to racial inequality.

The president's failure to define just what those solutions might be, coupled with the fact that almost all the "experts" invited to speak were white (except for a sprinkling of diverse international visitors), incensed many Afro-Brazilian activists and intellectuals. Some of the more strategic groups, however, refused to rebuff the political opening proffered by the Cardoso administration. Geledés Black Women's Institute, for example, accepted a National Human Rights Award from the president in 1996, and Geledés Coordinator Sueli Carneiro observed that it is impossible to ignore the historic significance of the Cardoso administration's official elevation of the problem of racism in the national consciousness (Personal communication, August 1996, São Paulo).

Since the mid-1990s, proposals for developing and implementing equal-opportunity affirmative actions have begun to reach beyond the domain of black activists and scholars of race relations to take hold in the discourses of labor movements, feminists, and public officials (all of whom until the mid-1990s had largely opposed such policies, even when their leadership was conversant with the rationales underlying affirmative action). The spreading use and discussion of the terms *diversity* and *multiculturalism*—directly subverting the time-honored tradition of a homogenous national identity—are pointing toward a radical rethinking of public and private policies to attack discrimination and social inequalities.

To Target or Not to Target: Off the Policy Hook?

The Cardoso administration's National Human Rights Plan of 1996 not only recognized the *negro* as a political subject, but it also marked the first time in Brazilian history that racial identity groups were officially recognized as categories for targeting of public policies. The idea of targeting, invariably translated as "quotas" in Brazil, has always been the most contested aspect of racial (and gender) politics. In the Datafolha study (1995, 101–5), 32 percent of the whites interviewed, 35 percent of mulattos, and 40 percent of *negros* agreed that places should be reserved for *negros* in the university and the workplace.

My own research among leftist party leaders and union officials revealed that support for quotas was highest among black men (56 percent), followed by black women (55 percent), white men (37 percent), and finally, white women (only 17 percent). Paradoxically, I found no clear relationship between awareness of discrimination and support for affirmative action measures in any group, nor did support for quotas correlate with support for training opportunities for black workers (Reichmann forthcoming).

At the time of my research, one of Brazil's largest labor confederations, the Central Union of Workers (Central Única dos Trabalhadores, CUT), had recently established a quota policy to ensure at least 30 percent participation of women in union leadership positions. The 1991 gender-quota policy was protested heatedly by both men and women, even within CUT's most progressive wings. Vicente de Souza, CUT president since 1994, remarked in 1992 that workers' positions on the policy cut across all existing factions.[29] Similar dissension later surrounded the controversial 1996 policy of the Partido dos Trabalhadores (Workers Party, PT) to guarantee 20 percent participation of women in municipal candidacies. In addition to the predictable claims that quotas would lower standards and delegitimize women leaders, a principal charge against the CUT's quota policy was that its importation was alien to Brazilian "reality."

Nevertheless, in the wake of these controversies, the Cardoso administration has almost effortlessly adopted the discourse of affirmative action and diversity. Early in the new administration, the president's wife, Ruth Cardoso (who, like her counterpart in the United States, was forced into silence on many issues early in her husband's term), first revealed how much things might be changing. In June 1995 at a World Bank conference on Education and Development in Latin America and the Caribbean, Dona Ruth remarked that the Brazilian education system is discriminatory and reproduces a "racist form of society."[30] A few months later, President Cardoso's Independence Day Address incorporated the idea of

29. Interview in Rio de Janeiro, November 1992.
30. "Ruth critica modelo educacional," *A Tarde*, 14 June 1995.

Brazil's cultural "diversity" (Fry 1996, 16), signaling a departure from his inaugural speech (made just nine months earlier), in which he celebrated the union of three races into a single national culture.

That year the Brazilian Foreign Ministry laid the groundwork for revolutionary equality policies in its report to the United Nations Commission on Human Rights in which it committed itself, in principle, to combat inequality *affirmatively:*

> In dealing with the issue of equality, the Brazilian Constitution proscribes unequal treatment, on the one hand, and imposes on the state an obligation to take positive action to promote equality, on the other. This often implies meting out unequal treatment to individuals. By treating unequal people unequally, to the extent of their inequality, the law will actually be providing substantively equal treatment for all. . . . According to the Brazilian Constitution, therefore, it is not illegitimate to discriminate positively with a view to improving the living conditions of a particular group or segment that has traditionally been denied privileges within the framework of society.[31]

In an astounding rejection of the doctrine of color blindness, the Ministries of Labor and Justice and the International Labour Organisation hosted a meeting on diversity policies. At this 1996 meeting and in a subsequent one in 1997, activists, scholars, and representatives of the private sector reviewed the diversity policies of multinational firms (in accord with a strategy developed in 1994 by the labor confederations).[32] In its final report, representatives of the government proposed policies to promote diversity in government employment and public relations, to offer diversity training in government-supported vocational programs, and, in awarding government contracts, to give preference to those firms that adopt affirmative actions (Ministério do Trabalho, Ministério da Justiça, e Organização Internacional do Trabalho [Ministry of Labor, Ministry of Justice, and International Labour Organisation] 1996).

Why has racial inequality risen so high on the political agenda of the Cardoso administration? Has the black movement accumulated so much political power that the Cardoso government was forced to respond?

31. Report Submitted by States Parties Under Article 9 of the International Convention on the Elimination of all Forms of Racial Discrimination, XIII Periodic Report of States Parties Due in 1994 (Addendum), Brazil, 23 November 1995, 4–5. This document contains the 10th, 11th, 12th, and 13th periodic reports due in January 1988, 1990, 1992, and 1994, respectively.

32. This conference was co-sponsored by the International Labour Organisation, the Ministry of Labor, and the Ministry of Justice.

Was the president himself—a leading analyst of racial inequality in his former life as a sociologist—firmly committed to antiracism? Did Brazil's racial problem become a foreign policy issue that had to be addressed before the eyes of the world?[33] What was the momentum in 1995 and 1996 behind the official discourse that suddenly embraced unheard of terms like *diversity* and *multiculturalism?* From the black movement's point of view, these were ideas whose time had come. Yet the Cardoso administration did not commit to any specific policies, and, oddly enough, despite its recognition of the need for affirmative actions, the Foreign Ministry's Report to the UN Commission on Human Rights remained firmly committed to the perspective that class factors explain racial inequalities.[34] Neither does the Report explicitly commit to race-based affirmative remedies, although it outlines the rationale for such remedies in the context of the Brazilian constitution's provisions for correcting racial inequality. Given the ambiguity surrounding the government's apparently revolutionary measures, will the movement, suspicious of the changing tide and ever-resistant to government co-optation, find common cause with its longstanding adversaries?

Brazilian Scholarship on Race

Until the late 1990s, Brazilian scholarship on race relations and Afro-Brazilian experience avoided confronting contemporary social inequality

33. Davis and Moore (1997, 174) have developed a typology to account for cases of transnational ethnic solidarity that may explain Cardoso's turnaround. Their model would suggest that the U.S. African-Americans' access to the U.S. power structure enables them to place demands on the U.S. government to be more responsive to Afro-Brazilians' conditions. Although these authors did not address the case of Brazil, this model implies that Cardoso either experienced, or anticipated experiencing, pressure from the United States.

As a Ford Foundation program officer, I visited the United States Information Agency (USIA) in Washington, D.C., in 1991 to seek additional sources of funds for black Brazilians to travel to the United States or for U.S. African-American public officials to visit Brazil. I was advised that this was not a priority area. Just a few years later, U.S. African-American scholars flooded Brazil with extensive speaking engagements supported by the USIA. During this period, U.S. State Department communiqués promoted U.S. support for democratic transitions around the world, specifically encouraging the inclusion of ethnic minorities' concerns in national debates and promoting dialogue with U.S. minority groups.

34. The Report concludes: "Statistics reveal a correlation between color and social stratification in Brazil, and that there is an inequality which weighs against nonwhites. . . . It is hard to gauge to what extent this is the result of racial prejudice or to differences in social status, income and education between whites and nonwhites, since these features are often cumulative. In other words, it is difficult to determine how independent race is as a variable influencing ways of life" (Report to the UN Commission on Human Rights 1996, 21).

and racial politics, perhaps because white scholars' identities are too vulnerable to the injuries of privilege and because for the 2.5 percent of Afro-Brazilians who go on to higher education (1990 PNAD), the wounds may be too recent and painful to wash professionally in the crowded laundry of academic politics. Rather than confronting inequality, the majority of Brazilian scholars in this century have adopted a lateral (or "encompassing," to use Da Matta's typology) approach to racial difference. They have focused on widespread syncretization of African, indigenous, and European religious, linguistic, and cultural forms; slave resistance and regional variations in slavery; the transition from slavery to free labor; and social relations in the immediate post-abolition period. The worst of this work has been folkloric, fixed on an idealized past. The best has meticulously documented the resilience of a spectrum of African survivals and appraised the enormous impact of black experience on Brazilian culture and identity.

Early Brazilian scholarship on race fixated on constructing an identity for the post-abolition nation. In the context of prevailing theories of scientific racism in the 1930s and 1940s, anthropologist Gilberto Freyre's works were widely hailed as the definitive portrait of Brazil's unique racial "paradise," formalizing the popular myth of racial democracy and giving it the legitimacy of a social scientist's stamp.

In succeeding decades, Donald Pierson (1942) and a Bahian social scientist, Thales de Azevedo (1953) articulated a hypothesis that today is still common wisdom: in Brazil, class inequalities exercise a more profound influence in everyday social relations than do race or skin color.[35] These scholars recognized that racial stereotypes and prejudices exist but did not view them as the source of discrimination; rather, they believed discriminatory behavior arose out of Brazil's rigidly stratified class structure, which *coincidentally* corresponds to racial stratification.

The idea that Brazil's racial democracy ignored skin color was so compelling that early in the 1950s UNESCO commissioned a group of scholars to seek the recipe for racial harmony in Brazil. Led by Florestan Fernandes, this group later became known as the "São Paulo school." The title that Fernandes chose for his landmark work, *The Integration of the Negro in a Class Society* (1969), reveals the school's hypothesis: class-based cleavages would eventually assimilate blacks. In coining the famous phrase that Brazil has "the prejudice of having no prejudice," Fernandes (1969) acknowledged that Brazil's fame as a haven of racial

---

35. The Foreign Ministry's 1996 Report to the UN Commission on Human Rights subscribes to this analysis.

tolerance was no substitute for equality. He reasoned that racial stratification persisted because blacks had been "handicapped" by slavery so that they were unable to "adapt" to the competition of the marketplace in the post-abolition period. Fernandes agreed with his Bahian counterparts, Azevedo and Pierson, and was joined by colleagues Fernando Henrique Cardoso and Otávio Ianni in São Paulo in concluding that the correlation of color with status was a transitory problem. Assuming a classical Marxist view of capitalist development, the São Paulo school claimed that economic growth and modernization would strengthen class identities and lessen ethnic differences, thereby simultaneously absorbing Afro-Brazilian workers into the industrializing economy and minimizing social inequalities among all groups, leading to a declining significance of race (see Cardoso 1962; Harris 1964; Azevedo 1966; Ianni 1972; Fernandes 1978).[36]

Thus, while many researchers in this period recognized the existence of racial discrimination, they proposed class-based arguments to explain both social and racial stratification. Sociologist Carlos Hasenbalg (1979), for example, suggested that capitalist elites reinforced the post-abolition racial stratification of the labor market by importing European workers to occupy semi-skilled positions, thus wedging African Brazilians into the market's most subordinate roles. Hasenbalg viewed racial segregation of the labor market as an effective means of maintaining competition for jobs among workers, deepening racial tensions and thereby preventing the emergence of strong labor organizations.

Until the late 1980s, the few scholars who attempted to analyze and distinguish the effects of class and race in contributing to racial subordination were confronted with the absence of reliable statistical data on race because the national census bureau had failed to collect and disaggregate racial data systematically.[37] As recently as the 1970 census, data collection for the color variable was skipped entirely, and it has only been since 1976 that the bureau settled on a consistent definition for its

---

36. U.S. researcher Carl Degler concurred with the São Paulo school, viewing racial inequality as a vestige of slavery. Citing the upward mobility of lighter-skinned Afro-Brazilians in the 1960s as evidence, Degler (1971) claimed that economic development would provide opportunities for racial integration in both the economic and social spheres—the traditional Brazilian notion of "whitening." Although many Brazilian scholars have now rejected a structuralist position in which economic and class factors are more determinant than interracial relationships in the reproduction of poverty, prevailing notions about Afro-Brazilians' social position approximate the views of some contemporary analysts of the U.S. case (e.g., Wilson 1989).

37. Thomas Skidmore (1992) discusses in greater depth lacunae in the contemporary literature.

color categories. (Rosemberg and Piza, in this volume, discuss census policy and shifts in color classifications throughout the history of the Brazilian census.) Sufficiently large and reliable sets of socioeconomic race data only became widely available to researchers in the 1980s, after the long-awaited release of the 1976 PNAD.

With the democratic opening in the early 1980s and the release of the 1976 PNAD data, Hasenbalg (1985) and demographer Nelson do Valle Silva (1985) undertook a series of analyses of racial differences that could not be attributed to class factors. Their landmark work documented racial inequalities in social mobility, employment, and wages, and it showed that blacks achieved lower financial returns than whites on their investments in education, particularly at higher education levels (N. V. Silva and C. Hasenbalg 1992). Charles Wood and Alberto Magno Carvalho continued in this line, examining child mortality data to show that even when socioeconomic factors are held constant, black Brazilians are subject to disadvantages that contribute to higher rates of child mortality. Scholars (including students trained by Hasenbalg and Silva, some of whom are contributors to this volume) continue to pursue these lines of inquiry. In addition, prestigious Brazilian economists, such as Ricardo Paes de Barros and Paul Singer, have recently taken account of race in analyses of human-capital development and inequality.[38]

Despite this progress, in the 1990s Brazilian scholars still face the barriers of scarce resources and official indifference, which are manifest in the government's inability to disseminate timely statistical data on race and to disaggregate socioeconomic indicators by race (or gender). Even when data are collected, they often become available only years later, and then researchers have difficulty gaining access to the information unless they are willing and able to pay for "special" tabulations. The census bureau has been so implacable that a group of scholars organized to pressure the government to make data more rapidly accessible and to disaggregate official socioeconomic data by gender and color (personal communication, Elza Berquó, 1993). As a result, that goal became one of the first priorities set by the Cardoso administration's Ministry of Labor's Working Group on the Elimination of Occupational and Employment Discrimination.[39] Another barrier resulting from meager fund-

38. Ricardo Paes de Barros and Rosane Silva Pinto Mendonça (1996) conclude that racial discrimination is responsible for half of Brazil's overall "super-inequality" in income. See also Barros, Mendonça, and Velazco 1996 and Singer 1996.

39. It is no coincidence that one of the key leaders in the crusade for improved statistics, Elza Berquó, and the head of the Working Group, Juarez Brandão Lopes, are both longtime colleagues of President Fernando Henrique Cardoso from the Brazilian Center for Analysis and Planning (CEBRAP).

ing is isolation. Researchers are forced to make sense of the uneven and limited data bases without the benefit of working with other researchers in the field of Afro-Brazilian studies. And since few Brazilian researchers in this field have had the privilege of studying English, they have had almost no access to the extensive international literature in their area of specialization.

Despite barriers, current Brazilian scholarship on racial dynamics is breaking new ground that adds to the ongoing scholarly work on culture and religion. In light of the black movement's success in formalizing the *negro* category, researchers are revisiting the construction of "race" and ethnicity and examining how they function in Brazil's unique social milieu. Scholars are looking more closely at policy implications of blacks' position, particularly by documenting inequalities in education and the labor market. More systematic attention is also being given to the role of the black movement in claiming Afro-Brazilian rights and in the evolution of Brazilian social movements. Recent articles by Elza Berquó and Luis Felipe de Alencastro (1992), Monica Mata Machado de Castro (1993), Reginaldo Prandi (1996) and Luiz Barcelos (this volume) are just beginning to examine black political participation.[40] Finally, Brazilian scholars are, for the first time, adopting comparative perspectives to explore how Brazil's racial imagination contrasts with its counterparts in South Africa and the United States (Guimarães 1996; Heringer 1996; and Ribeiro 1996).

In order to deepen the field of contemporary Afro-Brazilian studies, scholars face several challenges. A convincing theoretical approach is still needed to analyze the interlocking—rather than additive—systems of racial, gender, and class subordination.[41] Such a framework should build on recent empirical analyses of racial stratification (Barros and Mendonça 1996, and Silva and Hasenbalg and Silva in this volume) to disentangle the relationships among discrimination based on class, race, and gender, especially in education and employment. More interdisciplinary work is needed to clarify the cultural meanings of "race" in the media

40. Previous to the very recent work in this area, only two analyses were available of black political participation: Glaucio Soares and Nelson do Valle Silva (1987) and Amaury de Souza (1971). According to Prandi, de Souza and Machado de Castro concur with his conclusion that blacks are on the "margins of party politics" and therefore less interested in politics than whites (Prandi 1996, 76). Much remains to be done to develop this field of study. New work on political participation is potentially very promising, as Benedita da Silva's 1992 mayoral candidacy and Celso Pitta's 1996 victory in São Paulo were infused with racial politics.

41. The application of a racial formation perspective to analyses of social stratification would integrate analyses of national ideology, discourse and culture with the study of structural factors as a means of understanding what Winant (1992) terms 'racial hegemony' in Brazil. (See also Hanchard 1994.)

and the popular imagination, with attention to their implications for social policy.[42] Given the recent studies and public debates on racial attitudes, the field needs a timely analysis of the evolution of the Brazilian national identity, identity politics, and identity movements, particularly to assess their interactions with other social and transnational movements. Such an analysis in the Brazilian context promises to deepen the new social movements literature.

State and municipal programs and agencies serving the needs of Afro-Brazilians have accumulated almost two decades of experience, but their achievements in influencing social policy and public attitudes remain to be evaluated. Similarly, policy research is needed to evaluate Brazil's limited experiences with race-based interventions in education.

Finally, more work is needed on the role of the Brazilian state in constructing and consolidating racial categories. North American scholars (Marx 1998; Hanchard 1994; Nobles 1995) have examined how conceptual problems emanating from the state-defined color categories have thwarted the Afro-Brazilian movement and, in turn, tested the willingness of the popular masses of Brazilians to identify with exit strategies—either Africanist cultural celebrations or black movement protests against racism. While it does acknowledge that the authoritarian regime suppressed race-based activism and that a national identity based on the idea of racial democracy was in fact an official project, Brazilian scholarship has not fully explored the implications of the state's role and interests in defining a color-classification system.

This Volume

In a hit country-rock song called "Look at Her Hair," Northeastern Brazilian singer Tiririca berated a black woman's "steel wool" hair, likening its smell to a skunk. Just a few years earlier, Tiririca's bigotry/misogyny would have gone unnoticed, but in 1996 a judge banned the song after outraged cries from activists filled the national press. The CD's producer pulled it off the shelves, and Tiririca was forbidden to perform it in public (*Veja* 1997, 9).

This sudden public sensitivity to racism can be attributed to the voices

42. The Núcleo da Cor at the Institute of Philosophy and Social Sciences (IFCS) at the Federal University of Rio de Janeiro, the COR da Bahia program at the Federal University of Bahia and the Nucleus for Interdisciplinary Studies on Black Brazilians (NEINB) at the University of São Paulo are now training a generation of young scholars who are producing important work in these areas.

of Afro-Brazilians on the front lines (among them authors in this volume) and other black and white Brazilian authors who have worked quietly behind the lines for decades to systematically dispel the national myth of racial democracy. Whether by crunching numbers to show that across all social indicators blacks fare worse than whites of the same social strata, or by delving into how a tiny sliver of black professional women *fora do lugar* (who didn't stay in their place) achieved positions of power, the efforts of these scholars are finally reaching a wider audience.

Because *From Indifference to Inequality* focuses on contemporary policy-relevant topics, I have not included the rich literature on Brazilian racial history, culture, and religion. While honoring the critical historical meaning and import of those contributions, in this volume I have chosen to avoid romanticizing or "exoticizing" the African survivals that characterize parts of that literature.

The volume opens with a review of Brazil's color classification system and a set of studies designed to measure discrimination in schools, the workplace, and the courtroom. The section begins with a contribution by *Edith Piza and Fúlvia Rosemberg* that explores the purposes served by color categories in the national demographic censuses in Brazil since 1872. These authors examine how the traditional notion of "whitening" emerged within an official classification system designed to codify phenotype rather than ethnic heritage. Piza and Rosemberg posit that the classification system was designed to dilute ethnic identifications and enable individuals to shift between color categories, particularly with intermarriage, in the service of the national project to unify Brazil's three "races."[43]

Piza and Rosemberg's overview and analysis of color categories is followed by *Carlos A. Hasenbalg's and Nelson do Valle Silva's* landmark contribution to the literature on racial inequality in Brazil (originally published in 1990 in the academic journal, *Estudos Afro-Asiáticos*). Hasenbalg and Silva were the first Brazilian scholars to undertake statistical studies that convincingly disaggregated class variables from the effects of racial discrimination. Their findings were among the earliest to support activists' claims that racial stratification was not just an epiphenomenon of class or the result of a "culture" of poverty. Their chapter analyzes the unequal distribution of educational opportunities in Brazil, using national household survey statistics to show that a higher percent-

---

43. Nobles (1995, 77) argues that the Brazilian Institute of Geography and Statistics (IBGE) has "actively advanced, through its policy decisions and texts, a 'whiter' and/or 'mixed' national face."

age of black children enter school at a later age than white children. Further, the proportion of *preto* and *pardo* children who have no access whatsoever to school is three times larger than that of whites. The authors point out that family socioeconomic status and regional origin cannot explain racial inequality. Although higher socioeconomic status improves educational opportunities for children of all races, clear differences in access to schooling remain, even at higher per capita family income levels. Hasenbalg and Silva conclude that white children show significantly faster rates of progression through school than do *pretos* and *pardos*, and these differential rates of school achievement contribute to Brazil's profound racial inequality.

Silva's demographic analyses of employment opportunity and income distribution have also made a singular contribution to the field of Afro-Brazilian studies. In his chapter, *Nelson do Valle Silva* examines PNAD data to disentangle the effects of racial differences in socioeconomic levels from the effects of discrimination in the labor market, with particular attention to differentials in returns to schooling and to labor-market experience.[44]

Although both Hasenbalg and Silva have succeeded in discounting class as *the* explanatory factor underlying racial inequality, they have not attempted to explain how discrimination functions on a daily basis in Brazilian society. Taking up that challenge, *Nadya Araújo Castro and Antonio Sérgio Guimarães* investigate the dynamics of racial discrimination in the Bahian industrial labor market. To detect differential career paths for black and white Brazilians, they gather information on workers in two important Brazilian petrochemical companies located in Camaçari (Bahia), one state-run and one private. They discover racial barriers to low and semi-skilled jobs and to management positions in the industry. However, they find gender more significant than race as a barrier to mobility at the managerial and professional levels of the sectors studied. The authors attribute those findings to the "leveling" function of educational mobility and the relatively fluid nature of race relations in Brazil. Formal rules governing job mobility, such as those found in the state-owned plant, appear to protect individuals who might otherwise be discriminated against because of their color.

Maria Aparecida Silva Bento uses a qualitative approach to study discrimination in the workplace. She explores the distinct cultural represen-

---

44. Notably, although Silva did not find significant statistical differences among *pardos* and *pretos*, other authors in the volume (for example, Goldani in Chapter 10) have attributed significance to the *pardo* as distinct from the *preto* category.

tations of race in predominantly black sectors (construction, steel, public service, and domestic services) and in white-dominated sectors (finance, communications, software, and information services). This is one of the first and most comprehensive studies to explore how racism is experienced in the workplace (despite many Brazilian workers' insistence that racism does not exist). Through an analysis of seventy-five in-depth interviews with employers, human resources professionals, and employees, Bento's chapter uncovers how discriminatory practices function in a "racial democracy." Bento supplements her findings with an analysis of discourse on racial identity in the workplace and in the labor union. Finally, by assessing the likelihood that labor-union mobilization will decrease racial discrimination, Bento calls for legislative reform to promote nondiscriminatory labor policies.

While government jobs protect some blacks from discrimination, the Brazilian state appears to discriminate actively in the criminal justice system. To examine the role of the Brazilian justice system in perpetuating racial inequality, *Sérgio Adorno* analyzes a stratified sample of selected criminal trials in the municipality of São Paulo. His landmark study begins by profiling victims, assailants, witnesses, police personnel, prosecutors, defense attorneys, crime experts, and judges, as well as by collecting information on the outcomes of trials. Adorno offers evidence that police pursue black suspects more than whites and that blacks confront greater obstacles in exercising their constitutional right to legal representation. Blacks, consequently, tend to be subjected to more rigorous penal treatment (that is, a greater probability of being punished) than whites. All this indicates that color is a powerful instrument of discrimination in the distribution of justice. The principle of equality before the law, regardless of social differences, seems compromised by the biases present in Brazil's criminal justice system.

Also using examples from the Brazilian legal system, *Antonio Sérgio Alfredo Guimarães* examines how the Brazilian penal code defines discrimination and how affirmative action policies could be received. Guimarães asks why racial discrimination cases are rarely prosecuted despite Brazil's antidiscrimination laws, and why Brazilians resist adopting affirmative action. Guimarães shows that the ideologies underlying Brazil's antidiscrimination law have impeded legal battles against racism. According to Guimarães, Brazilians routinely cite three arguments against affirmative action. First, affirmative action policies require that ethnic and racial differences be recognized, which undermines the national myth that Brazilians are one and only one people, one and only one race. Second, "positive discrimination" can be interpreted as an attack on the universalist and individualist principle of merit, which is the new democracy's primary weapon against the personalistic and clientelistic practices that still dominate Brazilian public life. Finally, Guimarães concludes that Brazil's fluid color line precludes any practical possibilities for implementing affirmative action policies, but that economically targeted programs would effectively achieve the desired results.

The book's next section turns to the issue of mobilization in the electoral arena. *Luiz Claudio Barcelos* examines Afro-Brazilian political participation at the grassroots level and makes a significant contribution to the emergent Brazilian literature on new social movements organized around identity. He points out that the lack of legal race-based barriers in Brazil means that the message of a positive black identity must be supplemented with political education to overcome a culture that tends to discourage mobilization around "specific" identities. The black movement has become a relevant social actor, challenged today "to dismantle the mechanisms of discrimination and reproduction of racial inequalities and to strengthen links with the black community."

With the notable exception of Afro-Brazilian senator Benedita da Silva, few elected officials have pushed for judicial reform or legislation to confront racial discrimination. *Cloves Luiz Pereira Oliveira* explores that terrain in a case study of blacks in 1988 and 1992 city council elections in Salvador, Bahia, a predominantly Afro-Brazilian city. Through a comparison of socioeconomic profiles of men and women and blacks and whites, he illustrates the barriers to participation of women and Afro-Brazilians in an arena traditionally dominated by white male politicians. Oliveira finds that although black candidates in Salvador's 1992 municipal elections fared better than in previous races, white and Afro-Brazilian candidates had distinct socioeconomic profiles, with the white politicians controlling greater political capital. But he notes that although this election "was marked by a striking diversity of candidates' backgrounds, the overwhelming victory of men in the 1992 election marks politics as remaining a predominantly male realm."

"Gendered" racial identities are considered in the volume's final section on black women's struggle in Brazil. *Ana Maria Goldani* contrasts black and white Brazilian women's life patterns, focusing on marital status, motherhood, and life expectancy. Through demographic analysis, she shows that racial disparities reflect the interplay of economic, cultural, and regional factors that produce variations in the lives of Brazilian women. Despite the recent sea change in women's social and economic roles (marked by their massive entry into the labor force during the

1980s), Goldani finds that over the course of women's lives, race consistently shapes women's status. Goldani concludes by calling for differentiated public policies that identify and prioritize the needs of Brazil's most vulnerable group, black women.

Black women's experience in Brazil cannot be contemplated without attention to sterilization practices. Patricia Williams (1995, 9) has observed that around the world women deemed "undesirable" have been subjected to antinatalist policies. Black Brazilian women have had to endure their share of manipulation by social engineers. In this volume, black feminist Edna Roland and white feminist Elza Berquó interpret the sterilization debate from different perspectives. Although Roland and Berquó have collaborated in their research and activism to advance the rights of black women, their alliance does not preclude having radically distinct views about the meaning of sterilization practices in Brazil.

Edna Roland's chapter opens with her observation that a healthy democracy requires an explicit understanding of difference strong enough to create two distinct sides to an issue. Both the United States and Brazil supported population-control programs, but the U.S. black movement rallied an opposition to eugenics. In Brazil, Roland asserts that the unexpectedly precipitous decline in fertility rates for blacks during the past twenty years indicates the existence of a covert eugenics policy. Government officials and others try to explain the decline in black women's fertility by claiming that poor women are targeted for population control not because they are black but because they are poor. Although recent public debate and media coverage have led to some legislation and a congressional-level working group mandated to examine sterilization abuse, the black women's movement and other feminist groups have agreed only on one thing: the need to implement the Program of Integral Assistance to Women's Health (PAISM), a model preventive health program developed by Brazil's Ministry of Health.

Next, *Elza Berquó* documents Brazil's "culture of sterilization." Although tubal ligations are illegal, obstetrician-gynecologists perform them during cesarean births, and about one-third of all blacks and whites interviewed in her study admitted they had planned to have cesarean sections during childbirth in order to simultaneously undergo tubal ligation. In contrast to the claim that the Brazilian government sanctions eugenics policies aimed at controlling the growth of Brazil's black population, Berquó's data indicate sterilization is practiced in near-equal proportions by white and black women. Nevertheless, Berquó recognizes that the popularity of this birth control method surely stems from poor women's lack of information on contraception and alternatives. Berquó

concludes that the widespread availability of reproductive health resources would permit women—black and white—to make more informed choices about their fertility.

Sueli Carneiro discusses the challenges black women face in mobilizing alongside both a black movement and a feminist movement. Pointing
out that the "affirmation of a singular women's identity runs the risk of
ignoring the complexity of concrete social relations in Brazil," Carneiro
finds that the feminist movement focuses on the needs of middle-class
white women. At the same time, many black men "have helped erect the
barriers of women's subordination, creating an agenda for black men that
is distinct from that of black women." Carneiro critiques the tendency of
many black males to objectify black women as the least desirable and
least powerful of all social actors. Such a perspective, pervasive in Brazilian society, limits black women's potential within the black movement.
Carneiro calls for a consolidation of the black women's movement as a
mass movement—made up of differing political and ideological visions—
to sensitize both feminists and black male activists about the contradictions inherent in sexual and racial discrimination. She concludes that
"black women must constitute an independent political force capable of
dialogue on an equal basis with the women's and black movements, as
well as with other progressive sectors, joining with them for a more feminist and more black society."

In the concluding chapter, *Caetana Maria Damasceno* deconstructs
occupational niches in the Brazilian labor market that are "naturally" assigned to whites and nonwhites. She accomplishes this by comparing the
career trajectories of four women, two successful "nonwhites" and two
less successful whites. Within Brazil's profoundly segmented and hierarchical occupational universe, in which "whites" are concentrated in positions of authority and *pretos* and *pardos* are the majority in subordinate
positions, Damasceno asks which factors contribute to women's occupational success or failure, and what "success" or "failure" means. Where,
through whom, and most of all *how*, do "color" and appearance operate
as selective criteria? Damasceno documents the exclusion experienced by
the nonwhite women she interviewed, suggesting that perhaps the production of *boa aparência* ("good" appearance) is now increasingly combined with the production of "black" identity, not only in contexts that
politicize black identity, but also in work situations associated with
"progress and modernity."

These accounts of racial identity and dynamics, articulated by Brazilians themselves, are especially timely today as Brazilian civil society
struggles to guarantee democratic practice and demands that govern-

ment be accountable to the people. The entire configuration of discourse, practice, and policy surrounding race in Brazil is rapidly transforming. In 1992 I interviewed some of Brazil's most progressive political leaders about affirmative action and found a lack of knowledge, contradictory views, and ambivalence (Reichmann, forthcoming). But by 1996, Brazil's Foreign Ministry, and the president himself, came out with rationales to justify unequal treatment of (in other words, affirmative actions for) Brazil's poorest citizens in order to improve their competitiveness in society.

But the government's apparent goodwill should not be taken at its face value, as UNESCO Rapporteur Glèlè-Ahanhanzo reported after his fact-finding mission to Brazil:

> A degree of guile was necessary to draw from many of the official spokesmen a recognition of the existence of a cause-and-effect relationship between economic and social conditions, the marginalization and the poverty of Indians, people of mixed parentage and blacks and the historical circumstances which underlie the origins of Brazil. . . . Only a political will stemming from a clear-sighted and courageous analysis of reality can break the vicious circle of racial discrimination through negation and make Brazil the great nation it aspires to be in the 21st century. (Glèlè-Ahanhanzo 1995, 22)

This political will is now a transnational reality. International recognition of racial discrimination in Brazil and solidarity with Brazil's increasingly articulate Afro-Brazilian advocacy community has grown tremendously in the past decade. The international community must step up its demand for policy research on race and opportunity structures in Brazil to substantiate the black movement's claims and to inform and monitor the policies and programs of Brazil's political leaders. By giving an international voice to Brazilian scholars' own interpretations of racial dynamics in their country, this volume takes up that challenge, promising that if the full potential of half of Brazil's population can be realized, not only will the purposes of democracy be advanced, but the nation's wealth may finally be unleashed.

1

COLOR IN THE BRAZILIAN CENSUS

Edith Piza and Fúlvia Rosemberg

In Brazil, census collection of race data is not new, and recognition of racial issues is even older.[1] Brazilians classify themselves by phenotype—through a system combining skin color, physical characteristics (shape of nose and lips, hair color and texture, and eye color), and regional origin—rather by ethnic origin or race (Harris 1964; Harris et al. 1993). Thus, "color," not race, becomes the significant marker in racially identifying an individual. This chapter examines the complex process of racial self-identification and hetero-identification in the Brazilian census.[2] *Self-identification* refers to a color choice made by a census respondent; *hetero-identification* refers to a color attribution assigned by the census taker to the respondent. The range of possible choices for self- and hetero-identification is vast—encompassing both Brazil's official racial terminology as well as terminology commonly found in Brazilian society—any of which may or may not carry some association with symbolic or concrete social status.

The historical and social contexts for each of the eight censuses that collected data on race (1872, 1890, 1940, 1950, 1960, 1980, and 1991) are reflected in the "color" terms used by census takers.[3] The Brazilian Insti-

---

1. Authors such as Schwarcz (1993) date the recognition from 1871 with the declaration of the *Lei do Ventre Livre* (Law of the Free Womb). [Editor's note: this law declared free all children born to slaves.]

2. This chapter is the product of a larger study on education, gender, race, and age carried out at the Catholic University of São Paulo and supported by the Ford Foundation and the Carlos Chagas Foundation.

3. As of 1997, the data collection done in 1991 remains to be published.

tute of Geography and Statistics (IBGE), the government agency responsible for conducting the official census each decade, today uses only five
terms to designate color phenotypes: white, *preto* (black),[4] *pardo*
(brown), yellow, and indigenous. Studies have shown, however, that
most Brazilians recognize a much richer vocabulary. In the famous 1976
Pesquisa Nacional por Amostragem de Domicílios (the National Household Survey, PNAD), subjects gave more than 190 terms in response to
an open-ended question requesting self-identification.[5] (In that survey,
"white" was the category most frequently cited, followed by *moreno*.)

The literature on color, even that which distinguishes origin or ancestry from phenotype (Nogueira 1985a), has noted the fluidity of Brazil's
color line and the tendency toward "whitening," which is epitomized by
the paradigmatic expression "money whitens." Brazil's "racial democracy" has been the object of systematic studies by foreign researchers,
who point to Brazilians' use of an array of color terms (N. V. Silva 1992b,
37). Researchers have also documented social strategies that mask racism
(through faulty or nonexistent data collection on color in the censuses,
for example), while proclaiming Brazil's apparent racial tolerance evidenced by the miscegenation process (Skidmore 1991). Some scholars,
however, have reinforced the faith in Brazil's fluid color relations by
arguing that the spectrum of colors corresponds to purely economic
stratification.

The literature also points to the poor reliability of data collected in tripartite classification systems, such as that used in Brazil, when compared
to the bipolar systems, such as are used in Europe and North America
(Harris et al. 1993). Harris and colleagues discuss the differences between
the U.S. and Brazilian censuses' use of racial criteria by calling particular
attention to the classification of whites. Comparative studies have failed
to note that, unlike respondents in the United States, the portion of the
Brazilian population considering itself to be white is not conscious of its
race, color, or ethnicity as an important variable, despite the widespread
value placed on "whitening." This paradox explains the strenuous efforts
that activists and scholars must make to gain public recognition of race as
a factor in social inequality.

In a census someone declaring their color does so in response to both

4. In this article, "black" (*negro*) designates the racial group composed of those classified in
the census as *preto* and *pardo*.

5. PNAD's collection of data on color has been sporadic, with the first instance occurring in
1976 and becoming systematic only in 1985. Because of inconsistencies in the survey methods,
the 1976 data collection (which was one of the few years for which data on color was tabulated
and made available and one of only a few that has used an open-ended questionnaire that allowed for self-identification) has become a standard source for analysis. See Pinto (n.d.).

macro- and micro-structural determinants. Macro determinants have been the object of studies establishing a link between declaration of color and the individual (or institutional) attempts to "whiten." The most frequent question researchers ask about the Brazilian census is common to countries with a mestizo population: How do mestizos self-identify? The focus is usually on the correspondence of the respondent's answer to the criteria established by the census institution. Such studies thus question the data's macro dimension by disputing the categories through which the information itself is collected. For example, the growth since the 1940s of the *pardo* category in the Brazilian census, with a concomitant decrease in the white and *preto* categories, has been closely watched by demographers as evidence of the value placed on whitening. But few studies have analyzed changes in the subject's own *formulation* of racial concepts and the consequences of such changes for census data. This micro-level analysis needs closer attention. We are interested in how subjects understand the terminology of the census—the interchange between one's self-image and the other's projection that informs the definition of racial identity. In this chapter we consider the dialogue between the two perspectives in order to understand the processes of racial identification in Brazilian society.

Race and Nationality

In a study of the formation of post-independence Asiatic nations, Benedict Anderson (1991) noted the importance of understanding how in specific historical moments race becomes a salient element in demographic studies, whereas at other times it is largely ignored. Albert Hirschman found that census categories in Malaysia became more visible and exclusively racial as colonial consolidation proceeded (Anderson 1991, 165). Following independence, the categories remained rigid, but the racial hierarchy was reordered so that the formerly subordinate Malays assumed dominance as political elites.

A similar phenomenon is observable in the Brazilian census at several historical points. In 1872, when the colonial presence was still very strong (in spite of independence), color was recorded in all official surveys. In 1890, with the change from a monarchy to a republic and the end of slavery, the census was less concerned with race and more concerned with nationalities represented in the population. The 1940 census, carried out under a fascist-inspired regime for which race played an important role in the formation of a national identity, returned wholeheartedly to the use of the color variable and its racial derivatives. Compared with the Asian censuses of the previous century studied by Anderson, the innovation of that census was not just the "construction of ethnic/racial classifications, but . . . their systematic quantification" (Anderson 1991, 168).

The fact that color data was collected reveals a concern for the constitution of a Brazilian nationality, which emerged in the nineteenth century with proposals for a "virilization" of the race through the whitening by intermarriage with European immigrants.[6] Up to the 1920s arguments for the formation of a Brazilian nationality were clearly racial. After 1930, however, as a result of Gilberto Freyre's work (which viewed the three races as equally constituent of Brazilian culture), race became less salient. Race consciousness was even viewed as detrimental to a truly inclusive Brazilian national culture (Schwarcz 1993, 247), resulting, for example, in a government effort in 1940 to reeducate children of immigrants, who were viewed as trying unjustifiably to preserve their native cultures (Schwartzman, Homeny, and Costa 1984). Following the 1950 census, the color variable was collected twice, in 1960 and 1980, but the results were published only in a "skeletal" form, to use Skidmore's expression (1991).[7]

The poverty of statistical information, in both the collection and dissemination of official data, has been denounced as a strategy to keep race out of cultural, educational, social, and economic policy priorities. Since the political opening and subsequent mobilization of social movements, scholarly organizations have been able to analyze race relations at a macro level—using demographic profiles of mortality, fertility, labor-force participation, educational patterns, and women's well-being, based on PNAD and IBGE data.

Color in the Census

In the first general census of the Brazilian population (in 1872), abundant data were available from parish records, but they were of uneven value

6. Serva (1923), discussing the formulation of a "new" Brazilian social structure, noted that "we are a nation in formation, a chrysalis-like, nebulous, ethnic mass, still unformed, heterogeneous and plastic, which will assume the characteristics that the mental directors of its evolution will imprint" (79). He advocated "a campaign for the social and moral uplift of the subraces that inhabit the country" (122). C. C. M. Azevedo (1987) studied the Brazilian desire for "whitening" through intermarriage with European immigrants and pointed out white psychological projections about blacks and Asians in the years immediately before and after emancipation.

7. Notably, color data was collected only in one in every ten census interviews.

because color criteria were not explicit. The color of the population—white, *preto, pardo,* and *caboclo*—was established as a subcategory of socioeconomic condition, divided between slaves and free citizens. *Pardos* were those offspring of the union of *pretos* and whites; *caboclos* were the indigenous population and their descendents. Since the terms white, *preto,* and *pardo* are colors, and since *caboclo* is rooted in ethnicity, the 1872 census used a mixture of phenotypic criteria and ancestry to characterize the population. Reflecting a concern about miscegenation, the second general Brazilian census, in 1890, published data on color and civil status that used the terms white, *preto, caboclo,* and *mestiço.* Here a mixed methodology was again employed, but *mestiço* referred exclusively to the union of *pretos* and whites, and *caboclos* were still determined by ancestry.

Censuses carried out between 1900 and 1930, belonging to the so-called "statistics era," did not include color. The 1920 census justified the omission: "The responses in great part obscure the truth, especially with regard to the mestizos, who are numerous in almost all Brazilian states. . . . Individuals themselves do not always declare their ancestry, since the mixing generally occurred during the slavery period, or in a state of degradation of the mother of the mestizo. In addition, skin tonality leaves a lot to be desired as a discriminatory criteria, since it is inexact" (Lamounier 1976, 18). This justification reveals that the mixed classification system reflected respondents' difficulty in acknowledging their origins. Brazilians preferred to define themselves or be defined phenotypically by skin color.

The 1940 census, the first of a series of modern censuses, established the color categories of white, *preto, pardo,* and yellow (the term *indigenous* was added in 1991). The *pardo* category, which in the censuses of 1872 and 1890 had been reserved strictly for mestizos of *preto* and white origin, became a catch-all for persons who did not fit the *preto,* white, and yellow variables. By 1950 indigenous individuals were folded into the *pardo* category, which meant that *caboclos* lost their ethnic/racial reference and came to be designated by a color variable. The 1940 census was the first to explicitly state the procedures for collecting color data: interviewees were to classify themselves.

In 1950 interviewers were instructed that the *pardo* category should include Indians, *caboclos,* mulattos, *cafusos,*[8] and others. In 1970 no explanation was given for omitting color from the census, but the dictatorship showed little or no interest in social issues and tried to downplay

8. *Cafuso* is the term applied to those of black and Indian origin.

the significance of color. (The data might have revealed Brazil's blatant social inequalities.) During that decade, those interested in the data (including the black movement and scholars) made a strong argument for the future inclusion of a color variable (Costa 1974). But incorporating a racial variable into the census was not without its difficulties.

Collection of Color Data

Tereza Cristina Araújo Costa (1974) offered the most complete response to the problematic surrounding the color variable in the Brazilian census. She reviewed the sociological literature on interethnic relations and found that race, ethnicity, and color are used interchangeably. The lack of universal methods for gathering race data is a major problem. The United Nations, in *Principles and Recommendations for National Population Censuses* 1959 (cited in Costa 1974, 98), notes the difficulty of interpreting the meanings attached to color by the populations interviewed. In countries with mestizo populations, responses may reflect the social meaning that color holds either for those collecting the data or for those interviewed. According to the UN, the risk is that subjects will "falsify" color, affiliating themselves with a group of higher social prestige, or that the census taker may identify people who are upwardly mobile or, conversely, poor, according to their "economic" color.

The experiences of census takers demonstrate the difficulties in collecting color data. The reality of survey dynamics is complex. As Costa notes, "[I]n research settings, as in other social situations, [there is] a specific etiquette for relating, based in this case on the ideology of Brazilian race relations, which means that in fact there are various means of obtaining the data on color, involving both the interviewer and the subject" (1987, 17). In our own experience with collecting color data (Januário et al. 1993), we sensed moments when, in the two-way relationship between interviewer and respondent, the established criteria (self-identification according to the four color categories in use since 1940) posed a problem.

For example, in a study of the racial profile of adult literacy students in São Paulo, a young black woman—whose skin color and characteristics, according to the interviewer, showed no signs of miscegenation—was asked her color. After hearing the four alternatives (white, *preto*, *pardo*, and yellow), she unhesitatingly responded, "White!" The interviewer could not hide her surprise, but the student emphatically repeated her response. The interviewer faithfully marked an X next to the word "white," certain that this response was founded in the student's irritation with being asked the question—perhaps because of the obviousness of the answer. The problem with color categories is also reflected in the census's use of the term "yellow" to refer to people of Asian descent. Respondents took the term as a marker of illness (that is, of sallow, unhealthy skin) rather than as a marker of race or ancestry. Moreover, when they were referred to a list of popular color classifications, census respondents found it difficult to reconcile the array of tonalities with the arid *"pardo"* category.

Again referring to Costa (1974) and drawing on our own experience as subjects for the 1991 census, we note that when phenotypical characteristics appear sufficiently "objective," this can lead an interviewer to assign color to a subject. In Brazil, where color categories are abstract, having been constructed from a combination of physical characteristics, social status, and regional origin, the objectivity of color attribution is questionable (Pacheco 1987). Silva questions the validity of self-attribution, given that "informants are capable of changing their response from one interview to another," and he seems to suggest that interviews should combine self-identification with interviewers' assignation of a variable (N. V. Silva 1994, 70–71). Silva does not address the role of interviewers' color in shaping assignation, however, nor does he discuss under what circumstances the subjects' answers varied. It would be interesting to observe the variations in interviewers' attributions and subjects' responses according to *interviewers'* color.[9]

The problematic of the color variable in the Brazilian census reveals a dynamic rarely discussed in the literature on color. We lack knowledge about the proximity or distance separating hetero- and self-identification or racial belonging. We are not aware of any studies evaluating the convergence or divergence of hetero- and self-identification of color (anthropologists analyze primarily the diversity of linguistic designations). The ascribed color or racial group may be confirmed or negated by the census taker's response. Three recent studies suggest the need for better training of census interviewers with regard to the color variable, based on the differences in hetero-identification according to the color of the census taker.

Research in the city of São Paulo revealed immense variance in hetero-

---

9. Pacheco (1987) observed that much of the interview data obtained in her research was only available because she is black. She served as a point of reference for the subject. Under other circumstances, respondents may not express or relate their personal classification systems.

identification of color.[10] Similar variance may have occurred in all of the general censuses since 1940 as a result of interviewers coping with delicate situations, permeated by social etiquette, or confronting their own fatigue. For example, in order to practice attributing age and color according to official categories, census takers were presented with photos of adolescents and young adults. The subjects of the photos were of both sexes, from fourteen to twenty-one years of age, and represented a spectrum of phenotypes. Responses varied widely, and in only two cases did census takers fully agree on age and racial classification of the subjects of the thirty-four photos. More than half of the responses for the color variable were divided among at least three classifications. Staff of daycare centers in São Paulo were asked to classify photos of *preto*, white, and *pardo* children. The most provocative result was that the classifier's own color tended to be "recognized" in the child classified. Thus, a white staff person identified 89.3 percent of the photos as "white" children, while a black staff person identified only 26.2 percent of those same photos as being "white" children. This study suggests that the color of the classifier influences the classification process. It also suggests that white classifiers tend to "whiten" subjects (E. Oliveira 1994).

As part of her research among illiterate students in São Paulo, Leda Mohamed conducted interviews of census takers in the 1991 census. One white interviewer reported that, even though he had been trained to ask the subject's color and register the response, he marked the color category himself when: (1) the interviewee looked white; (2) the social etiquette of the situation demanded (as a more polite way) that he should avoid asking the subject's color; and (3) the fatigue and the monotony of the interview made him cut the survey short ("by the tenth questionnaire of the day, you just don't ask anymore"). He only asked for color if the subject was (in the interviewer's opinion) "black." This white census taker revealed his expectation that blacks would "whiten" their color in the census, noting, however, that nearly all the people of color who did not claim to be white declared themselves *negro* rather than *preto*.[11]

The Race Variable, Racial Criteria, and Racial Identity

Recent studies on the color of the Brazilian population have provoked important reflections on the problematic of "whitening," while at the

10. This research was conducted among census-takers-in-training and community organizers employed by the São Paulo State Secretariat for Children, Family and Social Welfare, during their training sessions (State of São Paulo 1993).

11. See the introduction for a discussion of the construction of the term *negro*.

same time the black movement has attempted to recover the dignity of racial identities expressed in the censuses by the colors *preto* and *pardo*. As recorded in the Brazilian censuses, color is a fragile approximation of a biological racial classification (T. C. N. A. Costa 1974), and as Seiferth notes, "The biological concept of the races has no instrumental use for the social sciences." Nevertheless, both authors agree that "the word 'race' evokes classifications of physical nature used to mark differences of a social nature [that] classify and hierarchize socially defined groups and persons according to subjective criteria that have nothing to do with the phenomenon 'race' " (Seiferth 1989, 54). Given that for many, color is a determinant of social hierarchy, Costa proposes the study of classifications used by the subjects of censuses in order "to arrive at a classification that reflects the various criteria utilized, and make more intelligible the ambiguity that seems to characterize ethnic identification in Brazilian society" (T. C. N. A. Costa 1974, 100).

Costa, noting the racism that underlies the use of color criteria, proposes revisions in the classifications to approximate cultural categories more closely. This strategy is also a goal of the black movement, but it could lead to a misreading of social categories, since, as Sieferth observes, "In multiracial societies there is a reductionist vision in which race determines culture" (1989, 54). By bringing color into the cultural spectrum, Costa seems to suggest that physical differences among individuals and groups of the same society determine cultural differences, which might be considered in the censuses as *real* (or essential) differences among members of the Brazilian population. The author did not propose an alternative, but the contemporary black movement (which was reactivated in the mid-1970s, when Costa was writing) coined the expression *negro*, which was later adopted by some academics and researchers.

What is a *negro*? In Brazil, the meaning of this term depends on who uses it. The black movement has used it in more than one way: to define the Brazilian population composed of descendents of Africans (*pretos* and *pardos*); to designate this same population as that possessing identifiable cultural characteristics; and to refer to those who descend from a differentiated and cohesive cultural minority group. For example, the minority condition of the "yellow" population leads to the application of criteria similar to that applied to *negro* or *pardo* groups: using a color term in defining a group by its ancestry (Munanga 1986, 1990).

Researchers of race relations and some demographers have also included *negro* in their vocabulary. Nevertheless, in the case of demographers, the term does not always hold the political-cultural-racial connotations that the black movement gives it. Research by SEADE (1992) on families and poverty in urban São Paulo used the color variable

in almost all of the categories it analyzed: housing, employment, education, family structure, fertility, and so forth. But by opting for the term
negro, SEADE did not distinguish the color term from the political-
cultural term. *Pardos* were not included in the *negro* category. Thus,
negro became synonymous with *preto* in this research, which had collected data using the four census categories (white, *negro, pardo,* and yellow). Here, the term was stripped of its political-cultural content.

Another aspect of the use of the term *negro* by white society and black
activists is discussed in a study by Yvonne Maggie, which revealed that in
purely cultural contexts, such as the festivities in honor of the centennial
of abolition, the term *negro* acquired an isomorphism with the term
white. Black culture and white culture were equivalent as cultural prod-
ucts whose difference did not imply subordination. Maggie notes: "During the centennial year, 'difference' was placed in culture, because it was
about origins and not the present. It was national identity that was
sought. But the year of the centennial revealed Brazilian's terror of
thinking in terms of blacks and whites, light-[skinned] and dark-
[skinned] as socially differentiated. . . . Black and white, light and dark-
[skinned], and finally *negro* are terms and oppositions socially applied to
communicate differences meaningful to Brazilian culture" (Maggie
1989a, 24). From this point of view, according to Maggie, to comprehend
the social meaning of color terms today—in which *negro* corresponds to
culture, black/white refer to socioeconomic differences, and light/dark-
skinned are euphemisms to mask social differences—would mean to
foreground color (not culture or origin) as the key element in concepts
of social differences in Brazilian society (24).

Regina Pinto's study of the constitution of ethnic identity in the black
movement in São Paulo (1993) points to a larger trend. For Pinto, the
process of construction of ethnic identity (to be *negro*) is relational because its product is (or becomes) an element of political identity. Thus,
groups in the process of constructing their ethnic identity tend to use
culture as a reference. Some aspects of culture are highlighted and others
are forgotten in a continuous reelaboration of the cultural referents for
political orientation vis-à-vis other ethnic groups. The author notes,
"Ethnicity is considered . . . to be a form of interaction among cultural
groups operating within common social contexts, insofar as the *negro* di-
alogues, or attempts to dialogue with society, as a carrier of a unique culture. Throughout this process, there is a continuous sensitization about
an 'us' in opposition to an 'other,' and therefore, strengthening of an ethnic-racial identity, as well as a *negro* culture" (Pinto 1993, 51).

From this perspective, the construction of ethnicity sheds light on power relations among groups and helps define strategies for confronting discrimination and its consequences. For example, the campaign "Don't Let Your Color Pass for White" attempted to encourage the national population to respond appropriately to the color variable during the 1991 census. That campaign, spearheaded by the black movement and researchers interested in racial issues, cannot yet be evaluated because processing of that census data on race has been delayed.

Finally, even considering the ideological connotations of color sustained by Brazil's "whitening" policies, the idea of whitening still represents the mainstream expression of identity of subjects who have no link to the black movement and who may not have developed an autonomous social and cultural consciousness. For the majority of subjects of the census, self-identification at the moment of the declaration probably is limited to defining physical characteristics that have nothing to do with racial or ethnic membership. The subject sees him- or herself as inserted in a group that is differentiated according to *other* signs of identity, beyond that which is being solicited. The numerous terms for self-identification used by the subjects of censuses might tell us not only about the social *values* that subjects assign to color or race, but also about the ambiguities faced by the interviewees as they insert themselves into a color system where color and only color defines their belonging to a *social* color group.

Moema Pacheco's 1987 study examining conflicts and ambiguity arising from hetero- and self-identification of color in low-income families in Rio de Janeiro illustrates the issue of self-attribution. Pacheco reveals the ambiguity of the color system in which her interviewees were inserted and the myriad forms these individuals found to approach the race issue outside of the discourse informed by the black movement. Among mestizo families, the author found a great variety of terms and combinations of terms referring to color, including those that refer to other phenotypes that support or confirm the color one attributes to oneself or another. Pacheco emphasized two key elements to understanding the classification system used by the *preto* and *pardo* women whom she interviewed. First, "It is in the *relationship* that a person's racial type is defined"; that is, the subject who attributes color to the other does so in function of his or her own racial attributes and defines the other in comparative terms. Second, the color classification system may also be associated with other attributes, such as the origin of the subject who is being assigned a color. "In sum, since the classifications are relational, they suggest a terminology system that allows for manipulation, which is accentuated due to the predominance of the mestizo element in the group" (Pacheco 1987, 89, 90).

In another study, Ivone Martins de Oliveira (1994) gathered evidence of bias among primary public school students and its effects on the self-concept of black and white children in the classroom. The students responded to the following questions: Who do I look like? and From whom am I different? The results were surprising. The black girls divided themselves into "lighter-skinned" and "darker-skinned" groups. The difference was constructed from phenotypical characteristics, especially hair and skin color. The boys also commented on phenotypical characteristics of their friends in a volley of comparisons. However, the comparisons gained a new element when the children, in addition to assigning physical similarities and differences, used a term linked to sexuality to reinforce the racial characteristics. Thus, *preto* and *pardo* boys were identified as boys who "grab" girls (regardless of whether they did, in fact, "grab" girls). The *preto* girls, in turn, claimed that the girls with lighter skin and straighter hair were the girls who were grabbed by both the white and black boys (I. M. Oliveira 1994).

This study confirms that the sexuality attributed to blacks defines boys and girls from their childhood and aesthetic tastes in beauty are conferred upon those who are closest to the white model. The identity of *preto* girls, with relation to *pardos* and whites, is most distant from a positive self-concept, not just because of the girls' physical attributes, but also due to the low power of sexual attraction attributed to the phenotype: the black girls are least "grabbed" and are frequently called "dirty" and "stinky." The black boys must construct their identity upon a referent of sexuality that many do not practice (Oliveira 1994a).

The children that Oliveira interviewed have not experienced an alternative construction of racial identity that many other young *preto* and *pardo* Brazilians seem to be experiencing: the process of constituting a positive racial identity based on cultural markers. The cultural markers constructed by social movements are important elements in the diacritical assignment of identity. Nevertheless, cultural differences, in order to become effective means of differentiation (to the point of being expressed as ethnic membership), need first to be absorbed in the process of identity development of individuals in each group. And as Cross (1991) alerts, the process of constructing ethnic identity is slow and takes place in stages. The stages include evolutionary moments of oscillation between stages of racial and/or cultural membership and of inward reactive moments to diacritical identity markers.

According to Cross (1991), there are five stages in the identity development of African Americans, and the oscillatory movement is present at each stage because racial identity (as an integral part of identity) is not formed as a finished product but as something constantly in process, mutable and mutating even when the sociocultural context may vary. (Cross analyzed the process of identity construction among African Americans in North America.) We seem to capture this movement in the studies about color in Brazil, where *pardos* make up a part of the population for whom color might determine cultural and social positions, depending on the color choice that the individual assumes and that may be socially attributed to him or her.

Racial Identities and the Color Line

This reflection on the identity of census respondents is an exploratory examination of factors that enter into the process of classifying the population according to color and of the relationships among color and other variables. In the absence of studies on Brazil similar to the U.S. study by Cross, we have to be content with conjecture. Our examination also problematizes the study of race relations based on census data and reveals the lacunae on the topic. The importance of Cross's work is that, in the context of labeling people's color, racial membership is not an immutable fact of life for most. We may hypothesize that in the life histories of many people, there will be changes in their internal process of self-identification.

In an analysis of data on education in São Paulo based on 1982 PNAD data, Germán W. Rama (1989) suggests that changes in the color line may occur in another sense—darkening of the population. Because the household is the unit of census collection and the heads of household attribute the color to younger members of the household, the data on color collected would be defined by the household head's racial membership. Rama suggests that racial membership declared in the censuses could vary according to the age of family heads.[12] This could mean that age differences internal to social groups determine their self-identification, which might alter over time. For example, a head of household may answer one way for the whole family, yet individual members in the future might alter their racial membership, especially if they become heads of families and gain more awareness of the social and political significance of their racial identification.

12. Among heads of household between forty and fifty-nine years of age, 74 percent identified themselves as whites, 6.5 percent as *preto*, 15 percent as *pardo*, and 4.2 percent as yellow. Among those between twenty and twenty-nine years of age, 71 percent identified themselves as white, 7.1 percent as *preto*, 18.6 percent as *pardo*, and 3.1 percent as yellow (Rama 1989, 25).

This hypothesis was also suggested by Wood (1991) in his study of changes in racial self-identification based on the technique of forward-survival estimates (that is, current cohorts should have the same proportions as exhibited in previous periods). Wood concluded that

> the technique of survival estimates shows that the number of *pretos* projected was well below the actual number collected in the 1980 census. The difference between the real and expected values suggests that about 38 percent of men and women that declared themselves *preto* in 1950 changed their identification to *pardo* in 1980. Among *pardos* and whites, analyses of projected populations and the actual census data indicate, moreover, that the predicted reclassification of *pardos* as whites was much less pronounced, if there was any, and that we cannot discard the reclassification of whites as *pardo* (1991, 104).

In addition to gaining insight into changes in the color line toward darker color, the suggestions of Rama and studies of Wood are even more interesting because they permit us to consider color as an independent variable. This has led researchers to ask which dimensions of social life might stimulate people to label themselves in the categories proposed by the census bureau. A consideration of the demographic variables of gender and age, for example, could lead to even more interesting results. Thus, we are suggesting the need to analyze color not just exclusively as an independent variable but also as a dependent variable.

Recent studies of racial composition of the Brazilian population and of interracial marriage in Brazil (Berquó 1991; N. V. Silva 1992b) analyze data as if the process of self-identification were identical among women and men. The data is analyzed under the assumption that it is objective information and fails to consider that occasionally the data may be an outcome of subjective classification processes (as suggested by the disproportionate number of women who self-identify as whites). Wood, for example, reports that color reclassification from one census to another is not identical, nor is it similar when comparing women and men separately (Wood 1991, tables 4 and 5, 100–101).

In studies of the color of children according to color combinations of their parents (that is, when heads of household classify members of the household), Hasenbalg and Silva (1992) observe (without discussion) that in contrast to the expectation based on genetics, "combinations with *pretos* tend to result in lighter-skinned [offspring] and combinations with *pardos* tend to result in *pardos*" (1992, 74). Berquó, Bercovich, and Garcia (1986) offer arguments about the psychosocial determinants of color attributions and the need to deepen the analysis. Based on special tabulations of the 1980 census, researchers found a "clear preference for declaring children under one year of age as white. In effect, approximately 152,000 children under age one are children of a mother of another color. This occurs among *preto* and *pardo* children: there are approximately 63,000 and 87,000 children whose mother is *preto* or *pardo* and the children are not" (36).

What transpires in the classification of a black by a white? Nothing is known about this act that permeates concrete social relations as well as research. What are the subjective guidelines for assigning color to another in a country known for racial inequality? Whether parents identify their children as being in the same or in a different group, or how whites classify blacks, are questions that remain unanswered.[13]

What to Do?

What is to be done in the face of ambiguity, of so many imponderables in the attribution of race in Brazil? Should we abandon the mapping of statistical information, with the certainty there is no solution? Nelson do Valle Silva believes we should not, since "the traditional form of measuring racial identity in official statistics is fundamentally valid and therefore the studies that use them . . . should treat with reasonable fidelity the racial dimension that they attempt to measure." With regard to the high correlation between the *moreno* response for open-ended question and the *pardo* response for the closed question (66 percent), Silva notes that "the only discrepancy in these patterns is the significant tendency of some *pretos* to designate themselves as *morenos*" (Silva 1992b, 41). For some, this may indicate a search for whitening. For others, the designation *moreno,* both in the self- and hetero-identification, could designate an attempt to remove bias in color names. The words used to name the color of people are not neutral vehicles but carry partiality and discrimination with them. The use of alternative terms allows for a distancing from and overcoming of those biases.

More attention is needed to understand how reformulation of color or race classifications in the census affect our interpretations of race. Our objective in this chapter has not been to propose new terminology but to

---

13. In the study of reclassification mentioned above, Wood (1991) fails to discuss the possible impact when the head of household assigns color to children.

examine the validity of terminology vis-à-vis the Brazilians' declaration of color. If those who formulate and assess the macro-level data were to rethink the use of categories, criteria, and collection practices, this might improve the usefulness of future census data. At the very least, it would encourage further research on the anthropological and psychosocial dimensions of color attribution.

2

RACE AND EDUCATIONAL OPPORTUNITY IN BRAZIL

Nelson do Valle Silva and Carlos A. Hasenbalg

The accelerated rhythm of industrialization and urbanization since the 1960s has radically improved living standards for most Brazilians. But in spite of massive structural transformations, a growing number of empirical studies indicate that the *pardo* and *preto* (or nonwhite) population is still systematically disadvantaged as measured by demographic and socioeconomic indicators such as infant mortality, life expectancy, social mobility, labor force participation, and income distribution. The evidence suggests that industrialization and modernization of the social structure did not eliminate race and color as determinants of social inequalities. This chapter will demonstrate how the structure of advantages associated with racial ascription influences performance in the educational sphere.

Current social science models in Brazil have led sociological research on education to neglect race and its effects on the distribution of social opportunities among population groups. An illustrative example is Zaia Brandão's 1982 review of state-of-the-art research on school truancy and delayed advancement through grade levels, which did not cite even one study that considered race or color as determinants of school achievement. This crucial variable is largely ignored by experts on this topic. Brazil is considered to be a racially homogenous or egalitarian society, and the great villains of history in regard to differential access to education are socioeconomic status and class inequalities.

An earlier version of this chapter was originally published in *Estudos Afro-Asiáticos* (Rio de Janeiro) 18 (1990): 73–91.

Only very recently has research on education begun to change, due mainly to black educators' and activists' identification of racially insensitive school curricula. Their criticisms center on the structure of school curricula (which excludes themes such as African history and black history in Brazil) and the stereotyped and biased manner in which blacks are represented in schoolbooks.[1] This work has demonstrated the deleterious effects of this curricula on the construction of racial identity among black students, and it has helped to put black activists, educators, and social scientists in contact with one another, opening up the debate about racism in the Brazilian education system. However, the focus on educational content has not addressed the underlying and complex factors that determine the educational experiences of *pretos* and *pardos*.

In a separate line of inquiry, recent sociological studies comparing the social mobility of whites and nonwhites have called attention to the role of education in race relations. Studies identify two tendencies in mobility of people of color: (a) *pretos* and *pardos* achieve educational levels consistently inferior to whites from the same socioeconomic levels, and (b) returns to education, in terms of occupational and income levels, are proportionately lower for *pretos* and *pardos* than for whites (Hasenbalg and Silva 1988). Together, these two tendencies reveal that nonwhites are confined to the base of Brazil's highly stratified social hierarchy.

The first trend suggests that throughout their educational careers, *pretos* and *pardos* are exposed to disadvantages tied specifically to their racial ascription. One of the rare studies of education and race to examine this was conducted by the Carlos Chagas Foundation in São Paulo. The study applied indicators measuring the educational careers of whites and nonwhites (*pretos* and *pardos*). Holding per capita family income constant, the study verified that (a) rates of schooling for nonwhites are lower than for whites; (b) fewer white students fall behind in school; and (c) nonwhite students attend schools that are apt to offer fewer classroom hours (see Rosemberg, Pinto, and Negrão 1986).

Official education statistics also dramatically document the inequality of educational opportunities for whites and nonwhites, and the accumulated effects of racial discrimination in formal education. In 1980 illiteracy rates of individuals 15 to 64 years of age were 14.5 percent for whites and 36.5 percent for *pretos* and *pardos*. At the other extreme of the edu-

---

1. See J. C. Silva (1988). For the reports of two conferences on this subject, see Melo and Coelho (1988) and "Raça Negra e Educação," *Cadernos de Pesquisa* 63, November 1987, Carlos Chagas Foundation, São Paulo. For a comprehensive review of research on racism in school texts, see Negrão (1987).

cational pyramid, 4.2 percent of whites and only 0.6 percent of non-whites had received a college diploma. In sum, not only were the illiteracy rates of nonwhites more than double that of whites, but whites had a sevenfold greater probability of completing college.

The diagnosis of differential educational careers for blacks and whites presented in this chapter is based on data from the 1982 National Household Survey (PNAD), which collected supplemental data on education.[2] Special emphasis will be given to the group aged 7 to 14 because this span represents both the normative and the legal compulsory age for children to attend primary school.

Inequalities in School Performance

Despite laws mandating compulsory school attendance, a surprisingly high proportion of the group 7 to 14 years of age either never finished the first grade or received no instruction whatsoever (see Table 2.1). Both legally and normatively, this group should represent approximately 12.5 percent of all cases; but the real figures are 32 percent for whites and almost 50 percent for *pretos* and *pardos*, suggesting problems in both access to education and late entry into the school system. The second group, 15 to 19 years old, represents a cohort that theoretically should have finished primary school (8th grade). Of whites in this age group, 5.5 percent had attended less than one year of school. The comparable figure for *pretos* and *pardos* was 17 percent, more than three times the rate for whites. Only 31.6 percent of the whites, 10.6 percent of the *pretos*, and 12.7 percent of *pardos* had managed to reach or finish the 8th grade.

Inequalities in educational opportunities between whites and non-whites are crystallized in the cohort 20 to 24 years of age. Approximately 90 percent of the men and 40 percent of the women in this group are already in the economically active population, limiting the possibility of returning to school. By this age, *pretos* and *pardos* are three times more likely than whites to have less than a full first-grade education. Whereas more than half of all whites in this group (52.8 percent) have completed at least the 8th grade, 71.6 percent of *pretos* and 68.7 percent of *pardos* have not. But the most accentuated inequality is in higher education. Only 1.6 percent of *pretos* and 2.8 percent of *pardos* enter college, compared to 13.6 percent of whites. Having white skin in Brazil means hav-

---

2. Only data for white, *preto*, and *pardo* groups were considered; *amarelo* (yellow), those who did not declare color, and "No response" (0.6 percent of the total sample) were excluded.

Table 2.1. Years of Schooling Completed for Individuals Ages 7 to 24, by Color (Brazil, 1982) (in percentages)

Years of Schooling	Age Range								
	7 to 14			15 to 19			20 to 24		
	Whites	Pretos	Pardos	Whites	Pretos	Pardos	Whites	Pretos	Pardos
Less than 1 year	31.9	49.7	50.0	5.5	17.5	17.3	5.1	15.4	14.4
1 to 4 years	55.2	46.1	44.9	31.8	45.8	44.7	27.2	37.0	37.1
5 to 7 years	11.6	4.2	5.1	31.0	25.9	25.1	14.7	19.2	17.2
8 years	0.3	—	—	12.7	5.9	6.2	10.7	9.7	8.7
9 to 11 years	—	—	—	18.1	4.6	6.4	28.5	16.9	19.6
12 years or more	—	—	—	0.8	0.1	0.1	13.6	1.6	2.8
No response	—	—	—	0.1	0.2	0.2	0.2	0.2	0.2
Total	100.0	100.0	100.0	100.0	100.0	100.0	100.0	100.0	100.0

SOURCE: PNAD, 1982.

ing 8.5 times more probability of starting college than *pretos* and almost five times more than *pardos* have. In this respect, Brazil more closely resembles South Africa than it does the United States, where in 1980 whites were 1.4 times more likely than blacks to enter college. In sum, this broad outline of differential outcomes in educational achievement shows that *pretos* and *pardos* experience more resistance in their journey through the school system, leaving them at a significant disadvantage as they begin adult life.

Access to Education

In a study that challenged assumptions about primary school teaching in Brazil, Philip R. Fletcher and Sérgio Costa Ribeiro (1987) suggested that entrance into the first grade is almost universal. Analyzing 1982 PNAD data, the authors concluded that 90 percent of those in each age cohort have access to education. In the most problematic region, the Northeast, only 79 percent of each cohort had entered the first grade. Thus, the Northeast, which accounts for 33 percent of the national school-age population, concentrates 70 percent of all those in Brazil who have no access to education. However, Fletcher and Ribeiro's conclusion fails to consider color differentials. Nonwhite children and adolescents are exposed to a series of disadvantages in access to education. First, at age 7, about 40 percent of whites and 55 percent of *pretos* and *pardos* have no access whatsoever to education. After age 7, absorption by the school system is rapid for whites, reaching 95 percent by age 11. From this point onward, the proportion of white children who receive no schooling stabilizes at about 5 percent. Among *preto* and *pardo* children, however, the decline in the percentage of children with little or no education slows as age increases, dropping to and stabilizing at about 15 percent by age 11. Thus, on the whole, nonwhite children enter school later than white children, with negative consequences for school performance, and the proportion of *pretos* and *pardos* that have no education at all is three times greater than for whites.

Access to the school system varies significantly by region, and within that, by level of economic development and urbanization. Thus, for example, in São Paulo, the proportion of children between ages 11 and 14 who never went to school is approximately 2 percent for whites and just under 5 percent for *pretos* and *pardos*. At the other extreme, in the Northeast, the proportion of the age group who never entered school oscillates between 16 and 20 percent for whites and between 22 and 31 percent for *pretos* and *pardos.* Certainly, in both relative and absolute terms, the greatest number of Brazilians who will become illiterate adults reside in the Northeast. With the exception of the Central-Western region, which ranks second lowest in educational performance, the proportion of school-age children in other regions of the country who have not entered school is lower than the national average, with the white group receiving the best access regardless of region.

What causes these racial disparities in access to education? Chances of entering school may vary with the socioeconomic level of the student's family, and *pretos* and *pardos* are known to be disproportionately concentrated among the poorest segment of the Brazilian population. But we might question the hypothesis that socioeconomic differences between white and nonwhite families fully explain the differences in school access between the two groups. To test this hypothesis, we controlled for per capita family income to see whether differences in school access would disappear at similar socioeconomic levels (see Table 2.2).

As expected, with increases in per capita family income, the proportion of children that have no access to school diminishes for all three color groups at all age levels. Among children from the poorest families (with a per capita family income of less than one-quarter of the minimum wage), the proportion of those in the 11 to 14 age group who never entered school is just above 10 percent for whites but exceeds 20 percent for *pretos* and *pardos.* At the other extreme, among children of the same age from better-off families (whose per capital family income is one to three times the minimum wage), entry into the school system is almost universal, with lack of educational access falling to below 2 percent for all groups, regardless of color.

The most important result seen in these data is that differential access to school for whites and nonwhites persists even when controlling for socioeconomic status. The differential is greatest among the poorest families. For example, in the 11 to 14 age group, differential disadvantage in access to education for *pretos* and *pardos* in relation to whites is about 10 percent for children whose family income is less than one-quarter of the minimum wage. This difference diminishes to close to 5 percent at the next income level (one-quarter to one-half of the minimum wage) and falls even more at the next two income levels.

Because of the limited nature of PNAD data, it is impossible to judge if differences in rates of educational access should be attributed to racial discrimination operating within the school system. However, because educational achievement is linked to *when* (or *if*) a student enters school, unequal access between whites and nonwhites in access to basic educa-

Table 2.2. Individuals Ages 7 to 14 Who Never Attended School, by Per Capita Family Income and Race (Brazil, 1982) (in percentages)

Age in Years	Age Range											
	Less Than 1/4 Minimum Wage			1/4 to 1/2 the Minimum Wage			1/2 to 1 Times Minimum Wage			1 to 3 Times Minimum Wage		
	Whites	Pretos	Pardos	Whites	Pretos	Pardos	Whites	Pretos	Pardos	Whites	Pretos	Pardos
7	56.3	62.2	64.9	41.0	46.8	47.9	30.5	38.6	41.1	19.9	31.2	21.7
8	30.0	47.5	45.1	12.5	27.3	24.9	5.5	7.6	11.3	1.8	2.6	4.8
9	19.9	35.5	33.7	8.0	11.7	14.1	2.6	8.8	6.7	1.4	0.0	3.5
10	14.7	30.8	29.0	5.1	1.2	11.2	2.0	6.7	8.2	0.8	0.0	1.0
11	12.1	21.8	22.1	4.5	11.4	8.7	1.4	0.8	5.4	0.7	0.0	0.0
12	13.6	28.6	24.2	4.9	9.5	10.0	1.5	2.7	4.0	0.7	0.0	1.5
13	11.3	24.5	20.6	3.6	10.2	10.2	1.2	2.5	4.7	0.9	0.0	1.8
14	12.0	22.5	21.7	4.8	13.4	9.8	1.2	3.1	4.1	0.9	4.5	1.1
Total	100.0	100.0	100.0	100.0	100.0	100.0	100.0	100.0	100.0	100.0	100.0	100.0

SOURCE: PNAD, 1982.
NOTE: Table omits income levels higher than three times the minimum wage because of the small number of cases at that income level. The minimum monthly wage is adjusted periodically to keep pace with inflation. In June 1995 it was R$100, or approximately US$92.

tion may perhaps be attributed to factors found in the family and society at large.

School Careers

After quantifying differentials in educational access for white and nonwhite children, we analyzed the careers of those children who entered school, and we found that *pardos* and *pretos* were less likely than whites to complete 8th grade. Most diagnoses of Brazil's school system point to the disproportionate concentration of students who fail to advance in the early grades as an illustration of the system's low productivity. PNAD data from 1982 confirm that for every 100 students entering the first grade, only 45 reach 4th grade and only 21 reach 8th grade. Disaggregated according to color, these figures are 100, 57, and 29 for whites; 100, 35, and 13 for *pretos;* and 100, 36, and 13 for *pardos.* Clearly, the participation of the two nonwhite groups diminishes significantly by the time children reach the more advanced primary grades. As a result, the proportion of *pretos* and *pardos* who succeed in completing their schooling is substantially lower than for whites.

Again, one might assume that the greater concentration of *pretos* and *pardos* in the poorest strata of the population explains this difference. To test this possibility, we controlled again for socioeconomic level and found the "class" explanation unsatisfactory (see Table 2.3).

There does appear to be strong a positive association between family socioeconomic status and the velocity of progress through school. Moving from the poorer to wealthier families across all three color groups, we find a 30 percent increase in the number of children who continue in school. However, within each income level, a higher proportion of *pretos* and *pardos* is clustered in the first three grades. Considering the comparable income levels, the advantages of whites in relation to *pretos* and

Table 2.3.   Individuals Ages 7 to 24 Who Attended the First Three Years of Primary School, by Race and Per Capita Median Family Income (Brazil, 1982) (in percentages)

Income Level	Whites	*Pretos*	*Pardos*
Less than ¼ minimum wage	78.3	86.2	84.5
¼ to ½ minimum wage	63.2	73.3	71.8
½ to 1 times minimum wage	52.1	60.3	60.3
1 to 3 times minimum wage	44.4	54.0	51.5

SOURCE: PNAD, 1982.

pardos oscillates between 6.2 percent and 10.1 percent. In contrast to the trends in educational access, the differences in velocity of promotion through the grades could point to the presence of discriminatory mechanisms within schools and the school system as a whole.

The slow progress of school-age children, particularly for nonwhite children, may be investigated by examining data on delayed advancement through grade levels (Table 2.4).[3] By age 8, about half of all white children and more than 70 percent of all nonwhite children have already fallen one grade behind their peers. From this age onward, across all three color groups, the proportion of children lagging behind grows, but it is particularly noticeable among nonwhite children. By age 10, a significant proportion (15.3 percent of whites, 33.3 percent of *pretos,* and 35.2 percent of *pardos*) are three or more grades behind their appropriate level. In these early years, late entrance into the school system can explain why children lag behind in grade level. As we have seen, nonwhite children are more likely to enter school at a later age than is legally mandated, but a late start is often compounded by a failure to advance at a normal rate, resulting in rapidly diminishing numbers of children who are at grade level, especially among *pretos* and *pardos.*

Late entry and delayed advancement create a cumulative effect, since children who enter school at a later age are more likely to have a slower and more difficult school career. And the cumulative effects tend to penalize *preto* and *pardo* children most severely. Although two-thirds of the *preto* and *pardo* children are lagging behind by three or more grades by age 13 or 14, this is the case for only two-fifths of white children. After age 10, the proportion of children who drop out of school tends to grow, reaching more than 20 percent by age 14. School drop-out rates are approximately the same for the three color groups, but nonwhite children who entered school at a later age and lagged farther behind tend to drop out with fewer grades of school completed than white dropouts.

Differential Rates of School Progress

Clearly, nonwhite groups progress through school at a markedly slower rate than whites. We applied a model to quantify the differential rates of school progress and test their statistical significance. We analyzed the determinants of individuals' educational levels by measuring the set of con-

3. Data for delayed progress in schooling were calculated by comparing age to the grade attended, assuming that children of age 7 should be in first grade, those 8 years of age in second grade, and so forth.

Table 2.4. Delayed Progress in Schooling for Individuals Ages 7 to 14 Who Have Attended School, by Race (Brazil, 1982) (in percentages)

Age in Years	Some Delay in Grade Advancement			Delay of Less Than Two Grades			Delay of More Than Two Grades			Total		
	Whites	Pretos	Pardos	Whites	Pretos	Pardos	Whites	Pretos	Pardos	Whites	Pretos	Pardos
7	100.0	100.0	100.0	—	—	—	—	—	—	100.0	100.0	100.0
8	48.5	28.6	27.7	51.5	71.4	72.3	—	—	—	100.0	100.0	100.0
9	39.0	14.2	18.6	61.0	85.8	81.4	—	—	—	100.0	100.0	100.0
10	31.3	12.9	12.5	53.4	53.8	52.3	15.3	33.3	35.2	100.0	100.0	100.0
11	27.6	6.5	9.8	48.5	41.9	41.3	23.9	51.6	48.9	100.0	100.0	100.0
12	23.3	5.5	8.2	43.7	33.4	32.6	33.0	61.1	59.2	100.0	100.0	100.0
13	21.0	6.3	6.3	41.8	27.9	29.3	37.2	65.8	64.4	100.0	100.0	100.0
14	20.8	4.6	6.1	38.4	18.2	24.6	40.8	77.2	69.3	100.0	100.0	100.0

SOURCE: PNAD, 1982.

ditional probabilities of educational progression, conceptualizing those determinants as a sequence of transitions between educational levels. The probabilities indicate the likelihood that an individual will reach a given level of education, provided that he or she completed the previous level. In other words, if we know to what point an individual has progressed in school (the last grade level completed), we may deduce all of the transitions between educational levels that he or she has completed. From that we can construct a sequence of dichotomous variables that express whether or not that person completed each level. In analyzing any particular transition, we only consider those individuals who completed the previous transition, because only they will be eligible to attempt the next level.

Therefore, for each grade level, the individuals apt to progress make up a subpopulation whose size diminishes as we move from lower to higher grade levels. The reduction in the size of the subpopulation, if the model is valid, is due to the process of selection of individuals primarily according to their socioeconomic background. The implication of this is that the subpopulations tend to remain relatively homogeneous with respect to determinants of their progress through the school system. This self-selection could limit the comparability of the effects between any two transitions, since it implies the modification of the marginal distribution of variables.[4]

However, when we applied our logistic model to the data on access to the school system, we found that significant differences *do* exist with respect to the rates of school access for the three color groups. We conclude that, in spite of the significant differences among all three groups, the difference between *pretos* and *pardos* in rates of access is relatively modest when compared with the differences between those two groups and whites. For example, the model estimates that the proportion of children who at age 14 have had access to school is 82 percent for *pretos*, 85 percent for *pardos*, and 95 percent for whites. Rates of access are more

---

4. To address this problem, Mare (1980) suggests that a logistic model should be applied to each transition, coded as a set of binary variables. This would ensure an appropriate analysis of alterations in educational inequalities, free of intervening factors such as intra-school selection processes, because the estimates of coefficients are not influenced by changes in marginal distribution of the variables. As Mare observed, "Differences in effects among subpopulations result from genuine differences of association between the variables measured" (297). Similarly, the effects of independent variables on a successful transition are not influenced by the proportions of those who make the transition as would be the case for simpler models (for example, a linear relationship), and the probabilities of a transition are asymptotically independent among themselves, allowing the equation in our model to be applied for each school transition.

rapid and predictable in urban than in rural areas, probably reflecting greater proximity of schools. In both urban and rural settings, all differences among the three color groups are statistically significant. Nevertheless, the dichotomous pattern for the overall population does not appear to prevail in urban areas where the *pardo* group clearly is differentiated from the *preto* group.

Our model proved reliable, sustaining the predictability of the transition between first and second grades, considered the most important within the school career. In that transition, differentials relative to whites are significant along with the age variable. In other words, not only in the total population but also in urban and rural areas, one observes a significant difference between *pretos* and whites in completion rates for first grade, but no difference between the rates for *pretos* and *pardos*. This dichotomous pattern appears clearly in both urban and rural areas. Translating these differences, we may say that the model's estimates of the proportion of children who reach, for example, age 12 and who have made the appropriate transitions through primary school is on the order of 84 percent for *pretos* and 86 percent for *pardos*. For whites, it is 96 percent.

By the time students reach the last transition—completion of the 8th grade—the effects of origin variables have been diluted. The explanatory power of the model is much reduced (a reduction in predictive reliability of 26.8 percent for the total population). Aside from the age variable, only the regression constant for the white group in urban areas—for the total country, by extension—appears to vary significantly. This implies that in urban areas all color groups have the same completion rates for the 8th grade but that while the white group presents a higher level of advancement (significantly higher than the others), the differences in chances of advancement are basically constant, regardless of the child's age. That is, the dichotomous pattern reappears, with no significant differences between *pretos* and *pardos*. However, only in this case is there a significant difference in whites' *level* of advancement, with no significant difference in the *rates* of advancement.

Summarizing the conclusions suggested by the application of our model of school transitions, we may conclude that in all transitions there is a clear difference between the white and the nonwhite groups. The only significant differentiation among *pardos* and *pretos* appears in the first transition, that is, access to the first grade of school. Nevertheless, even in this transition, the differences between *pardos* and *pretos* in rural areas are modest, which is not true for the difference between whites and *pretos*. We find a significant difference between *pretos* and *pardos* in access to first grade only in urban areas.

Conclusion

We have analyzed inequalities in educational opportunities in Brazil in terms of their dynamic components. The data from the 1982 PNAD survey indicate that with respect to school access, a high proportion of non-white children enter school late. In addition, the proportion of *pretos* and *pardos* who have no access to education at all is three times greater than for whites. Neither regional nor socioeconomic factors explain these inequalities. While a higher socioeconomic position may reduce the proportion of children who have no access to school, a clear difference in the levels of access between white and nonwhite children persists, even at the highest levels of per capita family income.

An analysis of students' delayed advancement through grade levels shows that in addition to the effects of late entry, school progress is slower among *preto* and *pardo* children: by age 14, at least two-thirds of the *preto* and *pardo* children are behind in school by three or more grade levels, whereas this occurs only among two-fifths of the white children. After age 10, the proportion of children who drop out of school—as a result of either repeating grades over and over or the family's need for the child to work—tends to increase rapidly. The problem of school truancy, therefore, is approximately the same for the three color groups. The result is that nonwhite children, because their progress through school is often delayed, finish their education with an average number of grades completed that is much lower than for white children.

By summarizing these educational dynamics with a formal model that attempts to capture the rates of individual school progress, we verified that in all of the transitions studied, differences among whites and non-whites persist: white children's rates of school advancement are significantly more rapid than those of *pardo* and *preto* children. These differences result in profound educational inequalities that separate whites and nonwhites in Brazilian society.

3

RACIAL DIFFERENCES IN INCOME: BRAZIL, 1988

Nelson do Valle Silva

On May 13, 1988, Brazil celebrated the first centennial of the abolition of slavery. Yet according to 1988 Pesquisa Nacional por Amostragem de Domicílios (PNAD, the National Household Survey), mean income for the white male population was Cr$96,153, compared to Cr$52,376 for *pardos* and only Cr$48,079 for blacks.[1] Standard sociological and anthropological treatment of social welfare data has underplayed or rejected outright the possibility that racially based discrimination has a role in the determination of socioeconomic standing in Brazilian society. This occurs in spite of substantial and enduring inequalities in social indicators such income, infant mortality (Garcia Tamburo 1987), and life-expectancy (Wood 1991).[2]

Two basic hypotheses characterize the literature on race relations in Brazil. The first assumes that social mobility is not influenced by race and that the disadvantaged position of nonwhites in Brazilian society stems from ongoing historical inequalities (e.g., Freyre 1933; Pierson

This chapter is based on a paper presented at the International Seminar on the Labor-Market Roots of Poverty and Inequality in Brazil, Rio de Janeiro, Brazil, August 1992. A presentation of the full statistical model and its analysis is available in English by contacting the author at the Laboratório Nacional de Pesquisas nas Ciências Sociais, Rio de Janeiro.

1. These are geometric means for individuals' monthly income in their main occupation. The reference population is male, twenty-five years or older, living in metropolitan areas. The corresponding figures for arithmetic means are Cr$164,405 for whites, Cr$77,082 for *pardos*, and Cr$72,166 for blacks.

2. A short summary of the relevant sociological literature on race relations can be found in Hasenbalg (1992a).

1955). This assimilationist hypothesis emphasizes the slave ancestry of the nonwhite population and concludes that over time racial groups will be incorporated into mainstream Brazilian society. Even theorists who acknowledge the existence of racial prejudice and discrimination believe that it arises from class discrimination (Ianni 1972) or is a cultural inheritance from the past (Fernandes 1972), a trait that will vanish as nonwhites progressively acquire adequate human capital.

2. The second dominant hypothesis in the literature on race relations suggests that mulattos hold a privileged position in Brazilian society. The "mulatto escape hatch" hypothesis (Degler 1971) expects mulattos to enjoy greater mobility than blacks, attaining higher educational, occupational, and economic levels. According to this line of thinking, widespread miscegenation in Brazil has attenuated the sharpness of race relations, and discrimination against individuals of mixed blood is weaker than against blacks.

These ideas were challenged only in the late 1970s. Both Carlos Hasenbalg and I called attention called to the possibility that racially based discrimination could play a significant role in labor-market exploitation and competition (Hasenbalg 1979; N. V. Silva 1978, 1980a). Instead of viewing prejudice and discrimination as an irrational cultural inheritance of the past, we suggested that discrimination is a rational reaction to group conflict over scarce social and economic resources, and thus racial stratification is fundamentally rooted in the current social structure of Brazil. Subsequently, empirical studies have attempted to measure the extent of racially based discrimination in Brazilian labor markets (e.g., Oliveira, Porcaro, and Costa 1981). I showed that blacks and *pardos,* contrary to expectations, displayed strikingly similar profiles (N. V. Silva 1978). This was particularly true with regard to patterns of economic returns to experience and schooling. Significantly, the claim that blacks and *pardos* compose a homogeneous "nonwhite" racial group apparently does not contradict reality. Rather than being a mere simplification, in some contexts the analysis of blacks and *pardos* together appears to be a sensible approach to the study of racial discrimination in Brazil.

My 1978 study also noted substantial differences in economic attainment between whites and nonwhites, even when controlling for relevant variables. Although the magnitude of income difference that can be attributed to labor-market discrimination may be considerably lower than in other countries, interracial difference in Brazil appears to be caused largely by discriminatory practices. In particular, even though nonwhites enjoy certain advantages at the lowest income levels, these advantages are superseded by the superior rates of return to experience and schooling enjoyed by whites. The net result is that nonwhites enjoy a relative advantage over whites only at the earliest phase of their entry into the labor market or at very low skill levels. Whites are much more efficient in converting experience and educational investment into monetary return, whereas nonwhites suffer increasing disadvantages as they try to go up the social ladder.

These results contradict the assimilationist and "escape-hatch" hypotheses so prominent in the Brazilian sociological literature. *Pardos* do not behave differently from blacks, and race significantly influences income levels. Whites enjoy substantial advantages over both blacks and *pardos* in the labor market. In a summary measure of labor-market discrimination in Rio de Janeiro, it was found that while 82.4 percent of white/*pardo* average income difference could be attributed to differences in labor-market composition and interaction, 17.6 percent could be attributed to discrimination in the labor market. The corresponding figures for blacks were 85.4 percent and 14.6 percent, respectively. This suggested the surprising conclusion that blacks tend to suffer relatively less discrimination than *pardos*, which contradicts conventional wisdom.

Using data from the 1976 PNAD, I extended my analysis to include more regions and additional variables not available for 1960 (N. V. Silva 1985). The results largely confirmed the earlier study: In 1976 about 33 percent of the white/*pardo* income difference could be attributed to discrimination in the labor market; the corresponding white/black difference was 26 percent. This reaffirmed that blacks appear to suffer less discrimination than *pardos*.

More recently, Lovell (1989) analyzed racial inequality in monthly income among male workers in all metropolitan areas in Brazil. Using data from the 1980 census, she estimated that mean income of the nonwhite population was about half that of the white population. With the same linear-regression standardization procedure that I had used (N. V. Silva 1980a), Lovell calculated the proportion of mean-income difference due to labor-market discrimination. The results show that for blacks and *pardos*, 25 and 32 percent of income difference, respectively, can be attributed to discriminatory practices. She concurred that nonwhites receive different treatment in the labor market, but contrary to my findings, she found crucial differences in the level of discrimination between blacks and *pardos*. Moreover, she found that income discrimination varies by region, industrial sector, and occupational position.

Data and Basic Model

In order to focus on clearly defined labor markets in this chapter, I limited the analysis of 1988 PNAD data to Brazil's nine metropolitan areas (plus Brasília). To enhance comparability with earlier studies and to minimize selectivity biases, I examined racial income inequalities only among men. I limited that sample to men over 25 because education is a major explanatory variable and because a significant proportion of younger men (particularly among the white population) have yet to complete school. Given that the more educated groups tended to progress faster through the educational system, a lower age threshold might underestimate racial difference. The final sample included 19,284 observations.

First, I applied a basic income-determination model relating the respondent's monthly income from his main occupation to his completed schooling and his age. This model evaluated the three main color groups: white, black, and *pardo*. (Asians, "yellow" in the Brazilian classification used, and nonrespondents constituted a minor fraction of the sample and are excluded from the analysis.) Two results were notable: first, model fit was much better for whites than for either blacks or *pardos*, expressed by the fraction of explained variance for each group; and second, returns to age and to schooling were considerably higher for whites than for nonwhites. Estimates for financial returns to schooling for whites was 13.3 percent per year, whereas for blacks it was 10.8 percent and for *pardos*, only 10.1 percent. Whites also exhibited higher returns to age, and the black/pardo contrast was stronger.

Analysis of differences among groups commonly employs a linear-regression standardization procedure (N. V. Silva 1978; Lovell 1989, 1992). This technique partitions income difference between two groups into three parts: discrimination, composition, and interaction. We start by estimating the earnings function for white and nonwhite groups and then standardize the income variable by using one group's average values and the other's corresponding regression coefficients (Althauser and Wigler 1972; Iam and Thornton 1975; Blinder 1973; Masters 1975; Thurow 1967). The "discrimination" component is indicative of the possible extent of discriminatory practices in the labor market and is measured as a function of the difference in the coefficients in the earnings model between the two groups. In other words, it represents the difference between predicted income in the hypothetical absence of discrimination in the labor market and actual income for the group discriminated against. Because it is model-based, this "discrimination" component is an unexplained residual difference.

Applying this decomposition procedure, I found that the total gap in income between blacks and white is 0.6931, implying a monetary difference of Cr$48,074 (Table 3.1). About 51 percent of this gap is an unexplained residual, normally attributed to discrimination. Thus, the expected mean income for blacks in the absence of discrimination is about 42 percent higher than the actual mean black income. On the other hand, the total white/*pardo* income gap is 0.6075, with discrimination accounting for about 46 percent. In the absence of discrimination, mean *pardo* income would be about 32 percent higher than it actually is.

The degree and quality of blacks' participation in labor markets is crucial when considering the determination of income, however. Brazil's regions exhibit tremendous variation in average income. This is particularly important when discussing racial difference because, as Hasenbalg (1979) has insistently pointed out, the geographic history of slavery and European immigration led to marked variation in regional distribution of color groups (Table 3.2). Whites are advantageously concentrated in the more developed metropolitan regions, but it is less obvious that blacks, in comparison to *pardos,* are concentrated in regions with more job opportunities. Whereas about 31 percent of *pardos* reside in the poorer Northeastern cities, the corresponding figure for blacks is only half that. On the other hand, 41 percent of the black population, compared to only 25 percent of the *pardo* population, live in the Rio de Janeiro metropolitan area. Thus, regional effects must be included in the basic model. To accomplish this, I added dummy variables to the model to represent the effect of residence in each of the nine metropolitan areas.

The models provided significant results, particularly in the cases of the

Table 3.1.   Decomposition of Average Income Differentials, by Color (Base Color Group: White)

	Color	
Component	Black (%)	Brown (%)
Difference		
$y^{-w} - y^{-n}$	0.6931 (100.0)	0.6075 (100.0)
Discrimination	0.3530 (50.9)	0.2772 (45.6)
Composition	0.2960 (42.7)	0.2460 (40.5)
Interaction	0.0441 (6.4)	0.0843 (13.9)

SOURCE: PNAD, 1988.
NOTE: w = white; n = nonwhite.

Table 3.2. Distribution of Color Groups, by Metropolitan Area

Metropolitan Area	Color Group		
	White (%)	Black (%)	*Pardo* (%)
Rio de Janeiro	24.2	41.4	25.1
São Paulo	44.8	24.9	23.8
Curitiba	5.8	2.0	2.0
Porto Alegre	8.7	5.7	1.5
Belo Horizonte	5.6	9.3	10.5
Fortaleza	2.2	1.2	8.0
Recife	3.1	4.6	13.7
Salvador	1.7	9.3	9.1
Brasília	3.0	1.5	5.7
Belém	0.9	0.1	0.6
Total	100.0	100.0	100.0

SOURCE: PNAD, 1988.

blacks and *pardos.* Not surprisingly, most regions showed significantly higher levels of income compared to the Northeastern cities of Recife and Fortaleza. Moreover, it is worth noting that the estimated rates of financial returns to age and schooling remained almost unaltered.

To test whether the equations for the three groups differed significantly, I introduced an interactive model with white- and *pardo*-specified dummy variables. This model uses these variables as a main effect and as interactive effects with each of the other independent variables. The results indicate significant interactions between color and several independent variables. More specifically, no regional contrast was significant for either whites or *pardos.* On the other hand, all black/white contrasts for the human-capital variables proved to be statistically significant. As for the *pardo* group, financial returns to age are significantly different from those for blacks (but only at the 5 percent level). The black/*pardo* contrast for private returns to schooling is not significant at any conventional level.

For the white/black comparison, the estimate for the unexplained residual gap drops to 0.2464 when applying the decomposition technique described above. This represents about 36 percent of the total interracial gap and implies that the black group, in the absence of discrimination, would register a 28 percent greater mean income. The results for the white/*pardo* comparison indicate a 30 percent unexplained gap, which, in the absence of discrimination, should be a 20 percent greater mean income. These finding represent statistically reliable estimates of the proportion of total income gap attributable to sporadic discriminatory practices in the labor market.

Racial discrimination can occur in the following ways:[3]

- *Human-capital discrimination*—mobility for nonwhites can be blocked when they are prevented from acquiring qualifications necessary to enter higher paying occupations;
- *Occupational discrimination*—nonwhites, regardless of their qualifications, can be prevented from entering better paying occupations;
- *Wage discrimination*—nonwhites can earn less for performing the same jobs as whites (unequal pay for equal work).

Human-capital discrimination often begins while individuals are still in school, before they enter the labor market. Occupational and wage discrimination take place after entrance into the labor market.

Human-Capital Discrimination

Schooling not only plays a central role in human-capital theories of income distribution but also has been found repeatedly to be a key factor in socioeconomic advancement (see, e.g., Blau and Duncan 1967; Haller and Portes 1973; Sewell and Hauser 1972). This has led to a concern for racial difference in educational attainment, but what are the determinants of educational attainment? In attempting to answer this, sociologists have increasingly incorporated a set of interpersonal and social-psychological intervening variables into their models (see, e.g., Sewell and Hauser 1975). Portes and Wilson (1976) used variables such academic performance, the influence of the "significant other," self-esteem, and educational aspirations to link parental background and intellectual attainment to educational attainment. In a study on blacks in the United States, they tentatively concluded that when one controls for parental background, mental ability, and other intervening variables, the net effect is actually positive on each of the variables included in the model describing educational attainment. In other words, there are strong indications that advantages for whites in regard to educational attainment depend directly on their initial advantage in exogenous variables such as parental background and mental ability. This reinforces the conclusion of

3. Discrimination can also occur through *employment discrimination*. Resources were inadequate to allow examination of employment status; therefore, employment discrimination will not be analyzed in this chapter.

earlier studies (e.g., Jencks et al. 1973) that lack of attainment in education for blacks is not due to any discernible discrimination, but to initial and historically conditioned disadvantages in the exogenous determinants of the process (Portes and Wilson 1976, 423). The study discussed in this chapter did not have access to exogenous and intervening variables. Therefore, what I present is a limited estimation of a model of educational attainment.

The 1988 PNAD gathered data on father's schooling and father's occupation (at the moment the respondent entered the labor market), which provided some information, albeit limited, on parental background. Respondents also gave their first occupation and age when entering that job. These questions were asked only to heads of households and their spouses, which reduced the sample to 10,782 respondents. More important, this may have introduced selection bias toward a more educated population.

To study the racial difference in schooling, I developed a third model to relate schooling (in years) to region of residence; to a dummy variable measuring whether or not respondent's father was employed in the rural sector ("rural origin"); to father's completed schooling (in years); and to a measure of father's occupational status, measured by a detailed socio-econometric scale based on 1970 Brazilian Census data (N. V. Silva 1973). The model suggests that whites are more efficient than nonwhites in converting parental achievement into advantages to offspring. Among whites, the father's schooling was the most important determinant of the son's educational level.[4] Father's schooling was 72 percent higher for whites than for blacks and 54 percent higher than for *pardos*. Patterns for father's occupation are similar, but the differences are slightly weaker. To investigate the joint effect that these differences in parental background might have on respondent's schooling, I ran the same regression standardization technique used previously.

The total white/black gap in schooling is estimated to be 2.89 years. Applying the decomposition technique, I arrive at an estimated discrimination of about 1.89 years or 65.5 percent of the total gap. In other words, educational level for blacks in the absence of differential returns to the explanatory variables should be 7.83 years, that is, around 30 percent higher than it indeed is. The corresponding estimate for the white/*pardo* gap is a

economic ties to cultural myths: blacks are lazy

---

4. There may be a problem of colinearity here, since the correlation between father's schooling and father's occupational status is $r = 0.627$. This might reflect the tendency of one compensating for the other: the higher the effect of father's schooling, the lower the effect of father's occupational status. For this reason, a better strategy might be to evaluate these variables together instead of separately so that they compose a joint "parental background effect."

their environment is ← want to party conducive to "squatter jobs" (ie carnival) total difference of 2.42 years, of which 1.70 years is the unexplained resid-ual. This amounts to about 70 percent of the total gap and implies an av-erage educational level in the absence of interracial difference for the *pardo* group about 27 percent higher than its current level.

The differences between the *pardo* and black groups are not statisti-cally significant except for small contrasts in father's occupational status and Rio de Janeiro or São Paulo residence. (For those variables, the con-trasts are only significant at the 5 percent level, and their estimates are ac-tually *lower* for *pardos* than for *blacks*.) On the other hand, all differences between parental background of whites and blacks are highly significant.

Taken together, these results suggest that whites are more efficient at converting family background into educational advantage than the non-white group. In this respect, differences within the nonwhite group seem to be relatively weak and insignificant, and if anything, *pardos* appear to be more disadvantaged educationally than blacks. However, because we cannot control for the effect of other potentially relevant variables, such as intellectual attainment and social-psychological attitudes, the attribu-tion of these differences to discrimination in schooling is problematic. The Brazilian case is similar to that described by Blau and Duncan (1967) for the United States. Both reflect the existence of a "double handicap," in which nonwhites are unable to convert either educational attainment or parental achievement to advantage as efficiently as do whites.

Finally, a related issue is possible "family-background bias" in the usual estimates of returns to schooling. Does the omission of variables for parental background and intellectual attainment significantly lower the estimates of investments in returns to schooling? Empirical evidence for the United States suggests that the effect of returns to schooling is completely mediated by the intervening variables normally included in attainment models (schooling, in particular), with no discernible *direct* effect (e.g., Sewell and Hauser 1972). Substantial evidence exists that parental background characteristics are important predictors of individ-ual economic outcomes (e.g., Pastore 1979). Therefore, the omission of this variable may introduce a bias in the previous estimates of labor-market discrimination.

To estimate the amount of the bias introduced by the omission of parental background variables, I created a fourth model by adding back-ground variables. I found significant *direct* effects of parental back-ground, besides those mediated by human-capital variables. Families possess resources (beyond simply the provision of formal education) that influence final economic outcomes for their offspring. This apparent bias favoring whites implies a *convergence* in the estimated rates of return to schooling, so that there were no significant differences between *pardos* and blacks, in comparison to whites. This result suggests that most of the interracial difference in returns to schooling is caused by differences in parental background. Family resources—from access to privileged family networks to direct monetary inheritance—may be the factors that make whites more efficient in converting schooling into income.

The only significant contrasts that remain after controlling for parental background are those related to returns to *experience*. I found that whites have significantly *higher* returns than nonwhites, and found *no* significant contrast between *pardos* and blacks. Therefore, advantages for whites appear to be related to better career and mobility opportunities, and perhaps this constitutes the core of labor-market discrimination.

Finally, I examined the effects of the omission of parental background on the measure of discrimination. If we assume that (a) parental background has both a direct and an indirect effect through the other intervening variables on income, and that (b) for a given level of parental background, the average nonwhite has lower or equal schooling than the average white, then it can be shown (N. V. Silva 1980b) that it is likely that the labor-market discrimination measure will be larger when parental background is included in the equation than when it is omitted. In other words, the measure of labor-market discrimination is, in this case, likely to *underestimate* the amount of discrimination. I have just shown that both conditions seem to hold for Brazilian society. Therefore, we should expect that applying a decomposition technique for the data on income determination would result in relatively higher estimates for the unexplained residual than was the case when parental background was omitted.

In fact, considering the white/black gap, total difference in income can be estimated at 0.68. The corresponding value for the unexplained residual labor-market discrimination is 0.31, or 46 percent of total gap (versus 36 percent previously estimated). Likewise, for a total 0.59 white/*pardo* gap, the estimate of labor-market discrimination is 0.19 or 32 percent of total gap (versus the 30 percent found previously). These figures imply that black income is 36 percent lower and *pardo* income is 21 percent lower than would be the case in the absence of labor-market discrimination.

Occupational and Wage Discrimination: An Exploratory Exercise

Having found significant racial difference in income, the next step is to ask: What are the labor-market processes that generate these differences?

As indicated before, racial differences in income occur in two ways. First, nonwhites can be prevented from entering better paying occupations, regardless of their qualifications (occupational discrimination). Second, nonwhites in the same occupations and having the same qualifications as whites can earn less for performing the same jobs (wage discrimination).

Implicit in this view is the argument that occupation is the basic labor-market variable intervening in the establishment of income differences among color groups. An individual earns income through the performance of an occupational role. Therefore, income differences between equally qualified individuals of different groups, in this case color groups, must ultimately be accompanied by differences either in occupational achievement (that is, performance of better paying occupational roles) or in pay within an occupation (that is, differences in economic reward for the performance of the same tasks). Many sociologists concern themselves with the study of occupational achievement, which is at the core of their analyses of social mobility. Although this is a well-established area of research, the analysis of the relationships between occupation and income attainment seems to be based on questionable procedures. Typically, in studies of economic attainment, occupation is introduced as a factor with purely additive effects on income. However, there are good reasons to view the labor market as stratified basically along occupational lines, and occupation should be viewed as not only having a net effect on income but also as possibly affecting the whole process of income attainment. In other words, occupation seems to affect the way the other independent variables are related to income attainment (see Stolzenberg 1975).

Workers often make tremendous investments in occupation-specific training, and the higher the level of that investment, the less likely it is that a worker will seek a job in another occupation. As an extreme example, physicians do not compete for jobs with lawyers or engineers. This observation supports the hypothesis that the labor market is segmented along occupational lines. But more important for the argument, certain socially determined factors, including racial discrimination, vary substantially from one occupation to another, and these factors affect the determination of wages. Hodge and Hodge (1965) and Stolzenberg (1973) have indicated that both the amount and direction of racial difference in returns to schooling vary among occupations. For these reasons, the analysis of racial difference in returns to labor within occupational groups should play a central role in the study of labor-market discrimination. Thus, the introduction of occupation in the analysis of racial difference in income leads us to the examination of intra-occupational earnings functions. This, in turn, calls for simplifications necessary to save degrees of freedom. Consideration of only two racial groups will be the first modification to the analytical framework since the number of blacks in certain occupational categories would be too low to guarantee an acceptable level of reliability in the analysis. We can overcome this problem by considering blacks and *pardos* to be a homogeneous group (a not unrealistic assumption, as I showed earlier).

The socioeconomic position of occupations can be estimated from the occupational-status scale used earlier to measure father's occupational status. Following the second model, we change the dependent variable to occupational status for the male population 25 years or older. The results for *pardos* and blacks are very similar, with no significant difference between these two groups. On the other hand, although returns to experience for whites appear to be slightly higher than for nonwhites, the differences in occupational returns to schooling are both very substantial and highly significant. Therefore, it appears that whites convert educational investments into occupational status more efficiently than do blacks. It must be kept in mind that advantages for whites in educational returns may be biased by family resources, as I noted earlier.

Mean occupational achievement for whites is 18.42 points, whereas for blacks, it is 11.04 points, and for *pardos,* 11.71 points. Decomposing the 7.38 gap between whites and blacks, we arrive at the estimate that 0.93 remains unexplained by other variables. This represents 12.6 percent of the total gap. Similarly, of the total 6.71 point gap between *pardos* and whites, 1.05 points remain unexplained, representing 15.6 percent of the total gap. These are the estimates for the extent of occupational discrimination as a labor-market mechanism, and the evidence presented suggests that this discrimination arises from the inability of nonwhites to convert educational investments into occupational gains as efficiently as do whites.

As shown above, a proper analysis of wage discrimination (unequal pay for the same job) should be performed *within* each occupational group. This allows occupation to interact freely with all the variables included in the model. But this drastically reduces the degrees of freedom for each analysis and requires some simplifications. One has already been suggested: the collapse of the black and *pardo* color categories into one "nonwhite" group. We must also reduce the number of variables in the equation. Therefore, for intra-occupational analysis, I restricted the predictors, in previous models, to the basic human-capital variables of age and schooling. To ensure reliability, I selected only the occupations having at least twenty incumbents from each color group, resulting in a total of sixty-nine occupations. The sample seems to be representative since it covers exactly 77 percent of each of the white and nonwhite groups in the sample. Correlating the proportion of nonwhites with other occupational characteristics (mean income and schooling), I found that whites and nonwhites have widely dissimilar occupational distributions. In fact, the proportion of nonwhites in each occupation is significantly (that is, at the 1 percent level) and negatively correlated with mean schooling ($r = -0.795$) and mean income ($r = 0.4854$). This result is expected, given the racial differences discussed earlier.

Although I have not provided here a detailed analysis of intra-occupational differences in returns to schooling and to experience between groups, qualitative and impressionistic evaluation strongly suggest that educational differences are very minor and are attributable to differences in returns to experience, since educational requirements tend to make occupational incumbents relatively homogeneous.[5] I do offer a summary evaluation of interracial differences in intra-occupational income attainment by measuring labor-market discrimination as the relative difference between expected and actual income. The results indicate that the mean level of discrimination is 0.229 and the relative difference is 0.272. Looking at the actual distribution of both indicators, we can say that there is a clear tendency for my measures of discrimination to be positive, indicating net gains for the white population. In fact, in only three occupations (high school teachers, bar attendants, and real-estate construction entrepreneurs) are the discrimination coefficients negative (that is, there is no evidence of discrimination).

The most interesting aspect of wage discrimination is not its existence as a labor-market mechanism but its variance, in both magnitude and direction, among occupations. Hypotheses have been advanced to explain certain aspects of wage discrimination against nonwhites. In a well-known article, the Hodges (1965) argue that nonwhites are in a weaker economic position than whites, which forces them to accept lower wages than whites receive for the performance of the same job. Because lower wages tend to reduce wages for everyone in the same occupation, these authors hypothesize that the larger the proportion of nonwhite workers in an occupation, the greater the resentment of whites against their non-white co-workers. The resentment translates into pressure on employers, which ultimately leads to higher levels of discrimination against

5. This is self-evident in the case of some professions, such physicians and lawyers, where educational requirements are fixed by law. Since educational levels do not vary, all interracial differences are necessarily derived from differences in return to experience. Incidentally, these two cases are among those in which the discrimination measures are highest.

nonwhites, neutralizing the downward effect on wages caused by non-white competition. Stolzenberg (1973) calls this the "economic-threat hypothesis."

Bergman's "crowding hypothesis" posits that certain occupations are open to nonwhites, whereas others are not. Consequently, the relative supply of labor in nonwhite occupations exceeds normal levels, which reduces wages. These jobs are performed by nonwhites and only those whites with a degree of occupation-specific skills that enable them to earn higher wages in the nonwhite occupation than they could otherwise earn in "white occupations" (Bergman 1971, 298).

Both the "economic threat" and the "crowding" hypotheses assume that higher levels of participation by nonwhites in a given occupation will produce downward pressure on wages in those occupations and lead to higher levels of wage discrimination. The plausibility of these hypotheses can be examined by correlating selected characteristics of the occupations with their associated absolute and relative discrimination levels.

Both discrimination measures correlate positively, but very weakly, with measures of socioeconomic status (income and schooling) associated with occupations. None of the correlation coefficients are significant at conventional levels. On the other hand, the proportion of nonwhites in the occupation correlates *negatively* and *significantly* to both discrimination measures. This pattern holds even when we control for the effect of the other occupational characteristics, clearly contradicting both the "economic threat" and the "crowding" hypotheses. This suggests that, holding constant the effect of other characteristics (particularly educational requirements), occupational exclusion is associated directly with wage discrimination: the higher the level of exclusion, the higher the level of intra-occupational income discrimination. When interpretations of the nature of wage discrimination are added to this, it appears that in some occupations (not necessarily the better paying ones), nonwhites suffer from a double handicap: not only is access made difficult, but once in an occupation, nonwhites find their career paths seriously blocked by discriminatory practices. However, the entrance of other nonwhites into a given occupation may moderate barriers to mobility.

no real incentive for the numbers/statistics to change drastically

Conclusion

In this chapter, I analyzed two hypotheses found in the Brazilian literature on race relations. One is the null hypothesis that racial discrimination does not exist in Brazilian society; the other, the "mulatto escape-hatch" hypothesis, posits a privileged position for mixed-blood individuals, which results in better prospects for upward social mobility. My analysis indicates that both hypotheses seem implausible. Not only is there a substantial, unexplained residual interracial difference in economic outcomes, but we also find *pardo*/black contrasts to be generally weak and insignificant. This suggests the existence of a white/nonwhite color line.   *comparison to U.S. → suggests the same*

Next I examined the role of parental background in the explanation of interracial differences. I found that parental background largely determines educational attainment. More important, parental background *directly* affects income attainment, suggesting the importance of familial *problem at the core?* resources in the determination of economic outcomes. Parental background can also be a proxy for *quality* of schooling, an effect that can have more weight than the number of years of schooling. This issue deserves closer investigation.   *back to incentive*

However, my analysis of parental background led to two important conclusions. First, interracial differences in returns to schooling, although still showing a net advantage for whites, seem to converge and become insignificant. That is, it seems that formally observed interracial differences can be explained by differences in familial resources. Second, the only significant differences between whites and nonwhites were in returns to experience, suggesting that whites enjoy advantages in career trajectories. In terms of occupational and wage discrimination, occupational attainment is determined by individual schooling. Similarly, interracial differences also rest on differences in returns to schooling. However, given the results obtained by the introduction of parental background indicators, it seems plausible to think that most of these differences in occupational returns to schooling might be contaminated by differences in familial resources.

Finally, wage discrimination was substantial and resulted primarily from differences in returns to *experience*. This is plausible, given that educational requirements for occupational entry tend to make incumbents somewhat homogeneous in regard to their level of schooling. As a consequence, estimates of returns to schooling (and by extension, estimates of differences) tend to become small and insignificant. Therefore, wage discrimination seems to stem from differences in career and mobility opportunities. Further, examining structural covariates of wage discrimination, it was found that the only significant predictor was the proportion of nonwhites in each particular occupation. Contradicting two well-known hypotheses, the "economic threat" and the "crowding" hypotheses, the data showed that wage discrimination is *negatively* related to the proportion of nonwhites, when other occupational characteristics were held constant.

Taken together, these results point to the existence of "multiple handicaps" for nonwhites. They are less efficient than whites in converting investments in schooling into better paying occupational positions; once employed, they suffer from fewer and inferior career and mobility opportunities, resulting in lower economic rewards; and they do not transfer advantages from one generation to the next as well as do whites.

4

RACIAL INEQUALITIES IN THE LABOR MARKET AND THE WORKPLACE

Nadya Araújo Castro and Antonio Sérgio Alfredo Guimarães

In Brazil, many studies of racial inequality have described and analyzed the entry of *negros* (blacks) and whites into the labor market (see Hasenbalg 1979, 1983, 1985, and 1991; Silva 1980a; Oliveira, Porcaro, and Araújo 1983, 1987a, and 1987b; Bairros 1987 and 1991; Porcaro 1988; Chaia 1989; Sandoval 1991; Bairros, Barreto, and Castro 1992).[1] But these studies have paid little attention to the career trajectories of people once they have entered that market. The literature provides almost no insight into the role of day-to-day work in reproducing racial inequalities (for an exception, see P. C. Silva 1993). While variables such as gender, age, or migratory experience have been used amply to measure the forms of subordination in the workplace, the same has not occurred with race. Labor-market studies need to problematize the social barriers to mobility founded in racial discrimination and reproduced in the microenvironment of companies and to examine individual strategies for overcoming those barriers.

How does race operate in selectivity within the labor market, as well as in the working conditions within the company? What barriers exist in each environment? What lines of congruence are there between them?

This chapter is an abridged version of "Desigualdades Raciais no Mercado e nos Locais de Trabalho," *Estudos Afro-Asiáticos* (Rio de Janeiro) 24 (July 1993): 23–60.

1. The terms *race* and *racial* are used here in the sense of "groups or quasi-groups to which are attributed characteristics of common behaviors" (Rex 1988), identified by phenotypes, the principal one being color, and not cultural features (ethnicity). In the same sense, we use the term *color groups*. Concretely, the terms will be used in reference to Euro-Brazilians and Afro-Brazilians.

Who are the people who overcome them? We will focus on these questions by analyzing two databases. For the study of racial selectivity in the labor market, we used household surveys conducted in the Salvador (Bahia) Metropolitan Region between December 1987 and September 1989.[2] For the study of professional trajectories and inequalities between racial groups in the factory context, we used information on workers in two important Brazilian petrochemical companies, one state-run and one private, located in Camaçari (Bahia).[3]

The empirical reality of the market and the work environment in modern industry in Bahia has certain advantages for our study. First, Salvador, Bahia's capital city, has the largest *negro* population of any city in Brazil; *negros* not only predominate numerically but also re-elaborate their cultural traditions with great vigor.[4] Important political-cultural mobilizations have been responsible for broad social activation of the ethnic symbols of "negritude." Second, the Salvador Metropolitan Region is conspicuous in its poverty and in the instability of its labor market (Fernandes 1986). And third, Salvador has profoundly transformed itself in recent decades through planned industrialization and heavy state subsidization (Azevedo 1975; N. A. Castro 1985 and 1988; Guimarães 1988), which has created new opportunities for occupational mobility even among impoverished and predominantly black (*negro*) social groups. Nevertheless, strong racial inequalities still persist in the Bahian labor market (Bairros, Barreto, and Castro 1992; N. A. Castro and Sa-Barreto 1992). One can spotlight the mechanisms behind these inequalities by analyzing the occupational insertion and career trajectories of those who have managed to overcome racial barriers.

2. Our data was drawn from the Research on Employment and Unemployment (PED) conducted simultaneously in several Brazilian metropolitan areas. The PED was a household survey aimed at capturing the conjunctural tendencies of employment and unemployment and was based on a common methodology defined by the Fundação SEADE and by DIEESE (Troyano 1985). The care in collecting the "color" query and, most of all, the availability of this information made this database a key source for analyzing variations over time in racial inequality in access to employment.

3. For the state-owned company, data collection took place initially in 1990, and the data were updated in January 1992. The hypotheses developed in two detailed studies on organization and management of labor in the factory by Guimarães (1988) and Rocha (1991) were broadly utilized in our analyses. The personnel files compiled by Elisa Amélia Rocha in 1991 were also used. For the private company, data collection, conducted by Nadya Castro, took place in 1992.

4. In this chapter we use the term *negro* (black) as the aggregate of two racial classifications employed by the PED and in official Brazilian statistics: *pardo* and *preto*. (*Branco* [white] is the third category generally utilized in statistical surveys in Brazil.) The categories of *pardo* and *preto* tend to present characteristics diametrical to those of whites (N. V. Silva 1980a). In the PED, the interviewer assigns a color category to the survey subject.

Negros and Whites in the Labor Market: In Search of Socially Valued Occupational Positions

Brazilian society, despite making a transition toward industrial capitalism, is far from having completed the integration of *negros* into its labor market. Hasenbalg, for example, has emphasized that "racist practices of the racially dominant group, far from being mere remnants from the past, are functionally linked to the material and symbolic benefits obtained by whites through disqualification of nonwhite competitors" (1985, 127). Two factors help reproduce these inequalities. First, the initial exclusion and retarded inclusion of *negros* in Brazilian industry is attributed to their delayed proletarianization. *Negros* remained segregated "in the predominantly agrarian and more underdeveloped regions of Brazil, where economic and educational opportunities are much smaller"[5] (Hasenbalg 1983, 180), or as occurred in São Paulo, they remained in agricultural activity a long time and entered the urban market only when industrial growth had already slowed. Thus, *negros* were left to contest the fringes of this market, and then only when the upward mobility of European immigrants or institutional regulation of the access to work (intended to benefit Brazilian nationals) created opportunities.[6]

Second, the reproduction of inequalities is attributed to discriminatory practices and symbolic violence exercised over *negros*. These mutually reinforcing factors have impeded upward mobility of *negros* so that they self-regulate "their aspirations in accordance with what was culturally imposed and defined as the 'appropriate place' for people of color" (Hasenbalg 1983, 181). In this way, social segregation complemented the "internalization, on the part of nonwhites, of an unfavorable self-image" (Hasenbalg 1985, 28).

In Bahia from 1987 to 1989, *negros* (that is, the sum of *pardos* and *pretos*), representing 84 percent of the workforce in the labor pool, constituted 83 percent of the employees in local industry. These figures attest

---

5. The poor Northeast provides an example of segregation of blacks in regions that are predominantly rural or agrarian. In 1950, 51.2 percent of all Brazilian blacks were employed in the Northeast; in 1980, after thirty years of intense transformation of Brazil's occupational structure, that figure was still 43.6 percent (Porcaro 1988, 177).

6. According to Hasenbalg (1991, 9), at the turn of the century foreigners monopolized 90 percent of the industrial jobs in São Paulo and Rio de Janeiro. In the 1940s the numbers, although smaller, still were revealing: in São Paulo, blacks held only 10 percent of the jobs in industry; seven of every ten blacks were stuck working in agriculture. Even in the Federal District—where nearly all employment was already located in urban markets—whites occupied 67 percent of all industrial jobs.

to the demographic weight of this group. However, equally important is the Bahian historical idiosyncrasy of intense industrial growth, expanding occupational opportunities, changing labor force management strategies, and progressive expansion and consequent positive valuing of features of black identity.

When the industrial boom took off in Bahia in the mid–twentieth century, an urban labor market already existed as a result of the commercial and financial history of the former colonial capital. And, as participants, *negros* were in the majority by far. Thus, Bahia's economic growth in the 1970s and 1980s not only expanded to already established tertiary activities but also created channels for upward mobility thanks to new occupational opportunities generated by industrial growth. How, then, did race interfere in an individual's access to these new opportunities?

We observed that a strong selectivity characterizes the world of emerging industry, exercised as much through ascribed characteristics (race, sex, and age) as through acquired characteristics (education and urban experience). Bahian employers are prone to discriminate based on race/color. Although 8 of every 10 industrial workers are *negro* (a ratio prevailing in the economically active population as a whole), this proportion drops to 7 out of 10 in the petrochemical industry, the premier sector of the economy and the local icon of modernity. Further, this selectivity appears to be increasing as *negros* are supplanted by white migrants from other states who are lured by the boom in Bahia's petrochemical industry.

The average length of urban residence was nearly perfectly balanced among whites and *pretos* employed in industry (Table 4.1). The tendency toward whitening of the labor force that is expressed in industry as a whole is also clearly perceptible in the petrochemical industry.

Race operates as much in the moment of establishing the buy-sell relation of the workforce (in the market) as in the opportunity for absorption of individuals by the occupational structure (in employment). The darker a worker's skin, the more likely it is that he or she will *not* find employment. Whites—and also significantly, although in lesser measure, *pardos*—have a greater range of occupations through which they circulated[7] and were concentrated in niches formed by high-level positions.

7. Analyzing the differentials for permanence of racial groups in the labor market, we find that whites more than blacks are the first to withdraw under adversity. For that reason, their rates of participation are extremely sensitive to socioeconomic changes. Analysis of the placement in the occupational structure shows that by possessing more job alternatives, and therefore greater command over their survival, whites can survive temporarily while awaiting access to better positions. Meanwhile, blacks are the first to react to adverse conditions, and they thereby disproportionately swell the ranks of the unemployed and underemployed (Bairros, Barreto, and Castro 1992).

Table 4.1. Migration and Whitening in Industry Overall and in Petrochemicals in Metropolitan Salvador, Bahia, from December 1987 to September 1989 (in percentages)

| | Length of Residence in Metropolitan Salvador (in years) | | | | | | | | | |
| | Industry Employees Overall[a] | | | | | Petrochemical Companies Employees[b] | | | | |
	Less Than 2	2 to 5	5 to 10	10 or More	Always	Less Than 2	2 to 5	5 to 10	10 or More	Always
Whites	23.0	21.3	23.7	19.6	12.1	34.0	43.3	23.4	30.8	23.2
Pardos	43.2	45.3	43.4	44.3	40.0	29.1	28.3	27.7	43.4	39.0
Pretos	32.9	33.4	32.9	36.1	47.9	17.0	28.3	28.9	25.8	37.8
Total	100.0	100.0	100.0	100.0	100.0	100.0	100.0	100.0	100.0	100.0

SOURCE: Pesquisa de Emprego e Desemprego (Survey on Employment and Unemployment), Sutrab/DIEESE/SEADE/Sine/Universidade Federal da Bahia.

[a]Chi square: 165.12842; significant.
[b]Chi square: 29.02308; 99.99% significant.

These positions include the activities of the legislative, executive, and judicial branches of government; ownership or management of companies; and professions of a scientific or technical nature. *Negros* were found in significant numbers in positions of intermediate authority over subordinate labor, but their niche is predominantly in manual occupations of production, particularly those requiring physical strength (Castro and Sá Barreto 1992, 6–7).[8]

In this respect, it is significant that of the approximately 130,000 individuals in the PED surveys, close to 9,000 were employed in industry, of whom about 900 were in the petrochemical industry. At the apex of the hierarchy of salaried workers, only 45 occupied the coveted title of engineer, 75 percent of whom (34) were white, 20 percent (9) *pardo,* and only 4 percent (2) *preto.* These numbers eloquently testify to the successive barriers faced by *negros* who seek access to socially valued occupations in cutting-edge industrial activity.

It is necessary, then, to study the specific mechanisms by which such discrimination is exercised, identifying the different barriers that apply to the movement of individuals both in the labor market and during the career trajectory. In our judgment, race determines occupational insertion in a complex and mediated fashion. It opens a range of possibilities, variable from individual to individual depending on a combination of distinctions of color and other characteristics, either ascribed (such as sex, age, and birthplace) or acquired (such as education), material characteristics (and those expressed in bodily features, such as sex and age) or cultural ones (expressed in attitudes or behaviors, in features of social distinction). All are pregnant with symbolic meaning and sustain their efficacy (as mechanisms of social selection) in shared, collective representations.

Gender is among the most prominent of these mediating mechanisms of racial selectivity in the labor market. Studying the ratios of masculinity among those employed in the modern petrochemical plants, we gathered evidence that in this industry not only was access more difficult for women than men *but it was prohibitive for preto women.* There were about 6 men of any race for each white or *pardo* woman, a ratio that increased to nearly 11 to 1 with regard to *preto* women, precisely those who carry the most evident racial features.[9] The eloquence of these find-

---

8. Working with a simple trichotomous scale of occupational prestige, we find that high-prestige occupations are numerically important only among whites; for nonwhites (and especially workers classified as *pretos*), positions of low prestige are dominant (Castro and Sá Barreto 1992).

9. This difference is notable and cannot be attributed only to Brazilian legislation that barred women from working swing and night shifts. If that were so, the data would indicate a reduction of the weight of feminine employment among *all* racial groups. In contrast, they point to a

ings suggests another social barrier: the condition of gender appears to function as a mediating element of racial exclusion.

Sandoval (1991) proposed a possible explanation. Analyzing life histories collected from São Paulo workers in different occupations, he verified that discrimination in the workplace is greatest in those occupations where *negros* must interact with the top echelons of management or with important white clients. The difficulty persists, though on a smaller scale, with regard to obtaining high-level positions that involve supervising other workers.

So in the case of *negras* (black women), gender blocks their access to direct-production jobs because of the laws against women's participation in shift work, while at the same time, race diminishes their chances of rising to higher level, skilled positions or administrative jobs.

To gain a better understanding of these barriers, we created a subsample, selecting workers in occupations in the petrochemical field that represent goals of mobility for different social classes: for the working classes, laborers or administrative or office workers; for the upper classes, engineers. For contrast, we provide data on manual laborers.[10] In this subsample, we found that of a total of 58 *pretos* working in petrochemical companies, only 12 (20 percent) were women, of whom no fewer than 10 (83 percent) were employed as maids, probably subcontracted by service companies. Only one *preto* woman (8 percent) worked as an engineer. Meanwhile, among the 11 white women, more than 50 percent of them (6) were office workers, 25 percent (3) worked as engineers, and only 18 percent (2) were employed as maids.

In industry generally, as well as in the petrochemical plants, *pretos* and *pardos* appeared to enter the workforce earlier, often before reaching adulthood. In the petrochemical industry, however, this association lacks statistical significance. While averages show that industry generally retains proportionally more whites, the petrochemical industry's need for stability in its workforce supersedes racial bias. Unlike industry as a whole, the barrier in the petrochemical plants is getting employment rather than keeping it. Once in the workforce, the petrochemical plants'

---

very unequal presence of women according to their color: although white and *pardo* women participate equally in the petrochemical industry, comprising 14 percent of their respective racial groups, only 9 percent of the *pretos* who manage to penetrate this area of modern industry are female (Castro and Sá Barreto 1992).

10. These four occupations make up less than 20 percent of the total PED survey interviewees who worked in the petrochemical industry; a total that includes both regular employees and subcontractors. Consequently, at this level of disaggregation, problems of representativeness appear, due to the sample design (that is, a household survey). Thus, it is prudent not to make inferences from this group to all employees in the sector.

universalist management rules mitigate toward a stable and technically reliable labor force, whether *preto, pardo,* or white.

The last characteristic that we studied, education, is a serious barrier to obtaining jobs in industry (Table 4.2) There is an undisputed association between level of education and race: although a majority in the industrial labor force, *preto* men had very little education (8 in every 10 have no more than an elementary school education, if they received any schooling at all). The reverse held true for white men (nearly 6 of every 10 completed at least high school). Overall women were better educated than men. The percentages of white women were almost evenly distributed across educational levels. However, when comparing figures for those who completed college in other racial groups, there was greater imbalance. While 23 percent of all white women workers completed college, only 6 percent of the *pardo* women and one percent of the *preto* women did so. Ethnic and class differences clearly limit access to higher education, and across both race and gender, the only population to attain a significant number of university degrees is white women.

Education not only seems to influence the possibilities for professional mobility among racial and gender groups, but it also becomes a mechanism of selection for obtaining high-level positions in industry. Across all occupations, women employed in industry showed higher levels of education than did men, and this difference was sharpest for women with the most advanced education. In the modern sector, typified by the petrochemical industry, educational gains were critical to winning jobs and job mobility. Fewer women were employed in the petrochemical industry than in industry on the whole, and gender inequalities kept them in more restricted occupational niches (because labor regulations excluded them from performing direct production jobs, such as equipment operator, and gender discrimination excluded them from "masculine" jobs, such as engineer). But in the petrochemical industry, among employees with high levels of education, we found almost double the percentage of women when compared to men (Table 4.2).

The comparison between industry as a whole and modern petrochemical plants suggests a hypothesis that possessing educational credentials can overcome barriers in a world where power (political, among administration and management, or technical, among skilled staff) emanates from white males. One can speculate that over-education qualifies women to enter modern industry, even in positions for which high levels of education are not formal requirements.

Education is thus simultaneously a mechanism of discrimination (that is, a barrier to mobility) and an instrument for achieving mobility. Seen

Table 4.2. Education, Gender, and Color in Industry Overall and in Petrochemicals in Metropolitan Salvador, Bahia (in percentages)

	Industry Overall[a]				Petrochemicals[b]			
	None	1st Grade	2d Grade	3d Grade	None	1st Grade	2d Grade	3d Grade
Men								
Whites	4.6	41.3	35.1	19.0	4.5	17.0	37.0	40.6
Pardos	6.3	59.2	29.0	5.5	6.8	39.8	43.3	10.1
Pretos	8.0	71.7	19.2	1.1	8.8	53.8	32.6	4.8
Total	6.8	61.7	25.8	5.8	6.8	38.2	38.4	16.5
Women								
Whites	3.4	33.1	39.8	23.7	2.7	8.1	32.4	56.8
Pardos	4.8	58.1	31.2	5.9	3.4	34.5	25.9	36.2
Pretos	7.1	64.9	26.6	1.3	7.4	59.3	18.5	14.8
Total	5.4	55.9	31.1	7.6	4.1	32.0	26.2	37.7

SOURCE: Pesquisa de Emprego e Desemprego (Survey on Employment and Unemployment), Sutrab/DIEESE/SEADE/Sine/Universidade Federal da Bahia.

NOTE: Data collected between December 1987 and September 1989.

[a] and [b]Men: Chi square: 544.97071; significant.

[a]Women: Chi square: 149.59137; significant.

[b]Women: Chi square: 161.89253; significant.

from the perspective of occupational positions held by women, educational attainment is indicative of women's use of over-education as a mechanism to compensate for gender disparities. This was corroborated by the even higher level of education among *negras* (black women) employed in the petrochemical industry than in industry in general (Table 4.2). While only one in every 100 black women employed in industry completed college, this figure swelled to 14 in every 100 in the petrochemical industry. However, in petrochemicals, the occupational range open to *negros* is appreciably *smaller* than in industry overall, and gender barriers at the high end of the occupational hierarchy operate against *negras* (black women) who are seeking occupations that require college degrees. The double discrimination against color and gender reinforces the attainment of education as a mechanism to compensate for those biases. This hypothesis can be evaluated more rigorously by analyzing the data on position and professional mobility in the company.

Labor Management, Inequality of Access, and Racial Discrimination in Petrochemical Companies in Camaçari

To determine the mechanisms of discrimination as they operate through management policies and the organization of work, we collected data on color,[11] gender, age, year hired, current job and jobs previously held, number of promotions and the intervals between them, and the number of high-level positions held by employees in two petrochemical plants in Camaçari. The state-owned plant employed 845 people, of whom 16.9 percent were white, 24.2 percent *moreno,* 21.1 percent mulatto, and 37.6 percent *preto.* Of this total, 21.5 percent (212) were women (Table 4.3). These percentages had remained essentially unchanged since 1987, despite a downsizing policy based on voluntary resignation and nonreplacement of retirees that resulted in a 20 percent decrease in the company's number of employees. The private plant employed 401 people: 28 percent white, 22.2 percent *moreno,* 16.5 percent mulatto, and

11. The data on color were collected by classifying photographs in the personnel files of the two companies using the categories white, *moreno,* mulatto, and *preto.* The classification was based on physical characteristics, such as color of skin, shape of nose and lips, and hair type. *Morenos* were distinguished from mulattos by having more white features; mulattos, in turn, were distinguished from *pretos* by having lighter skin. We thank Genice Batista de Araújo for the report on these data.

33.3 percent *preto*. Only 13 percent (53) were women. This company was undergoing a major restructuring in an attempt to overcome the crisis that hit the industry in 1990, and it had already dismissed many employees.[12]

The state-run company followed a bureaucratized, formal, and universalist management policy that favored the entry and retention of socially subordinated groups, such as *negros* and women.[13] *Pretos,* both men and women, were a majority in this plant, reflecting little inequality in the distribution of color groups by gender (Table 4.3). In the *moreno* and mulatto groups, men outnumbered women by only 1 percent, and the difference increased only slightly when comparing whites and *pretos:* among whites, there were 6 percent more women than men, and among men, 4 percent more *pretos* than women.

The impact of the private management style on recruitment of blacks and women in the industry was evident when comparing the number of women employed in the two firms: the private firm employed markedly fewer women and considerably more whites than the state-owned company. We attributed the greater presence of men compared to women to the fact that the private company's administrative sector, where women are traditionally utilized, is very small. Women are clearly favored as administrative personnel, particularly in the mid-level, and the private company's preference for whites spanned nearly all occupational groups (Table 4.4) but was particularly apparent in skilled jobs requiring a university education. The preference appears to whiten subordinate jobs, affecting administration, production, and even semi-skilled office work. Even in the state-owned company, the racial and gender inequalities discussed here were more evident when we studied the composition of occupational groups.

Company Hierarchy, Occupational Groups, and Color

In the petrochemical industry, management's rigid division between those who have college degrees, on the one hand, and technicians, craftspeople, and specialized workers, on the other, has had a strong influence

---

12. As yet, no data are available to evaluate if downsizing affected one racial or gender group more than another.

13. A detailed description of the personnel policy of this company can be found in Guimarães (1988, chaps. 4 and 6).

Table 4.3. Composition of Employees by Sex and Color in Two Petrochemical Plants in Camaçari

Color	State-Owned Company[a]			Private Company[b]		
	Men	Women	Total	Men	Women	Total
White	103	40	143	83	28	111
% line	72.0	28.0	100.0	74.8	25.2	100.0
% column	15.6	22.0	17.0	24.1	54.9	28.0
Moreno	162	42	204	74	14	88
% line	79.4	20.6	100.0	84.1	15.9	100.0
% column	24.5	23.1	24.2	21.4	27.5	22.2
Mulatto	141	37	178	61	4	65
% line	79.2	20.8	100.0	93.8	6.2	100.0
% column	21.3	20.3	21.2	17.7	7.8	16.4
Preto	255	63	318	127	5	132
% line	80.2	19.8	100.0	96.2	3.8	100.0
% column	38.6	34.6	37.7	36.8	9.8	33.3
Total	661	182	843	345	51	396
% column	78.4	21.6	100.0	87.1	12.9	100.0

SOURCE: Author's 1992 field research data.
[a]State-owned plant: Chi square: 4.22373; significant at 76 percent.
[b]Private plant: Chi square: 28.4312; significant.

Table 4.4. Percentage of Employees, Women, and Whites in
Two Petrochemical Plants

	% Employees		% Women		% Whites	
	State	Private	State	Private	State	Private
Industrial Jobs	55.8	63.8				
Engineers	9.9	8.2	6.0	9.1	33.3	62.5
Trained technicians	38.1	39.9	2.5	6.9	15.2	20.8
Semi-skilled technicians	7.8	15.7	3.0	0.0	6.1	6.3
Administrative Jobs	44.1	36.2				
Lawyers, auditors,						
M.D.s, and economists	5.1	5.5	30.2	27.3	27.9	52.4
Other professions	5.2	6.2	36.4	36.0	22.7	48.0
Skilled office workers	28.0	17.5	54.0	31.4	15.3	35.3
Semi-skilled office workers	5.8	7.0	20.4	7.1	8.2	25.0

SOURCE: Author's 1992 field research data.

on social relations within the company.[14] Because of the barrier represented by education, the jobs were usually classified as being high- or mid-level. At the high end, engineers (chemical, mechanical, electrical, and civil) stood out. More numerous, they monopolized the technical and hierarchically important positions. Next were found high-prestige professions, such as lawyers, doctors, administrators, and economists, used in special departments. Finally, there were the mid-level support professions—accountants, librarians, nurses, nutritionists, systems analysts—in addition to a residual group whose level of college education was so little relevant that it was diluted in the common, generic designation of "professional."

Predominating in the mid-level jobs were occupations demanding the equivalent of a high-school education (chemical analysis, industrial design, instrumentation, electromechanics, accounting, secretarial, equipment inspection) or specialized training courses (operation of petrochemical processes, industrial security). Access to other mid-level occupations, ranging from craftspeople prized by the industry (mechanics, solderers, electricians, lubricators) to "complementary craftspeople" (carpenters, painters), required less education. From this, we developed seven occupational categories: (1) engineers; (2) lawyers, auditors, doctors, administrators, and economists; (3) other college-trained pro-

14. The designation of "technicians" is reserved for those who have received secondary technical training or a high-level, specialized training course, and for craftspeople who have technical training or practical command of a craft or trade.

fessions; (4) skilled industrial workers; (5) skilled office workers; (6) semiskilled industrial workers; and (7) semiskilled administrative workers.

Analyzing the average education for individuals within each group, we noted that formal education appeared to be an occupational requirement: only very rarely was it circumvented and only in less prestigious careers in the plant's occupational hierarchy (such as the residual group of "professionals" and the systems analysts, at the university level, and transportation operators and some craftspeople, in mid-level occupational groups).

By examining the pattern of distribution of people across these occupational groups, we found, when controlling for color, that in the state-run plant 37.7 percent of its employees were *preto* but that they were a majority only in mid-level occupations. Whites and *morenos* were concentrated in positions of greater social prestige and authority; *pretos* were more numerous in the less skilled and subordinate jobs. Mulattos were generally more evenly distributed across all occupations. This pattern of distribution was not specific to this company and was congruent with what occurs in Bahian society in general, as we described earlier when discussing occupational selectivity in the labor market.

In the private plant, whites outnumbered other groups. Examination of the racial composition of occupational groups indicated that the privilege of whites cannot be attributed to coincidence, given that in practically all the groups, with the exception of manual labor in production, the number of whites was one-third to three times more than in the state company (Tables 4.5 and 4.6). An explanation can be found in informal mechanisms present in recruitment and selection processes, which we will explore below.

In both companies, unequal distribution of individuals by occupation did not appear to affect all racial groups in the same way. Where, then, was the line of demarcation of this inequality? Between whites and non-whites, as suggested by several recent analyses of data from the Brazilian labor market (Hasenbalg 1979; Silva 1980)? Between lighter (whites and *morenos*) and darker (mulattos and *pretos*), as in studies that suggest that discrimination increases with gradations of darkness in skin color? Or between *pretos* and other groups?

To answer this question, we calculated indices of dissimilarity among racial classifications (see Table 4.7),[15] which clearly show that in the state-

---

15. The index of dissimilarity measured social distance or inequality among racial groups by plotting the distribution of these groups in variables, such as position in the occupational hierarchy, level of education, salary, indicators of occupational mobility, and so forth. It varied from 0 (perfect equality) to 10 (total dissimilarity) and was calculated by adding the absolute values of

Table 4.5. Distribution of Employees, by Occupation and
Color, in the Private Plant

	Whites	*Morenos*	Mulattos	*Pretos*	Total
Engineers	20	9	1	2	32
% line	62.5	28.1	3.1	6.3	100.0
% column	18.0	10.2	1.5	1.5	8.1
Lawyers, auditors,					
M.D.'s, and economists	11	7	2	1	21
% line	52.4	33.3	9.5	4.8	100.0
% column	9.9	8.0	3.1	0.8	5.3
Other professions	12	7	1	5	25
% line	48.0	28.0	4.0	20.0	100.0
% column	10.8	8.0	1.5	3.8	6.3
Trained technicians	33	33	29	64	159
% line	20.8	20.8	18.2	40.3	100.0
% column	29.7	37.5	44.6	48.5	40.2
Skilled office workers	24	19	14	11	68
% line	35.3	27.9	20.6	16.2	100.0
% column	21.6	21.6	21.5	8.3	17.2
Semi-skilled technicians	4	8	15	36	63
% line	6.3	12.7	23.8	57.1	100.0
% column	3.6	9.1	23.1	27.3	15.9
Semi-skilled office workers	7	5	3	13	28
% line	25.0	17.9	10.7	46.4	100.0
% column	6.3	5.7	4.6	9.8	7.1
Total (in numbers)	111	88	65	132	396
Total column %	28.0	22.2	16.4	33.3	100.0

SOURCE: Author's September 1992 field research data.
NOTE: Chi square: 86.56911; full significance.

run plant, *pretos* suffered the greatest inequalities in occupational position, whether compared to whites, *morenos,* or light-skinned individuals
(*claros*). Mulattos occupy an intermediate position in this terrain, separated equally from whites, *morenos,* and *pretos.* It is interesting to note
that in this plant, the distance between *"brancos da terra"* or *"brancos da
Bahia"* (as people used to say in Bahia when referring to individuals considered "white" even though they had black forebears) and mulattos and

---

the differences in distribution of the selected variable in the groups of analysis and dividing the
result by two (Andrews 1992a). The measurement indicates the percentage of individuals who
would have to cross from one category to another in the variable under consideration in order
to reach perfect equality in distribution of racial groups.

Table 4.6.　Distribution of Employees, by Occupation and Color, in the State-Owned Plant

	Whites	*Morenos*	Mulattos	*Pretos*	Total
Engineers	28	34	17	5	84
% line	33.3	40.5	20.2	6.0	100.0
% column	19.6	16.7	9.6	1.6	10.0
Lawyers, auditors, M.D.'s, and economists	12	16	8	7	43
% line	27.9	37.2	18.6	16.3	100.0
% column	8.4	7.8	4.5	2.2	5.1
Other professions	10	20	5	9	44
% line	22.7	45.5	11.4	20.5	100.0
% column	7.0	9.8	2.8	2.8	5.2
Trained technicians	49	61	69	143	322
% line	15.2	18.9	21.4	44.4	100.0
% column	34.2	29.9	38.2	45.0	38.2
Skilled office workers	36	62	58	79	235
% line	15.3	26.4	24.7	33.6	100.0
% column	25.2	30.4	32.6	24.8	27.9
Semi-skilled technicians	4	6	13	43	66
% line	6.1	9.1	19.7	65.2	100.0
% column	2.8	2.9	7.3	13.5	7.8
Semi-skilled office workers	4	5	8	32	49
% line	8.2	10.2	16.3	65.3	100.0
% column	2.8	2.5	4.5	10.1	9.6
Total (in numbers)	143	204	178	318	843
Total column %	17.0	24.2	21.1	37.7	100.0

SOURCE: Author's September 1992 field research data.
NOTE: Chi square: 86.56911; significant.

pretos was greater than the distance between them and whites, possibly because whites are a minority in the local labor market. It bears repeating that the disadvantage of *pretos* was much more defined in relation to all the other groups. This pattern of differentiation makes the division between light-skinned and dark-skinned people more important in terms of aggregate classification.

In the private plant, the disadvantage of *pretos* in relation to other color groups was aggravated by the disproportionate advantage of whites, resulting most likely from the company's preference for recruiting outside Bahia. The distance between whites and *morenos* was equal

Table 4.7.   Index of Disparities Among Color Groups in Access to
Occupational Groups in the Two Plants

	State-Owned	Private
Whites/*Morenos*	6.95	14.99
Whites/Mulattos	19.50	36.09
Whites/*Pretos*	30.08	47.70
Whites/Darks[a]	25.24	33.57
Whites/Nonwhites	18.92	40.20
Morenos/Mulattos	17.46	21.10
Morenos/*Pretos*	33.26	33.33
Morenos/Darks	23.75	25.83
Pretos/Mulattos	18.01	15.55
Pretos/Nonwhites	23.69	30.17
Lights[a]/Mulattos	17.73	28.50
Lights/*Pretos*	31.38	40.38
Lights/Darks	23.47	32.88

SOURCE: Author's 1992 field research data.
[a]Darks = mulattos and *pretos;* lights = whites and *morenos.*

to the distance between mulattos and *pretos,* making the division between lights and *pretos* equivalent to that between whites and nonwhites.
That is, in the private plant, the polarity between whites and *pretos* was
very marked, whereas the pattern of disparity between *morenos* in relation to the other groups was similar in the two companies.

These data indicate, therefore, that a more bureaucratic and universalist labor management produces more graduated differences, although it
still leaves *pretos* in a disadvantaged position. Management that is freer of
formal hiring rules, on the other hand, permits a greater favoring of
whites in relation to all other color groups (even *"brancos da terra"*)
while at the same time accentuating the disadvantage of *pretos.*

Color and Education

To what can we attribute this inequality in the position of *pretos?* An obvious answer lies in differences in education, given that education was a
defining factor in job status. By analyzing the correlation among variables, we found a strong relationship between education and occupational groups, which supports this assumption. As a consequence of its
modernization and rationalization policies, the private-company employees exhibited an increasing trend toward higher levels of education,
which is seen in the correlation between educational level and year hired.

In the same fashion, women in this company had more education. In both companies, correlations between color and occupation and between color and education show that color functions as a barrier to access because *negras* (black women) have fewer years of schooling. However, it is probable that racial inequality in the composition of occupational groups reflected more than the simple inequality in formal education, although that may have been the most important factor.

In our survey, *pretos* had less formal education than other groups. There was a big gap in level of schooling between employees in the light-skinned group (that is, whites and *morenos*) and those in the dark-skinned group (that is, mulattos and *pretos*); however, differences between whites and *morenos,* on one hand, and *pretos* and mulattos, on the other, are more attenuated. That is, for all races, access to the desirable petrochemical industry jobs is more difficult than access to education. This is especially true with respect to private employers.

This pattern of inequality was more pronounced among men than among women. In the state-run firm, *preto* women had more education than mulatto women; but in the private firm, *preto* women had the least education of all racial groups. In view of the sparse distribution of *pretos* in positions of higher pay and greater power in the company, we can conclude that educational level constitutes a barrier for people of color. Nevertheless, there may be a racial and gender component in these occupational and educational inequalities. What mechanisms reproduce such inequalities? Are they external to the plant, with the inequality related to restricted access to, and progression through, school? Or is inequality also reinforced by mechanisms that operate within the workplace? To respond to these questions, we examined over-education, that is, the situation in which employees have more education than required for the positions held.

Over-Education: Under-Utilization or Strategy of Mobility?

Over-education among people with college degrees occupying mid-level jobs was not specific to a racial group, although it was more intense among whites in the state-run company and among *morenos* in the private company. (For a detailed description of the statistical analysis supporting these claims, see Castro and Guimarães 1993.) Thus, we can discard the hypothesis that these companies are indifferent to the education of blacks, given that no systematic under-utilization exists in regard to skilled black labor. On the contrary, these results seem to reveal either a reasonably diffuse strategy among skilled workers regardless of color that uses college education as an instrument for social and occupational mobility, or an over-qualification among women in the workforce. Over-education was an attribute mainly of administrative workers, whose chances for occupational mobility by means of formal education appear to be more effective; but it was also used by women to compensate for the handicap of their gender in these work contexts.

To what degree was over-education a strategy for occupational mobility versus a mere under-utilization of the workforce, principally women? Over-education can signify a strategy of usurpation of places (when it is effective), or, if it lacks effectiveness, it can also express the difficulty of realizing this usurpation by keeping those who resort to it under-utilized. To shed some light on this question, we examined individuals in the group holding higher level jobs but having entered at mid-level, probably with a high-school education. That is, we looked at a group for whom the strategy of over-education appears to have been successful. The composition by gender and color of this group of individuals in the two companies shows that it was women and *pretos* who most generally used the strategy of over-education. In the state firm, the ratio of women who were hired into mid-level jobs and those who were hired already having completed college was 0.62.[16] In the private firm, the same ratio calculated for *pretos* suggests that twice as many were hired into mid-level jobs as into others. In both cases, it seems clear that this strategy to achieve mobility was often used by disadvantaged groups. It is also interesting that these companies are permeable to these strategies of mobility.

We also examined distributions by gender and color, controlling for year hired. In doing so, we verified that in the first ten years of operation, when the companies' structures of organization and power were less consolidated, the success of a strategy of over-education for occupational mobility was much more common than it has been recently. This is true for both sexes and for all color groups alike. In addition, the data indicate that recruitment and selection policy has changed in recent years to favor the hiring of better educated people. In the private firm, for example, in its first five years of operation, the average educational level for new hires was less than a full primary education; later it rose to more than a high-school education. These results suggest that:

16. For blacks, however, we could not make statistically significant attributions.

- in the last ten years, the plants have counted on a better educated labor pool than in the first ten years of operation, having thereby increased de facto the formal education requirements for semiskilled and auxiliary positions;
- women responded to the elevation of educational requirements more than did other groups;
- *pretos*, more than the other color groups, experienced difficulties keeping up with this increase in educational requirements;
- educational level can function simultaneously as a barrier to access by *pretos* and as a passport for entry by women in the plants.

Career Performance Among People of Different Sex and Color Groups

Let us now establish another possible form of discrimination: the differential in pace of career advancement between whites and *negros* (blacks). We examined a technical career—process operators—and observed the distribution of people in all jobs according to color. We did not find any relevant relationship between job held and the worker's color. Notably, in the private firm, there exists a predominance of whites in managerial jobs within this specific technical career. Blacks are well represented in jobs requiring semi-qualified technical skills: at least 30 percent of all individuals in those positions were *pretos*.

If we look at career performance by measuring the average number of promotions and the average interval (in years) between those promotions, we find a curious phenomenon. The structure of the process operator's career, as well as the pattern of advancement, was very similar in the two firms, as evidenced by similar averages for both the number of promotions and the intervals between them. Despite this, we see that in the private firm the intervals between promotion were markedly shorter for white operators than for other color groups. Whites, concentrated in managerial jobs within the process-operator career, not only progressed more rapidly but were initially hired into higher-level jobs. Six of the twelve managers were born in Southeastern states. We noted that their progress was much faster than that of Bahians or Northeasterners, who hailed from states that are considered poorer and less developed (Table 4.8). This privileged pattern was also seen among skilled office workers in the private firm. However, the same did not occur in the state-owned plant. Although the average total number of promotions in the two companies was similar for the skilled office workers, in the state-owned plant

Table 4.8. Average Time in Years Between Promotions for Process Operators and Office Workers in the Private Company, by Place of Origin

	Process Operators		Office Workers	
Place of Origin	Intervals	Cases	Intervals	Cases
Salvador	2.4874	33	4.7640	27
Metropolitan Salvador and Recôncavo	2.9543	21	5.4159	5
Interior B.A.	2.5411	15	5.2121	15
Northeastern region	2.8863	2	9.9644	3
Southeastern region	1.5884	6	4.9635	3

SOURCE: Author's 1992 field research data.

we found less discrimination. Nevertheless, in the case of the office workers, whites who are native Bahians are numerically insignificant, which seems to indicate that discrimination operates through color and not only place of origin (Table 4.7).

In the case of the state-owned plant, the data were also surprising. If the pace of progression was slower for *pretos,* we would expect to find longer average intervals of time between promotions. Yet in the state firm, the *inverse* was true: the darker the worker, the *shorter* the intervals between promotions. Only in the average number of promotions does one find that mulattos and *pretos* perform worse than whites and *morenos.*

From the analysis of the data on mid-level careers, we can conclude that there was little racial discrimination in the state-owned plant in regard to either standards for promotions or career advancement. The signals of discrimination seem to be external to the career, whether it be in terms of access, by means of educational requirements, or because of preferential selection based on physical attributes that are socially (de)valued. In regard to the private plant, it seems clear that the privilege of whites is not limited to access to the better position, but also extends to standards for promotion and career advancement.

This last observation was used to synthesize the analysis of data on higher-ranking personnel. In the case of the state-owned plant, the distribution of color groups into three occupational categories (ranked by social prestige) indicated that, even when they were a minority, *pretos* are found in the less prestigious occupations (Table 4.9). However, once employed, the data suggest that we can no longer speak of discrimination in career advancement. In the state firm, *pretos* and whites were relatively similar, not only in pace of promotion but also in regard to achieving high-level positions. The major difference lay in the number of promo-

Table 4.9. Average Length of Interval Between Promotions, Number of Promotions, and Number of High-Level Positions Occupied by High-Level Personnel, by Color

	State-Owned Plant			Private Plant		
Color	Length of Interval	No. of Promotions	No. of Positions	Length of Interval	No. of Promotions	No. of Positions
Whites	3.98	1.33	2.33	3.15	1.46	0.93
Morenos	4.17	0.81	1.44	2.55	1.78	0.70
Mulattos	3.39	0.52	1.18	3.54	1.00	0.50
Pretos	4.70	1.12	1.87	5.45	2.25	0.25

SOURCE: Author's 1992 field research data.

tions for whites (2.33) versus that for mulattos and *morenos* (1.15 and 0.89, respectively). However, among high-level professionals, *pretos'* career performance (measured by number of promotions and high-level positions previously held) was better than that of mulattos and even of *morenos*.

In summary, in the state-owned company, we did not find the expected association between color and career. Formal rules for job mobility appeared to protect individuals who are discriminated against because of their color. In the case of the private company, however, the situation was different. Despite *pretos* receiving more promotions, the average interval between these promotions was much longer than that of other racial groups. Furthermore, the number of managerial jobs held by *pretos* was half that of mulattos, nearly one-third that of *morenos,* and close to one-fourth that of whites. For their part, whites control access to the high-level positions in both plants, although in the private firm this was even more evident. This suggests that in positions that are more vulnerable to the arbitrary and discretionary criteria of nomination and appointment—as appears to be the case for high-level positions—inequality of access for nonwhites increases.

Gender inequality was also generalized, regardless of the type of management. Gender discrimination was evident not only in the low number of women engineers but also in the fact that the average number of high-level positions held by men was more than triple that held by women. Having determined the gender composition of high-level jobs, we discovered that in the state-owned plant only 4 women in 26 (15 percent) held high-level jobs (as an administrator, an accountant, an economist, but only one engineer), compared to 34 of the 100 men. Men, monopolizing the plant's top-paying jobs, held 89 percent of the high-level positions (and almost 100 percent of the engineering jobs). But the inequalities did not stop there. In the state-owned company, we found an even more serious problem: women experienced an average delay of a year more than men between promotions over the length of their careers. Gender inequality, although reflected most noticeably by the overwhelming presence of men in engineering jobs, affected all higher level, managerial positions in the company. Women also suffered disadvantages in the private company: only 6 percent of women employees were in high-level jobs, the number of their promotions was always less than that of men, and the average interval between promotions was slightly greater than those of male employees.

Race, Gender, and Salary

In a capitalist company, an employee's salary is perhaps the most synthetic index of his or her professional competence and importance to the organization. Consequently, it is also a good indicator of relative power. In the private firm, we collected the following data on salaries (given in 1992 U.S. dollars): whites, $1,312.09; *morenos,* $1,071.01; mulattos, $830.55; *pretos* $827; men, $1,026.79; and women, $957.26. What stands out is the relationship between salary and color, on the one hand, and salary and gender, on the other. Salary level is determined by position in the occupational hierarchy, length of employment, level of authority, level of education, age, gender, color (white or nonwhite), and birthplace (born in Southeastern or Southern states, foreigner, or native Bahian). Using a correlational analysis, we found that salary level was determined by position in the occupational hierarchy. It was the decisive variable, explaining 53 percent of the variation in salary. In descending order of importance were length of employment, level of authority, education, and age. (Gender, color, and birthplace were found to have only slight explanatory power.)

We divided the variables into those that are neutral in relation to race or gender (length of employment and age) and those that, in contrast, are negatively associated with them (position in the occupational hierarchy, education, and level of authority). The first are universalist criteria; the second are more subject to particular influences.

This division is accurate, broadly speaking, with the following caveat: length of employment and age can hide alterations in hiring policies. In the case under examination, we established that the population hired tended, over time, to be lighter skinned and to have a smaller proportion of men. This was probably due to a hiring policy that emphasized the selection of somewhat more mature people and those with more education. This means, therefore, that *pretos* and mulattos tended to have more seniority, and they thus earn a higher wage than they would earn were they to have been hired more recently. Women, in contrast, suffer discrimination in all the variables that influence salary level.

Discrimination in the state firm is mediated by explicit criteria: education (limited education equates to limited access to jobs); courage and physical strength needed to work in the conditions found in a petrochemical plant (considered masculine attributes); industrial experience, intelligence, and discipline (regarded as cultural attributes belonging more to whites and people of more developed regions). But, of these, education is the principal barrier to mobility into high status jobs, and it is a principal determinant of salary level.

Conclusion

Our analysis indicated that the state-owned company presented mild forms of racial discrimination, attributable more to practices existing in the surrounding society than to managerial practices themselves. The most common form—the restriction of *preto* men's access to more skilled and better remunerated occupational positions—was strongly associated with the educational levels of those men. Even so, when compared to other petrochemical companies throughout Brazil, the state-owned company showed greater permeability to *negros* and women. In the same way, the performance of *pretos* and mulattos throughout their careers clearly showed that the organizational norms of hiring and promotion in the state-owned company were not greatly discriminatory in regard to race. In the private company, in contrast, we found not only barriers of access for *pretos* but also mechanisms that prevent their occupational mobility.

Seen as a whole, our data indicated that the most glaring form of discrimination affected the occupational mobility of women in the state-owned company and of women and *pretos* in the private company, which suggests the generalized presence in entrepreneurial and organizational practice of a strong discriminatory pattern in regard to gender.

One of our most important findings was that the inequality of *pretos* in relation to the other color groups was a striking indicator of color discrimination. Where a more universalist management policy was in force, we found better career performance for mulattos and *morenos*, in an evident tendency of *whitening,* in the sense that Thales de Azevedo (1956) and Oracy Nogueira (1955) lent to that term. But even under these policies, *pretos* remain noticeably subordinated. When more arbitrary and less regulated policies were in force, the privilege of whites increased notably in relation to all other color groups. However, even when the distance that separates whites and *morenos,* on one hand, and *pretos* and mulattos, on the other, widens and is the same on each side, it is *pretos* more than all the other groups who most intensely suffer the consequences of these policies.

We noted, finally, another result of important theoretical consequence. The universalist and bureaucratic management rules that impeded racial discrimination did not ease gender discrimination. Why? Probably because gender and race are distinct modes of classification that operate in distinct ways, producing distinct forms of inequality and discrimination.

Instead of separating and hierarchizing groups of people (whites, blacks, Asians, Hispanics, etc.), Brazilian racial classification seems to follow a principle that absorbs persons and hierarchizes them in a single whole (whites, *morenos,* mulattos and *pretos;* light-skinned and dark) (Da Matta 1985). Instead of an abstract notion of race, signifiers that are employed are concrete, physiognomic, and phenotypic (color of skin, straightness of hair, fullness of lips, shape of the nose, etc.). It is these features, not belonging to a race, that irredeemably form the racial capital of a Brazilian. And this capital is in strict relation to other ascribed properties (physical features such as gender, age, height, corpulence, and "normalcy"), converging to form the general phenotypic capital. To this are associated acquired qualities, among which two stand out—"good education" and the "network of relations" (Da Matta 1985)—to constitute a person's social capital. Scholars would have reason, then, to point out that racial groups in Brazil function principally as groups of prestige.

The overwhelming presence of persons (rather than groups of people) in our system of cultural reference deconstructs race or ethnicity into its original genetic and cultural elements so that they can be diluted along with other physical and cultural characteristics. Racism would exist, therefore, in the fact that Negroid features and African cultural heritage (which includes illiteracy) are negative in this calculation, whereas Aryan features and European culture carry positive associations.

Such a thesis adapts itself well to the results that we found in the state-owned company, which was organized under universalist labor management. In that plant, we did not find discriminatory mechanisms affecting career performance, even though we have shown that color can represent either an advantage or a handicap in gaining access to careers. One may speculate that some occupations were more black and others more white. But for all occupations, education most influenced access, functioning as the great leveler, at least in industry.

All this leads one to believe that the dilution of racial features into phenotypic features within a more inclusive classification inhibits the operation of labor force discrimination when rules for hiring, career promotion, and evaluation are followed uniformly. The only evidence that we found to the contrary—the concentration of whites (in detriment to *morenos,* mulattos, and *pretos*) in higher level jobs in the state-owned company—seems to be more an exception that confirms the rule. First, high level jobs were often the least bureaucratized positions and were not especially subject to universalist rules; and second, the engineers with the most seniority were concentrated in the highest level jobs, and among them there were more individuals from other regions of Brazil where whites are whiter.

Women, in contrast, even when inserted into a highly regulated environment, progressed more slowly and had fewer promotions than men, regardless of their color. Why? Probably because, unlike race, *gender* is socially and culturally constructed from abstract principles that reorganize the differences of sex. The agents can freely employ these principles, coloring the operation of universalist rules of labor organization: this or that activity is or is not appropriate for women; this or that quality is *feminine* or not, and it does or does not deserve to be considered as a promotional criterion; this or that job requires *masculine* qualities, and so forth.

Unlike what occurs with the differences of color—in which inequality of education justifies the inequality of positions—in the case of work relations between men and women, it is the inequality of education that underlies the equality of positions between the sexes. One can surmise that women, in order to compensate for gender subordination, need more educational capital than men.

5

SILENT CONFLICT:

Discriminatory Practices and Black Responses in the Workplace

Maria Aparecida Silva Bento

This chapter's examination of workplace discrimination in Brazil reveals an ongoing and silent conflict between blacks and whites in daily life on the job. Businesses and their human-resources representatives block the progress of black workers, reinforcing the denial and obfuscation of racial discrimination that is a fundamental characteristic of Brazilian racism. The racial criteria used by Brazilian employers in developing a profile on which to base recruitment, selection, and promotion decisions are never made explicit, yet black employees' narratives expose the persistence of these criteria in blocking their career paths. All this points to the need for public policy that would regulate employer-employee relations and for public disclosure of discriminatory processes affecting occupational mobility. But public policies that promote equal opportunity in the labor market must be based on understanding of the complex mechanisms that reproduce racial discrimination in the workplace. Fundamental to the design of effective antidiscrimination policies is an understanding of black workers' individual responses to discrimination as well as their collective resistance in the union movement.

The Brazilian Ministry of Labor, the Ministry of Culture, and the Center for Afro-Asian Studies of the Candido Mendes University of Rio de Janeiro supported the research described in this chapter. The chapter also reports on the author's research during the 1980s, which received initial support from the São Paulo State Council for the Participation and Development of the Black Community.

Racial Inequality in the Brazilian Labor Market

In spite of the inclusion of a color category in the Brazilian demographic census of 1872, it was only in 1980 that Brazil's official census agency, the Institute of Geography and Statistics (IBGE) began to analyze and disseminate race data systematically. Other governmental institutions and nongovernmental organizations began to study the conditions of blacks and whites in the labor market only after the political opening during the 1980s. Although labor market discrimination in Brazil is dramatic, fifteen years of official data documenting the problem have not resulted in even minimally satisfactory responses from either the private sector or the government.

According to the 1990 census, blacks made up almost 44 percent of the Brazilian population.[1] Yet studies undertaken to date reveal significant differences in rights and opportunities for blacks and whites, manifested in persistent racial segmentation of Brazil's labor market. The labor market analysis by Porcaro and Araújo (1988) concluded that more than half of the black labor force is concentrated in predominantly low-paying, manual occupations. Only about 13 percent of black workers are employed in nonmanual services compared to a figure of 24 percent for whites, and whites earn about twice as much as blacks in the higher paying nonmanual service-sector jobs. Porcaro and Araújo also noted that recruitment and selection procedures are more rigorous for blacks, resulting in their higher unemployment rates.

But income differences document discrimination even more clearly. According to 1990 national census data (IBGE 1994), black women and men had the lowest incomes nationwide. Average income for white men was 6.3 minimum salaries, while for black men it was 2.9 minimum salaries (with the comparable figures for women being 3.6 for whites versus 1.7 for blacks). Conditions for black women reach shocking levels: in the Northeast region, the overall average monthly income of that group is 90 percent of the legal minimum wage, and in rural regions it is only 30 percent.

Such evident inequality suggests that racism in the workplace strongly affects blacks, confining them to inferior economic circumstances and creating conditions for the aggravation of conflict among ethnic groups. It is a vicious cycle of exploitation and unequal treatment that is real but that has been systematically ignored by society in spite of official statistics and research.

1. "Blacks" includes both *preto* and *pardo* individuals.

Both domestically and abroad, Brazilians prefer to broadcast the idea that their country is an unbiased, egalitarian society. Brazil has disseminated this basic premise, which underlies the ideology of a "racial democracy," for strategic political reasons. Perhaps the most damaging result of the myth that blacks and whites enjoy the same opportunities is that it places responsibility for blacks' inferior socioeconomic and political position on blacks themselves. The persistent denial of the existence of discrimination by institutions, the media, and schools creates enormous difficulties that blacks must overcome in order to organize to struggle against racism.

To confront the contradictions between black's ongoing experience of racial discrimination and the official discourse that Brazilians "are all equal before the law," we examined the institutional mechanisms reinforcing discriminatory practices in everyday life. We specifically sought to reveal the way in which daily practices, under the pretext of official discourse, reconciled a denial of racism with discriminatory actions that have resulted in disadvantages to blacks.

A brief review of social science research on race in Brazil shows that from the end of the nineteenth century to the middle of the twentieth, the belief in the innate inferiority of mestizos and blacks, along with a general denial of violent horrors that slave owners had inflicted on blacks, grew and spread (R. N. Rodrigues 1945, Freyre 1933). These ideas evolved into strategies to perpetuate racial inequality, and they have become the basis for the biased idea of a "Brazilian style" of race relations. For four decades, studies explicitly combating the myth of Brazil's racial democracy have been heralded for their efforts to overturn these ideas. This campaign was led by, among others, Octávio Ianni (1972), Florestan Fernandes (1978), Emilia Viotti da Costa (1982), and Sueli Robles de Queiroz (1977). These authors all began with the assumption that slavery was rooted in violence and exploitation, which allowed the institution to continue; in other words, racial democracy had always been a myth. Moreover, the reality of specific racial inequalities in Brazilian society proved that it was a false concept. Nevertheless, Fernandes and other authors analyzing class relations could not avoid strengthening existing black stereotypes and even creating new ones, such as the notion of the black individual "deformed" by the slave experience. While slavery involved two parts of society (that is, black and white), the personality that was deformed by the institution, according to Fernandes, was the black part: "Slavery deformed its agents of labor, impeding blacks and mulattos from being able to fully enjoy the fruits of post-abolition free labor—in which they had to compete with other human beings" (Fernandes 1978, 1:52).

Under pressure from the black movement, researchers in the last two decades have found new linkages between race and class resulting from the consolidation of industrial capitalism in Brazil. Their studies demonstrate that racial inequality is not only being perpetuated but is reasserting itself in certain places, such as the Southeastern region, which has the highest level of economic development in Brazil. The most outstanding work among these analytical explorations of race relations are those of Chaia (1988), Porcaro e Araújo (1988), Carneiro and Santos (1985), Rosemberg (1987), Bairros (1991), and Hasenbalg (1979).

To examine discrimination and black workers' responses to it—phenomena systematically ignored by Brazilian scholars—we turned to Norberto Bobbio's concept of resistance in his studies of passive and active opposition documented in Europe during the Second World War (1986, 1114). Bobbio characterized resistance as a reaction more than an action, a defense more than an offense, a diffuse phenomenon that is not localized geographically and that takes many forms, but which is always present when oppression occurs. We also referred to literature on labor relations and education (Apple 1989; Giroux 1983; Enguita 1989; Anyon 1990). These authors confirm that blacks' reactions to discrimination cannot be reduced to the interpretations of classical political analysis in which individuals are viewed as being passive in the face of a dominant ideology. Authors in this school emphasize that people are not mere receptors; they interpret the values dictated by the dominant ideology and reproduce them with their own subjective interpretations (Apple 1989, 31–32). These authors also describe a pendulum-like effect in the nature of oppressed peoples' aspirations that makes them advance and retreat from institutional requirements. For some theorists, resistance is not necessarily conscious, directed, or collective (Apple 1989; Anyon 1990. Nevertheless, it is always present, and in our case, it is associated with racial identification.

Methodology

To deepen our understanding of workplace discrimination from the workers' point of view, we collected seventy-five employment histories of black men and women working in metropolitan São Paulo in 1989. These individuals were employed in a variety of occupations, ranging from unskilled workers to independent professionals. The sample was stratified by sex and educational level. In addition to recording occupational histories, we also formed discussion groups with twenty-five black union leaders to examine the position of black workers in the labor market and the unions' efforts to address the situation of blacks in the workplace.

Because of the ideology of whitening, not all descendants of blacks identify themselves as "black." For that reason, we included in our sample individuals drawn from membership lists of black movement groups and Afro-Brazilian groups or organizations affiliated with unions, universities, companies, associations, and government agencies. When it was necessary to use other sources, we selected from photographs those individuals who were without a doubt black, that is, those who are usually identified as "ink black" (negros retintos). We also sought to include subjects with diverse patterns of mobility. That is, among people working in the same profession, preference was given to those who had worked in a variety of capacities. For example, a lawyer who had worked in public organizations, been a manager, and also had experience as a university professor would be selected over a professional whose experience was limited to a private practice.

Our first sample contained 310 names, and from that we selected the seventy-five people who were interviewed. Of those subjects, 80 percent had, at some point in their careers, performed manual jobs. Women had worked as seamstresses doing piecework, and men had worked as manual laborers. Few of the subjects had held management positions; when they had, it was in industry, government administration, or labor unions. The majority of our interviewees were employed in the banking sector and financial institutions, with most of the remainder in sales.

In addition to discussing workplace experiences, our interviews explored the subjects' family and school backgrounds in regard to the formation of racial identity and racial conflict. An overall reading of the testimonies revealed that the daily experience of black individuals is plagued by intense discrimination that provokes a constant sense of danger and preparedness for confrontation. Stories revealed a pattern of human relations far removed from the famous Brazilian "cordiality" that white Brazilians would like to believe exists.[2] Contrary to the studies that have claimed that Brazilian blacks are passively docile in the face of discrimination, we found that blacks must continuously summon up responses and stage resistance to discrimination in the workplace.

---

2. Historian Sérgio Buarque de Holanda (1995) was the first to label Brazil's race relations as "cordial."

Discriminatory Practices in the Workplace

Our research highlighted two aspects of Brazilian discrimination: First, the testimonies of subjects contradict many studies of Brazilian race relations that view discrimination as occasional and episodic in black people's lives, or as something that is perpetrated only by fanatics. Second, our findings refute studies that attribute blacks' difficulty in "integrating" into Brazilian society to the legacy of slavery, which supposedly has forever crippled the black identity (Fernandes 1978). Racial discrimination as described by our subjects is a permanent set of daily practices that guarantees both economic and symbolic privileges to white workers. The interviews revealed that integration in the workplace is not hindered by blacks themselves, but by whites, who block blacks' entrance into and mobility in the job market.

Recruitment and On-the-Job Discrimination

Discrimination was reported in personnel recruitment and selection in all types of jobs, whether among domestic servants, unskilled laborers, or professional workers. Officially, racial identity is not evaluated by personnel professionals. However, testimony from interviewees indicated otherwise, as one woman's report reflects:

> Two women, both of whom had more than five years experience in television production, applied for a job. I routed their forms to Mr. Pires, the manager. His assistant came back and said there was just one job opening. I called Mr. Pires and asked him if he was losing his mind. He had just told me there were two positions open for production work. He said, "Ah, dona Rosane, you didn't tell me one was a *crioula,* you didn't tell me that." I said, "Mr. Pires, it's too bad you don't have a video screen on your phone so you could see me." Then I hung up.

Blacks' access to jobs is blocked by subterfuge and complex configurations of racism, as another interviewee recalled:

> A feature of government jobs filled by competitive exams is that the boss has to accept as employees those who pass the exam; an employer can't reject someone who passes. But this doesn't guarantee that racism won't be present. If the boss can't discriminate

in the selection of an employee, he can when you start the job. Managers can make you feel that they don't have confidence in you, or they won't tell you things you have to know to do your job. Limiting your responsibilities is another way of humiliating an employee, especially when its implies that you can't be trusted.

Many interviewees recounted that they were told they were hired for their "competence" but were considered an exception. They would be subjected to comments such as, "You don't seem like a black." Co-workers often treated these "exceptional" employees as if they were whites, encouraging them to keep other black workers at arm's length. But when conflicts arose, these same employees would be reminded of their race by colleagues, with remarks we heard reported in many of the subjects' interviews: "It had to be a black," or "It could only have been a black."

Subjects also repeatedly pointed to provocations in the workplace and identified an overload of day-to-day responsibilities when compared to the levels of work required of white employees. When blacks occupied positions of authority or management, clients devalued their competence, and colleagues and subordinates were disrespectful or mistrusted their performance. Confirming the official statistics on wage differentials (IBGE 1990; SEADE 1992), blacks consistently reported that when they carried out the same functions as whites, their job titles and salaries were below those of their white counterparts. Conversely, other subjects observed that even when they had the same job title and salary as a colleague, they were not always allowed to carry out the same duties. For example, blacks often reported being blocked from performing jobs entailing the handling of money and equipment or involving access to sensitive areas of the firm. Even when an employee's level of responsibility was high, discrimination could be at play: "I was one of five people (among the company's forty thousand employees worldwide) who traveled on business. I flew more than an airline pilot, but I never saw a good promotion, even after sixteen years in the same position!"

Employment Mobility

The research also revealed that the more job mobility a black experienced within a firm, the more uncomfortable his or her white colleagues became, and the more intense and visible the discrimination inflicted on the employee. Many whites refused to accept the idea that blacks might be in positions of power. One of the interviewees, Joanna, recounted, "I was promoted to head of the department—a position directly reporting to the department chair, one of the highest posts in the university—but when people came into the office looking for Dr. Joanna, they would go to the white clerks, until finally a young male clerk once exclaimed, 'Listen, do you think I look like a Joanna, Professor?' "

As they rose in the hierarchy of the workplace, subjects reported the setting of "traps"—strategies to get them to make an error. As one interviewee noted, "They went as far as to accuse me of allowing them to cheat on the test. The students got together and sent one pupil to ask me something; as soon as I got distracted answering his question, the others copied from each other. . . . Then they turned it around and charged me with letting them cheat!"

Many of the blacks interviewed in the study reported salary levels that were below the market average, and they also complained that they had had difficulty in getting training to prepare them for better jobs. This type of discrimination was most accentuated when it involved black women. Sixty percent of the women interviewed began their working lives as domestic workers, and 40 percent of them had to return to this occupation in times of economic crisis. Black women were rarely promoted to management positions or to jobs involving contact with clients or with authority figures in their own firms. In a culture obsessed by the cult of the body, women are subjected to great pressure in regard to their personal appearance. Black women are particularly harmed by this criteria, since standards of beauty are based on a European physique.

Although hiring for government jobs is less discriminatory because candidates compete by taking impartial civil service exams, opportunities for professional growth within the public sector are still limited for blacks. Of the 75 percent of our subjects who had been engaged in public service at some point in their lives, virtually all felt that racial discrimination had interfered with their promotion. Blacks who specialized in training colleagues reported that white coworkers trained by them often got promotions or even became their supervisors, whereas the black worker's position remained unchanged. Other blacks with special qualifications were not rewarded with salaries and benefits commensurate with their professional knowledge, experience, and skills. All the subjects interviewed who had reacted explicitly to discriminatory practices at work reported having been reprimanded, demoted, or in extreme cases, fired. Marcos, one of the interviewees, recounted that his own boss had declared, " 'I don't like you . . . for a very simple reason, you are black. I don't like the fact that in a business like this we have a black at the reception desk . . . I want to throw you out of here!' And imagine, he was my boss! 'Be careful because with the first mistake you make, you are out of here.' "

When, despite negativity and obstacles, a black is promoted to a position of leadership, he or she can immediately sense an increase in the intensity of rejection and discrimination. Christina, another person interviewed during the research, explained, "My relationships here at work are very difficult; I have made them difficult, I have made the other employees dislike me because I am a very demanding person, a perfectionist, a detail-oriented individual. I have had arguments with people, and they have resisted when I gave them direction; they don't want to take orders from a black, you see?"

Joanna, in her testimony, says that she was always worried about being fired. "I had a high visibility job. . . . I reported directly to the President, and I was the first black and the first women to be a manager . . . whatever happened, I clung to my position, knowing that others were after my job." It is important to note the reference to being "the first" or "the only one" in a position never before occupied by blacks. On one hand, there is evidence that institutional discrimination over decades has placed white men in the positions of power; on the other hand, there is also evidence of the exceptional resources of individuals who, under certain circumstances, break barriers. This extraordinary situation also reveals the burden of accepting additional responsibilities, which carries with it the obligation to prove that nonwhites, that is, all the categories that compose the notion of "the other," are also competent human beings. Part of blacks' burden as "pioneers" arises from not having role models on which to rely.

Black Workers' Resistance

According to Manuela Carneiro da Cunha (1985) and Edgar Carvalho (1985), racial identification is a form of resistance to discrimination, a political response of people living apart from their places of origin. This can create a "diaspora culture," which affirms racial identity and the consciousness of difference. However, many researchers have demonstrated that in racist societies, groups suffering discrimination may have great difficulty in self-identification and may even consider members of their own racial group to be inferior (Hasenbalg 1979, 254). Evidence of this appeared frequently in our interviews.

Although black workers' responses to discrimination varied in intensity, explicitness, and levels of conscious awareness, the boundaries of the reactions were consistently defined by workers' conscious or uncon-scious evaluation of the balance of potential losses and gains that a reac-tion might generate. In the workplace, this meant assessing the risks involved in maintaining or improving one's position on the job. These balance-sheet calculations constitute what we call *survival strategies.*

Most interviewees who experienced discrimination responded to it in some way. Their reactions ranged from silence and retreat to verbal and physical aggression. At one extreme, we found blacks who believed that discrimination did not affect them directly or who attributed their diffi-culties to factors not related to race. This response appeared in various forms: black workers' negation of their own racial identity, their con-stant criticism of other blacks, their efforts to associate with white col-leagues and "appear white," and their wish to avoid behaviors stereotyped as black. Some individuals even attempted to hide their black features and avoided altogether associating with blacks. We also observed responses of withdrawal, depression, loss of energy, and failure to make future plans—all of which frequently translated into job loss.

Some interviewees confronted discrimination by obsessively accumu-lating knowledge about their jobs to prepare for daily racial confronta-tions or by attempting to deconstruct the stereotype of inferiority by demonstrating their aptitude and excellence. These blacks strove to be "the best," the most competent, the most honest on the job, and to achieve "unexpectedly" higher results than their coworkers. Other indi-viduals attempted to maintain strictly formal professional relationships with whites, confining their contact with them to the workplace.

A smaller but significant number of subjects responded to discrimina-tion with aggression. This more overt reaction appeared at moments in respondents' lives in which their racial identity was mobilized. The re-sponses that we gathered suggest that as racial identity grows, blacks try to make discriminatory practices more visible by involving whites and, principally, other blacks in the issue. This reaction may stimulate others to denounce discriminatory practices: blacks begin to encourage other blacks to identify with their negritude, and at the same time they attempt to strengthen and support the blacks with whom they work.

Organizing Strategies

Cross (1991) characterizes the taking of initiative in organizing blacks against workplace discrimination as a mature form of resistance. Actors involved in collective resistance may choose the union as the best place to assemble and deliver responses to workplace discrimination. However, the Brazilian union movement has until very recently been unreceptive to the racial issues confronted by black workers. Unions are definitively beginning to incorporate racial issues, if only because of the strong pressure exerted by its black leadership and because of the pressure from black women who are members of women's councils within the unions. In my estimation, this trend is growing rapidly. If it were not for these pressures, the unions would have remained focused only on class.

The reports from our subjects indicate that union discourse urges black workers to forget their daily confrontation with racism; it tries to convince them that they are equal to all workers (that is, nonblacks) and asks them to abdicate their racial identity in the name of class unity. As a result, some black union leaders we interviewed strongly opposed recognizing and addressing discrimination. They used expressions such as "the totality." In their view, effective union actions are based on the workers' struggle as an undifferentiated "totality." From this rationale is derived the idea that the "race issue" (or discrimination) has nothing to do with the union. The fear also persists among union leaders that specific demands voiced by subgroups could undermine the unity, indivisibility, and homogeneity of the workers' struggle. The significance of discrimination against black workers is therefore devalued, resulting in the unions' silence on race issues.

Given the unions' silence on racial discrimination in the workplace, we question the assertions of Ricardo Antunes (1991) and other scholars that all union action is based on daily struggles of the working classes, since the everyday experience of racial discrimination is not on the union agenda. What is the color of the workers that Antunes and his colleagues are talking about? Since blacks do not seem to have support from the union movement in their daily struggle against racism, it appears that the intellectuals' vision of the union is pasteurized.

Nevertheless, the labor movement's disregard has not stopped black workers from organizing and searching for a systematic, institutional means of securing visibility and support for their struggle against racial discrimination. In some cases, we found that unions had encouraged black workers to voice their reflections on racism, since the workers viewed the union as a legitimate place to struggle against injustice.

Our research on Brazilian labor unions suggests that black workers and labor leaders have begun to organize to increase pressure on the labor movement to respond to a problem that affects almost half of the Brazilian labor force. Since 1990 the Center for the Study of Labor Relations and Inequality (Centro de Estudos das Relações do Trabalho e Desigualdades, CEERT) has been offering courses to union locals in twelve Brazilian states. The goal of these courses is to examine the intersection of syndicalism and racism in the labor market. That effort was vital to the creation in 1992 of the National Commission Against Racism (Comissão Nacional contra o Racismo), formed by union leaders within the Workers' Central Union (Central Única dos Trabalhadores, CUT). Among the Commission's achievements are:

- the decentralization of antidiscrimination efforts within the CUT through the creation of state-level commissions;
- heightened visibility, resulting from a national-level conference held in August 1993 involving the participation of 102 delegates from forty unions in eight states;
- the formation of a political environment that made possible the approval of an unprecedented antiracist platform during the 1995 National Meeting of the CUT.

Brazil's second largest labor confederation, Força Sindical (Syndical Force), now also has a Special Agency in the Fight Against Racism, and the General Confederation of Workers (CGT) has formed a National Commission Against Racism.

In November 1994, the three main Brazilian labor confederations, all affiliated with the AFL-CIO, organized a conference to examine North Americans' experiences in combating racism in the workplace and to establish formal linkages with U.S. unions. In August 1995, these three Brazilian confederations participated in the Second Inter-American Conference on Racial Equality, which was held in the United States. As a result of the joint effort, the Inter-American Union Institute on Racial Equality was established in Brazil in November 1995, with the participation of unions from both countries. Additionally, the collaboration of Brazilian unions and the Brazilian government resulted in the creation of a Working Group on the Elimination of Occupational and Employment Discrimination, sponsored by the Ministry of Labor, the goal of which is the implementation of the International Labour Organisation's Convention 111. This group consists of eight representatives from the Brazilian federal government, three union representatives, five representatives of employers from industry and the business community; and one representative from the Ministry of Labor, a cabinet-level agency that regulates employment.[3] A decree signed by Brazilian President Fernando

3. CEERT was elected by the labor confederations to participate and to give technical assistance to government representatives in the Ministry of Labor's Working Group.

Henrique Cardoso and the Brazilian Minister of Labor and published in the official government record in March 1996, commissions the Working Group "to design steps to combat discrimination, propose strategies to implement those steps in both industry and in the professions, and suggest normative policies as necessary."

This represents a potentially promising initiative if only because of the opportunity it presents for an unprecedented dialogue about race among workers, business people, and the government. Moreover, the Ministry of Labor's participation signals the possible strengthening of the state's role in enforcing antidiscriminatory policies as well as increasing the quantity and quality of suits pursued in the judiciary. In his 1995 pronouncement to the United Nation's Commission on Human Rights, Minister of Justice Nelson Jobim reinforced the state's new role, anticipating some of the principles that would be announced in the Cardoso administration's 1996 National Human Rights Plan. The goals of the Plan include the introduction of the "color" category in public-information data systems, which would aid in the implementation of Convention 111, and the refinement of antidiscriminatory legislation.

Conclusion

This chapter has illustrated the ongoing and often subtle discrimination against blacks experienced in daily life on the job. In order to design effective antidiscrimination policies, an understanding of black workers' individual and collective responses to discrimination is needed. Our study examined the institutional mechanisms reinforcing racially discriminatory practices in everyday life. We specifically sought to reveal the way in which daily practices reconciled a denial of racism with discriminatory actions that have resulted in disadvantages to blacks. The testimonies of our research subjects contradict studies of Brazilian race relations that view discrimination as occasional and episodic in black people's lives, and they refute studies that attribute blacks' difficulty in "integrating" into Brazilian society to the legacy of slavery. Instead, racial discrimination is described as a permanent set of practices that guarantees both economic and symbolic privileges to white workers. The interviews revealed that integration in the workplace is not hindered by blacks themselves, but by whites who block blacks' entrance into and mobility in the job market. It is within this ongoing environment that black workers must constantly invoke survival strategies to balance potential losses and gains that might result from a fight to move up the job ladder.

Thus, despite potential advances in race relations made possible by the Brazilian government in recent years, it is still within an extremely discriminatory environment that innovative antidiscrimination policies must be developed for the workplace. The union movement should be leading the working class in this effort. Although it is heterogeneous and pluralistic, the working class faces its greatest challenge in promoting and defending equal opportunity for *all* workers, differentiated but united.

6

RACIAL DISCRIMINATION AND CRIMINAL JUSTICE IN SÃO PAULO

Sérgio Adorno

The principle of equality before the law is a legacy of classical political thought, solemnly proclaimed in the 1789 Brazilian Declaration of the Rights of Man and of the Citizen. This principle claims that all citizens are subject to the same laws regardless of class, gender, ethnicity, regional origins, or religious or political convictions and that all citizens enjoy the same constitutionally guaranteed rights. In short, the law cannot promote the exclusion of some in favor of others. Forged into the liberal architecture of the modern state, this principle was embodied in democratic constitutions and codified to allow for the peaceful articulation of individual and social identity and private interests with the goal of guaranteeing the common good (Bobbio 1986 and 1988; Neuman 1964; Rawls 1971; W. G. Santos 1981; Vachet 1970).

Intense social struggles, mostly in Western Europe and North America, during nearly a century, brought citizens of the popular classes into the public arena, challenged the bourgeoisie's economic and social privi-

This chapter reports on a research study supported by the Ford Foundation, Fundação de Amparo à Pesquisa do Estado de São Paulo/FAPESP, and the Conselho Nacional do Desenvolvimento Científico e Tecnológico/CNPq. The research team was Leila Maria Vieira de Paula and Sônia Maria P. Nascimento (Geledés Institute); and Cristina Eiko Sakai, Amarylis Ferreira Nóbrega, Marcelo Gomes Justo, and Jacqueline Signorretto (NEV-USP). Eliana Blumer Trindade Bordini (Fundação SEADE) provided statistical assistance. Dr. Angélica Mello de Almeida provided assistance with legal research. My special thanks goes to Túlio Kahn and Renato Sérgio de Lima, who collaborated in the computation, and to Nancy Cardia for her invaluable assistance in revising this chapter. Carlos Cesar Grama, Mário Baldini, and Raquel Uyeda also lent their support to the project. However, I take full responsibility for the content of the essay.

leges and established new terms for political relations, thus diminishing the historical asymmetries between the governing elites and the governed. This process reduced immense social inequalities, laying the groundwork for the rule of law and establishing a historical nexus between social justice and judicial equality.

Despite its universalizing propositions, the principle of judicial equality was widely accepted only in those societies where advanced capitalist development had already brought a level of well-being to the working classes. In modern societies where capitalist development had not consolidated, the acceptance of this principle often was merely symbolic. The gap between the ideal and the concrete reality of discrimination and exclusion contributes to the weakening of universal criteria of judgment intended to resolve conflicts and disputes in intersubjective relations. In such situations, only *some* citizens enjoy access to justice, and judicial decisions are often discriminatory.

This is true of Brazil, where large segments of the population live excluded from full rights despite reconstruction of the democratic order following twenty-one years of authoritarian rule (Pinheiro 1984 and 1991; Zaluar 1985 and 1986). Different factors contribute to this situation: un- or under-employment, lack of professional training, insufficient education, gender, regional origin, age, and above all else, color. Blacks—men and women, adults and children—find themselves situated on the lowest rungs of the social hierarchy in Brazilian society, as numerous research studies have demonstrated (Hasenbalg 1979; Jaguaribe 1986 and 1989; Jaguaribe et al. 1990). Among the poor, blacks receive the lowest salaries and receive the least education (Oliveira et al. 1983).

Social exclusion is reinforced by prejudice and stigmatization (C. C. M. Azevedo 1987; Bastide and Fernandes 1959; Schwarcz 1987; Skidmore 1976). Black citizens are commonly perceived as potential disrupters of social order (Fausto 1984). Perhaps for that reason they also constitute a target for police investigations (Paixão 1982 and 1988), although there is no empirical scientific evidence of blacks' greater criminal activity (Adorno 1996). If crime is not a characteristic of the black population, punishment seems to be. This certainly is not a phenomenon exclusive to Brazilian society. Elsewhere, socioeconomic discrimination frequently is associated with and reinforced by ethnic or racial discrimination. In the United States, where there is a long tradition of social confrontation between whites and blacks, the issue has been the subject of many scientific investigations (Barry and Blassingame 1982; Comer 1985; Epstein 1981; Kuntz II 1978; Lane 1979 and 1986; Reiss Jr. 1974 and 1976; Silberman 1978; Simon et al. 1976; Wolfgang 1972; Wolfgang et al. 1976; Wright 1987).

What appears to differentiate Brazil from other societies is Brazilians' extreme tolerance for racial discrimination. In the United States, particularly in the 1950s and 1960s, fierce resistance grew against this form of discrimination and manifested itself in the intense civil rights struggle. In Brazil, in contrast, the average citizen believes that race relations are harmonious. Our political and historical traditions have failed to denounce discrimination, thus helping to solidify this myth. The myth of racial harmony freely circulates in civil society as well as among political actors who formulate and implement public policies to preserve human rights. The myth is endowed with such extraordinary symbolic efficacy that it has even seduced social scientists.

A very small circle of people—intellectuals, politicians, human-rights activists—has denounced Brazil's racism in organized public protests, electronic media and the press, and most of all in their own research (Adorno 1991a, b; Adorno and Bordini 1989; Benevides 1983; Campos Coelho 1980; Fausto 1984; Paixão 1983 and 1988; Pinheiro 1982 and 1984; Zaluar 1989a, b). Their studies find that government agencies charged with controlling crime also promote discrimination through police intimidation, punitive sanctions, and harsher treatment for "the youngest, poorest, and blackest" suspects and prisoners. On the other hand, middle- and upper-class citizens who commit crimes, including those individuals mixed up with sophisticated criminal organizations, receive better treatment and lighter punishment. Inequalities in sanctions based on the class of the accused are neither few nor irrelevant. Among the most flagrant is the privilege granted those holding university degrees. For this population, the government has established a special prison, where inmates are isolated from contact with "common" prisoners. Despite having committed ordinary crimes, this "jail apartheid" means that the well-educated are not subject to the same prison conditions affecting most of the wards of the Brazilian penal system.

The survival of authoritarianism in its multiple manifestations—isolation, segregation, prejudice, lack of rights, injustices, oppression, assaults on civil and political liberties, in short, human rights violations—indicates that the forces committed to democratic advancement in Brazilian society have not managed to overcome the forces committed to the conservative and authoritarian heritage left by the colonial past of patrimony and slavery (Da Matta 1979 and 1982; Lebrun 1987; Martins 1984; O'Donnell 1984, 1986, and 1987; Pinheiro 1984 and 1991; Reis and O'Donnell 1988; A. Stepan 1988).

Many obstacles impede the universalization of full citizenship rights. Among them are persistent, extreme social inequalities—despite impressive economic and social development in Brazil during the second half of the twentieth century—along with accentuated corporatism that introduces a serious imbalance into the organization of collective interests, and the low level of participation of citizens in the organizations that represent different social groups. These features converge to maintain a profoundly divided society, crosscut by elite cultural identities, lifestyles, and patterns of consumption that work against the common good. Regulation of Brazilian society relies on interpersonal and private relationships, in which the rules of conduct do not obey the same legal principles that regulate the state. Therefore, conflicts tend to be resolved based on relations of dominance/submission between the powerful and the weak without mediation by public institutions and laws (M. Santos 1991).

Entrenched in the judicial apparatus are impediments that ensure the failure of an effective distribution of social justice. The criminal justice system is marred by conservatism and a rigid corporate structure—both of which sustain a patrimonial style of public administration (Adorno 1994; J. E. Faria 1989 and 1991; Lopes 1989). The result has been the consolidation of a criminal justice system that restricts individual rights and thus approaches failure in its political function of maintaining civic order (Adorno 1991a).

In this chapter, I consider social processes that lead to the Brazilian state's restriction of rights, and I try to answer the following questions: In what circumstances and in which stages of criminal procedure do black defendants accused of violent crime become targets of penal sanctions as compared to white defendants in identical situations? What are the possible causes of the differential judicial treatment applied to black defendants in relation to white defendants? How does inequality in distribution of rights and access to justice manifest itself?

Crime and Ethnicity

In any great metropolis, fear of crime constitutes one of the main issues on citizens' lists of insecurities and uncertainties (Wright 1987). In Brazilian society the feelings of fear and insecurity are no longer restricted to those living in the big cities, and there is a widespread perception that anyone, regardless of race, class, gender, age, or ethnic or regional origin, may become the victim of a criminal offense. This feeling is not unfounded. Official crime statistics indicate an increase in every category of crime, especially those involving violence.[1] Substantial

1. Many studies have shown that official crime statistics suffer grave methodological difficulties. These studies, used by social analysts as indicators of change in levels and patterns of crime, are better used to identify effects of changes in penal legislation as well as decline in the efficacy

changes in conventional patterns of crime as well as in the profile of people involved in criminal activities have accompanied this growth. A widening internationalization of organized crime, especially drug trafficking, is also being experienced worldwide (Enzenberger 1967).[2]

Common wisdom and collective opinion associate crime with a socially constructed profile of the potential criminal. Criminality is widely believed to be biologically determined, with certain "races" being more inclined to delinquency (Goffman 1961). Black citizens, in particular, appear in the collective consciousness as potential criminals. Physical and cultural attributes of blacks have stigmatized them with the blame for the growth of violent urban crime. In Brazil the substratum of these beliefs lies in historical-cultural roots. Since colonial times, slave owners judged blacks to be "lazy, corrupt, and immoral" (Bretas 1991, 54). Throughout the nineteenth century, political elites concerned with Brazil's development and progress (as measured against Europe and the United States) found in racial ideologies a balm for its dilemmas.

However, no contemporary study confirms that blacks are more inclined than whites to commit crimes. On the contrary, since the late 1920s, U.S. studies have shown the extent to which social and cultural prejudices, especially racism, compromise the neutrality of court trials and the universality of applying criminal laws. Sellin (1928), in a classic study, demonstrated the selective preference of penal sanctions for blacks. Shaw and McKay (1931), studying the distribution of crime in major U.S. cities, sought to demonstrate that in some residential areas where crime was endemic, delinquency persisted despite substantial changes over time in the ethnic or racial compositions of these neighborhoods. Unlike areas with lower rates of delinquency, these neighborhoods "were characterized by physical deterioration and declining populations, the economically underprivileged, ethnic cultures, high crime rates among adults, and a disintegration of traditional institutions and neighborhood organizations with the failure of the functioning of the community as an organ of social control" (Reiss Jr. 1976, 64–65).

Nevertheless, subsequent studies contested the supposition that delinquency was disproportionately concentrated among groups of lower socioeconomic status or among certain ethnic groups such as blacks. Some

---

of police performance. Compare, among others, Gurr 1977; Curtis 1985; Wright 1987; Robert et al. 1994; Paixão 1983 and 1986.

2. The tendency toward increase in violent crime, especially crimes of intentional homicide, is worldwide (see Gurr 1977; Morris 1989; Weiner and Wolfgang 1985; Graham and Gurr 1969). The rapid internationalization of drug trafficking has had its impact on Brazil (Zaluar 1985, 1989a and b, and 1993, among others), but increase in violent crime is not limited to "Third World" countries.

critiques sought to demonstrate that no statistically significant differences in crime existed according to social class or ethnic group. Others tried to accentuate the biased nature of official crime statistics that incriminated individuals from low-income social groups.

With those debates as background, this chapter will focus on the preliminary results of a research study on race in the criminal justice system in a democratic order, including the role of the judicial apparatus as a mediator of social conflicts. In a democracy, it is expected that justice, through its institutions and practices, is an effective instrument for mediating both intersubjective conflicts and conflicts in relations between social classes. Rather than being an instrument of social conformity, the justice system should ensure the rights consecrated in the constitutional pact. In this view, democratic justice supposes a game of reciprocities capable of translating differences and inequalities into group rights; that is, it should be able to construct a sociability founded on solidarities (Ewald 1993). However, it is widely believed that defendants from different social strata do not receive the same legal treatment upon committing identical crimes (Caldeira 1991; Cardia 1994). Often those who have resources seem less vulnerable to punishment, or at least less susceptible to the rigors of criminal laws.

In this perspective, a fundamental challenge is the evaluation of this hypothesis: *Black defendants are more vulnerable to penal sanctions precisely because, in comparison with white defendants, they face greater obstacles in gaining access to criminal justice, including equitable access to legal assistance.* In order to evaluate this hypothesis, we designed a study to analyze information from criminal trials for robbery (including armed robbery), drug trafficking, rape, and extortion through kidnapping that were first heard in 1990 in the municipality of São Paulo. The research base was a stratified sample statistically representative of the universe of trials in each of the categories of crime in cases tried across all the criminal jurisdictions that make up municipal São Paulo. For each case, we sought to characterize the criminal incident, the social profiles of victims, assailants, witnesses, and "practitioners/operators,"[3] and the outcome of the trial. We took care to respect the sequence of the penal process in its four phases: police investigation, filing of charges, presentation of evidence, and verdict and sentencing.

---

3. According to Corrêa (1983), practitioners/operators comprise, within the criminal justice system, police detectives, police chiefs, prosecutors, defense attorneys, crime experts, and judges.

Methodological Considerations

The study was designed to examine the hypothesis stated above that whites and blacks contribute to crime in proportion to their representation in the urban population. According to the Instituto Brasileiro de Geografia e Estatística (IBGE 1982), the racial composition of the population in the municipality of São Paulo in 1980 was 72.1 percent white and 24.6 percent black (*pretos* and *pardos*).[4] Therefore, one would expect that white citizens would commit roughly 70 percent of the crimes, with blacks committing the remainder. The costs and technical considerations required to verify this were insurmountable, so we relied on previous studies, particularly on the long tradition of U.S. analyses, which shows that no one ethnic group demonstrates a greater inclination to commit crimes. In support of this thesis, our research found no significant statistical differences in the social profiles of black and white defendants, except in regard to educational background and occupation. Black defendants had higher levels of illiteracy and unemployment, which confirms observations that black citizens are, on average, the poorest segment of the poor population.

A second methodological consideration was the category of the crime. Because sentences vary in extent (the *quantum* of punishment), depending on the category of the crime, the comparison between white and black defendants must be drawn from crimes of identical nature. This methodological imperative called for the design of a complex mechanism of technical control and required that a separate analysis be made for each type of offense. In this chapter, we focus only on aggravated robbery with accomplices (as defined in Article 157, para. 2, I, of the Penal Code), which represented 37.9 percent of all crimes in the sample.

A third methodological concern was the designation of color. During the course of the criminal procedure, suspects and defendants are submitted to distinct instances of questioning, during which various forms are filled out. The official in charge may use his or her own discretion in designating the suspect's race on those forms or may simply transcribe information taken from previously completed forms or witnesses' depositions. In some situations, the defendant may be asked to self-identify. Obviously, procedures of this nature cloud reliability. Furthermore, transcripts and documents from the penal proceedings revealed a process of "whitening" for many black defendants. To exercise a "control" over

4. Data from the 1980 census were used because data for 1991 were not available.

the color variable, the study sampled the defendants' color at three points: in the Record of Criminal Occurrence, in the police investigation, and in documents from the criminal proceedings. The data that support our analysis here used the color registered in the police investigation as reference.[5] In view of these difficulties, we used two classifications, "whites" and "blacks," an option certainly subject to criticism, yet one adopted with a view toward avoiding dispersion of data into multiple color categories.[6]

Finally, the analysis also examines variables measuring the right to legal representation and access to justice. These involved determining the quality of legal representation, whether a defendant pleaded guilty, and whether a defendant called witnesses.

Defendants and Their Rights

Brazil's criminal justice system, heir to Portuguese penal traditions, is constituted around an investigation-trial-sentencing sequence during which criminal responsibility is assigned. The Brazilian penal tradition accepts the principle of *nulla poena sine lege* (no crime exists without prior definition in the law), and thus its point of departure is the recognition of a crime or legal violation. Whenever an incident is reported to a public authority,[7] it should in principle launch a police inquiry that includes field investigations, expert reports, and depositions by victims, assailants, and witnesses.[8] In the initial police inquiry, the suspect is not yet formally accused and does not have the right to legal representation, although he can be accompanied by a lawyer. As Lima has pointed out (1989 and 1990), these procedures heighten police power. They often in-

5. If the results are "tied" to color, as reported in the Record of Criminal Occurrence or the criminal trial, it is likely that rates of distribution of black and white defendants according to selected variables would change. The degree to which these changes compromise the results reported here remains to be determined.

6. See Adorno (1994) for a detailed description of other equally thorny methodological problems not covered in this chapter.

7. In Brazil the Military Police, organized along military lines even though it is not part of Brazilian military, is responsible for vigilance and the repression of crime. The Civil Police, a nonmilitarized public organization, is responsible for criminal investigations. A criminal act discovered by the police authorities results in the filing of a Record of Criminal Occurrence, which leads to an inquiry.

8. In practice, these procedures do not always follow a consistent pattern. For example, in crimes of public accountability (i.e., littering, polluting, etc.), the procedure is initiated by police investigation rather than by filling out the Record of Criminal Occurrence. Moreover, it is estimated that only one third of all incidents result in a police investigation (Adorno 1991b).

volve illegal police practices—including torture, abuse, and extortion perpetrated against suspects or witnesses; sequestering of relatives or friends of the accused; and using informants—all as ways to pressure those who find themselves caught in the web of police scrutiny.

After the inquiry, the case is forwarded to the criminal courts and from there to the Public Ministry, which, in turn, is responsible for deciding whether to file charges. If the case is admitted, it goes to trial, and the citizen under investigation becomes a defendant.[9] In the judicial phase prosecution is based on the principle of rebuttal. The defendant may receive ample legal representation, including legal assistance; demand the presentation of evidence (documentary and expert evidence and that of witnesses); plead not guilty; rebut depositions and witnesses; and demand provisional freedom, release on bond, or the filing a writ of habeas corpus. Following the legal proceedings, the judge issues a final sentence, which can be conviction, acquittal, extinction of punishment, or dismissal of the case (see Adorno 1995, 79–80).

Inequalities in Access to Criminal Justice

To what extent is inequality in access to justice reflected in trial outcomes? To answer that question, we examined racial differences in the conduct of the police inquiry, the type of legal counsel available to defendants of different races, and differences in use of witnesses for black versus white defendants. To what extent is inequality in access to justice reflected in trial outcomes? We found that the type of legal counsel and the use of witnesses differentially influenced verdicts handed down in cases involving blacks and whites in Brazil's criminal justice system.

In our study, blacks were more subject to arbitrary police investigation than whites. More black than white defendants (58.1 versus 46 percent) were arrested during the commission of a crime, and more white than black defendants were released before trial (27 versus 15.5 percent) (see Table 6.1). There is no evidence that blacks exhibit a special inclination toward crime; on the contrary, they seem more vulnerable to police pressure and surveillance. Arbitrary arrest, persecution, intimidation, and greater police presence in lower class neighborhoods all point to the targeting of blacks by repressive police (Campos Coelho 1978; Paixão 1988; Zaluar 1989b).

---

9. In simplified and ideal-type terms, this is standard procedure for crimes tried in trial courts. Cases submitted to juries, such as murder trials, follow slightly different procedures.

Table 6.1. Status of Defendants Tried for Aggravated Robbery, by Race,
According to Incarceration, Municipality of São Paulo (1990)

	Defendants' Race	
Status	% White	% Black
Provisional detention	3.2	1.3
Arrested during commission of crime, in custody	46.0	58.1
Preventive custody	7.9	3.2
Detained for another case	6.3	11.6
Arrested during commission of crime, free on bond	9.5	10.3
Free, awaiting trial	27.0	15.5
Total	100.0	100.0

SOURCES: São Paulo State Judiciary, Núcleo de Estudos da Violência/Geledés.

Nevertheless, it appears that police tactics in the interrogation phase
tend to pressure white defendants more than blacks (Foucault 1980; see
Rabinow 1984). Similarly, black defendants faced greater obstacles in
gaining access to their right to legal representation. While in police detention, more whites than blacks confessed to committing crimes (65.3
percent versus 59.1 percent); fewer white than black defendants denied
the charges against them (34.7 percent versus 40.9 percent) (Table 6.2). In
contrast, during the judicial phase, the pattern was reversed: fewer whites
than blacks confessed to committing crimes (7.1 percent versus 11.2 percent).

As has been seen, black prisoners were more likely to be caught during
the commission of a crime. Under these circumstances a confession is not
necessary, nor is it a basic element needed by the police to build their

Table 6.2. Defendants Tried for Aggravated Robbery, by Race, According
to Confession, Municipality of São Paulo (1990)

Confession		Race	
		% White	% Black
Police phase			
	Yes	65.3	59.1
	No	34.7	40.9
Judicial phase			
	Yes	7.1	11.2
	No	92.9	88.8
Total	100.0	100.0	

SOURCES: São Paulo State Judiciary, Núcleo de Estudos da Violência/Geledés.

case. Consequently, black prisoners caught *in flagrante delicto* are less likely to become targets of corruption and abuse during interrogation. On the other hand, insofar as more white defendants than black defendants have yet to be charged during the police inquiry, and that more black than white defendants are in custody after being caught in flagrante delicto, it is probable that whites are more vulnerable to police extortion to extract a confession. Threatened with serious accusations and fearful of incarceration, mistreatment, and the possibility of being convicted, the white suspect relents and confesses. Not infrequently this involves a bribe, often provided by the suspect's family, relatives, or friends. In this way, confessions and corruption are inexorably paired during police interrogation.

Following the police investigation phase, systematic threats of violence or mistreatment appear to dissipate. Confessions seem to lose their weight as the presentation of information, indictments, and evidence become paramount. The focus shifts to the ability of the defendant's lawyer to elaborate a defense to counter the police charges. To claim innocence in the judicial phase requires discrediting the accuracy of police investigations and their conclusions. A high proportion of defendants, white as well as black (92.9 percent and 88.8 percent, respectively), plead innocent in the judicial phase. Notably, although the statistical differences are small, fewer blacks than whites avail themselves of this right at this decisive moment in the proceedings, probably because a convincing defense— requiring the presentation of evidence and witnesses—is costly to mount.

Unequal access to criminal justice is revealed by the frequency with which blacks rely on public defenders. Black defendants use public defenders more than they use private or court-appointed attorneys[10] (45.2 versus 38.1 and 16.8 percent, respectively); corresponding figures for white defendants are 30.6 versus 60.5 and 8.9 percent. It is likely that this inequality in representation is a result of the lesser socioeconomic status of blacks. Being poorer, black defendants must rely on free legal aid. Other factors may also heighten blacks' greater dependence on public legal aid. Attorneys in Brazil are predominantly white, and white citizens, especially those from the popular classes, hire attorneys drawn from among their relatives and acquaintances.[11] It is less likely that a

---

10. Public defenders are on the payrolls of state attorneys' offices. Given the low number of these professionals and the high volume of criminal court cases, the state must also name private attorneys to render free aid to defendants. These constitute the court-appointed defense.

11. There are few black attorneys in Brazil. It was recently reported that a magistrate in a judicial hearing had before him two citizens, one white and one black. He proceeded to address

black defendant will be personally acquainted with a lawyer, which reduces his options for selecting a defender.

The presentation of witnesses also reveals inequality in access to criminal justice. Guaranteed by the 1988 Constitution, the right of rebuttal
allows defendants to contest the charges against them, yet our research
found that only 25.2 percent of black defendants called witnesses in contrast to 42.3 percent of the whites. It is at this point in the judicial phase
that the presence of an experienced lawyer is especially critical to the defense. Committed to the cause he or she has chosen to defend, a private-
practice attorney carefully selects witnesses, strategically directing them
on what to say and not to say. An effective lawyer does not hesitate to
recast evidence and depositions according to her or his own interpretations, drawing on insights that only legal practice can teach: reconstructing facts and events, inventing attenuating circumstances, drawing telling
moral portraits of the victims or the aggressors (Corrêa 1983).

Even if the lawyer is committed to the case and has the necessary experience, locating witnesses to testify in favor of black defendants may
be more difficult, and potential witnesses may be intimidated by having
to appear before those who sit in judgment. Results of this nature once
again support the hypothesis that guided our research: black defendants
seem unfavorably positioned before the courts compared to white defendants. Discrimination in access to justice is reinforced by the high cost of
lawyers' fees, the ignorance among the poor of their legal rights, and
their reluctance to appear before the courts due to mistrust or resignation
(B. de S. Santos 1995). This "poverty of rights" is characteristic of societies with extreme social inequality.

Among white defendants who did not call witnesses, 30 percent were
acquitted and 70 percent convicted; among white defendants who called
witnesses, 48 percent were acquitted and 52 percent convicted. In other
words, for white defendants, the probability of acquittal increased when
defense witnesses were called. The reverse is true for black defendants.
Among blacks who did not present witnesses, 32 percent were acquitted
and 68 percent were convicted. However, among blacks who called defense witnesses, 28.2 percent were acquitted, while 71.8 percent were
convicted.

The importance of calling witnesses is heightened by the Brazilian
penal tradition, which provides the judge with considerable discretionary leeway and places him at the center of the Brazilian criminal justice system. As Lima notes:

---

the white as the lawyer and the black as the defendant. With great embarrassment, the white citizen told the magistrate that he was the prisoner not the lawyer.

Brazilian legislation that governs the criminal trial establishes the principle of judicial discretion. According to Brazilian jurists . . . , this legislation adopted an alternative system to that of legal proof, which has come to be the system in which the judge has the liberty to make a decision based exclusively upon his [or her] own conscience. According to the Brazilian system (articles 157 and 381, Code of Criminal Process), the judge should make a decision abiding by his [or her] own judgment, though limited to what he or she derives from the files. . . . A criminal judge is expected to show total impartiality toward the prosecution and the defense. (Lima 1994, 24)

The judge controls the entire trial and has the power to question defendants and witnesses, request more detailed investigations, order the gathering of evidence, accept or reject petitions, and recognize or reject indictments that might lead the case in a direction contrary to the one that appears in the police report. This level of authority has led to a collective sentiment that the justice system does not necessarily restrict itself to the facts and evidence contained in legal documents. Verdicts often seem to be influenced by tangential and "extrajudicial" factors. To what degree do these characteristics of the Brazilian criminal justice system affect the trial outcome?

In our study, among the 289 prisoners accused of aggravated robbery, there were 182 convictions, or 62.9 percent of the total. Of these convicted individuals, 58.2 percent were black and 41.7 percent were white. Of the 96 individuals acquitted, about half were black and half were white (see Table 6.3). Broadly speaking, one could say that for every two convictions there was one acquittal. That result challenges the common idea that Brazilian law enforcement and the courts are "soft" on crime.[12] We did find, however, that more blacks were convicted than whites (68.8 and 59.4 percent, respectively) and, conversely, that more whites were acquitted than blacks (37.5 percent and 31.2 percent, respectively).[13] Convictions of black defendants are disproportionately high when compared to their distribution in the population of the municipality of São Paulo (where approximately 72 percent self-identify as white and 25 per-

12. It is true that the judiciary may be even more rigorous in other settings. In France, for example, approximately nineteen out of twenty defendants in criminal trials are convicted, whether by correctional judges or juries, confirming that exemptions from punishment or acquittals are minimal. See Robert et al. 1994.

13. These disturbing observations do not necessarily indicate the existence of racism among judges. The trial outcome results from complex interactions among competing agents, innumerable specialized procedures, and cultural practices.

cent as black). This suggests a certain "elective affinity" between race and punishment. Difference between acquittals and convictions among whites is 21.9 percentage points, whereas the comparable figure for blacks is 37.6 percentage points. Thus, the distribution of convictions and acquittals is more balanced for crimes allegedly committed by whites. In cases where the defendant is black, that imbalance is more accentuated.

As we have seen, black defendants are significantly more dependent on legal aid provided by public defenders than on private legal aid. Attorneys in private practice defend only 38.1 percent of black defendants. A defendant's dependency on free legal aid is associated with a probability of being convicted (Adorno 1994). Not rarely, public defenders or court-appointed attorneys for assorted reasons limit their actions to the cold letter of the law and legal codes. They restrict themselves to procedural formalities, and few exert themselves on their defendant's behalf. They present arguments half-heartedly, do not rely on jurisprudence, and do not file appeals. In contrast, as noted above, most private-practice lawyers elaborate a defense, call witnesses, base their argument on jurisprudence, and take maximum advantage of opportunities offered by documentary evidence, witnesses, and expert testimony. An experienced and shrewd lawyer orients the defendant and witnesses' testimonies and takes advantage of loopholes in penal law to win an acquittal or a light sentence.

Conclusion

The analysis thus far suggests that the constitutional right to legal representation is not guaranteed for black defendants. It appears that blacks do not enjoy the same access to justice as whites: they have greater diffi-

Table 6.3.   Defendants Tried for Aggravated Robbery, by Race, According to Type of Defense Representation, Municipality of São Paulo (1990)

Category	Race	
	White Prisoners	Black Prisoners
Public defenders	30.6	45.2
Court-appointed attorneys	8.9	16.8
Private attorneys	60.5	38.1
Total	100.0	100.0

SOURCES: São Paulo State Judiciary, Núcleo de Estudos da Violência/Geledés.

culty in exercising their rights; the exercise of rights benefits black defendants less than white defendants; and black defendants are more vulnerable to arbitrary police activities and judicial practices and procedures. Black defendants tend to be pursued more by police and confront greater obstacles in exercising their constitutional right to legal representation. Consequently, they tend to be subjected to more rigorous penal treatment, represented by a greater probability of being punished in comparison to white defendants.

This is illustrated in regard to the right to call witnesses. For several reasons, black defendants call fewer witnesses. When witnesses are called, it appears that lawyers for black defendants may make less than optimal use of them in elaborating the defense. This reveals the inequality of access to criminal justice and, more seriously, establishes that "rights" apply to white defendants but not to most blacks who find themselves in the clutches of the criminal justice system.

Although further analysis needs to be done to disentangle the effects of socioeconomic class from race, our study appears to indicate that color is a powerful instrument of discrimination in the distribution of justice. The principle of equality before the law, regardless of social differences, appears compromised by the biases present in the Brazilian criminal justice system.

7

MEASURES TO COMBAT DISCRIMINATION AND RACIAL INEQUALITY IN BRAZIL

Antonio Sérgio Alfredo Guimarães

The struggle to assure equal treatment and equal opportunities for Afro-Brazilians has been fought on three different fronts: racial exclusion,[1] racial inequalities in the distribution of goods and services, and racial inequalities in the distribution of positions of power and leadership. The Brazilian black movement has faced obstacles to convincing Brazilians of the need for affirmative action policies to break through the inertia of the nation's inherited hierarchies. This chapter examines ideologies and interpretations that have hindered the adoption of more effective policies in Brazil's battle against racism. It tries to answer two questions: Why does racial discrimination still go widely unpunished in spite of our already having passed specific antidiscrimination laws? Why do Brazilians vigorously resist adopting affirmative action policies?

Why Does Racial Discrimination Still Go Unpunished?

In 1989 a small-business owner, who first identified himself as being white and later as *pardo*, was arrested for hurling racial epithets at a black woman. The police reported that "the victim was rudely insulted by the accused, who called her a 'vulture,' 'monkey' and *'negra,'* in an act of racism. . . . After . . . having ordered the offender not to call her 'nigger' or other words insulting to her race, the accused, in the presence of the

1. Editor's note: This is the only type of discrimination recognized in Brazilian law.

police, again called the victim a 'sickening *negra.*' " Having witnessed this, and with the testimony of three witnesses who stated that the abusive behavior of the accused had continued for more than two years, police authorities concluded that they were dealing, not with a misdemeanor, but with an offense against the color and race of the victim, and they filed an indictment for racial discrimination *in flagrante delicto* (Auto de Prisão em Flagrante Delito—Crime de Racismo, Article 5, Subsection 42 of the Federal Constitution, City of São Paulo Civil Police).

This indictment was based on the constitutional law that reads in part: "The practice of racism constitutes a crime for which bail may not be posted." Yet Law 7716, passed in 1989 to define crimes of prejudice based on race or skin color, fails to specify that racist epithets constitute a crime. Even though the law does not cover slander, the victim's attorney, appointed by Geledés Institute, a black feminist antiracist organization, argued that the case fit under Law 7716, subsection 14, which defines racism as "the act of impeding or blocking, in any manner or form, . . . the social or family life of an individual." Although the victim, the arresting officers, and the prosecution attorney interpreted the incident as a crime of racism, the judge did not deem it serious enough to merit that indictment. Instead, he opted for a limited interpretation of Law 7716, claiming that the intent of the legislation was to punish "any act impeding or blocking, in any manner or form, marriage or a relationship" in the private sphere, *not* harassing a person in public "with slanderous language. The victim, who, we infer from the documents, had every reason to be revolted by the conduct of the accused, should have initiated a penal suit for private injury," citing a crime against her reputation.

How does such confusion arise? My argument follows two theses. First, Law 7716 limits itself to banning a segregationist form of racism, which has never been widely practiced in Brazil. Thus, the law is effective only against gross and openly racist acts and misses the more subtle and invisible forms of racial discrimination that operate in Brazil. Second, the way in which Brazilian racism is practiced not only makes the law inoperative but also systematically confuses the police, who tend to take defamation for racism (invoking Law 7716), whereas the courts deem what otherwise might fall under the purview of Law 7716 to be crimes of defamation (*crimes contra a honra*).

Racism as Defined by the Brazilian Judiciary

The critical failure of Law 7716 is its definition of racism (as interpreted by the Brazilian judiciary) as being limited to an *act* of segregation or exclusion based on skin color or race. In the writing of this law, all behavior considered criminal is described with verbs related to exclusion ("prevent," "restrain," "deny," and so forth), and these are set in contexts relating to public services, business establishments, or family life. In these arenas, however, segregationist practices are rare in Brazil today. When they do occur, they are camouflaged so that the true racial motive is disguised by a metonymy or trope, such as physical traits (*boa aparência* or good—that is, white—appearance), occupational division (dark-skinned people use the service elevator), ownership ("this property is exclusively for the use of members only"), technical (educational merit), or even cultural criteria (tacit qualifications or clientele's preference).

A narrow interpretation of Law 7716 makes it inapplicable to the kind of racism that actually exists in Brazil, a racism that is embedded in hierarchical inequalities—an ascribed status difference between aggressors and victims—while social relations between classes and races are remarkably friendly and informal. In this context, an insult to someone who has overstepped racial boundaries may serve as an instrument "to keep blacks in their place" as a means of maintaining the racial hierarchy.

Three types of racism typically occur. First, a black person may become a suspect in a crime simply because of his or her skin color. Second, racial insults may be used to question or break the authority of a public official or professional. Finally, racial insults can function to trivialize a black person in a position of high status.

Reality would support public suspicion, since bank robberies, prostitution, and petty thefts are committed most often by the poor, who in Brazil are mainly black. Many blacks find it hard to convince themselves and others of the racial motivation behind the act of being searched or being asked to show identity cards even when these acts are accompanied by racial slurs, such as the simple word *negão* (big black).[2] Ironically, Brazilian blacks live with the absurdity that if they are the victims of racially motivated slurs, the crime might not be interpreted as an act of racism. A judge will usually rule that slurs are defamatory and not prosecutable under Law 7716, which covers only acts of gross racial segregation.

The logic of treating blacks this way is simple: blacks are relegated to inferior social positions by means of impersonal mechanisms—insufficient formal education, job insecurity, poverty, and a culturally different lifestyle. They are classified socially based on their skin color, dress, ac-

---

2. Editor's note: The notion of "probable cause" has never been incorporated into the Brazilian justice system. Suspects may be arbitrarily detained without legal recourse.

cent, and even the way they behave in public. Brazil's traditional lack of legal segregation, in other words, the country's "racial democracy," has led to the development of an etiquette in which overt racially based treatment has disappeared to the point that even openly classifying people by race is considered to be offensive and rude. If a black person obviously belongs to a high social class, it is an offense to identify him or her as a black because that would be classifying the person by race rather than by socioeconomic status. Cultural or socioeconomic markers, not race, should identify a person. But for most Brazilian judges, transgression of this social etiquette is regarded not as what it really is—racial discrimination—but as defamation or a crime against a person's "honor." That interpretation is extremely perverse not only because it discounts the racial motivation behind an insult that violates the fundamental rights of black citizens, but also because it even dilutes the case for a conviction based on slander. After all, one can always argue that a designation of a person by color is simply an objective classification of the color of the skin and not racial in nature.

Police Classification of Crimes of Discrimination

My survey of thirty-one police reports on cases of racial discrimination filed in Salvador, Bahia, between 1989 and 1996 reveals noticeable discrepancies in the way the crimes were classified. For example, most discrimination claims affecting the rights of the consumer (especially unfounded suspicion of theft in supermarkets and department stores) were classified as crimes of defamation rather than as cases of infringement on the individual's freedom or right to engage in commerce (rights covered by Law 7716). To my amazement, most cases that I classified as being solely an attack on someone's reputation (and not having any racist motive whatsoever) were classified by the police as crimes of discrimination.

Were the police simply interpreting Brazil's particular brand of racism—consistent with the belief in the country's "racial democracy"—as the act of verbally and offensively characterizing a person by his or her skin color? Within the norms of Brazilian racial etiquette, even when skin color triggers discrimination, it is largely ignored—unless the racist attitude is verbalized. After all, when the police arrest, search, and detain a working-class suspect, most Brazilians regard it as "normal."[3] On the other hand, the police view racially motivated offenses as disgusting, even when they are limited to interpersonal relationships. In their minds,

3. Editor's note: The lack of privacy rights is critical to understanding racism in Brazil.

the law against racism must have been created to punish verbal excesses rather violations of an individual's rights.

The research also showed that the victim's sex plays a role in how crimes of racial discrimination are categorized. Law 7716 is very harsh, since it considers racism to be a crime for which bail cannot be posted. Thus, the police are likely to distinguish among crimes that would fall under the purview of Law 7716, preferring to classify as discrimination those cases that involve verbal offenses against men, but as defamation similar crimes perpetrated against women.

Although the data from my fieldwork are too preliminary to allow me to draw definite conclusions, some interesting hypotheses have emerged. First, the wording of Law 7716 is key to the difficulty in prosecuting acts of racism—that is, that particular brand of Brazilian racism that "assimilates" blacks while treating them as inferiors. Second, judicial interpretation limits even further the possibility of classifying real cases under the law, given that the interpretations are limited to considering the explicit public behaviors covered by Law 7716, while ignoring the fundamental rights of citizens. Third, paradoxically, making explicit the racial motives behind such crimes has tended to disqualify them as crimes of racism and has relegated them to the purview of private penal law.

Fourth, when members of the working class or blacks are involved, the likelihood is greater that a racist remark will be interpreted as evidence that racial discrimination (that is, segregation or exclusion, according to Brazilian law) occurred. At the same time, the likelihood is also greater that police and judges will misinterpret a racist *verbal* offense as a violation of the antidiscrimination law (when, in fact, the law covers only acts of segregation or exclusion). Given that police often "soften" charges against an aggressor who victimizes a black woman (by classifying the crime as one against the woman's honor rather than as an act of discrimination), a fifth and last hypothesis is that gender, possibly along with other conditions of social subordination, may make racial discrimination even more invisible. If further research corroborates these hypotheses, lawmakers will need to expand the current antisegregationist law to curb everyday discriminatory practices, affirming the citizenship of those Brazilians who are not yet part of a "racial democracy."

The Brazilian Debate over Affirmative Action

The Brazilian controversy over public policies to benefit Afro-Brazilians has just begun. Initially, the debate took place only within black-movement organizations and certain academic spheres, but more recently the federal government has promoted more public and frequent discussion on affirmative action.[4]

Thus far, the arguments against affirmative action have taken three forms. First, to some people, affirmative action involves recognition of ethnic and racial differences among Brazilians, which would belie the national myth that we are one and only one people, one and only one race. Second, there are those who see "positive discrimination" as an attack on the universalist and individualist principle of merit, which is the main weapon against the personalistic and clientelistic practices that dominate Brazilian public life. Finally, still others believe that Brazil's fluid color line precludes any practical possibilities for implementing affirmative action policies. Let us examine each argument in greater detail.

On November 11, 1968, *Diários Associados,* a Brazilian news conglomerate, published an open letter from Raquel de Queiroz addressed to the minister of labor at the time, Jarbas Passarinho.[5] In the letter, the writer indignantly disputed a comment made by ministry officials who had acknowledged that racial discrimination exists in the Brazilian labor market. The officials were quoted in *Jornal do Brasil* as saying that they were in favor of potential legislation setting quotas for businesses that would require hiring a percentage of "colored employees" into company jobs (the exact rates were to be determined by a set of the company's specific characteristics). De Queiroz's indignation over this proposal was rooted in a belief that "what we must not do is seal a pact with the crime of discrimination, quarrel over discrimination, or acknowledge its existence. . . . It is preferable that we continue coexisting with covert and illegal discrimination, however widespread it may be, than to allow the government to acknowledge it officially—since any regulation would imply a recognition of discrimination" (*Diário de Notícias* 1968, p. 4).

De Queiroz's point of view, despite its vehement polemic, was and still is shared by wide segments of Brazilian society, including many well-educated individuals. Among social scientists, for example, the self-censorship of the word *race* in scientific and scholarly texts (and its replacement with the term *ethnicity*) has been a common practice for fifty years. Because the antiracism of the postwar period had as its goal to extirpate racism through a denial of the empirical existence of different

---

4. Apart from the initiatives introducing affirmative action legislation made by Abdias do Nascimento, Florestan Fernandes, and Benedita da Silva, I know of only one publicly stated position on affirmative action made prior to the 1970s, that of the writer Raquel de Queiroz (1968).

5. Jocélio Teles dos Santos kindly drew my attention to this document.

races, it made sense to combat racial discrimination, as Raquel de Queiroz wanted, by having it outlawed in the penal code and ignored in public policy.

This romantic form of antiracism has been supported by an equally romantic view of Brazilian society. De Queiroz expresses it well: "How can we distinguish who is and who is not black among us? A rigid color line exists in the United States and South Africa, and anyone who is not 100 percent white is considered black. In Brazil, the tendency is to consider every person who is not visibly colored to be white. The great majority of our population consists of people of mixed blood. Brazil is a nation of mestizos. What about all these people? How would they be categorized?"

The refusal to recognize the existence of racial discrimination is transformed by de Queiroz into a statement that discrimination cannot possibly exist in Brazil since all Brazilians are people of mixed blood and, therefore, not white. This national consensus, however, crumbles under closer examination. If we are not white, why do we "consider every person who is not visibly colored to be white"? Do we categorize people by color, or don't we? Do we consider some people "white" and others "black," or don't we? Do we discriminate among people in terms of color, or don't we? In this romantic version of antiracism, everything is constructed as if one were trying to deny a reality while at the same time profoundly accepting it. Race is declared nonexistent, but the categories "black" and "white," borrowed from the United States, are used as if they were an empirical racial classification. It is as if American whites were pure, "one hundred percent" white, with no individuals of mixed blood among them. By extension, Brazilian whites of mixed blood would be considered "black" in the United States. In truth, it is against this "hateful" categorization that would turn all of us "black" that we become provoked, causing us to deny the existence of the races and, at the same time, the possibility of discrimination among us. But what "us" is this, one might ask? Who is included in this "we"? Apparently, all those who "are not visibly colored." But can anyone objectively define who that would be? Certainly not. Thus, so as not to ruin things with a loose classification—one that allows, maintains, and denies discrimination according to skin color—it is better simply not to speak of it, not to study it, not even to pronounce the word, and certainly not to make it a public issue.

A second constellation of arguments crystallizes around the defense of the ideal of treatment according to merit, an ideal that affirmative action policies could threaten to destroy. Here, just as in the United States, the argument is over the illegality or immorality of affirmative action. From the legal point of view, legislation requiring the use of positive discrimination has its precedents. Marcelo Neves synthesizes an argument made by Celso Antônio Bandeira de Mello (1993) about the legal aspects of the principle of equality:

> In a rigorously positivistic perspective, Bandeira de Mello emphasizes that the constitutional principle of equality involves legal discrimination among people, things, facts, and situations. He discusses whether the act of discrimination in itself corrupts the principle of equality. He also points out three requirements: the presence of differentiating features in people, things, facts, or situations; logical correlation between the discriminatory act and the resulting inequality; and consonance of the discriminatory act to the values protected by the Constitution." (Neves 1996, 9)

Neves then considers these parameters to claim that "*the more historically solid and effective negative racial discrimination becomes* against a specific ethnic-racial group, principally when it implies impeding the exercise of rights, *the more legal affirmative action is justified* in favor of the members of that group. It is presumed that this positive discrimination should mitigate toward an egalitarian integration of everyone in the society and the State." He concludes that "legal affirmative action in favor of the integration of blacks and indigenous peoples is in harmony with the fundamental principles of the [Brazilian constitution], set forth in art. 3, subsections III and IV"[6] (Neves 1996, 10).

Along these same lines, Sérgio da Silva Martins reminds us that "the 1988 Constitution created the Brazilian constitutional tradition of recognizing material inequality among [*social*] sectors and proposes protections that imply the positive presence of the State" (1996, 206). As an example of the Brazilian government's official recognition of policies aimed at banning racial discrimination, Martins turns also to the 1996 Plano Nacional dos Direitos Humanos [National Human Rights Plan], which proposes "to develop affirmative actions to enable the access of blacks to professional training and university courses in leading technological fields." Additionally, he points out as further legal justification for affirmative action that Brazil subscribes to several international conventions on discrimination (including conventions against employment

---

6. These are III: "eradicate poverty and marginalization and reduce social and regional inequalities" and IV: "promote the well-being of all, without regard to origin, race, sex, color, age, or any other form of discrimination."

discrimination, discrimination in education, and the elimination of all forms of discrimination).

Thus, there is no doubt that, as has happened in the United States, it is possible to prove the moral correctness and constitutional justification for affirmative action policies in Brazil. However, in Brazil, as in the United States, what seems to be at stake is much more than the constitutional or ethical principles that guide public life. It is the meaning of the nation and of citizenship itself (that is, of civic life itself) that is being questioned—who are the "we" protected by the laws and actions of the state?

The third constellation of arguments against affirmative action is historical and empirical. Brazilian society has not yet managed to constitute a society sustained by objective market mechanisms and rules of social interaction based on formal, universal, and impersonal criteria. In this context, the main political objective of progressives has been to strengthen universal mechanisms for rewarding merit in order to reduce personalistic and clientelistic practices. From this point of view, the urgency of broadening democratic access to resources runs counter to advocating particularistic policies at the expense of broader universalist policies. Márcia Contins and Luiz Carlos Santana explain: "In the Brazilian case, a markedly hierarchical context perverts the modern principles of egalitarianism. The effects of affirmative action policies might mean one more twist in the screw, favoring—rather than discouraging—a hierarchy of social relations" (1996, 200).

This concern is perfectly wedded to an obvious conclusion: since most blacks are poor, the worst racial inequalities in Brazil could be reversed easily by means of universalist policies to eradicate poverty. Without a doubt, policies promoting mass education, basic sanitation, affordable housing, increased employment, and land distribution would proportionally benefit more blacks than whites (as was the case in revolutionary Cuba).[7]

The irony is not coincidental. The individualistic aspects of affirmative action policies and their targeting of only the relatively small segment of society that would qualify for "set asides" would mean that the poorer of the poor black population might be overlooked, which many members of the black movement find unacceptable. Contins and Santana have clearly recorded that reaction in their surveys: "In general, the debate among black movement activists is centered on the concern that affirmative action could create a 'black elite' without effectively solving racism " (1996, 217). They quote a black union militant: "Quotas and affirmative

7. On this topic, see de la Fuente 1995, 7–43.

actions are forced on Southern Hemisphere countries, but these policies only attempt to be effective, since the core questions, the ones that really matter, remain untouched" (218).

Another substantive consideration is how to implement affirmative action policies in the absence of a well-defined and strict racial (or color) classification. Who would be the beneficiaries of these policies? And moreover, given the uneven distribution of black mestizos and indigenous populations inside Brazil, how can the regional nuances in the way race is conceptualized be dealt with?

Let us analyze these arguments. First, we must be absolutely clear on the point that what are generically called "affirmative action policies," *tout court,* are not limited to one special or particular mechanism based on goals to be achieved or quotas to be fulfilled. Policies to expand access to university education, job promotion, preferential contracts for materials or services, and so on, can benefit only a small part of the black population—those who have the skills and qualifications to attend college, run a company, or supply needed goods or services. Such policies would affect the profile and size of the black middle class far more than the living standard of the majority of poor (black) Brazilians. Thus, affirmative action policies must be anchored in universalist policies to improve public elementary and high-school education, provide universal medical and dental assistance, build basic infrastructure, and expand the civic participation of the poor.

Furthermore, affirmative action policies cannot be implemented without first establishing policies to expand universal civil rights, as in the United States. The issue is not a simple alternative between universalist versus particularist policies. What is at issue is whether Brazilian blacks should wait for this "revolution from above"—the expansion of civil rights and social opportunities for the poor—or immediately and *pari passu* demand more urgent measures, albeit limited ones, that would enhance blacks' access to both public and private universities as well as expand and strengthen their business relationships in order to enlarge the black "middle class."

The moral, ethical, and constitutional justifications for taking more urgent measures do not need to be repeated. Another invalid objection, in my opinion, is that affirmative action policies that affirm universalist norms of nondiscrimination will undermine the universality of those very norms. After all, democratic countries worldwide have made exceptions in order to protect and benefit certain segments of society, and they have done so without diminishing the quality of their democracy. Take, for example, measures that benefit inhabitants of certain geographic regions, veterans of war, women, indigenous peoples, and so on. Hence, the question should be: Do blacks deserve to be among the beneficiaries of those sorts of policies?

This issue was raised by two participants in a recent workshop on affirmative action held in Rio de Janeiro, organized by the feminist journal, *Estudos Feministas*. Edward Telles emphasized the scant importance Brazilians attribute to racism: "In Brazil, racism is only one among many of democracy's unsolved problems, and race still is not considered an element underlying inequality" (1996, 194). Sérgio da Silva Martins was even more direct: "We can assert that a substantial commitment to eliminating racial inequality in Brazilian society—fundamental to the adoption of affirmative policies—has yet to be made" (1996, 203). Despite a recognition that blacks are discriminated against and deserve compensatory policies, many Brazilians still doubt that affirmative action is either feasible or effective. But let me address those reservations.

Ever since affirmative action was first proposed, many have argued that we are not able to say objectively who in Brazil is black or, consequently, who would benefit from affirmative action. As we saw earlier, the romantic version of this argument is unsustainable given that it mixes existing racial identities—how people define themselves and how they are defined in terms of color in Brazil—with pseudoscientific identities or racial identities used in different cultural contexts. In contrast, I maintain what I have said elsewhere (Guimarães 1996): A compensatory policy only makes sense if the target population is truly compensated for their overall disadvantages and relegation to low status. Compensatory policies cannot eliminate the disadvantages they seek to correct. Who would care to suffer the injustices of a black all his life just to benefit during adolescence from preferential access to universities? When an indigenous group goes to the government to demand its rights, it will forever be perceived as indebted, reinforcing the state's system of patronage. The examples are endless.

So how can the state compensate blacks when it refuses to racially identify its citizens? Today in Brazil only a few agencies track race or color. These characteristics are not shown on identification cards, driver's licenses, *carteiras de trabalho* (a record of jobs held by individuals, which is maintained by the Labor Ministry), or elsewhere. Given that fact, it makes sense to ask how a just distribution of goods could be achieved for those who occasionally self-identify as blacks. This brings us back to the crucial point made by de Queiroz in 1968: compensatory policies mean universal recognition of race and color, something that deeply undermines Brazil's imagined national character.

Yet another unsupportable objection to affirmative action is that the unequal distribution of the mestizo population within Brazil represents an obstacle to affirmative action. On one hand, this objection is based on in an essentialist or biological conception of race. Yet how "black identity" is defined varies regionally. A black from Bahia may have different phenotypic characteristics from a black from Porto Alegre. The problem is not whether race or color is defined differently across regions. "Race" and "color" are not real or objective in and of themselves, but they do demarcate real situations and experiences of discrimination.

Some also argue that the black population may become a demographic majority, at least in certain places. In that case, what would be the applicability of policies designed to compensate minorities? I find implausible the supposition on which this objection to affirmative action is founded. According to the Pesquisa Nacional por Amostragem de Domicílios (the National Household Survey, PNAD), Salvador has the greatest number of people who declare themselves to be *preto,* but the rate is only 15.6 percent. There is no indication whatsoever that the 64.9 percent of Salvador's population who declare themselves *pardo* want, or might someday wish, to become black. And on the day that the 80 percent majority of *pretos* and *pardos* identify themselves as black and have full access to universities, for instance, there will no longer be a need for affirmative action policies in Salvador.

Another variant of this objection is that in Brazil the majority of the people are black mestizos, and therefore, rather than affirmative action, what is needed are universalistic actions to expand citizenship. I believe I have demonstrated that this statement is false: we cannot classify most of the Brazilian population as "black" because they do not define and identify themselves racially in this way. The truth is that very few individuals want to be (or are not able to avoid being) black. It is these people, those who suffer discrimination the most, to whom affirmative action policies should be directed. (Table 7.1 summarizes the main arguments over affirmative action for blacks in Brazil.)

Conclusion

What can we conclude from the debate? In my opinion, it is important to highlight the points that have not yet been considered in the Brazilian debate. First, government affirmative action policies are very unpopular everywhere in the Western world—Europe and the Americas. Even when these policies are demonstrably compatible with individualist and universalist ideals, most white populations oppose them. This is a fact.

Table 7.1.   The Brazilian Debate About Affirmative Action

Against	In Favor
Affirmative action requires recognition of racial distinctions, which contradicts the Brazilian creed that we are one people and one nation.	Though it is unacknowledged, race already is the primary criterion used in Brazilian society to distinguish between individuals. This must be acknowledged in order to end discrimination.
Affirmative action is impossible in Brazil because there are no rigid or objective distinctions between the races.	Rigid or objective distinctions between the races do not exist anywhere. Positive or negative discrimination functions on the basis of the social constructs of racial identity.
Because of the fluidity of racial identity in Brazil, opportunists could easily take unfair advantage of affirmative action policies.	The risk is real, and affirmative action policies do require an official recognition of racial identities. Nevertheless, affirmative action will not immediately put an end to discrimination. Thus, it is unlikely that opportunism would be widespread.
Universalist measures would have the same effect.	Universalist measures cannot break the momentum of social exclusion.
There is no consensus in Brazilian society about the relationships between social inequality and race or color differences.	Affirmative action policies could help to legitimate such a consensus.
Affirmative action policies would reinforce privilege and hierarchical inequality.	Affirmative action would reverse inequality, and in so doing would lay bare the absurdity of the prevailing order.
Affirmative action policies are unconstitutional because they exclude certain groups.	There is no legal basis for the claim that affirmative action policies are unconstitutional.

SOURCE: The author.

Second, it seems impossible to prove that white opposition to such policies evolves from a "new racism," rooted in individualist values. Sniderman and Piazza (1993) have resourcefully demonstrated the opposite. While racists oppose affirmative action, they are not the majority of those who oppose affirmative action.

Third, it is inadvisable to criticize the individualist and universalist val-

ues that sustain western democracies solely because they still harbor biased particularism and favoritism. At this moment, envisioning a society
that is proportionalist (that is, with ethnic representation in all strata of
social life) or collectivist would be utopian. Whether the utopia be proportionalist, socialist (banning all social inequalities, including racial
ones), or populist (taking immediate, substantial, and far-reaching steps
to confront social inequalities), awaiting its arrival to act affirmatively on
behalf of the Afro-Brazilian population would be shirking our responsibility. Feasible and effective policies are needed here and now.

Having made these observations, I would like to focus on what seems
to be a significant change in antiracism worldwide in the mid-1990s, a
change that appears to be at the root of the Brazilian intellectuals' resistance to affirmative action policies. We all know that scientific racism has
only recently expired (some even doubt that it is, indeed, dead). Despite
UNESCO's postwar effort to demystify and denounce racial theories
and categories as pseudoscientific and ideological, the very concept of
race has neither vanished from people's minds nor, more gravely, have
the social and "hard" sciences ceased to use those concepts. In the social
sciences, banishing the use of racial categories by means of the excessive
use of quotation marks (to denote race as a native or a socially constructed category) lost its meaning when deconstructionist critiques revealed that in the end more immediate notions such as "skin color" or
"hair type" are not inherently different from the notion of "race" itself.
As far as the biological sciences are concerned, the concept of race continues to be used in the same essentialist and naturalist manner in which
it has always been used.

This all seems innocent until one realizes that the concept of race has
reappeared in political speeches—on the right and the left alike, and
equally in both racist and antiracist discourse. This is leading some social
scientists back to the antiracist ideals of the 1940s and 1950s, as they once
again preach that racial categories must be banned not only from political
speeches but also in social-science debate itself.

Although I understand the reasons and the intent that motivate these
intellectuals, I cannot agree with them. First, the strategy they defend has
been tried, and it failed despite UN support. Second, banning the concept
of race may result in a sort of political paralysis in the social sciences—
after all, the most visible reality at the turn of the millennium is articulated by the reinvention of social identities. To the contrary, rather than
banning the word, I believe the antiracist agenda must construct a strictly
sociological concept of race and then popularize it. This new concept of
race would displace the biological concept of race from the intellectual

mind. I intentionally say "intellectual mind" rather than social imagination because I'm sure that in the latter the naturalization and essentializing of concepts is irreversible, which, to paraphrase Colette Guillaumin (1992), is instrumental to any technique of social domination.

To conclude, I would like to reiterate what I consider to be truly problematic for the implementation of affirmative action policies in Brazil. In my research (Guimarães 1996, 45), I have noticed that racial discrimination is linked to forms of status-based discrimination, that is, discrimination based on the assumption of natural privileges for certain groups and classes of people. The naturalization of racial inequalities, the submission of people to a circumscribed network of social relations (Da Matta 1979), the subordination of people's rights to property rights,[8] all prevent racial discrimination from being acknowledged and regarded as a major barrier to equal opportunity for blacks in our society. In reality, for everyone, it is this fundamental inequality of citizens before the law and the government that seems to be—and actually is—the decisive social factor in the interplay of discrimination and subordination in Brazil.[9] This is at the core of the common affirmation that in Brazil the issue is not about race but about class. That statement is based on the correct perception that we are not all equal, nor are we all treated as equals.

Our greatest challenge as a nation, therefore, is to avoid falling into a paralysis that is, at the same time, relativistic and fatalistic. In other words, we must not accept as a defining feature of our national identity that which we contest. We must not continue to publicly treat as equals those who, in fact, are treated as a separate group (*estamentalmente*). Above all, affirmative action policies are a commitment to the ideal of equal treatment for all. And for that reason, and only for that reason, at certain moments for certain social groups, we must be willing to privilege the underprivileged.

8. This hypothesis was proposed by Sérgio Adorno to explain the levels of violence in urban Brazil.

9. This idea was popularized by an expression coined by Donald Pierson, "a multiracial society of classes" (although Pierson gave the expression a very specific meaning) (see Guimarães, forthcoming).

8

STRUGGLING IN PARADISE:

Racial Mobilization and the
Contemporary Black Movement in Brazil

Luiz Claudio Barcelos

Social groups mobilize to demand collective services and social goods and to fight against mechanisms and practices that lead to the reproduction of their subordination. In Brazil, race[1] has a significant effect on life opportunities, which generates enormous inequalities.[2] Although consensus mobilization along racial lines is not easily reached, racial grievances based on these inequalities have developed into social and political mobilization. What are the features of racial mobilization in Brazil? What does the black movement's trajectory tell us about Brazilian racial politics? This chapter maps racial mobilization in Brazil from the 1920s to the 1980s and integrates at an analytical level the components of the racial mobilization across time and in three regions: São Paulo, Rio de Janeiro, and Salvador. This chapter also calls attention to theories in the social movement literature that have largely been ignored by students of racial mobilization in Brazil. It demonstrates how the construction of meaning in social movements, following Klandermans and Tarrow (1988), operates in Brazilian racial mobilization. In dealing with the contemporary period, the focus is on the black movement and the challenges it has confronted.

A version of this study was published in *Afro-Ásia* (Salvador) 17 (1996): 187–210.

1. I understand race as a historically constructed social classification that permeates the relationship between individuals and the social structure.

2. In the growing literature on racial inequalities in Brazil, I would highlight the studies that inaugurated a new approach, including Hasenbalg (1979), Oliveira, Porcaro and Araújo (1983), and N. V. Silva (1978); and recent reviews, including Hasenbalg and Silva (1992) and "Laboratório de pesquisas sobre desigualdades raciais" (1992).

Two points are significant in introducing the Brazilian racial context. First, lacking unequivocal political mobilization along racial lines, activists and researchers take a plethora of collective manifestations as expression of racial identity and mobilization. These manifestations denote the "many ways of being black," in Berriel's (1989) thoughtful phrasing, and are seen in different degrees as cases of racial mobilization. Second, perceptions of race relations in Brazil are central to the political participation of blacks. The myth of "racial democracy" is one link, perhaps the strongest one, in a chain of idealizations involving the Brazilian sense of nationality (Rufino 1988). This self-representation of Brazilian society thwarts the black movement's ability to mobilize the black community as well as other sectors of civil society.

Theoretical Background

Structural transformations in twentieth-century society, the appearance of new forms of collective action in the post–World War II period, and theoretical controversies in the social sciences have generated two major paradigms in studies of collective actors: "resource mobilization" and "new social movements." The former dominates the debate in the United States; the latter, in Europe (Klandermans and Tarrow 1988; Johnston, Laraña, and Gusfield 1994; Eyerman and Jamison 1991). Klandermans and Tarrow (1988) show that the "resource mobilization" and "new social movements" paradigms emphasize motivational and structural elements, respectively, which represent distinct aspects of collective mobilization. The authors propose a notion of "consensus mobilization" that links internal attributes of a social movement to characteristics of the political system. On the other hand, Brazil's racial mobilization is an interesting example of how local traditions can be reinforced while selectively incorporating symbols and practices generated in other contexts. These dynamics provide social groups with diacritical symbols to construct their identity, which largely replace *ideology* as a reference point in the analysis of social movements (Eyerman and Jamison 1991; Johnston, Laraña, and Gusfield 1994). Individual, collective, and public identities interact in social movements. By articulating alternative views of identity and elaborating new social identities, or by redefining those already in existence, social movements not only try to maximize the effects of their collective actions but pose new cognitive projects for society.

In the 1970s a literature that predominantly deals with "urban social movements" developed in Brazil (Boshi and Valladares 1982; Cardoso

1983; L. A. Silva and Ziccardi 1983). This literature characterizes collective actors, the "popular sectors," as impoverished groups who are excluded from political decisions but who organize as pressure groups to demand goods—such as potable water or sewage services—for collective consumption.

The focus on these new collective actors is not trivial in a literature that has held the concept of class as central (Larangeira 1990). The contradictions of urban life seem to blur or even to deny the class struggle. Simultaneously, the weakening of traditional means of social control, such as patron-client authority, prompts new forms of contestation. These circumstances motivated European students of social movements, especially scholars in France, to revise the Marxist paradigm, and these new studies have had a strong influence on Brazilian social scientists (Cardoso 1983).

Thus, as a consequence of the absence of race in the Marxist paradigm, and consequently in the new social movement approach as well, the theme of race relations has been overlooked in research on social movements in Brazil. One tries unsuccessfully to find in the literature the race or color of the popular sectors. If race is mentioned, it is not incorporated in the analysis. On the other hand, studies on racial mobilization, which mostly are based on the works of Florestan Fernandes and Roger Bastide, do not pay close attention to the debate on social movements (with the remarkable exception of Pinto's 1993 literature review). In short, the relationships among racial mobilization, civil society, and the state are not thoroughly depicted in the literature.

Moreover, considering the features of Brazilian society, racial politics cannot be isolated from the struggle for the citizenship of subordinate groups, classified by Souza-Lobo (1991) as "emergent citizenship."[3] Therefore, racial mobilization occurs in a fragile democratic framework and is an issue "invisible" to most of Brazilian society. Proponents of racial mobilization, especially in the contemporary period, face three principal tasks: (1) to overcome the dominant racial ideology, (2) to unify blacks and mulattos under a common banner,[4] and (3) to fight against racial subordination, whether socioeconomic inequalities or negative

---

3. Souza-Lobo focuses on gender relations, but her observations could be applied to race relations as well. She points out that "women's problems are coincidental with the social issues debated in Brazilian society. This explains the noncentrality of the issues of female equality and rights, as well as a weak and diffused consciousness regarding discrimination. Democracy, now at the center of the debates, is traversed by the problem of extending citizenship" (1991, 12).

4. Some issues related to the Brazilian system of racial classification cannot be addressed in this study. See Maggie (1989b), Sansone (1993), and N. V. Silva (1994).

stereotypes. Put differently, the black movement's major challenges are its "real representativeness"[5] and its ability to extend consensus mobilization along racial lines.

Racial Mobilization in the Early Twentieth Century

A network of Afro-Brazilian cultural and recreation associations and a black press emerged in São Paulo in the 1920s. The first explicitly political Afro-Brazilian organization, the Frente Negra Brasileira (FNB), was founded in 1931.[6] Although the FNB had a political agenda from the beginning, it became a political party only in 1936.

In this period of racial mobilization the living conditions of the black population were highlighted, but there was no critique of race relations as such. Pinto (1993) calls attention to concerns with moral and social behavior proclaimed as adequate in the black press. She also notes that the newspapers expressed hostility toward European immigrants, who were seen as competitors in the labor market (although they were also heralded as models for their dedication to work and education). However, it is vital to point out that the FNB opposed them not on a racial or ethnic basis but as foreign groups. Pinto (1993, 268) comments on the black Brazilian press's treatment of racial integration in Brazil, which it portrayed as superior to race relations in the United States. It is not an exaggeration to say that this assertion was anathema to the black movement some decades later.

After this phase of racial mobilization ended under the pressure of the authoritarian regime inaugurated in 1937, it reemerged in the mid-1940s and 1950s, marked by the Teatro Experimental do Negro (TEN). Under the leadership of Abdias do Nascimento, the TEN organized many seminars and meetings, in addition to producing theater events, in Rio de Janeiro and São Paulo (Hanchard 1994; Maués 1991; Müller 1988; Pinto 1993). In adhering to the Négritude Mouvement—a movement of West Indians and French-speaking Africans of literary expressiveness but di-

---

5. Boshi and Valladares (1982) call attention to this in their analysis of the movement of favela residents' associations in Brazil. They note the significant costs involved in participating in social movements and that high levels of activity are usually short-lived. These observations are relevant when evaluating the success of the black movement.

6. Pinto (1993) provides the most complete analysis of this period, with special emphasis on the FNB. Mitchell (1977) focused on this period of black mobilization in a study that has not been reproduced to cover contemporary black movement politics. See also Andrews (1991 and 1992b) and Nascimento (1989).

vergent politics—the intellectuals related to the TEN were unable to solve the original contradictions of that movement. In referring to the TEN as an elitist mobilization, authors have agreed with the harsh assessment made by Moura (1983), who with vehement rhetoric dismissed this mobilization as meaning nothing to the vast majority of blacks living in poverty. The validity of this criticism notwithstanding, the TEN had a critical perspective of race relations in Brazil. Müller (1988) alludes to a document elaborated in one meeting sponsored by the TEN, which recommended, among other measures, that racial discrimination be considered a criminal offense. Pinto calls attention to another document because it used the term Afro-Brazilian "to designate blacks, [in addition to] the valorization, yet incipient, of the Afro-Brazilian religions, until then largely ignored by the black elite, the acknowledgment of organizations, called popular in the document, such as carnival groups" (1993, 348). These elements, it is worth noting, became crucial in the next period of racial mobilization.

Contemporary Racial Mobilization

From the 1970s onward, two decisive features shaped racial mobilization and, in particular, the black movement in Brazil.[7] The first feature is that rather than addressing the black community itself, black movement organizations have tried to generate actions that question the mechanisms of discrimination leading to the reproduction of racial inequalities in Brazilian society. The second feature is the existence of a strong pole of racial mobilization outside the Rio–São Paulo axis. In Salvador there are original and unique forms of mobilization.[8] In this Northeastern city, appropriation and redefinition of urban spaces is more visible as the realms of work, residence, leisure, religion, and politics mix in spatial and symbolic terms (da Cunha 1991).

The phenomenon known as "black soul" in some sense initiated the racial mobilization in the 1970s. Young blacks in large cities, mainly in Rio de Janeiro and Salvador, gathered at musical parties, inspired by cul-

7. In this chapter, the black movement is considered to be a component of contemporary racial mobilization. Nonetheless, according to Pinto (1993, 213), this term appears for the first time in 1934 in a text published in *A Voz da Raça*, the FNB newspaper.

8. Although Damasceno, Giacomini, and Santos (1988) and Santos (1986) catalogue organizations throughout the country using broad criteria for inclusion, the literature focuses on experiences in the country's three largest cities. Unquestionably, this has to do with racial dynamics, but also with the country's academic structure, which is concentrated in those cities.

tural developments in the United States marked by afro hairstyles and Motown records.[9] "Black soul" was expressive as a leisure option for young blacks outside carnival boundaries; and in spite of the difficulty of politically motivating youth through cultural activities, it influenced the careers of important activists.

Parallel to the U.S. music used as a language of black soul, the U.S. civil rights movement as well as the decolonization of African countries inspired many organizations. Intense mobilization took place in the 1970s: in 1971 the Centro de Cultura e Arte Negra was founded in São Paulo and the Grupo Evolução was founded in Campinas; in 1974 the Grupo Negro and the Bloco Afro Ilê Aiyê were founded in Salvador; in 1974 and 1975, respectively, the Sociedade de Intercâmbio Brasil-África and the Instituto de Pesquisa das Culturas Negras were founded in Rio de Janeiro; and in Niterói the Grupo de Trabalho André Rebouças, which organized the Semanas de Estudos to discuss the evolving race-relations literature and provide valuable opportunities for exchange be-tween activists and intellectuals, was founded (Monteiro 1991, Turner 1985). Additionally, the Centro de Estudos Afro-Asiáticos was founded in Rio de Janeiro to promote study groups and meetings among activists.

The most specifically political project in the contemporary racial mo-bilization came to life with the Movimento Negro Unificado (MNU), founded in 1978.[10] Two traits stand out in the profile of the MNU. First, the organization integrated race and class into its practices. Second, it at-tempted to incorporate groups and organizations acting in that moment. The definition of the organization's name illustrates these characteristics. At its first rally on July 7, 1978, it called itself the Movimento Unificado Contra a Discriminação Racial. In a meeting in São Paulo on July 23, it was decided to incorporate the word *negro* in the original name, so it be-came Movimento Negro Unificado Contra a Discriminação Racial. A national congress held in Rio de Janeiro in December 1979 shortened the name to Movimento Negro Unificado. These alterations bear relevant symbolic and political meanings. A clear racial point of reference hin-dered a broad agglutination of subordinate segments, as had been the in-tention of some activists. A rupture with the original project occurred, and the "fight against racism was redefined, creating a black organiza-

9. On Black Rio, see Hanchard (1994) and Monteiro (1991); and on Black Bahia, see da Cunha (1991) and Risério (1981).

10. On the MNU, see—in addition to the pioneer studies by Gonzalez (1982 and 1985) and Moura (1980 and 1983)—Andrews (1991 and 1992b), Covin (1990), Hanchard (1994), Pinto (1993), Nascimento (1989), and G. G. Santos (1992).

tion, independent of the structure and guidance of the left, yet the class principle in the struggle against racism was preserved" (G. G. Santos, 1992, 60). The MNU organized in many cities and states, making it the first black national organization after the extinction of the FNB.

Racial Mobilization: Issues and Challenges

It is possible to represent the repertoire of racial mobilization graphically, where the vertical axis indicates the political-cultural continuum and the horizontal axis gives the position regarding the hegemonic discourse about race relations in Brazilian society (see Figure 8.1).[11] As a whole, the racial mobilization lies in the identity pole, in opposition to an ideological pole, which has been a major focus of the analysis of contemporary collective movements.[12] In manipulating identity, social movements activate symbols that express affiliation and try to ensure transmission of values and behavior norms.

The groups and organizations involved in the racial mobilization in the 1920s and 1930s aimed to increase the black community's education and skill levels, which would help integrate blacks into the developing national economy. The TEN typified the racial mobilization in the mid-1940s and 1950s. Although racial mobilization in both periods was assimilative, in the latter it became more critical of racial relations in Brazil and manipulated the discourse of contrasting identity.

In the 1970s and 1980s, racial mobilization generated a radical critique of race relations in Brazil.[13] In this context, black soul can be placed in a conflictive dimension because it carved out a leisure domain different from those perceived as traditionally appropriate for blacks in Brazil. The profiles of two carnival groups also exemplify the change in the perspective on the participation of blacks in Brazilian society. The symbols, discourses, and positions professed by the Afoxé Filhos de Gandhi and the Bloco Afro Ilê Aiyê represent a shift in the understanding of race re-

11. This map draws on Paulston's (1993) analysis. He suggests a cartographic representation in identifying social actors and their discourses.

12. Racial identity has been a major research theme in the Brazilian literature on race relations, although it is most often analyzed in reference to anthropological theories rather than within the discourse of social movements (see, for example, Agier 1992, Berriel 1989, Monteiro 1991, Pinto 1990 and 1993).

13. Comparing the racial mobilization in the 1970s and 1980s to that in the first half of the century, it is clear that the press played a much more important role in mobilizing blacks in the early part of the century (Pinto 1993). There are, nevertheless, more sophisticated literary initiatives today, such as *QUILOMBO HOJE* (Kennedy 1986).

Figure 8.1.   Map of Racial Mobilization in Brazil, 1920s to1980s

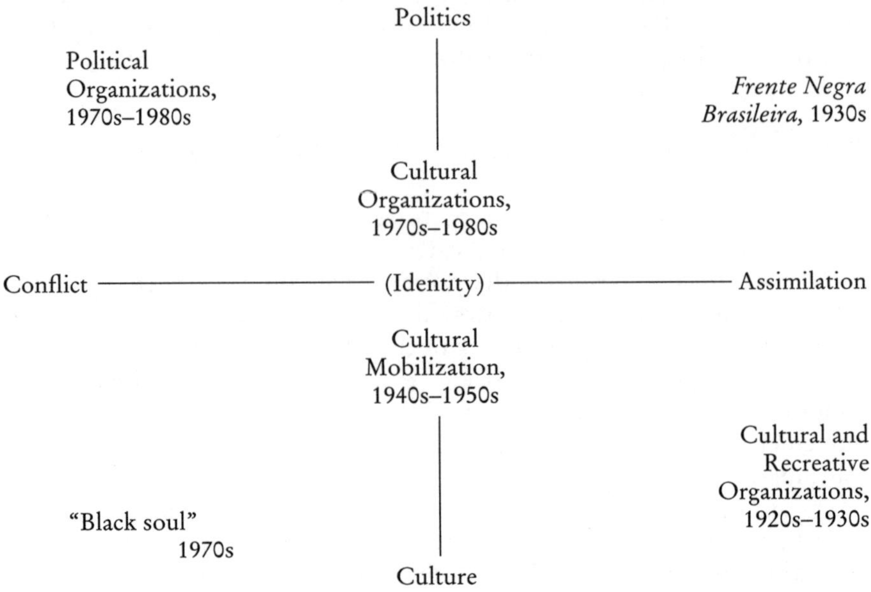

Politics

Political
Organizations,
1970s–1980s

*Frente Negra
Brasileira*, 1930s

Cultural
Organizations,
1970s–1980s

Conflict ———————————— (Identity) ———————————— Assimilation

Cultural
Mobilization,
1940s–1950s

Cultural and
Recreative
Organizations,
1920s–1930s

"Black soul"
1970s

Culture

lations in Brazil. Both carnival groups express the black community's mobilization in the carnival context, but the Bloco Afro Ilê Aiyê, which admits only blacks in its carnival parades, is undoubtedly a significant element in articulating and opening up new forms of participation for blacks (Morales 1988 and 1991).[14]

Nowadays, the political-cultural cleavage pervading racial mobilization is more salient. "Black" culture has been claimed for political goals, and many organizations have a double, perhaps ambiguous, presence in the two realms. Activists use cultural messages for consensus mobilization among the black movement's potential constituency; analogously, those in cultural organizations claim to be involved in consciousness raising. The strategy reinforces the distinction based on cultural factors

14. In Salvador the carnival experienced a "reafricanization" (Risério 1981), providing blacks with new forms of participation. Meanwhile, in Rio de Janeiro, the appropriation of "black" themes and references to "black" roots from Bahia transformed carnival parades into a spectacular show (Cavalcanti 1990), which may have alienated the black community's participation in the event (Rodrigues 1984).

in order to open paths to a political project specific to the black commu-nity. Nonetheless, conflicts have arisen in this process. J. C. Silva (1988, 285–86) recalls concerns of activists in Salvador who called for more ex-plicitly political actions, and he mentions that they pointed to the cul-tural element as a barrier for the MNU. Da Cunha (1991, 169) depicts the tension between activists connected to political organizations and to carnival groups. In Rio de Janeiro, the relationship between the black movement and soul participants was always precarious, in spite of—or because of—efforts to mobilize the latter. In Sebastião Soares's analysis,[15] there was little gain in "terms of activism and consciousness for the black movement. Very few of those who attended the soul parties became mili-tants of the black movement."

Debates about the effectiveness of strategies adopted by the black movement and about culturalism as an instrument of political mobiliza-tion permeate the literature (Winant 1994). In studying how activists, which she calls a "black intellectual elite," formed the black movement in Rio de Janeiro in the 1970s, Monteiro concludes that "the fight against racism was translated into cultural manifestations in which the socioeco-nomic aspects of living conditions of blacks did not became visible" (1991, 115). For Maués (1991), the problem lies in the gap between the "common black" and the model of "Africanized black" (clothes, hair-styles, diet, names for children, etc.) adopted by militants.[16] Hanchard (1994) further elaborates this argumentation. For him, "culturalistic" practices, as opposed to cultural ones, undermine the efficacy of dis-courses challenging racial hegemony. In his view, by reinforcing the bias that black identity is confined to the realm of folklore, the black move-ment reproduces the reification that the dominant culture imposes on black symbols.

In a more complex analysis of political mobilization through cultural means, Agier (1992, 109) looks at the formation in Salvador of a political arena occupied by the language of ethnic identity. He argues that the reappropriation for political aims of a cultural repertoire is a common trait in the religious, cultural, and political fields, in spite of ideological differences among them. In talking about reappropriation, Agier put in new terms what Fontaine (1985) had referred to as power relations. Fontaine argues that blacks in Brazil hold leadership positions at the

15. Black activist interviewed by Monteiro (1991, 76).
16. Figueiredo (1994) shows that new occupational opportunities appear in this process. She studies the labor market and professionalization in Salvador motivated by what she calls "new black esthetics," especially related to hairstyles.

local level but are excluded from them at regional and national levels. If this is correct, the issue is how to make local control abet the struggle against racial discrimination and inequality.

These difficulties have been tangible in electoral politics, despite the increase of black candidates in electoral races.[17] Berquó and Alencastro (1992) identify a move toward an "ethnic vote," but Hasenbalg and Silva (1993) detect evidence of resistance against racial mobilization. In analyzing a survey in São Paulo, they show that blacks and whites generally believe that all Brazilians have access to the same rights, although they also think that there is discrimination in the labor market and in police treatment of blacks. Most strikingly, however, people do not believe in a singular solution for the problem, but they believe blacks and whites must join together to end it. For the authors, this response indicates a preference for avoiding conflict in dealing with racial discrimination. They note also that this conciliatory attitude does not apply to work relations, since the majority accepts strikes as a legitimate means of pressure.

These analyses suggest that the obstacles for the black movement lie beyond the difficulties of communication within the black community or the cultural component of its practices. The obstruction of political mobilization along racial lines happens because Brazilian political culture has not historically recognized identities other than class affiliation. In this sense, it is interesting to examine how the black movement interacts with other sectors of civil society, and how the state answers its demands.

Maio (1993) describes a coalition that mobilized blacks and Jews in Rio de Janeiro in 1993 following highly publicized neo-Nazi attacks that targeted Jews, blacks, homosexuals, and Northeastern migrants. The author analyzes documents and speeches delivered in the short period of the coalition's existence and highlights the troubles Jewish and black leadership encountered in trying to find common ground. In the end, the coalition decided to characterize the attacks as a threat to citizenship, calling for the mobilization of a "Brazilian and democratic majority." The limitation of this strategy "exposed the difficulty of affirming ethnic identity as constituent of citizenship, which is an important Brazilian dilemma" (Maio 1993, 181). In other words, for political purposes one can be a Brazilian, a citizen, or a democrat, but not a Jew or a black.

Thus, the black movement is confronting a political culture that tends to discourage mobilization around specific identities. At the same time,

---

17. On electoral politics and race in São Paulo, see Pereira (1982), G. G. Santos (1992), and Valente (1986); and in Salvador, see C. Oliveira (1991). Curiously, there are no studies with a similar focus for Rio de Janeiro.

much like other social movements, it confronts topics such as autonomy, subordination, and cooperation, vis-à-vis the government and political parties, which are constantly discussed among both activists and students of social movements. Democratization, beginning in the late 1970s, renewed the preeminence of these issues, especially with the victory of politicians involved in the consolidation of democracy and receptive to the demands of civil society. They created channels of communication between the state apparatus and social movements by establishing consulting agencies and appointments to administrative positions.[18]

The black movement's reactions to these initiatives, their efficacy, the possibility for future consolidation beyond administrative and political-party bases, and the extent to which they help to democratize the state become crucial subjects. The experience of social movements has demonstrated that the state is as much an enemy to be confronted as an agent of legitimization. It reacts selectively to collective demands, even as it may democratize itself through contacts with social movements.[19] These contacts cannot be ignored as a means for bringing qualitative changes in the exercise of the citizenship that must surpass the mere performance of democratic rituals.

Conclusion

Mapping racial mobilization in Brazil since the early twentieth century reveals the complexity of the mobilization and features of the black movement. The task of that movement is to critique race relations and to uncover the sinuous paths of the dominant racial ideology. It is not that people ignore discrimination, but activists must persuade them that collective mobilization is the appropriate response. As a strategy to transform consensus mobilization into action mobilization, activists rely on a common cultural heritage and claim, now more than ever before, positive aspects of the black identity. These initiatives try to invert the tendency toward national appropriation of ethnic and racial symbols. Efforts to-

18. The first of such agencies was a state council dedicated to women's rights created in São Paulo in 1983. Governor Franco Montoro appointed a black feminist to the council after extensive lobbying by black organizations (Alvarez 1990, 201) and created a black community council in 1984 (G. G. Santos 1992). In Rio de Janeiro, Governor Leonel Brizola appointed three blacks, among them a woman, to cabinet-level positions in 1983, and in his second administration, he created a state secretariat devoted to racial issues (Motta and Santos 1994).

19. Cardoso (1983) emphasizes these arguments, and Alvarez (1990, 195) mentions differentiated points of access in the relations between state agencies and social movements.

ward establishing Zumbi and November 20th as significant symbols for
the black community are the most vivid examples (M. Santos 1991).
However, since there are no legal race barriers, the black movement must
undertake a long process of political education. In the short run, the
message of a positive identity may be more effective in the urban spheres
of leisure and culture than in the political realm.

There is much that we do not know about the black movement: Who
are the activists in socioeconomic terms? Who are the participants in activities organized by the black movement? How were new practices
forged by organizations such as the Geledés-Instituto da Mulher Negra
in São Paulo, the Centro de Articulação das Populações Marginalizadas
in Rio de Janeiro, and the Casa Dandara in Belo Horizonte? The government agencies responsible for racial issues, and the—at least formal—
concern of political parties on the topic, prove the black movement's
potential. The study of these agencies as channels of absorption of demands and managers of public policies, and of their influence on the
black movement and on the activists and organizations associated with it
should be part of the research agenda.

Despite obstacles, the black movement has become a relevant social
actor. This is said not to idealize the movement but to properly situate it.
The complexity of the black movement's challenges cannot be underestimated. As demonstrated in this chapter, activists have been relentless in
struggling to extend consensus mobilization along racial lines in order to
mobilize resources and support for the fight against mechanisms that reproduce racial inequalities in Brazil.

9

STRUGGLING FOR A PLACE:

Race, Gender, and Class in Political Elections in Brazil

Cloves Luiz Pereira Oliveira

Since the 1940s a major theme in the sociological literature has been the influence of gender and race on the participation of individuals in Brazilian society. Studies have mainly analyzed gender or race in regard to women and Afro-Brazilians and their participation in the labor market, their pattern of educational attainment, and their social mobility (Andrews 1991, 1992a; Bairros 1987; N. A. Castro 1993; Sá Barreto 1993; Hasenbalg 1979; Lovell 1992; Wood and Carvalho 1988). These works reveal that Brazil has a strong pattern of racial and gender inequality that, operating either alone or together with other ascribed or achieved characteristics, has historically restricted competition and participation by women and Afro-Brazilians (Bairros et al. 1993; Lovell 1992). Only a few studies, however, have attempted to analyze how gender and race influence the participation of women and Afro-Brazilians in politics, and even fewer have examined how these groups perform both as voters and as politicians running for office in Brazil (Tabak 1987; N. A. Castro 1993; Souza 1971; Valente 1982; Oliveira 1991). This body of literature chooses to focus on the participation of *either* women or Afro–Brazilians but fails to compare the two groups. Nevertheless, a comparative approach would illuminate the similarities and differences that mark the participation of women and Afro-Brazilians in an arena traditionally dominated by white male politicians.

I thank Wanderlin Barbosa, Judge of the Second Electoral Zone of the Tribunal Regional Eleitoral da Bahia (Regional Electoral Tribunal of Bahia, TRE) in Salvador, who kindly allowed me to consult the TRE archives.

Women and Afro-Brazilian politicians occupy fewer than 10 percent
of the seats in the Brazilian state legislatures (Castro 1993; Tabak 1987;
C. Oliveira 1991; Valente 1986). Whether studying gender and politics or
race and politics, authors identify four problems to explain the failure of
women's and Afro-Brazilians' candidacies. First, both women and Afro-
Brazilians are stereotyped as passive, irrational, dependent, and lacking
in leadership and entrepreneurial ability. Because those characteristics are
not associated with the exercise of power, women and Afro-Brazilians
tend to consider themselves unfit to be candidates, and when they do
run, the electorate tends to refuse to vote for them. The old saying in
Brazilian political culture that "Women do not vote for women, and
blacks do not vote for blacks" seems to be a synthesis of this culturalist
argument.

Second, the restricted supply of women and Afro-Brazilians competing for political office contributes to their electoral failure (N. A. Castro
1993; Randall 1982). According to Bourdieu (1989), politics is a place
where the symbolic can legitimize the group because, like art or religion,
politics requires that the participant have symbolic capital, including, for
candidates, masculinity (Randall 1982). The presence or absence of symbolic capital can predetermine a person's willingness to participate in the
political system. The predominance of sexist and racial prejudice is seen
in the tendency to exclude women and Afro-Brazilians from political
power. However, as some authors point out (Tabak 1987; Borges Pereira
1982; Oliveira 1991), both women and Afro-Brazilians in politics have
been characterized by their common position as victims of symbolic violence as well as for their attempts to redefine their identities and to use
identity to force their grievances onto the agendas of political parties and
to gain access to the political apparatus. It is not always a disadvantage to
be a woman or a minority in politics because this identity can be a basis
for political alliances.

Third, neither group has had much success in running for political office, which means they lack political experience and often exhibit ama-
teurish political styles. These groups are also disadvantaged in regard to
education and occupation, both of which strongly influence political recruitment (Randall 1982, 88). Traditionally, Brazilian candidates are professionals and business owners (F. H. Cardoso 1978).

Fourth, the very logic of political recruitment influences the participation of women and Afro-Brazilians (Barreira 1993). By "logic" I refer to
the institutions governing recruitment, the roles assigned to political
elites, and their power to regulate entrance into parties. Pointing out the
prevalence of subjective criteria used in political recruitment, Randall ad-

mits that it is difficult to know "whether women who may experience discrimination might, in addition, lack qualifications for political office" (1982, 99).

This chapter sketches a profile of the 1992 candidates for city council in Salvador, Bahia. The choice of Salvador to study the influence of race and gender in politics lies mainly in demographic, socioeconomic, cultural, and political factors. First, Salvador, the capital of the state of Bahia, is the third largest city in the country, with a 1992 population of about 2.2 million inhabitants, 52 percent women and 80 percent Afro-Brazilians (in contrast to 46 percent Afro-Brazilians in the overall population). As has occurred elsewhere in rapidly industrializing and urbanizing areas of Brazil, Afro-Brazilians are concentrated in the lower economic strata (Castro and Guimarães 1993). However, Salvador differs from other regions of Brazil because it embodies a significant Afro-Brazilian cultural tradition. In the late 1970s Salvador was a center for an Afro-Brazilian cultural and political movement that has framed the national discourse of racial pride and Afrocentricity and has sparked an explicitly political discourse questioning the position of Afro-Brazilians in society (Agier 1992). All the same, whites hegemonically dominate the major economic and political positions in Salvador, as in the rest of Brazil. This chapter examines the actors who emerged in 1992 to struggle for a place in the political-institutional arena of Salvador.

Data and Methods

Data were gathered from the files of candidates registered for the 1992 elections with the Tribunal Regional Eleitoral da Bahia (Regional Electoral Tribunal of Bahia, TRE). Twenty-two parties, registering 1,149 candidates, contested 35 seats.[1] The TRE uses a standard registration form and requires a specific set of personal documents from each candidate.[2]

---

1. It is significant that compared to the 1988 elections this represents a 27 percent increase in the number of candidates.

2. Brazilian elections are regulated by a federal electoral code administered by a national system of electoral courts. Candidates must be nominated by a political party or coalition of political parties that is registered with the courts. All candidates must speak Portuguese and be in full possession of their political rights, but the age limit depends on the political office for which a person is running (candidates for city council must be at least 18 years old). Council members are elected by proportional representation. The city council is the lowest ranking political office in Brazil but is invested with powers of impeachment, appeal, and budget auditing as a means of control over the mayor (Brazil Election Factbook 1966).

This information provided a record of a candidate's socioeconomic background and, in certain cases, political background.[3]

Traditionally, studies on race relations in Brazil, especially those dealing with demographic data, encounter obstacles in identifying individuals by race or color. The major problem is that most Brazilian institutions tend to be color-blind in their bureaucratic procedures. The TRE is no exception. This study identified color from other documents in the candidates' files. For men, a major source was the Army Certificate of Registration, which includes a photograph and a written statement of color. Because 88.5 percent of the candidates were men, this document proved invaluable. The main source for women was the "declaration of property," which contains a short self-description.

The color classification applied to the data followed a sociological method traditionally used in many studies on race relations in Brazil that categorizes people in two groups, "white" and "nonwhite" (with the latter encompassing *pardos* and *pretos*) (Andrews 1991; Bairros 1987; Hasenbalg and Silva 1993; Lovell 1992; Wood and Carvalho 1988). In this chapter, the "nonwhite" category is synonymous with Afro-Brazilian. I added a third category, *moreno*, because approximately 10 percent of the sample represented a phenotype whose traits fell somewhere between "white" and "nonwhite." One objective of the study was to determine how patterns of candidates' political participation varied among whites, *morenos*, and nonwhites (that is, those individuals that I identified as Afro-Brazilians).

Parties and Electoral Laws

The advent of an election presents a strategic moment for party recruitment. Of the candidates running in the 1992 city council race in Salvador, 75 percent joined their parties only on the eve of the elections. It is impossible to know whether a candidate had run for office previously, but the data definitively suggest that many newcomers broke into the professional political arena in 1992.

Most of the twenty-two parties competing in the city council race were national-level parties, the oldest ones having been founded after the 1979 electoral reforms that ended the bipartisan structure installed by the military regime in 1966 (Lamounier and Meneguello 1986). There were

3. The TRE administered one form to about 80 percent of the candidates and another form to the remainder. The first asked the candidates' profession; the second did not. Fortunately, by piecing together a variety of data it was possible to determine the profession of most candidates.

three main divisions: left, right, and *partidos de ocasião* or "opportunistic parties," as political analysts like to call them (Valle 1987). The ideological profile of a party, its prestige, and its electoral strategy influenced the number of candidates it registered.[4] In most parties, approximately half of the candidates recruited were Afro-Brazilian. Color did not appear to be associated with party affiliation, and Afro-Brazilians were found in parties across the political spectrum, from left to right.

The left-wing parties, running 313 candidates, created a coalition marked by its ideological overtones and its recruitment of the fewest candidates. Most parties espoused a right-wing ideology and recruited large numbers of candidates based on their political capital (that is, the capacity to gather votes) rather than on their ideological identification. The opportunistic parties recruited fewer candidates than the right-wing parties. According to Valle, these parties organized to provide an outlet for the personal political aspirations of individuals who had shown leadership ability or who were involved in the defense of a specific, ephemeral issue. Most opportunistic-party candidates leaned to the center or right ideologically, but recruitment in those parties was much less the result of a candidate's ideological commitment than his or her potential to win votes. Additionally, party leadership recognized that recruitment of a charismatic candidate helps to legitimize the party. In sum, both right-wing and opportunistic parties were characterized by political-ideological inconsistency, *personalismo*, clientelism, and a weak sense of loyalty to the party on the part of members and voters (F. H. Cardoso 1978; Lamounier 1978).[5]

Brazil has a proportional representation system in which the parties are the focus of the election. Proportional representation establishes that the number of votes that a party achieves in the election grants it a proportion of seats in the assembly. Within the party, seats are distributed according to a ranking of candidates based on the number of votes each has received in the election. For example, if a party wins five seats, the five highest polling candidates will be seated. It is the party's overall performance—not the candidate's individual performance—that determines

4. The Brazilian electoral system rules that each party can register a number of candidates up to twice the number of seats available on the city council, which, in the case of Salvador, would be 70 candidates. Coalitions, however, can register three times the number of seats available.

5. However, with the emergence of the PT, PDT, and the legalization of the communist parties in the 1980s, some authors (e.g., Moises 1993) have observed changes in party structure and political culture, marked by a crystallization of party ideology, at least among left-wing parties, the emergence in the electorate of a sense of political rights and duties, and growing criticism of the performance of political institutions and politicians.

who will win a seat in the representative body (Brazil Election Factbook 1966; Dias 1991). Thus, proportional representation systems are characterized by instances of the seating of candidates who received fewer votes than other candidates running in the election. This weakens party solidarity because party members compete to rank first in the organization, and it allows candidates with less real support among the electorate to become representatives.

Race and Gender in the 1992 Election

What kind of women and men were most likely to participate in the 1992 Salvador elections? Only one out of ten candidates were women (11.5 percent women versus 88.5 percent men), and this gap was apparent across all three racial groups. The disparity in the rates of participation of men and women directly touches on a central issue in women's relationship to institutional politics: the low number of women who aspire to political careers (Randall 1982; Tabak and Toscano 1982).

Even in political recruitment a sexual division of labor appears to operate. Women candidates in the Salvador election were more likely than their male counterparts to be better educated, single or divorced, and employed as public servants (28.6 percent), teachers (26.7 percent), business owners (17.0 percent), or professionals (16.1 percent).[6] Significantly, 67 percent of all Afro-Brazilian women candidates were teachers or public servants compared to 55 percent of all women candidates and 43 percent of all white candidates, regardless of gender. As in the general population, white women politicians were, to a significant degree, more likely to be professionals or business owners (45 percent) than were Afro-Brazilian women politicians (22 percent). Women were much more likely to be better educated than men, with 56 percent having had some college education compared to 42 percent of the men. Fewer than 5 percent of the women had only primary schooling compared to 17 percent of the men.

Class, in contrast, influenced recruitment of women and men about equally. When measured by neighborhood of residence, men and women had nearly the same class background, with the majority of the candidates, independent of gender, drawn from the working class, followed by

6. Some studies (Tabak and Toscano 1982, Randall 1982) claim that certain occupations, including social work, education, and charity, provide a strategic base to launch a woman's career as a politician. These are female-dominated professions in which women may gain experience in leadership roles.

a significant segment from the middle class and only a small proportion from the upper or upper-middle class. Women candidates were as likely as their male counterparts to join their parties only on the eve of the elections. In regard to age, both groups were predominantly between 30 and 60. But male candidates were drawn from a wider range of occupations, which may indicate that, directly or indirectly, their professional activities have given them greater exposure to politics. Thus, political recruitment differed for women and men, especially in regard to education and occupation, with women being more likely to have more education and to work in occupations usually characterized as "female."

While women were underrepresented among the candidates in the 1992 election, 575 Afro-Brazilians (54.1 percent) competed against 377 whites (35.6 percent), and 100 *morenos* (10.3 percent) for 35 city-council seats. Given the rate of participation of women and *morenos,* it appears that this electoral race was disputed mainly by white and Afro-Brazilian *men.* In general, white candidates were better off in terms of education, employment, living conditions, and class position than the Afro-Brazilians. In socioeconomic terms, most *morenos* fell somewhere between white and Afro-Brazilian politicians.

Afro-Brazilian candidates comprised more than two-thirds of all those candidates who had only a primary education. Of all the Afro-Brazilian candidates, almost 20 percent had only a primary education, almost double the rates for whites and *morenos.* The rates for those who completed high school but went no further was 48 percent for Afro-Brazilians and 38 percent for whites. It is striking that almost 50 percent of the white candidates were college educated, compared to only 42 percent of the *morenos* and 32 percent of the Afro-Brazilians. However, it is important to point out that among those who had attained a college education, the size of the white candidate pool was only slightly larger than the size of the pool of Afro-Brazilian candidates (190 whites and 171 Afro-Brazilians). Given the traditional pattern of political recruitment in Brazil that tends to "privilege" college-educated candidates, the 1992 Salvador city council election was unusual for its high proportion of candidates with only a low or intermediate level of education.

Overall, Afro-Brazilian candidates were drafted from the working class, whereas whites came from the upper-middle and middle classes, and *morenos* from the middle class. The occupational profile of candidates tended to match the general pattern of racial segmentation that exists in the local labor market, where, according to N. A. Castro (1993) and Sá Barreto (1993), whites and Afro-Brazilians work in exclusive niches. Castro (1993) notes that whites are concentrated in high-ranking positions in both the public and private sectors, and many are business owners. Afro-Brazilians, on the other hand, are found in blue-collar jobs and the service sector. Racial segmentation in the labor market means that whites command positions of power and own the means of production, whereas Afro-Brazilians are more likely to be manual laborers, service workers, or first-line supervisors.

Not surprisingly, Afro-Brazilians made up approximately two-thirds or more of all candidates working in the armed forces (73 percent) or as public servants (66 percent), teachers (64 percent), blue-collar workers (76 percent), and transport workers (82.5). White candidates were concentrated (55.5 percent) in the professional occupations, traditionally associated with the image of the prestigious professional politician. Only 38 percent of the Afro-Brazilian candidates and 7 percent of the *moreno* candidates held professional occupations. Among business owners, who ran the gamut from corner grocery store and news stand operators to magnates of large companies, whites and nonwhites were about equally represented: 43.2 percent and 44.3 percent, respectively, with *morenos* lagging far behind.[7]

Class affiliation is especially apparent when one considers the neighborhoods in which the candidates lived. Whereas 65.5 percent of the candidates living in upper- and middle-class neighborhoods (16.8 percent of the total candidate pool) were white, almost 64 percent of the Afro-Brazilian candidates, versus about one-third of the whites, were drafted from working-class neighborhoods or the outskirts of Salvador. Put differently, two out of three white candidates came from either upper- or upper-middle-class neighborhoods, compared to only one out of three Afro-Brazilians candidates. Among the nonwhite candidates only 8.1 percent lived in upper-class or upper-middle-class neighborhoods.

The higher socioeconomic status of white candidates is also confirmed by the number of properties a candidate owns. Thirty-one percent of the candidates claimed they owned no property; most of that group (61.2 percent) was Afro-Brazilian. Inversely, more than half of those who claimed they owned seven or more pieces of real estate were white, but only one-third were Afro-Brazilian (35.9 percent) and about one-tenth *moreno*. Thus, among the richest candidates, Afro-Brazilians were the least represented, whereas among the poorest, they were significantly in the majority.

In conclusion, white, Afro-Brazilian, and *moreno* politicians are char-

7. According to N. A. Castro (1993, 49), only 5 percent of Afro-Brazilians in Salvador are business owners.

acterized by strikingly different backgrounds. In this sense, it is possible to say that white and Afro-Brazilian candidates have distinct profiles. One out every two white candidates was a professional or a business owner, college-educated, and from upper-middle-class and middle-class neighborhoods. The other half were more likely to have completed only elementary or high school (9.9 percent and 37.6 percent, respectively). In terms of occupation, few white candidates worked in blue-collar work, services, and the public sector.

For their part, 60 percent of the Afro-Brazilian candidates were employed as public servants, blue-collar workers, teachers, transport workers, and sales people (with an additional percentage artists, self-employed, retired, or students). Afro-Brazilian professionals (9.2 percent) and business owners (17.2 percent) also had significant presence, but their numbers were still small when compared to their white counterparts. The working-class background of Afro-Brazilian candidates is reaffirmed by the observation that two-thirds of the candidates lived in working-class neighborhoods or the outskirts of Salvador.

The small population of *moreno* candidates does not present a sharply defined set of features; however, it appears that they were primarily professionals and business owners (39.1 percent) as well as public servants and sales people and that approximately half came from middle-class or upper-middle-class neighborhoods.

The most interesting finding comes from the analysis of the pattern of voting distribution. At first glance, the electoral race appeared highly competitive, since 1,149 candidates were fighting to get one of the 35 seats on the city council (an average of 33 candidates fought for each seat). The lowest-polling successful candidate received 1,306 votes. Yet using that figure as a baseline for measuring serious competitors, it is striking to see that only about 10 percent of the candidates polled more than 1,200 votes, whereas more than 40 percent received between only 2 and 200 votes. Of that 40 percent, 60 percent were Afro-Brazilian candidates, which indicates that nonwhites were disproportionately dismissed by the electorate as "non-candidates."

Clearly the race was marked by candidates who possessed a very unequal distribution of political capital. What social, ideological, and political factors mobilized those who polled fewer than 200 votes to enter this electoral contest in the first place? One hypothesis suggests that this type of candidate would represent the leadership of a small group of friends or coworkers, a professional community, or a neighborhood association. As Piven and Cloward (1979) suggest, changes in the political structure, such as in the representation of politics and politicians within Brazilian society, and macro socioeconomic crises in Brazil may have reshaped the political arena.

Who Won the Race for City Council?

The 1992 Bahia election appeared to be characterized by highly democratic political recruitment; nevertheless, the race was contested by candidates with unequal political capital (including socioeconomic capital and prestige). Two candidate profiles predominated. One comprised well-educated, married, middle-aged, middle- or upper-middle-class men, a profile exemplifying the traditional Brazilian politician (F. H. Cardoso 1978). The second profile also comprised married, middle-aged men, but in this case, men drafted from an urban, working-class background. Notably, these candidates came from occupational groups that have been actively involved in strikes and labor struggles in Bahia. Unlike the candidate pool, winners presented more homogeneous characteristics. They were overwhelmingly male, college-educated, married, between 35 and 60 years of age, professionals or businessmen, living in affluent neighborhoods.[8]

The 1992 election reflected two major changes in the process of political recruitment in Salvador. The number of Afro-Brazilian politicians elected jumped from four candidates in the 1988 election to twelve in 1992, and a significant proportion of working-class candidates (17.1 percent) also won seats. In this election, Afro-Brazilians and workers seem to have been less intimidated by discrimination and prejudice, which usually regulates their aspirations and relegates them to their "appropriate place." Further research is needed to understand the mechanisms for the emergence of the second group as political actors in an arena where class boundaries (delineated by education, cultural capital, and socioeconomic capital) have traditionally discouraged their participation.

Despite these developments, old patterns of political recruitment are deeply rooted in society. One aspect of that Brazilian tradition is the tendency to reelect incumbents (Brazil Election Factbook 1966; Tabak 1987). About half of the winners in 1992 had served as council members

8. The municipal council in Salvador is a male domain. Only one woman, the highest polling candidate in the entire election, succeeded in winning a seat on the council. However, this victory means little in regard to women's struggle to enter the political arena because her husband was already an established politician in Bahia. Compared to the 1988 election, when two women were elected—both of whom had accrued political capital mainly as a product of their militancy—women lost heavily in 1992.

during the 1988–92 term. Although the 1992 race was marked by a striking diversity of candidates' backgrounds, the overwhelming victory of men in that election marks politics as remaining a dominantly male realm.

The profile of male and female candidates showed that both groups tend to emerge from across all segments of society. But women candidates were better educated than their male counterparts. They also were more likely to come from a narrow set of occupations that includes social workers, teachers, public servants, and professionals. Women from traditionally "female" occupations were clearly favored in political recruitment.

The most striking difference in candidate profile was color. White and Afro-Brazilians candidates emerged from different social environments. The white candidates, regardless of gender, were more likely to be college-educated professionals or business owners from affluent neighborhoods. Afro-Brazilians were more likely to hold working-class occupations and live in working-class neighborhoods. Nevertheless, candidates from all color groups emerged from all class segments.

Thus, this profile indicates the emergence of a wave of new actors in the professional political arena in Salvador. The increase in the participation of Afro-Brazilian politicians from 11.4 percent in the 1988 election to 34.3 percent, along with the emergence of working-class candidates (17.1 percent), definitely reshaped the political battleground. Nevertheless, the Salvador city council continues to be dominated by whites (57.1 percent) rather than Afro-Brazilians (34.2 percent) or *morenos* (8.6 percent) and by college-educated, affluent individuals who are overwhelmingly men.

10

RACIAL INEQUALITY IN THE LIVES OF BRAZILIAN WOMEN

Ana Maria Goldani

The lives of Brazilian women have undergone profound transformations in recent decades and today reflect a diversity of roles both at home and in the labor market. Hard-won rights are significantly redefining women's position in society and their status as citizens (Jatobá 1990; M. G. Castro 1989; Goldani 1989; Henriques and Silva 1989; Oliveira, Porcaro, and Araújo 1987a). This chapter's discussion of racial differences in the organization and pattern of Brazilian women's domestic life is guided by two assumptions. First, although the lives of *preto, pardo,* and white women are all predominantly oriented toward marriage and motherhood, these roles are influenced by a woman's racial affiliation and social opportunities. Thus, the "normative" or expected domestic pattern for Brazilian women varies in relation to race. Second, racism shapes the organization and trajectory of domestic life for Brazilian women, as is shown by a growing body of research demonstrating that during the course of their lifetime *pardo* and *preto* women have fewer and inferior opportunities as compared to whites (Hasenbalg 1990, 4).

The persistence of racial differences in Brazil calls for a broader examination of both white and nonwhite families and their historical context resulting from the clash of European and African cultures, Catholic and syncretic beliefs, and slave and nonslave experience. This chapter touches on some of these elements, but the emphasis here is on contemporary mechanisms of discrimination and racism associated with racial inequali-

I thank Elide Ruggai Bastos and Edward Telles for their insightful comments on this chapter, but I assume full responsibility for the results and opinions presented here.

ties in the lives of Brazilian women. This chapter attempts to illustrate these mechanisms through an analysis of the demographic dynamics of discrimination against people of color and the consequences for women's lives and the pattern of their domestic arrangements.

In Brazil, women are commonly expected to live out a pattern of domestic life that is defined by the traditional sexual roles embedded in the "organized and legitimated" model of the family that until recently was sanctioned by both church and state (Leers 1987). Both church and state equated the family value system with monogamy, indissoluble union, and legitimacy of offspring. This view of the family as a monolithic institution left no leeway for alternative models and led to a view that single-mother households were deviant and that divorce was synonymous with family instability. For many years the 1940 Civil Code reflected this perspective. Legal recognition of birth outside of matrimony occurred only in 1940, and the federal government legalized divorce only in 1977 (Goldani 1990). While the institutions of church and state promoted an "ideal" family model, recent studies have emphasized that concrete living conditions also determine family structure (Samara 1989; J. C. Silva 1988; Corrêa 1982; Stolcke 1982; Macedo 1977; Bilac 1978).

The Condition of Women: Color and Domestic Patterns

Few studies have been done on women's changing position in the Brazilian family, their active participation in social transformation, or the implications of these changes for women's domestic life. Likewise, research on the situation of Brazilian women at different moments in the country's history reveals almost nothing about differences by race. The scarcity of information reflects how Brazilians treat racial issues. The myth of "racial democracy," which reigned at least until the mid-1970s, permeated the social sciences, and only recently has racial discrimination been acknowledged and debated (Hasenbalg 1990). The perception of the black woman's role is part of this evolving context and touches on the debate over the stability of the black family under slavery.

Official historiography long maintained that the licentious environment of slave quarters and the destructive action of slavery created unstable families. Critical revision of that argument claimed that despite the violence, slaves married and maintained unions, but their stability depended on a close relationship to the family cycles of the slave owners (Metcalf 1990). Other studies have also noted similarities between slave families and those of free poor people, with both marked by a high proportion of single men and single-mother households (Slenes 1987; Costa, Slenes, and Swartz 1987; Samara 1988).

On the São Paulo plantations, the slave woman not only performed domestic tasks and child care but also worked in the fields, sorting coffee and cultivating subsistence crops (Andrews 1986, 517). But many slave women were also domestic workers and participated in small trade in the urban areas. This enabled them to purchase their freedom, thus creating conditions leading to the prevalence of families headed by women. After slavery, according to the classical argument, both black women and black men were excluded from capitalist expansion. But according to Fernandes (1979), black women played a decisive role as mediator between races and classes, and they were at the center of the "unstable" or "incomplete" black family. Evidence for the "incomplete family" is found in the disproportionately large numbers of consensual unions, separations, and illegitimate children among nonwhites. Inspired by the work of Gilberto Freyre (1933), this view of the black woman's role emphasizes biases against the nonwhite population that assume that instability in domestic life results from differences based on class and not on race; that is, difference is due to the inferior socioeconomic position blacks occupy (Ianni 1972; Fernandes 1978). The idea of the black woman as an engine of social mobility and as key to the reproduction of the incomplete black family marked the post-abolition period and, until very recently, permeated analyses of black women's condition.

The hypothesis that black families are supported by black women and that black men hold a lower social and economic position than their female counterparts is now being questioned, largely because median incomes are consistently higher for black men and because there are significant differentials between black men and women in their rates of economic participation (Oliveira, Porcaro, and Araújo 1987a). Nevertheless, reports of ongoing family "instability" in the black population, represented by a preponderance of black single mothers, calls for a discussion about differences in the family arrangements of whites, *pardos,* and *pretos.* The argument that the incomplete black nuclear family after abolition did not reflect lack of a tradition of domestic organization but rather the family's "cultural and material" destitution (Rios 1990) appears to gain explanatory strength in light of existing racial differences in family arrangements.

Yet in the past two decades accumulated empirical knowledge has shown that racial inequality is a classifying principle, not just a question of class. Sociodemographic profiles demonstrate that even when controlling for the social condition of individuals, *pretos* and *pardos* risk higher mortality rates, suffer greater matrimonial instability, receive less education, earn lower salaries, and so forth (Goldani 1989; Berquó 1988; Wood and Lovell 1986; Lovell 1989; Wood and Carvalho 1988). Today a new consensus seems to have developed. *Pretos* and *pardos* (the black population, as some prefer) suffer under society's worst economic conditions, and race constitutes the common basis for that discrimination. Though generalized, these conditions are differentiated by sex (Hasenbalg, Silva, and Barcelos 1989; N. V. Silva 1985; Oliviera, Porcaro, and Araújo 1987a).

Demographic Profile of Brazilian Families

In the early 1990s approximately 74 percent of all Brazilian families consisted of couples with or without children, 16 percent were single-parent households comprising a mother or father living with children, 7 percent were households with people living alone or in groups without family ties, and another 3 percent consisted of some other type of arrangement. Broken out by color groups, we find that 58 percent of all Brazilian households were headed by whites, 36 percent by *pardos,* 6 percent by *pretos,* and the remainder by Asians (Goldani 1989). These domestic arrangements are marked by a greater proportion of single-parent households among *pretos* (21 percent) than among *pardos* (18 percent) or whites (14 percent). At the root of these differences are the demographic dynamics of discrimination. For example, the persistent contrast in life expectancy (nearly seven years less for *pretos*), the lower probability of marriage, lower *preto* birthrates (until 1960), and elevated birthrates among *pardos* may explain the differences in family structure (Tables 10.1 and 10.2) (Goldani 1989; Berquó 1988).

The proportional growth of female-headed families constitutes one of the most important factors affecting the structure of the family. In the past thirty years the percentage of households headed by women has doubled, from 10 to 20 percent. This has been accompanied by an increase in the proportion of these families living below the poverty line, so that by 1989, 33 percent lived in poverty. Of those, 49 percent were families headed by *preto* women, 45 percent by *pardo* women, 21 percent by white women, and 7 percent by Asian women. Finally, this increase is accentuated in urban areas and the poorest regions of the country. Between 1978 and 1986 households headed by women grew 18 percent nationwide compared to 33 percent in metropolitan areas, with the greatest

Table 10.1. Demographic Profile of Brazilian Women, by Color (1980–1984)

	White	*Pardo*	*Preto*	Total
Overall fertility rate	3.14	4.42	4.37	3.64
Marital fertility rate	6.42	8.39	9.32	7.23
Life expectancy	70.29	61.79	61.79	65.7
Marital status				
First marriage	66.4	72.0	62.1	70.9
Divorced/Separated	15.0	22.4	30.7	18.6
Widowed	4.3	5.6	8.3	5.0
Remarried divorcée	60.0	64.0	62.0	62.1
Remarried widow	64.1	54.0	47.0	56.7

SOURCE: PNAD, 1984.

Table 10.2. Distribution of Brazilian Women, 15 to 54 Years of Age, by Marital Status and Color (1980–1984)

	Single with Children	Number of Times Married or in a Consensual Union		
		1	2	3
White	10.70	92.1	7.3	0.6
Pardo	7.63	93.8	6.0	0.2
Preto	13.36	89.8	9.1	1.1
Total	20.60	87.9	10.7	1.4

SOURCE: PNAD, 1984.

increase occurring in urban areas of the Northeast, the poorest region of Brazil (Barros and Fox 1990).

Traditional and Alternative Domestic Patterns: The Role of the Sequence and Duration of Events

For Brazilian women, the normative course of domestic life between the ages of 15 and 50 follows a pattern of marriage at about 22 years of age with reproduction between about 20 and 29 years of age, resulting in a family of 2 to 4 children. A woman who marries, has at least one child, and keeps her first marriage intact until she reaches 50 years of age could be considered as fulfilling the domestic pattern of the average Brazilian woman. The distribution of all Brazilian women across birth cohorts shows that the number of women meeting the normative pattern has increased proportionally. Of women born between 1890 and 1894 who reached adulthood, nearly 41 percent followed the expected pattern. For women born between 1930 and 1934, the figure is 59.7 percent (Goldani 1989), representing an increase of almost 50 percent in only forty years. Among other factors, this may be attributable to declining mortality rates resulting from widespread eradication of infectious diseases.

Despite the pattern in which growing proportions of Brazilian women reach age 50 with children and married, it is far from universal. The proportion of women who opt not to have children or to divorce has also increased. At the same time, because of the diversification of women's roles, we can see a change in the sequence and duration of the events throughout a woman's life. These trends are reflected in the marital and maternal trajectories of women, and they differ by race and age cohort. In examining the alternative life trajectories followed by Brazilian women, we must take into account that premarital pregnancies and births as well as marriage[1] are important events in the process of forming the Brazilian family and that these do not necessarily constitute a deviation from the "normal" pattern.

This fact is supported by data from the 1984 PNAD, which showed that about 15 percent of Brazilian women between ages 15 and 54 who had married had had one child or pregnancy before marriage; for unmarried women, the figure was about 11 percent. Family formation varies among racial groups, however. The percentage of *preto* women who never married and reported having at least one child (20.6 percent) contrasts sharply with the figure for white (7.6 percent) and *pardo* women (13.4 percent) (Table 10.2). Among married women who had had children before marriage, *preto* women presented the highest percentage (18.6 percent), compared to white women (14.4 percent) and *pardo* women (16.5 percent).

In most societies becoming a father or mother is one of the most important social roles for individuals in the young-adult phase. Pressures among young adults assume different forms. In Brazil, the long pronatalist tradition of the state and the Catholic Church, and a marked sexual division in family roles may influence young people to become parents. At an individual level, this pressure primarily comes from the family lifestyle. For example, at family celebrations relatives and friends constantly question young couples without children. However, the strongest pressure seems to be in the association of the role of parent with the achievement of adulthood.

---

1. Marriage in this study refers to unions regardless of the type of bond. Thus, marriage here can refer to consensual unions or civil and/or religious marriages.

Motherhood as a vital event is often characterized as occurring at one of two extremes: an "early" entrance, in which adolescents become mothers, or a "late" entrance, in which older women, generally those over 30, become mothers. Implicitly these classifications of "early" and "late" obey a certain notion of order, sequence, and timing of events that characterize a normal life cycle. Using the statistical averages of age relative to occurrence of life events,[2] I have tried to identify the typical point at which women experience motherhood during their life trajectories.

In 1984 about half of all Brazilian women who were married or had been married had become mothers at age 21 (the age range was from 18.8 to 24.3 years, with a median of 21.3 years). As might be expected, the variation is closely related to age at first marriage[3] (a range from 17.7 to 23.3 years, with a median of 20.1 years). From the set of these relative ages, it seems reasonable to assume that in Brazil the normative age for achieving motherhood is between 18 and 25 years of age. Thus, an "early" entrance would mean having a child before 18, and a "late" entrance would mean having a child at 25 years of age or older. The results show that 16 percent of married Brazilian women became mothers early, and 21.5 percent, late. Approximately 62 percent had their first child "on time" (Table 10.3). Racial differences in the timing of motherhood show a strong deviation in the pattern for *preto* women.[4] When racial groups are compared with the norm, the proportion of *preto* women who became mothers "on time" (56.4 percent) is lower than the 62 percent average for Brazilian women, and the percentage of *preto* women entering motherhood late (25.3 percent) is greater than the national average (21.3 percent).

Demographic and structural changes in the country suggest that the timing of motherhood has undergone alterations. Thus, the "typical" age at motherhood would have changed over time and, as the analysis by different cohorts suggests, racial differences are becoming attenuated (Table 10.3). The hypothesis of a possible attenuation of racial differences in the normative timing of motherhood is verified in the younger cohort (30 to 34 years old). Across all racial groups, 63 percent of the women became mothers between 18 and 24 years of age. But in the older group (45–49

---

2. The relative ages refer to the age at the beginning of the interval of an event's occurrence. These are called "relative ages" because they are based on interviewees' ages and attributed to women at the same stage of reproductive life (Rodriguez and Hobcraft 1980).

3. Throughout, the term *marriage* refers to either cohabitation or formal marriage.

4. The 1984 PNAD research sample consisted of close to 137,000 women 15 to 54 years of age, 57 percent of whom were white, 6.5 percent *preto*, and 36 percent *pardo*. The *pardo* label included many racially mixed categories, such as mulatto, mestizo, *índio*, *caboclo*, *mameluco*, and *cafuzo*.

Table 10.3. Distribution of Women by Age upon Reaching Motherhood
(Brazil, 1984)

	Early (b. 18)	On Time (18–24)	Late (25+)
Brazil Nationwide			
White	13.8	63.6	17.5
Pardo	19.9	61.5	18.6
Preto	18.3	56.4	25.3
Total	16.2	62.3	16.2
Cohort 45 to 49 Years of Age			
White	14.3	66.1	19.5
Pardo	20.7	64.0	15.3
Preto	19.6	60.1	20.3
Total	16.3	65.6	18.1
Cohort 30 to 34 Years of Age			
White	9.8	63.2	26.9
Pardo	15.3	63.9	20.8
Preto	12.7	62.9	24.4
Total	11.9	63.4	24.7

SOURCE: PNAD, 1984.
NOTE: Only women who have been married or in a consensual union are counted for this
table. For the age cohorts, only those who had children before reaching age 30 are counted,
because those who had children after age 30 accounted for only 4.3 percent of the total.

years) that figure varied from 66 percent for white women to 64 percent
for *pardo* women and 60 percent for *preto* women. This tendency among
the younger cohort toward uniformity in the age of reaching motherhood may be associated with a lifestyle in which vital events are increasingly regulated and institutionalized. Therefore, the length of the
transitions between vital events, and even the sequence of those events,
may be governed increasingly by the demands and age-related norms of
an industrialized and urban society.

Despite the tendency toward homogenization in the normative age for
motherhood, different color groups diverge in the timing and order of
vital events. The sequence of marriage and first child has shifted toward
more premarital pregnancies, and this change has varied according to a
woman's race and age cohort. Between the periods 1945 to 1954 and 1975
to 1984, the percentage of marriages that involved premarital pregnancies
increased from 14.3 percent to 19.3 percent on average.
Premarital pregnancies in 1984 ranged from 19 percent for *preto*

women to 16 percent for *pardo* women and 14 percent for white women. These differences were due basically to the elevated proportion of premarital births among *preto* women (8.4 percent) in relation to white and *pardo* women (4.8 percent and 7 percent, respectively). With time, premarital pregnancies have increased for all racial groups. Nevertheless, the differences between racial groups today have diminished primarily because of an increase in the rate of premarital pregnancies among white women.

In conclusion, marriage across all racial groups seems to be less and less a determining factor in fertility. This fact, added to the generalized use of contraceptive methods, points to new conditions of reproduction with direct implications for the process of family-building (see Goldani 1990 on racial differences in patterns of family-building). Alterations in the sequences of vital events in women's family life can be linked to changes in duration of family roles, with important implications for women's lives, such as assuming sole responsibility for children.

Duration of Maternal and Marital Roles

To investigate the impact of demographic factors on the length of time that women of different color and age groups spend in the roles of wife and mother, we used demographic indicators and a macro-simulation model known as the Family Status Life Table, proposed by Bongaarts (1987).[5] We reconstructed the length of time that Brazilian women could expect to spend as wives and mothers using data for different cohorts at two moments in the country's demographic history (Goldani 1989). The "post-transition cohort" comprises women whose reproductive years were concentrated in the period *after* 1965, when national fertility rates had declined, and who were between 15 and 49 years of age in 1984. The "transition cohort" comprises women whose reproductive years were concentrated in the period *prior* to 1965, and who lived through a demographic trend that saw Brazil's fertility rate drop significantly. The interpretation of results followed the logic of the concept of life expectancy. On average, women who survived to age 15 during the post-transition

5. The Family Status Life Table is a technique used to analyze multiple events. It involves a type of tabulation of length of an individual's position within the family, a refinement of the more basic methodology using longevity tables. It is a macro simulation model of an individual's history within the nuclear family. In this study, I primarily used a computer program, FAMTAB, which John Bongaarts (1987) developed, and which he kindly put at my disposal. For more details about this methodology, see Goldani 1989.

period could expect to live another 52 years, during which time they
would spend about 29 years married, 10 years single, 7 years divorced,
and 6 years widowed.

Time Spent as a Wife

Comparing transition and post-transition cohorts showed that women in
the latter group could expect to spend a longer time married. Women in
the transition cohort could expect to spend 25 years married, but in the
post-transition cohort, that figure rose to 29 years. The number of years
that a woman could expect to spend as an ex-wife rose from 8 to 13 years
(Table 10.4). But these figures varied when disaggregated by color. For
both cohorts, white women had a greater probability of remaining married longer than did *pardo* or *preto* women. In the transition cohort, a
white woman could expect to be married for 29 years, compared to 22
years for a *pardo* woman and 19 years for a *preto* woman. These differences increased over time, with post-transition white women remaining
married for 33 years, an increase of 4 years, while *pardo* and *preto*
women extended the length of their marriages by only 3 years. The
greater life expectancy for white women, nearly 8 years longer when
compared to nonwhite women, may partially explain these differences
for color groups in regard to the length of time spent in marriage. But
patterns of marriage also play an important role. Despite the similarity in
mortality rates for *pardos* and *pretos,* and the overall increase in years
spent in marriage across all three color groups in the post-transition cohort, *preto* women continued to spend about 3 fewer years married than
did *pardo* women.

Comparing cohorts, the increase in the number of years women were
ex-wives (separated, divorced, or widowed) was greatest among whites,
rising from 8 to 14 years, while for *pardo* women that figure grew from 9
to 13 years and for *preto* women from 10 to 15 years. This indicates a
higher proportion of separations and divorces for white women, making
them the ones who "lost" more of the potential time as wives that their
longer life expectancy offered.

Verifying that improved mortality rates are more important than shifts
in patterns of marriage and divorce in determining the time that Brazilian
women spend as wives is an important element in discussing the weakening of the family institution, something commonly attributed to the
growing disruption in marriages. Thus, the number, size, and new types
of family arrangements have been shaped by lengthened life spans, which
increase the likelihood for disruption of a marriage. Such "matrimonial

Table 10.4. Marital Status of Brazilian Women, According to Color and Cohort (in years)

	Years Lived Beyond Age 15	Married	Single	Widowed	Divorced/Separated
White					
Post-transition[a]	56.38	32.89	9.98	6.75	6.76
Transition[b]	44.62	28.87	7.93	4.91	2.90
Pardo					
Post-transition cohort	48.68	25.39	9.72	6.08	7.49
Transition cohort	37.67	22.31	6.88	4.92	3.55
Preto					
Post-transition cohort	48.48	21.49	11.68	6.43	9.09
Transition cohort	37.67	18.81	8.54	4.10	6.21
Brazilians overall					
Post-transition cohort	51.92	28.60	10.48	6.07	6.77
Transition cohort	40.76	24.70	8.16	5.01	2.88

SOURCE: Family Status Life Table, calculated from the marital and fertility data in PNAD, 1984.
[a]The post-transition cohort comprises women whose reproductive years were concentrated in the period *after* 1965, when national fertility rates had declined, and who were between 15 and 49 years of age in 1984.
[b]The transition cohort comprises women whose reproductive years were concentrated in the period *prior to* 1965 and who lived through a demographic trend that saw Brazil's fertility rate drop significantly.

disruptions" do not, therefore, indicate a weakening in the institution of the Brazilian family. Instead, they are a reflection of a changing demographic pattern in life expectancy.

Time Spent as a Mother

The time that a woman spends as a mother of young children is interpreted as a period of great responsibility because it is the period when offspring are considered the most demanding. In Brazil the growing need for women to work outside the home and contribute to supporting the family, the lack of public daycare, and limited free health care and education all help to make child rearing a weighty responsibility.

The application of the Family Status Life Table, a mathematical model that describes the life histories from birth to death of members of an age cohort, shows that most women become mothers, but women in the post-transition cohort had fewer children. A decline in birthrates and an increase in life expectancy was decisive in this change. For example, our results show that in the transition period, women 35 years of age had given birth to an average of 4.7 children, with one child not surviving; women 50 years of age had given birth to approximately 6 children, with 26 percent not surviving. For the post-transition cohort, women 35 years of age had given birth to an average of 3.3 children; by 50 years of age, they had given birth to approximately 4 children, with 12.5 percent not surviving. Women of the transition cohort spent an average of 29 years as mothers compared to 36 years for the post-transition group. Thus, despite a 25 percent decline in birthrate, the improved mortality rate meant women who had fewer children spent more years as mothers.

The duration of motherhood varied by racial group, and as occurred with the time spent as wives, the differences were also strongly associated with rates of mortality. Thus in the post-transition period, with its greater life expectancy, married white women spent the longest time as mothers, 40 years. Despite higher birthrates, the comparable figures for *preto* and *pardo* women were 34 and 32 years, respectively. The impact of lower mortality and birthrates on the duration of motherhood is something considerably more complex because it requires the incorporation of a marriage variable. Nevertheless, our simulation exercises allowed us to conclude that the simple decline in mortality permits an even greater increase in the duration of motherhood (Goldani 1989).

Finally, the combined effects of changes in rates of mortality, birth, and marriage demonstrate that the effect of the decreased mortality rate compensates for the shifts in birthrates and marriage, increasing by 3 years the probability that women in the post-transition period would remain mothers in a conjugal-type family. The increase in time that women spent as heads of household (that is, as single mothers) was even greater, increasing by 4 years. This increase was more marked among *preto* women. For example, in the more recent cohort, *preto* women spent 13.3 years as single mothers compared to 11.6 years for *pardo* women and 11.5 years for white women. Despite the increase in time spent as single mothers, even today most Brazilian women spend more than two-thirds of their lives as mothers in a conjugal-type family arrangement, albeit with racial variations. For example, among women in the post-transition cohort, the time spent as a mother in a conjugal family varied from 71 percent for whites to 66 percent for *pardos,* and 58 percent for *pretos* (Goldani 1989).

Conclusion

In the mid-1980s, nearly 72 percent of Brazilian women who lived to age 50 had followed the normative pattern of domestic life; that is, they married and had children. The remaining 28 percent had remained single, had not had children, or had been widowed, separated, or divorced. The proportion of women who followed the normative pattern increased over time, primarily as a result of the improved life expectancy for both sexes.

Despite the prevalence of the normative pattern, there are important variations. With more women having premarital pregnancies, the sequencing of marriage and birth of children has been modified, and there has been a tendency to postpone marriage (including consensual unions) and the conception of the first child. The implications of these changes on other dimensions of women's lives are seen in the redefinition of priorities and relations within the family, which in turn redefine the nature of the normative domestic pattern.

In demographic terms, failure to follow the normative pattern occurs basically as a result of the increase in separations and divorces. The higher levels of separation and divorce in the post-transition period has meant that Brazilian women can expect to live twice as long separated or divorced than women in the transition cohort, who married during the 1950s. The effects of these marital disruptions appear clearly in the formation of alternative family models, especially in the growth of single-mother families, where *pretos* predominate.

The racial inequalities in the organization of women's domestic pattern of life appear to confirm the hypothesis that women adopt different strategies in the face of a structure of opportunities in which race appears fundamental. The results for the more recent cohort indicate that *preto* women today can expect to live more than half their adult lives unmarried or without a partner (56 percent), longer than *pardo* women (48 percent) or white women (42 percent). These differences were amplified by the propensity for white women to remain married longer.

Among the elements explaining differences among racial groups in duration of time spent in various marital states, the nearly 8 years longer life expectancy for white women stands out as well as marriage patterns, which vary according to race. These demographic elements reflect the different "life opportunities" for *preto* women in a structure of unequal economic, social, and cultural capital. Thus, given the normative pattern, this picture of greater "instability" in the domestic experiences of *preto* women, which leads to a greater diversity of family arrangements, must be understood above all as different strategies these women employ in the face of a structure of opportunities that is determined objectively as well as subjectively.

Racial groups' use of different strategies in the process of family formation assumes particular importance when viewed in the more global perspective of the lives of women. An example is the relationship that this has with the dimension of work in a woman's life. A women's economic participation in the labor force varies markedly when she becomes a mother and even more when she has more than one child. The level of female workforce participation is higher as women's level of education increases (Bruschini 1989).

The changes in Brazilian women's life trajectories are important in and of themselves. But they gain special relevance because of their consequences for family functioning and because they place new demands on society, especially public policy. This study shows that demographic changes have caused a progressively greater proportion of women, regardless of race, to superimpose roles throughout their family lives. For example, even though they spend more years married and as mothers because they live longer, they spend a relatively lower proportion of time in those roles. Thus, Brazilian women potentially have more time to devote to other activities. Related to this is the redefinition of obligations and expectations for family members, which in turn may shift traditional family obligations onto the community and/or the state. In the case of single mothers, the absence of public institutions providing support for female-headed households means that civil society and the state should assume greater responsibility for the support of these families.

The consequences of the profound transformations in women's life trajectory, whether on family unity or society in general, have not been evaluated. Despite new constitutional rights and the creation of women's councils and special agencies within Brazil's institutional framework, social policies have ignored women's multiple roles and the responsibility women shoulder for domestic duties and dependent care. The lack of social policies that address these new conditions can be partially rectified by enacting laws based on women's social rights that were incorporated into the Constitution of 1988. In this regularization process it is necessary, nevertheless, to guard against adverse effects. For example, the Constitution assigns to the family, society, and the state the duty of supporting the elderly, and it proposes that this support take place at home. This emphasis on "home-based programs for the elderly" may mean greater hardships for women, who are already overburdened with dependent care and who are in the midst of crucial changes in their own lives. Racial differences indicate the need for differentiated social programs because—despite the needs of the majority of Brazilian families—when establishing the state's priorities, the overall scarcity of resources demands identification of the country's most vulnerable groups. The racial differences in women's domestic life patterns noted in this study contribute to the urgent discussion of these issues in Brazil.

11

THE SODA CRACKER DILEMMA

Reproductive Rights and Racism in Brazil

Edna Roland

The perception of racial differences is embedded in a nation's dominant ideology, legal system, economy, and political culture. As a social construct, Brazilians and Americans perceive race in radically different ways. Brazilians have long claimed that their nation is a racial democracy, while Americans have fought, often violently, over the issue. A comparison of the two countries shows, however, that regardless of ideology, concrete practices—in our case, those relating to population control of blacks—support racist agendas. A reflection on reproductive rights for black women in Brazil and the United States highlights how social institutions maintain the perception of race (and gender) and in doing so reinforce racist (and sexist) practices.

Racist Agendas and Reproductive Rights in the United States

The history of the struggle for reproductive rights in the United States is marked by dramatic ethnic and racial explicitness, characteristic of American society, that allows for clear action and reaction of democratic forces. The United States has produced the Ku Klux Klan *and* the civil rights movement, eugenics laws *and* the abortion-rights struggle. In the conflict over sterilization and abortion, black American women have experienced a harsh onslaught of social forces seeking to restrict the growth of the U.S. black population. As Angela Davis shows in *Women, Race, and Class* (1981), poor (black) and working-class women, on the one hand, and middle-class (white) feminists, on the other, are sharply split over reproductive rights issues.

Although desired by almost all women, reproductive rights only became a legitimate demand when women's rights in general became a goal of the organized women's movement. However, feminists emphasized birth control as a means of advancing their professional careers and educational levels, goals beyond the reach of poor women with or without birth control (Gordon 1976, Davis 1981). With the drop in white fertility rates at the end of the nineteenth century, the fantasy of "racial suicide" had emerged in official circles in the United States. Pro-birth-control feminists, such as Margaret Sanger, began to popularize the idea that the poor had the moral obligation to restrict the size of their families because large families drained resources and because poor children had fewer opportunities for achievement (Gordon 1976). Thus, according to Davis (1981), what was first demanded by the privileged as a "right" became interpreted as an obligation for the poor. Margaret Sanger, who at the beginning of her crusade for birth control had a close relationship with the working class movement, was swayed by the influence of the eugenics movement (Davis 1981).

By 1932 twenty-six U.S. states had approved compulsory sterilization laws. This resulted in the performance of contraceptive surgical procedures on thousands of women considered "unfit" for reproduction. In 1939 the Birth Control Federation of America launched a "Negro Project," which it attempted to promote through black ministers. For people of color, contraception was proposed not as an individual right to control fertility, but as part of a larger racist strategy to control the black population. A backlash against these and other racist initiatives gradually formed, but laws to prevent involuntary sterilization were approved only in 1974.

Although bigotry and racist policies abound in the United States, the struggle over reproductive rights has been and is being played out openly and primarily within the nation's democratic institutions. However, in Brazil the denial of race as a social hierarchical category has made the struggle more difficult. Brazilian policy makers and politicians use the class label "poor" without acknowledging that this category refers to a disproportionately high percentage of blacks. This maneuver successfully obscures the battlefield for those who would change the socioeconomic reality of Brazil.

Racist Agendas and Reproductive Rights in Brazil

Brazil is a country of continental dimensions, with great cultural diversity. Of its more than 150 million inhabitants, three-quarters live in urban areas. In official terms, the population is classified in five color categories: *preto* (black), *pardo* (brown), white, yellow, and indigenous, with the *negro* (black) population understood here as the sum of *pretos* and *pardos*. Blacks (that is, *pretos* and *pardos*) compose about 44.2 percent of the population, making Brazil the second largest black country in the world, after Nigeria. As a result of the prevalent ideology of "whitening," miscegenation is widespread in Brazil, and *pardos* account for about 39.3 percent of the population, whereas *pretos* account for only about 4.9 percent, according to the 1990 PNAD.

Gilberto Freyre, one of Brazil's foremost social analysts, interpreted this extensive miscegenation as proof of Brazil's harmonious race relations and its racial democracy (Freyre 1933). However, the numbers belie the country's acclaimed racial democracy: whereas the income of 15.5 percent of whites is below minimum wage, for the black population that figure is 27.6 percent for *pretos* and 24.8 for *pardos,* according to the 1989 PNAD. The 1990 PNAD showed that the average nominal income of a white Brazilian was Cr$32,212, whereas it was Cr$13,295 for *pretos* and Cr$15,308 for *pardos.* Illiteracy rates reflect similar inequality: 12.1 percent of all whites are illiterate, compared to 29.3 percent of all *pardos* and 30.1 percent of all *pretos.* These data speak for themselves in debunking the myth of racial democracy in Brazil. Mortality rates are not officially available by color/race; however, studies have demonstrated that in 1960 the infant mortality rate of children born to white women was 44 percent below the infant mortality rate of children born to *preto* women and 33 percent below the mortality rate of children born to *pardo* women. Only twenty years later, in 1980, children of black mothers (*preto* and *pardo*) reached the level recorded in 1960 for white mothers. Those differences were maintained even when controlling for the mothers' level of education (M. G. Castro 1991).

According to Elza Berquó (1993b), the Brazilian government has never had a specific population policy. But the government's implicit policy is based on the idea that poverty can be ended by ending the poor. And in Brazil, as in the United States, most of the "poor" are black. Nevertheless, the idea that a drop in fertility could reduce poverty has been proven false: women are having ever fewer children, but poor women remain poor. Fertility has been reduced, but at a very high price to those women who sought the impossible dream that fewer children would mean greater wealth, something that will never be realized without altering the cruel concentration of income in Brazil.

While the harsh reality experienced by the black population in Brazil demonstrates that Brazil's "racial democracy" is not working, it nevertheless continues to function efficiently as an ideology. Data on racial inequality are frequently devalued, even by progressive sectors of the Brazilian intelligentsia. How is this possible? Most Brazilians claim that it is mere coincidence that being *negro* is synonymous with being poor and deny the link between discriminatory policies targeting the black population and social and economic realities. As Sueli Carneiro affirms, "In Brazil a very sophisticated, perverse and competent form of racism developed, in which racial intolerance masked itself in equal legal rights and concretized itself in absolute inequality of social opportunities" (1995, 1). After the abolition of slavery, blacks were not banned from voting; they simply did not meet the literacy requirement. There is no apartheid-like pass law on the books, but even today an unemployed black who does not have a work card could be arrested. There are no *Bantustans,* but Brazil's *favelas* are home primarily to black people.

Although in Brazil there are sharp regional differences in terms of income and education as well as in the distribution of the population by color, inequalities between black and white remain within each region. In spite of the existence of a strongly worded article in Brazil's 1988 Constitution, which deems racism a crime for which bail cannot be posted, discriminatory practices abound in all areas of social life. This discriminatory behavior has been denounced, especially since the 1980s, by black organizations, and it receives coverage by the media. Discrimination has been documented in a great variety of situations, including labor-market recruitment, salary levels, career advancement, housing, and access to public facilities, such as restaurants and hotels. Many instances of discrimination have become legal cases yet have been difficult to prosecute under the country's antidiscrimination laws, since judges tend to disqualify charges of racism.[1]

The distance between legality and reality is made possible by the *jeitinho brasileiro,* the famous Brazilian way "around" a problem, avoiding resistance or conflict. Let us see how it works in the area of reproductive rights.

In 1995 Brazil's population growth rate was about 1.22 percent per year. The white population was in the majority in 1940, but from the

---

1. Editor's note: see Chapters 6 and 7.

1940s to the 1980s, the size of the *preto* and white populations declined in relation to the *pardo* population. Miscegenation and the higher fertility rates of *pardo* women, which offset that population's high mortality rate, may explain this expansion, both numerically and in relation to other racial classifications. The *preto* population declined consistently during these decades as a result of high mortality, low fertility, and miscegenation. Until the advent of modern contraceptive methods, the white population had lower mortality rates and higher fertility compared with the *preto* population. After 1965, as a result of the use of the pill as well as because of miscegenation, the white population also began to decline.

Demographers thus predicted that the 1990 PNAD would reflect a continued shrinking of the white population, stability in the size of the *preto* population, and even greater growth in the *pardo* population. Mortality rates had been decreasing nationally, and it was assumed that this would be reflected in the *pardo* population. Lower fertility resulting from contraceptive use among *pardo* women would be offset by the decline in mortality rates coupled with miscegenation. Because of the anticipated decline in the size of the white population and the anticipated increase in the black population, demographers expected the survey to reveal that the *negro* population (*pretos* and *pardos*) had surpassed the white population in size (Berquó 1993a).

To the great surprise of the experts, the 1990 PNAD did not confirm these predictions. Within the overall Brazilian population, for the first time in five decades, the size of the white population had grown somewhat; the *preto* population had diminished slightly; and the *pardo* population had remained about constant (see Table 11.1 and Table 11.2).

How can this be explained? Levels of endogamy have not changed perceptibly since 1980 (Berquó 1993b), so the absence of growth in the

Table 11.1. Brazilian Population in Absolute and Percentage Figures, by Color/Race (1980 and 1990)

	1980		1990	
	N	%	N	%
White	65,540,467	54	81,407,395	55
Preta	7,046,906	6	7,264,317	5
Parda	46,233,531	39	57,821,981	39
Yellow	672,251	1	811,181	1
Total[a]	119,011,052		147,305,524	

SOURCES: For 1980, IBGE 1980. For 1990, IBGE; and PNAD, 1990, excluding northern rural region.
[a]Total excludes undeclared respondents.

Table 11.2. Growth Rate of the Brazilian Population Between 1980 and 1990,
by Color/Race

Color/Race	Percentage Change
White	2.6
Preta	0.3
Parda	2.5
Yellow	2.1
Undeclared	−10.0
Total	2.4

SOURCE: IBGE, 1980; PNAD, 1990.

pardo population could not be attributed to a change in levels of miscegenation. There was, however, a significant reduction in the growth rate
for the pardo population, from a 1980 level of 4.1 percent to 2.5 percent
per year. This is noteworthy in that it reverses the pardo population's
consistently higher growth since the 1940s. Equally noteworthy, the
growth rate of the white population increased from 2.2 percent in the
1980s to 2.6 percent, a rate even higher than that of the pardo population
(IBGE 1980 and the 1990 PNAD).

The PNAD survey thus indicates that Brazil's black population, rather
than becoming the majority, is shrinking. How can we account for this
shift in growth-rate patterns? Either mortality rates are higher than was
expected or blacks are reproducing more slowly compared to the white
population. The second hypothesis is the more likely one.[2]

The overall fertility rate in Brazil fell from 3.5 children per woman in
1986 to 2.3 in 1995. In the Northeast region of Brazil, the estimated fertility rate is much higher: 4 children per woman. That figure is mislead-
ing, however. Although out of line with the national average, it
represents an enormous decline from the 1970s, when the region's fertility rate was 7.5 children per woman. Given that blacks make up 71 percent of the population in the Northeast, we can assume a substantial
reduction in the fertility rate for blacks in that region over the past two
decades.

Contributing to that decline were birth-control programs that targeted

2. Because the Ministry of Health has only recently begun to note the color or race of an individual on death certificates, accurate data on mortality rates of different color groups are not
available, although they can be estimated. Mounting pressure from political groups has forced
the Ministry to begin to compile these statistics. It is true that mortality rates have always been
higher for the black population (Berquó 1988); however, there is no reason to expect that they
might have increased in 1990 as compared to 1980.

the Northeast throughout the 1980s. The Brazilian government has relied on abundant donations from private organizations interested in supporting the birth-control effort in that region. The programs were
"successful"; consequently, the Brazilian region with the greatest concentration of blacks and poor experienced the greatest reduction in fertility rates.

Elza Berquó's study (1989) based on the official 1986 PNAD appeared
to reveal a greater tendency for women in the North and Northeast to
undergo sterilization than women elsewhere in Brazil. Her research also
demonstrated that the pill was the only readily and widely available
alternative to sterilization. In 1986, 66 percent of Brazilian women of reproductive age who were sexually active used some form of contraceptive, including 27 percent who were sterilized and 25 percent who used
the pill (World Bank 1993). According to the Population Council, in
1990 69.2 percent of Brazilian women used some form of contraceptive.
Of this total, 43.9 percent were sterilized, accounting for 30.4 percent of
all Brazilian women of reproductive age.

More recent studies have demonstrated that the Northeast continues
to have the highest rates of sterilization, whereas in the country's richest
region, São Paulo, sterilization rates appear to have dropped (Berquó
1993a). In the Northeast in 1991, women who had undergone sterilization represented an unimaginable figure of 62.9 percent of all women
using some contraceptive method. To have an idea of the process underway in the Northeast, the same figure for 1986 was 47.2 percent, revealing an increase of more than 15 percent in five years! At the same time,
the use of the pill had fallen from 32.1 percent in 1986 to 22 percent in
1991 (BENFAM/DHS 1991). Sterilization appears to be the inexorable
destiny of Northeastern Brazilian women, where in 1991 19 percent
were sterilized by age 25. A measure of the speed of this process is the
fact that five years before, the figure was only 5 percent (Berquó 1993a).

Covert Eugenics?

The most extraordinary part of this process is that it has taken place not
only in the absence of eugenic laws but also within the context of a legal
framework that, at minimum, left sterilization open to interpretation as
constituting bodily injury. Given the ambiguity of the law, the public-
health system would not provide sterilization. This is where the *jeitinho
brasileiro* enters: many of the cases of sterilization in Brazil occur when
women undergo cesarean deliveries. As Rebecca Reichmann (1995)

notes, "Women have been subjected to unnecessary Caesarian sections performed as a cover for tubal ligation . . . [and the federal government] did not take any concrete measures to curb the abuse until April 1995." The public-health system paid for the Cesarean, while the patient paid clandestinely for the sterilization. Other women are sterilized for free in clinics sponsored by population-control agencies, which train doctors to perform sterilizations with the complicit approval of the public health authorities. Employers are cited as one source of pressure for sterilization of Brazil's female population. They "have been known to conduct covert pregnancy tests during 'routine' admission health check-ups or to demand proof of sterilization in order to try to circumvent their obligation under the employment law to provide paid maternity leave" (Reichmann 1995, 41).

Brazil's public-health system, having fallen victim to structural adjustment policies, is being dismantled, and it fails to offer alternative contraceptive methods. Consequently, women are forced to "choose" sterilization. Black women activists have been involved in a major debate with researchers, congressional representatives, and white feminists in a campaign to stop mass sterilization by showing that poor black women are a target in a process that forces them to accept sterilization.

Although researchers have presented data that show no difference in levels of sterilization for white and black women in different regions of the country, black activists have responded by questioning the methodologies of those researchers and arguing that regional differences point to a policy directed to the Northeast.[3] These activists have questioned the use of a statistical technique that matches samples of black and white women across all variables, such as education, income, and age, even though the demographic indicators for the two groups are completely different. If there were no social differences between black and white women, one might expect no differences in their reproductive behavior. However, social and economic differences between black and white women are dramatic in Brazil, making the generalization to the entire population of survey results based on matched samples suspect. What researchers miss is that black women are poor and undereducated *because* they are black, since Brazilian society distributes resources based on a racial hierarchy through a variety of social mechanisms that range from the infamously low salaries paid to the workforce (the case of the domes-

3. For example, in São Paulo 28 percent of white women and 27.2 percent of black women have been sterilized, whereas in the Northeast the figures are 38.5 and 37.5 percent, respectively (BENFAM/DHS 1991; CEBRAP 1992).

tic workers should be highlighted) and unequal distribution of public services and resources, to discriminatory employment and social practices. If researchers were to use samples with variables stratified according to the existing differences in the real world, it seems to us that the results would be more reliable.

How is it possible to have no differences among sterilization rates of black and white women if the black population declined while the white population grew, probably as a result of a decline in black fertility, and while we know that sterilization was the principle instrument in causing that decline in fertility? Some try to explain away the differences by reasoning that Northeastern women are targeted because they are poor, not because they are black. This is the reasoning that politicians and intellectuals use when they claim that the black population is discriminated against because it is poor, not because it is black. They do not ask themselves *why* the black population is poor. In a revision of the old idea of racial democracy, progressives now talk of "social apartheid." This concept incorporates a recognition of the excluded classes, but not a recognition of their race. Such reasoning seems to bring up the same dilemma posed by a popular television commercial for soda crackers in Brazil: "Do Tostines sell faster because they are fresh, or are they fresh because they sell faster?"

It is important to remember that for sterilization to be abusive, it is not necessary to submit a woman to open coercion; all that is needed is subtle influence to sway her decision. In Brazil employers often require proof of sterilization before agreeing to hire a woman, and many doctors and other health professionals insist on sterilization for poor and black women, who they believe incapable of making informed decisions concerning their own reproduction.[4] Certainly, many women actively seek tubal ligations, but usually the underlying reason is that no alternative is offered to them. The availability of contraceptives in the public-health system is practically nonexistent, and abortion is illegal except in cases of rape or risk to the woman's life. Rosalind Petchesky, researcher at Hunter College of New York, claims that "sterilization abuse always occurs when the procedure is carried out under conditions that . . . pressure an individual to agree to be sterilized, or obscure the risks, consequences,

---

4. While I served as consultant to the Women's Health Program for the City of São Paulo Health Department, my colleagues and I frequently encountered strong skepticism among the doctors we approached to discuss the possibility of introducing barrier contraceptive methods into the public health network. These physicians considered barrier methods unsuitable for the poor and undereducated women who represent the majority of the public health system's clients.

and alternatives" (Petchesky 1990). If she is right, under the condition of ever-increasing poverty, dismantlement of the public-health system, and circumstances under which sterilization has often taken place—during unnecessary Cesarean surgeries and in an environment impeding access to alternative contraceptive methods (including safe legal abortion)— most of the estimated 12 million cases of sterilization of Brazilian women can be considered abusive.

Conclusion

Positions differ within the black Brazilian women's movement and within other feminist groups over the appropriate response to Brazil's implicit population policy. Debates have resulted in legislative proposals, a congressional inquiry on sterilization abuse, and, in several states, fo-rums against mass sterilization, as well as in research initiatives and media coverage. Some black militants do not accept the regulation of sterilization because they consider it an instrument of genocide, whereas others, among whom I include myself, feel that bringing sterilization into the open is necessary to establish socially acceptable limits and regu-late medical procedures. Without such steps there will be no instrument to curb the sterilization of girls as young as fifteen, a practice that has been documented by the 1986 PNAD. Within the national feminist movement, opinions have ranged from the belief in the need for legal regulation to the argument that sterilization is a radical choice that women should have the right to make without legal interference. The most vocal position now is that sterilization should be regulated but only available to women over the age of 21.

Out of this has come concurrence between black women's groups and the feminist movement on the need for the implementation of the Pro-gram of Integral Assistance to Women's Health (PAISM), an exemplary health program developed by the Brazil's Ministry of Health in conjunc-tion with the women's movement. PAISM, based on a broad concept of women's reproductive health, provides prenatal and childbirth care, con-traception, and prevention and treatment of sexually transmitted diseases and gynecological and breast cancer. In recent years, a progressive ad-ministration in the city of São Paulo adopted a PAISM-style program, demonstrating that political will can bring rapid change to Brazil's lam-entable reproductive health and rights situation.[5]

5. On January 12, 1996, after this chapter was written, Law 9263 was approved, amending paragraph 7, art. 95, of the Federal Constitution of Brazil, the statute that regulates the use of sterilization and other contraceptive methods. After an extensive legislative battle, President

As Rosalind Petchesky (1990, 12) notes, "Women make their own reproductive choices, but not as they would like, not under conditions that they create, but under restricted social conditions that they as mere individuals are impotent to change. . . . We should focus less on the issue of choice and more on the question of how to transform the social conditions of choice, of work and reproduction." What does the right to choose mean when one has no power to determine the social conditions in which that choice is made?

In the United States the struggle against sterilization abuse has been led principally by Puerto Rican, black, Chicana, and indigenous women. Not by chance, in Brazil it has also been black women who have reacted most strongly against the shocking levels of female sterilization. But in the United States our sisters have the advantage of fighting against an explicit enemy, one that, as such, is easier to confront. Because conflicts in the United States are open, it is easier to "win, bargain, lose, concede, conquer rights," whereas in Brazil we have to face additional difficulties because "ambiguity is the regime" and we "live between deliciousness and disgrace, between the monstrous and the sublime."[6]

Fernando Henrique Cardoso initially vetoed all articles referring to sterilization, having viewed it as a possible interference by the Catholic Church. The president subsequently recognized his political mistake and dropped the vetoes when the women's movement loudly complained. The new law requires a minimum age of 25 for both women and men, the presence of two living children, informed and written consent by the interested party, and a minimum period of sixty days between the request and the performance of the surgery, during which time other contraceptive methods and counseling must be offered to discourage precocious sterilization.

6. This is borrowed from the lyrics of Caetano Veloso's famous song, "Americanos."

12

STERILIZATION AND RACE IN SÃO PAULO

Elza Berquó

A serious polemic surrounds the issue of sterilization in Brazil. On one side are those representatives of the black movement who view sterilization as an attempt to reduce the black population. On the other side are researchers who have shown that there is no statistical difference in sterilization rates of black and white women (Morell 1994; Berquó 1993a). The practice of sterilization, traditionally more common among upper-class women, has spread in recent years to poorer strata of the Brazilian population. In the face of a near-total absence of public health services and a lack of contraceptive options, poor women, the majority of whom are black, turn to tubal ligation as a means of regulating their fertility. This chapter attempts to add to the debate over this controversial issue by demonstrating that a network, both familial and social, exists that creates a "culture of sterilization," which permeates race, class, and age divisions throughout Brazil.

The Contraceptive Setting and Race in the 1980s

An overview of fertility regulation in Brazil reveals high rates of contraceptive use. Official data from the 1986 Pesquisa Nacional por Amostragem de Domicílios (the National Household Survey, PNAD) found that 70 percent of all women of reproductive age who were living with partners used some form of contraception. Among all women (independent of conjugal status) the rate was 43 percent. Most used oral hormones (41 percent) or female sterilization (44 percent), with the two methods together accounting for 85 percent of all contraceptive use among women of reproductive age. The elevated prevalence of these two contraceptive methods is the result of the extreme lack of contraceptive options available to women in Brazil. Although contraceptive practice varies by region, prevalence of these two methods is the rule throughout the country.

In the state of São Paulo, 68 percent of all women used some form of contraception, but of those, fully 40 percent used the pill and 39 percent were sterilized. In greater metropolitan São Paulo the situation was similar, with 67 percent of the population using contraceptives, and of those, 41 percent using the pill and 39 percent sterilized. Among women of reproductive age[1] in the state of São Paulo who were living with partners, 22 percent identified themselves as black, and of those, 60 percent were urban residents. Throughout the state, more white women used contraceptives than blacks, with 71.4 percent of white women in the interior of the state using a contraceptive method, compared to 59.6 percent of black women (Table 12.1). In metropolitan São Paulo, sterilization was much more popular among white women than among black women, whereas oral contraception was more popular among black women than among their white counterparts. In the interior of the state the reverse was true, with white women preferring—by a slight margin—the pill to sterilization and black women preferring sterilization to the pill, also by a slight margin.

In greater metropolitan São Paulo, the higher prevalence of sterilization among white women than among black women held true regardless of level of education (see Table 12.2). Women, but in particular black women who had completed one to three years of education, showed a higher rate of contraceptive use than did women with more education. However, among those women with more than three years of education, contraceptive use stabilized at an average of 67 percent for both blacks and whites. For all women with more than three years of education, regardless of color, sterilization diminished, while the use of the pill and other methods increased.

On the one hand, if we look only at those individuals within the group of white women who used some form of contraception, we see that the proportion who had undergone sterilization had fallen from 55 percent for the group who had less than one year of education to 29 percent for the group with nine or more years of education, a drop of 26 percent. Sterilization was the method used by slightly more than half of all white

---

1. Reproductive age, for the purposes of this chapter, is defined as being between ages 15 and 49.

Table 12.1. Prevalence of Contraceptive Use by Women of Reproductive Age, by Color (1986)

Method	São Paulo State		Greater Metropolitan		Interior	
	Whites	Blacks	Whites	Blacks	Whites	Blacks
Contraceptive user	70.1	61.4	68.7	62.7	71.4	59.6
Pill	27.2	31.0	25.6	35.6	28.7	23.9
Sterilization	27.9	22.2	30.5	18.7	25.5	27.7
Other method	14.9	8.2	12.5	8.3	17.2	8.0
No contraceptive	29.9	38.6	31.3	37.3	28.6	40.4
Total	100.0	100.0	100.0	100.0	100.0	100.0

SOURCE: M. G. G. Morell, "Anticoncepção em São Paulo em 1986: prevalência e características," in *A Fecundidade da Mulher Paulista* (São Paulo: Fundação SEADE), Informe Demográfico, no. 25 (1994).

Table 12.2. Prevalence of Contraceptive Use by Women of Reproductive Age, by Education and Color (Greater Metropolitan São Paulo, 1986)

Years of Education	Contraceptive Method	Whites	Blacks
Less than 1	Pill	18.7	15.6
	Sterilization	35.4	21.2
	Other	9.7	4.1
	Total	62.9	40.9
	None	37.1	59.1
1 to 3	Pill	22.1	37.2
	Sterilization	36.7	21.9
	Other	13.4	6.3
	Total	72.2	65.4
	None	27.8	34.6
4	Pill	22.9	35.2
	Sterilization	36.8	19.3
	Other	9.6	9.6
	Total	69.4	64.1
	None	30.6	35.9
5 to 8	Pill	30.7	43.2
	Sterilization	29.7	12.6
	Other	6.5	11.4
	Total	66.8	67.2
	None	33.2	32.8
9 or more	Pill	27.3	43.0
	Sterilization	20.2	13.4
	Other	21.1	11.3
	Total	68.6	67.6
	None	31.4	32.4

SOURCE: M. G. G. Morell, "Anticoncepção em São Paulo em 1986: prevalência e características," in *A Fecundidade da Mulher Paulista* (São Paulo: Fundação SEADE), Informe Demográfico, no. 25 (1994).

women with four or fewer years of education, and this rate began to fall only within the group having five to eight years of education.

On the other hand, if we look only at those individuals within the group of black women who used some form of contraception, we see that the proportion who had undergone sterilization had fallen from 52 percent for the group who had less than one year of education to 19 percent for the group with five to eight years of education, a drop of 33 percent. Unlike the white group, sterilization levels among black women declined by 21 percent in the group with four or fewer years of education and another 12 percent within the group having five to eight years of education. (Among the group with nine or more years of education, the percentage of those black women sterilized rose very slightly, to 20 percent.)

Contraceptive Use According to Color in São Paulo

The Black Women's Reproductive Health research project, organized by the Brazilian Center for Analysis and Planning (Centro Brasileiro de Análise e Planejamento, CEBRAP) made it possible to do a more current analysis of the relationship between race and contraception. Carried out in 1992 in the greater metropolitan region of São Paulo, the project included a survey of women's reproductive health taken from a sample of 1,026 women between the ages of 15 and 50, half white and half black. In order to guarantee more accurate results from the survey data, which was being collected in people's homes, interviewers were matched with respondents of the same self-identified racial classification.

We found that 73 percent of black women and 81 percent of white women used some form of contraception. In 1992, as had been the case in 1986, the rate for those using contraceptives continued to be higher for whites than blacks, and there was great consistency between the groups with respect to the use of highly effective methods of contraception (Table 12.3). Of the women interviewed, 48.7 percent of whites and 43.5 percent of blacks used the pill or sterilization, or their partners had had vasectomies. Despite greater use of contraceptives among whites, both groups had about the same number of pregnancies and the same number of live births. This holds true across educational levels, with the highest number of births occurring among the women with the least education.

It is important to note that the CEBRAP study did not find a significant difference between rates of sterilization for black and white women, even when controlling for education and monthly per capita income. (Table 12.4 demonstrates that the chi-square, with one degree of freedom, is not significant in the comparison between races at each level of education. Table 12.5 shows that no contrast among blacks and white women according to monthly income was statistically significant.)

The "Culture" of Sterilization: Equally Present Among Black and White Women

Every year many women put an end to their reproductive capacity through sterilization. Of the women who have undergone sterilization, 80.6 percent of the blacks and 81.3 percent of the whites gave as the rea-

Table 12.3. Women Ages 15 to 50 Using a Contraceptive Method, by Color (São Paulo, 1992)

Contraceptive Method	Whites	Blacks
Pill	24.0	20.0
Sterilization	22.0	20.1
Vasectomy	2.7	2.5
Condom	4.3	2.9
Natural methods	3.9	3.5
Other	6.3	3.5
Total using contraception	63.2	53.4
No contraceptive use	36.8	46.6
Total	100.0	100.0

SOURCE: Black Women's Reproductive Health Project, CEBRAP, 1992.
NOTE: A positive response for contraceptive use was registered only for women who indicated they were using a contraceptive at the time of being interviewed.

Table 12.4. Percentage of Women Sterilized, by Education and Color (São Paulo, 1992)

Level of Schooling	Blacks	Whites	X^2	Probability Values
Did not complete primary school	24.6	20.0	1.082	30%
Completed primary or secondary school	20.5	28.1	2.689	10%
At least some college education	15.2	18.1	0.526	40%

SOURCE: Black Women's Reproductive Health Project, CEBRAP, 1992.

son for their decision the desire not to bear more children and the present-day difficulty in rearing children. The absence of a wider selection of contraceptive options (both because of the scarcity of public programs on sexual and reproductive health and the general difficulty of obtaining pills, condoms, or other reversible methods) leaves women with only one choice: a tubal ligation or future pregnancy. This situation is reinforced, given the complicity among women and health professionals. Tubal ligations are prohibited by law, but obstetrician-gynecologists regularly perform the surgery during Cesarean births. One-third of the black women interviewed and almost one-third of the white women said that they had decided to have a Cesarean in order to have a tubal ligation, and 80 percent of both groups had, in fact, actually done so during their last pregnancy.[2] Despite an awareness of the irreversibility of the practice

2. It is widely believed that more tubal ligations are performed in Brazil than in any other country despite the illegal nature of the procedure. Because tubal ligations are outlawed, the technology used to perform them is primitive compared to that of most Western nations.

Table 12.5. Percentage of Women Sterilized, by Income Level and Color (São Paulo, 1992)

Per Capita Income Level	Whites	Blacks	X^2	Probability Values
0 to 1/4 the minimum salary	27.4	20.0	1.04	31%
1/4 to 1/2 the minimum salary	28.2	21.6	1.3	25%
1/2 to 1 minimum salary	19.2	21.9	0.36	55%
1 to 2 times the minimum salary	14.6	22.7	2.10	15%
2 to 3 times the minimum salary	12.5	28.6	2.77	10%
3 or more times the minimum salary	6.2	18.5	1.26[a]	26%

SOURCE: Black Women's Reproductive Health Project, CEBRAP, 1992.
[a]The Fisher Significance Test in this case yielded P = 39 percent.

(95 percent of both black and white women stated that they knew that tubal ligation was irreversible), 50 percent of the women were sterilized before reaching the age of 30.

Some of the data suggest that the dissemination or diffusion of sterilization—from mother to daughter, from sister to sister, from friend to friend—creates a "culture" of fertility regulation favoring an irreversible method. First, 52 percent of sterilized women were daughters or sisters of sterilized women, reflecting inter- and intragenerational dissemination of information about sterilization. Second, 89 percent of sterilized women welcomed the method's security because it freed them from worrying about birth control and allowed them to have a desired number of children. But this satisfaction creates a demonstration-effect for other women. Third, nearly two-thirds of these women said they would recommend tubal ligations to other women, which is further evidence of the diffusion of the "culture" of fertility regulation among women. Finally, in terms of the future, of the 39 percent of the women living with a partner who said they planned to have a tubal ligation in the near future, the desire was strongest among the youngest group, that is, women between fifteen and twenty-four years of age (Berquó 1993). The research survey indicated a marked consistency among black and white women with regard to these points; that is, the "culture" of sterilization is equally present in both groups.

Conclusion

A social and family network aids the diffusion of the practice of sterilization. It permeates generations, racial groups, and other segments of society. Notably, the prevalence of pairs of mothers and daughters or sisters who have been sterilized increases in number with educational level, although it is present as well among women with no education. Satisfaction with sterilization registered by black women was nearly constant at all levels of education, and among white women it increased slightly as educational level increased. Age did not affect the degree of satisfaction—both the youngest and oldest groups expressed similar satisfaction, independent of race. In addition, the tendency to recommend a tubal ligation to other women did not vary significantly with either education or age.

The highest levels registered for both black and white women who intended to undergo sterilization occurred among those with a medium level (that is, five to eight years) of education; women with more education were less likely to consider sterilization. Given that sterilization emerged initially among the upper class in Brazil, we may conclude that the middle class now embraces what was once a prerogative of the elite.

Although the intention to have a tubal ligation diminishes with age, 30 percent of women who are between ages 35 and 50 plan to undergo sterilization. This level seems high given that the probabilities for pregnancy decline in this phase of the reproductive cycle. In regard to reproduction, a long road must be traveled in daily life from a woman's desires to the satisfaction of those desires. The availability of reproductive-health resources, free of discrimination, would permit women—black and white—to make informed choices and allow them to satisfy their desires.

13

BLACK WOMEN'S IDENTITY
IN BRAZIL

Sueli Carneiro

As a project in construction, the shaping of women's identity today calls for an ongoing battle to guarantee women's citizenship rights. But will those rights guarantee full citizenship for all Brazilian women? In our struggle for women's rights, are we promoting the construction of a single "universal" identity for women? If women's identity is historically determined, is it the same for all Brazilian women?

When we feminists condemn the myth of feminine fragility that historically has justified the paternalistic "protection" of women by men, which women are we talking about? As black women, we are part of a contingent of women—probably the majority—who never found ourselves in this myth because we have never been treated as fragile. We are women who for centuries have worked hard in the fields as slaves, or in the streets as vendors or prostitutes. When we struggle to guarantee equal opportunities for men and women in the labor market, for which women are we guaranteeing jobs? We cannot understand what feminists are talking about when they call for us to "take back the streets" and go out to work.

When we feminists speak of breaking out of the myths of the "home," the private sphere, where we are a muse idealized by poets, which women are we talking about? Black women are not ideals of anything;

Preliminary versions of this text appeared in *Cadernos Geledés 4: Mulher Negra* (São Paulo: Geledés Instituto da Mulher Negra, 1993); *Revista de Cultura Vozes* II (March/April 1990); and Heleieth Saffioti and Monica Muñoz-Vargas, *Mulher Brasileira É Assim* (Rio de Janeiro: Editora Rosa dos Tempos, 1994).

we are portrayed as the anti-muses of Brazilian society because the aesthetic model for Brazilian women is white. We are women identified as objects. Job advertisements that require a "good appearance" exclude black women. Yesterday we were in the service of frail mistresses and rapacious plantation owners; today we are domestic workers for "liberated" women and housewives or mulattas-for-export. When we say that woman is a subproduct of man, made of Adam's rib, what woman are we talking about? Black women come from a culture that has no Adam. We come from a violated, folkloric, and marginalized culture that is treated as primitive, diabolical, and alien to our own national culture.

The public health system ignores us because Brazil's myth of racial democracy, alive in each of us, precludes asking the race of patients for hospital and clinic records. Consequently, we know almost nothing about the health conditions of black women in Brazil, even though we know that in other countries white and black women have significantly different health profiles. At the same time, we have been the object of special attention by our public officials, who have planned mass sterilization campaigns for black women because they knew that if the black population continued to grow, by the year 2000 we would be the majority and would dispute political power in our country.

The affirmation of a singular women's identity runs the risk of ignoring the complexity of concrete social relations in Brazil. That complexity implies that there are differences among women as well as among men. Black women have lived a unique historical experience. The classic feminist discourse on women's oppression fails to account for the qualitative differences in oppression suffered by black women, and the effects those multiple oppressions had and still have on black women's identity. Because the women's movement has failed to comprehend this, its victories tend to benefit white women. In a similar way, the minor gains made by Brazil's black movement have primarily benefited black men, who are still barely conscious of sexual discrimination.

The Brazilian Women's Movement

The women's movement was reborn in Brazil in the mid-1970s, as a reconstituted civil society struggled to end the military dictatorship and establish democracy. Women mobilized in amnesty campaigns for political prisoners, in mass movements against torture, and in protests for day care or against high costs of living, among other issues. Women who had had contact with feminist movements while in political exile in Europe and North America introduced into this political context the critique of gender inequality. Private life was politicized. Sexuality and domestic violence, for example, were transformed into political issues. The new feminist vision called for organizing women politically and introduced the issue of gender into the political agenda of political parties, unions, and other social institutions, such as the church. Gender contradictions raised by feminists were appropriated and adapted by women from the popular classes, producing increasingly strong interconnections between gender issues and wider social struggles.

Over time, Brazilian "Feminist Encounters" incorporated demands of women from very different social sectors—rural women workers, domestic workers, black women, women unionists, and so forth. The growing participation of women from different social sectors broadened feminists' understanding of the many facets of discrimination against women in Brazilian society, and they responded by taking on new social struggles that attempted to account for the diversity of women's issues.

This process did not occur without conflict and contradictions. But over the past twenty years, women have formed organizations all over Brazil to address violence against women, labor-market inequality, day-care rights, decriminalization of abortion, regulation of paid domestic work, parity with men in employment and social security rights for urban and rural workers, equity in domestic law, racism, and the implementation of universal preventive women's health care.

This robust process of women's organization has resulted in eleven national Feminist Encounters; Women's Police Stations in seventeen states; assistance for women victims of domestic violence; programs in women's studies and gender studies at Brazil's principal universities; women's rights councils at the municipal, state, and federal levels; and the creation of other government agencies charged with implementing public policies responsive to women. Women's gains in the 1988 Constitution give a picture of the breadth of the struggles for equal rights and opportunities waged by the women's movement in Brazil:

> As a result of intensive organized feminist lobbying, Brazil's 1988 Constitution reflects women's demands for official mechanisms to combat violence in the home, female rural workers' rights to welfare benefits, employees' rights to employer-provided daycare facilities, four-month maternity leave and five-day paternity leave, equal pay for equal work, social security for domestic workers, family planning as a constitutional right, and land rights for women, irrespective of their marital status. (Reichmann 1995, 41)

There is still much to be done, including the decriminalization of abortion, regulation of sterilization, parity for women's representation in political parties and union leadership, effective curbing of domestic and gender violence, and implementation of universal preventive women's health policies.

Brazil's Black Movement

Parallel to the women's movement, the black movement also reemerged in the 1970s. The authoritarian government had repressed black Brazilians ever since 1937 when it banned the Frente Negra Brasileira, the largest post-abolition black political organization. The black movement revived with the first signs of political *abertura*, and this movement too was influenced by the struggles of minority groups internationally, especially by the African liberation movements and the U.S. civil rights movement. Two specific cases in Brazil, the murder of a black worker by military police and racial discrimination against two black athletes in a São Paulo club, detonated a process that had been gestating for many years (Andrews 1991). Headed by black militants, artists, and intellectuals, the Unified Black Movement (MNU) was founded in July 1978. It placed before the Brazilian public the problems of racism and discrimination as structurally imposed by capitalism to maintain Brazil's social and racial inequalities.

The MNU's political vision required that class and race be confronted together in any proposal to eliminate social inequality, particularly in Brazil's multiracial society. In an attempt to sensitize human rights organizations to racial violence in the daily life of black people, MNU categorized as one and the same police violence, violence suffered by common prisoners, and torture suffered by political prisoners. Black organizations across the country responded, and they were joined by progressive sectors of the left. Although differing in their political visions, all black organizations were engaged in demystifying the myth of racial democracy, heightening race consciousness among black Brazilians, incorporating race issues in party and government policy proposals, gaining institutional space, and transforming black cultural events into a means for affirming ethnic identity and fighting racism.

Results of the Women's Movement and Brazilian Black Movement

In spite of similar trajectories, the black movement and the women's movement achieved very different outcomes. Although women's inequality has persisted over twenty years of struggle, Brazilian society, nevertheless, has been much more receptive to women's critiques and demands than to those of the black movement. Despite all the black movement's attempts to break the conspiracy of silence surrounding racism and racial discrimination, race persists as one of Brazil's greatest taboos.

Since its beginning, the women's movement has counted on the support of significant numbers of middle- and upper-class women who brought social, political, and intellectual capital to the movement. Through a dialogue with elites and important sectors of civil society, as well as with the international feminist movement, they facilitated the incorporation of many women's issues into mainstream society.

In contrast, in its attempts to enter political parties and academic institutions and gain support from financing agencies, the black movement encountered as an obstacle the taboo of race. Moreover, the black movement is led by an activist community with weak academic and political experience; with virtually no social, economic, or political capital; and with no tradition of vying for political power. The movement is an advocate for a black population still imprisoned by the myth of racial democracy and the ideology of whitening, and it must confront stubborn resistance to racial issues even in so-called progressive sectors of society. These conditions interact to hobble black organizational development in Brazil, limiting blacks' ability to construct meaningful political alliances, to give wider visibility to the race problem, or to consolidate international exchange and support.

The First National Encounter of Black Organizations, in November 1991, confirmed this when declaring that the movement's first priority is to strengthen black organizations, train activists, and support political actions that confront racism. Nevertheless, the 1988 Constitution's principle establishing racism as "a crime, subject to imprisonment, for which bail may not be posted" has raised the race issue to a new level in Brazilian society by recognizing and criminalizing the practice of racism and calling into question the equality of rights and opportunities exalted by Brazil's myth of racial democracy.

Failure of the Black Movement Vis-à-vis Black Women

For black Brazilian women, the black movement also exhibits internal weaknesses and contradictions that have limited its usefulness as an arena for mobilization. In Barbosa and Rufino dos Santos (1994), Joel Rufino dos Santos exemplifies fundamental assumptions in the thinking of many Brazilian black men—assumptions that have helped erect the barriers of subordination, creating an agenda for black men that is distinct from that of black women, an element forcing black women to forge an autonomous movement.

Rufino's story objectifies black women as Volkswagens that socially mobile black men "trade in" for Chevrolet Monzas (white women). The story, purportedly about the social mobility of black men, inadvertently illustrates two great Brazilian fallacies. First, it assumes that the act of trade is equivalent to the exercise of real power. Yet a black man in Brazil, no matter how famous, no matter how great his social ascent, has no real power. He owns no banks, controls no great companies, has no political presence or recognized intellectual or academic importance. These are the concrete elements that invest people or segments of our society with power. Whatever power the black man exercises, he exercises it only by delegation of white men, who can dismiss him at any time. Moreover, black men who owe their success to their own personal talents are impotent to transfer their personal prestige to their racial group.

Second, the story presents interethnic sexual relations as contributing to the "transformation of a state of hostility or of antagonism, real or potential, into a state of peace and of alliance. The woman, circulating through the network of marital exchanges, is the instrument of this conversion" (Balandier 1976, 38). This interpretation masks the racial tensions present in Brazilian society. The myth of Brazilian racial democracy is rooted in the miscegenation ensuing from the colonial rape of the black woman by the white man. Rufino uses the sexual appropriation of the white woman by the black man to symbolize black social mobility, but this is a subterfuge that disguises the black man's use of the white woman's aesthetic and social primacy as collateral with which to satisfy his desire for belonging and alliance in a world restricted to white men. For Rufino, the white woman fulfills a strategic function of rescuing the black man from secular humiliation, lending him the emblematic penis of her whiteness, symbol of power everywhere, which places him closer to the white man and supposedly enables the black man to share his power. In contrast, Rufino deliberately devalues black women, but this hides a narcissistic wound: the idea that black women were complicit and found pleasure in the sexual assault of white men. The racial and macho rancor and cynicism present in Rufino's tale indicate that something very deep escaped his control in this story and exploded in hatred toward black women for their supposed historical lack of fidelity. Rufino knows that no white woman or black woman can erase the marks left by history, but he avenges himself on *them*, treating white women as luxury items of his macho proselytism and black women as second-rate objects available in the market for a cheap little price.

The black poet Arnaldo Xavier considered *machismo* the only space of effective complicity between black and white men. They could agree and be accomplices at least in this, in the right that both give themselves to oppress, discriminate against, and dehumanize women, white or black. But in truth, Rufino uses women as a smoke screen to obscure a fight between males that he dares not fully explain, in which the need to conquer the white woman reflects the envy of the white man's power, the resentment and hatred accumulated in nearly five centuries of racial domination and inequality. In this context, the objectification of the white woman as a *thing* symbolizes the alliance with that dominant white universe that produces and reproduces racial and sexual discrimination and inequalities as much in the concrete universe as in that of consciousness. The real target, albeit disguised, is the white man, and toward him is directed the imperious need to flaunt a white woman.

Rufino's stereotype lends itself to the construction of a new meaning, not for women, not even for interethnic relations, but rather for black men. In freezing women in these stereotypes, he promotes the "new" black man, freed from his stigmas and the *subject* of a discourse about women. The dehumanization of women in the text functions as an element in affirming the "humanization" of the black man, because it enlists him in the dominant masculine logic; and in doing so, it "elevates" him to the same category as white men, which consequently ratifies the myth of the black man's social mobility.

As long as the black man seeks out the white woman in order to present himself—alleviated of the castration complex—before the white man, the black movement will lack a place for black women. This fundamental ambivalence on the part of some black men toward the world of white power has required the creation of an autonomous black women's movement.

The National Organization of Black Women: Political Perspectives

Since the mid-1980s a new social actor in Brazil—the black women's movement—has emerged at the intersection of the women's and black movements. The search for black women's political affirmation began with the inadequacy with which their issues were treated in both the women's movement and the black movement. The marriage of racism and sexism against black women and the lack of solidarity among some feminists and black activists has meant that the victories of the women's movement end up benefiting white women and the victories of the black movement tend to benefit black men.

This has imposed a double militancy on black women: from their own perspective, they must take up the causes of both the black movement and the women's movement. But for double militancy to be meaningful, they need their own independent organization of black women in order to constitute themselves as a political force capable of dialogue on an equal basis with other social movements and social institutions. The construction of the black woman as a new social actor has called for creativity in demarcating a political identity in dialogue with women's issues and black issues. Creativity is needed because the mere transposition of the women's or black movement's organizational forms will not speak to black women's more complex organizational needs. Today's black movement organizations are modeled on leftist parties and organizations with a highly centralized vision of democracy. In contrast, the women's movement has historically sought more horizontal forms of organizing by creating collectives and networks. Both traditions are present in black women's political experience, and the challenge now is to redesign from these experiences new forms of organization conducive to more democratic decision making and struggle.

In 1988, the centennial of abolition in Brazil, black women mobilized nationally around their own issues. It proved to be a particularly important year for black Brazilian women, who advanced their internal organizational process while uncovering the contrasting ideological-political visions threaded through their movement. The centennial was a political moment for black women to gain greater visibility and seek increasing organizational strength to defend their interests. This process culminated in December 1988 with Brazil's First National Encounter of Black Women, in which 460 activists, representing seventeen states, participated.

The existential and political need to organize black women as a separate force demonstrates the limits of both the women's and black movements. The critique offered by the black women's movement is generated from the subordination of black women's issues in both the black and feminist movements. In recent years this subordination has begun to change as we have become increasingly effective in articulating our demands. Important segments of the black women's movement have begun to reject the theses of the women's movement. Black male leaders have similarly subordinated black women, "tutoring" them through control mechanisms that range from attempts at ideological control of the black women's movement to various forms of devaluation of our political importance. Confronting these patronizing attitudes is even more crucial when we consider that black women are often the majority who participate in black organizations in Brazil. Yet, our participation does not translate into political or public visibility in the same proportions as it does for black men. Our social and cultural situation as women is supposed to condition us to accept a subordinate role in black organizations even while we take on important responsibilities within them.

Four Perspectives Within the Black Women's Movement

In sum, the insufficiency with which black women's issues are treated by the feminist and black movements determines that black women must develop a specific platform for political action. All groups of black women share this basic critique, but because we have developed different perspectives, this position alone is not enough to engender our unity. There are at least four political positions on the role that Brazil's black women's movement should play.

The first position recognizes the gravity of black women's condition in Brazilian society but believes that above all, it represents just one more aspect of the oppression and marginalization of blacks. As such, black women's issues should be treated in conjunction with, or subordinated to, the black movement's agenda, as was proposed by some participants in the First National Encounter of Black Women (December 1988, in Vassouras, State of Rio de Janeiro). There was no consensus on this issue at the Encounter, so a resolution was approved that sought to account for the divergent positions. The compromise resolution proposed that black women's meetings, both national and regional, be coordinated in conjunction with those of the black movement, but without being subordinate to them. Restricting our discussions of black women's concerns to the calendar of the black movement was supposed to address the latent concern that black women's political actions should not break the supposed unity of the "general" struggle of blacks or disperse activists into different spheres of action. The resolution also revealed some black women's fear of competing with black men for political space.

A second position understands that the black women's movement must assume a feminist character and maintain its autonomy in relation to the black movement. The women's movement today represents an important segment of organized social movements in Brazil. But many issues must be debated and incorporated—among them, black women's issues.

A third position articulates black women's issues as one aspect of the need to organize all oppressed social sectors within the class struggle. In this view, black women's organizations acquire a tactical importance within a broader strategy of social transformation. This instrumentalist vision of black women's issues limits the potential of our approach, since it is precisely through our transformation of older approaches and ideologies that our own organization is justified. Political action developed under these circumstances is restricted to exhaustively reiterating general ideological principles appropriate to any situation of oppression without reflection on black women's own political identity. The following statement illustrates this position: "Our organization depends on the comprehension of what we are, within our specific issues, as it *serves as an instrument* of struggle to advance our larger plan, which is the liberation of all exploited and oppressed sectors of society" (Encontro Estadual de Mulheres Negras, 1993, emphasis added).

Finally, a fourth view seeks a more complex synthesis of the black women's movement, conceived of as a mass movement made up of differing political and ideological visions. In this view, unity may be forged around common platforms for struggle. This view necessarily articulates the black women's movement with the other two movements, which are reinterpreted though the synthesizing experience of black women. Our experience permits us to sensitize the women's and black movements to the contradictions inherent in racial and sexual discrimination and to introduce them to new issues for reflection and political practice.

For the women's movement, this means recognizing and acting politically against inequalities between white and black women due to racism, because "if the sexual division of labor configured roles for women that the feminist movement seeks to question and redefine, the racial division of labor establishes roles and functions differentiated within women where the evaluation of cost-benefit earned expresses the different levels of exploitation and oppression that belongs to women from different racial groups" (Encontro Estadual de Mulheres Negras 1993, 44).

For the black movement, the fourth position is equivalent to recognizing and acting politically against existing inequalities, even among black men and women, as a function of sexism. Available statistical data show that "black men, with regard to racism and racial discrimination, when compared to women, enjoy advantages that can only be attributed to their sex. That is, analysis of social indictors shows that black men are born with certain social opportunities unavailable to black women. The inequality based on sexual differentiation is more accentuated when considering that the educational differences among black men and women

... are irrelevant to explain the differences in income" (Carneiro and Santos 1985, 30–31).

Therefore, this fourth position asserts that black women's double militancy—as women and as blacks—must sensitize the two movements to take on racism and sexism as fundamental, not peripheral, to any project seeking a just and egalitarian society. However, for this double militancy to be consequential, black women must constitute an independent political force capable of dialogue on an equal basis with the women's and black movements, as well as with other progressive sectors, joining with them for a more feminist and more black society.

Conclusion

The diverse positions presented here constitute latent tendencies or embryonic positions in the black women's movement. None of them enjoys political hegemony. They will consolidate or not to the degree that they are consonant with the real needs of black women. The four positions often intertwine, their interests influencing each other and even converging upon certain common objectives. The attempt to delineate these incipient positions demonstrates the potential and vitality of voices in the emergent movement of black women as well as revealing the influences on black women's thought of the black and feminist movements, political parties, the church, and other social institutions. Proponents of any one of the positions would agree that our struggle is for black Brazilian women's full citizenship beyond the constitutional rights achieved by the women's movement but including, as well, the struggle against all forms of racial discrimination.

In this sense, it is imperative that the black women's movement give special attention to the constitutional provision for "protection of women in the labor market, *through special incentives,* in terms of the law" (Constitution of Brazil, Chapter II, Article 7, emphasis added). This constitutional provision may be conceived of as a legal instrument defining government policies and encouraging private-sector incentives to promote equal opportunities for socially marginalized groups. That is, compensatory policies should be developed to eliminate the disadvantages historically experienced by groups suffering from discrimination and to better prepare them—through education and training—to compete in the labor market under conditions equal to other groups in society.

Black women's struggle also includes the demand that government agencies collect and analyze race data in all official censuses, because we have the right to know how many we are and what our living conditions are like. Official treatment of statistics and race data masks inequalities among racial groups in Brazilian society. The "color" variable is arbitrarily applied (or not) in official tabulations, and data on it is rarely disseminated.

The struggle of black women includes enforcement of the constitutional ban on racial discrimination, legalization of abortion, eradication of conditions that obligate poor women to turn to abortion, and the transformation of social conditions to allow women and black couples to care for the number of children they choose to bear. This means that we must fight for housing, health, sanitation, and antiracist and antisexist education—basic conditions to break the vicious cycle that confines the black population, and black women in particular, to the subterranean levels of Brazilian society. Finally, black women's struggle is for a multiracial and multicultural society, where difference is experienced not as inferiority but as equality.

WOMEN WORKERS OF RIO

Laborious Interpretations of the Racial Condition

Caetana Maria Damasceno

In this chapter, the anthropological *démarche* consists of deconstructing occupational positions in the Brazilian labor market that are "naturally" assigned to "white" and "nonwhite" individuals.[1] Using this approach, I will compare career trajectories by focusing on occupational histories of four women working in the Rio de Janeiro labor market. I selected these histories from a set of interviews conducted between August 1992 and January 1995 that were part of a broader investigation into the social construction of racial and gender inequality in the world of work.[2] The interview subjects were working in occupations categorized as being "appropriate" for individuals of a certain race (or color).[3] The interviews, with their narrative peculiarities, guided me through a territory whose

1. The expression "nonwhite," combining the official terms *preto* (black) and *pardo* (brown), came into usage in empirical analyses of race relations in the 1970s. Although the "yellow" group falls under the same rubric, it is not included in this study because the size of the Asian population is Brazil is so small.

2. This study was part of larger project, the first phase of which was supported by the Ford Foundation, conducted by the Center for Afro-Asian Studies in Rio de Janeiro. Although this chapter analyzes only women's occupational careers, the scope of the project also included men's careers.

3. I designate color in quotation marks to emphasize the semantic complexity of race relations in Brazil. "White" (*branco*), "black" (*preto*), and "brown" (*pardo*) are the categories used in official censuses. In Brazil, a myriad of designations exists—from "mulatto" (mixed race) to *moreno* (brunet)—whose symbolic strengths can vary depending on the social situation. The central issue for the social scientist using categories of native racial classification is to understand that they are not natural essences but rather categories of moral, ethical, and aesthetic perception.

borders have not been rigidly delineated. For this reason, the text has a
pilot-study format intended to produce interpretive hypotheses by constructing an object through its exploration.

Within a profoundly segmented and hierarchical occupational universe, in which "whites" are concentrated in positions of authority, and
"blacks" and "browns" are the majority in subordinate positions, the
question is where and how to locate factors leading to the occupational
success of a few "black" women, and how to understand the meaning of
that success in their careers. Inversely, where and how do we locate factors leading to occupational failure of a few "white" women and the
meaning of that failure in their careers? Where, through whom, and most
of all, how does "color" operate as a selective principle?

Revisiting a Few Paradigms

In culturalist studies of the 1930s—exemplified by the work of Gilberto
Freyre—the perception of "Brazilian racial democracy" was strongly related to the theme of *boa aparência,* or "good appearance," an expression
as ingrained in daily life today as it was then. The transition from a basically rural society to a class society, produced through urbanization and
industrialization, became the central paradigm of race-relations studies
in Brazil. As a corollary to this evolutionist perspective, miscegenation
and "good appearance" played an important role in overcoming racially
based contradictions and conflicts during the passage from one type of
social organization to another. In *Sobrados e Mucambos* (1936 [*The
Mansions and the Shanties,* 1963]), Freyre expressed this paradigm in
terms of shifts of values from the nineteenth-century plantation house
and rural slave quarters to the modern townhouse and urban shanties
(see "The Rise of the Professional and the 'Mulatto,' " chap. 11, which
discusses this process).

This unilateral theoretical perspective, long dominant in Brazilian sociology, inhibited new paradigms that might have stimulated research on
the conditions—while not always homogeneous or universal—governing
the social ascent of "blacks" and "mestizos" and the construction of new
socioracial identities (Pierson 1971 [1942]; Azevedo 1955; Fernandes
1968). Michel Agier identifies the pasteurized and psychologized results
forged by this paradigm: "[A] *negro* identity would not fit the theory of
modern social relations. In it might only enter psychological dramas,
dilemmas, and maladjustments, always transitory, generally observed
among blacks out of place, that is, in a situation of social ascension"
(1992, 99).

In turn, the studies UNESCO sponsored in the 1950s, although meant to demonstrate to the post-Holocaust world how Brazil had developed "harmonious racial relations," revealed contradictions. The results of some of these studies—especially those developed by Florestan Fernandes—for the first time put "Brazilian racial democracy" under strong suspicion. The São Paulo school of sociology undertook similar studies in the 1960s and 1970s (Bastide and Fernandes 1959; Fernandes 1974 [1965], 1968, and 1972).[4] Although the early studies in this school broke from the ideology of racial democracy, they theoretically subordinated race to class. For the new urban-industrial model of competitive social relations, the principles of racial hierarchizations "typical" of the slavocratic society and inherited in the new order were anachronistic anomalies. In that view, São Paulo was a case study of Brazil as a whole. An important result of this theoretical perspective involved the now widespread expectation that racial prejudice decreases in proportion to industrial development.[5]

It bears noting that Guerreiros Ramos (1954) and Oracy Nogueira (1954) were the first intellectuals to raise the issue of the relative autonomy of racial condition in relation to class, a topic that would be revisited only in the 1970s. Unlike previous studies, this new model indicated the reproduction and even expansion of racial inequality in Brazil in direct proportion to the increase in urban and industrial growth. The paradigm shift during that decade was related to the efforts of the Brazilian Institute of Geography and Statistics (IBGE) to systematize the collection of statistical data on race or "color,"[6] as well as to the resurgence of

4. Thales de Azevedo recalls that it was Charles Wagley who designated this set of studies as the "São Paulo school of sociology." Florestan Fernandes was among the most noteworthy authors, and Azevedo counts among its affiliates Roger Bastide, Donald Pierson, Oracy Nogueira, Otávio Ianni, and Fernando Henrique Cardoso. UNESCO sponsored contemporaneous studies—in Rio de Janeiro, Bahia, and Amazônia—on which Azevedo and Wagley worked, along with L. A. Costa Pinto, Marvin Harris, W. H. Hutchison, and Ben Zimmerman. This division of academic social research, noted by Azevedo in the preface of the book by Nogueira, *Tanto preto quanto branco: Estudos de relações raciais* (1985), seems to indicate diverse theoretical perspectives that deserve careful treatment. It is significant that sociologist Guerreiros Ramos is characterized in the same preface almost as an outsider of Brazilian sociology of the period.

5. In 1968 Florestan Fernandes, seeking the limits imposed on "true social ascension" of the "negro" and the "mulatto," asserted: "Urban expansion, the industrial revolution, and modernization *still* have not produced sufficiently profound effects to modify the extreme racial inequality that we inherited from the past" (Fernandes 1972 [1968], 48, emphasis mine).

6. In 1976 the Pesquisa Nacional por Amostragem de Domicílios (National Household Survey, PNAD) introduced the innovation of an open-ended question where the subject could choose the terms with which to self-identify racially. The study registered more than one hundred terms expressing shades of color—from "darker" to "lighter"—which are replaced by the official categories of "black," "brown," and "white." From that moment on, debate heated up in

institutions of the *movimento "negro"* (Brazil's black social movement) especially in the state of São Paulo.

Analysis of the quantitative data produced by the empirical sociology of the 1970s indicates that the "nonwhite" population does *not* enjoy opportunities that favor mobility of "place" in the Brazilian social structure. Furthermore, the greatest disadvantages fall to "nonwhite" women (Berquó 1991; M. G. Castro 1991; Aguiar 1994). The social negativity through which "black identity" emerges as an element of constant individual depreciation no doubt strongly influences how this issue is approached. Racism is no longer a mere inheritance from slavery but—from the logic of practical reason (Sahlins 1979)—a singular instrument of manipulation "serving the complex and diverse interests of the racially dominant group in the present" (Hasenbalg 1979, 118), eager to reproduce, in homogenizing fashion, the subordination of the "nonwhite" mass of workers, excluding it from industrial modernization and social mobility. From this angle, the institution of racism remains a social and moral problem of "blacks" and "mestizos" and not an issue that Brazilian society assumes as its own.

This new generation of sociologists argue that in the hierarchical structures of the labor market and the school system, "whites" and "nonwhites" progress differentially, with the latter exhibiting very negative results. Even when "nonwhites" make the same investments in education and have the same experience in the labor market as the "white" population, the dividends—mainly in terms of wages—do not favor them. This pattern of inequality did not improve during the "Brazilian economic miracle" of the 1970s, and it appears to have worsened during the economic crisis of the 1980s (Aguiar and Silva 1992; Hasenbalg 1991; Lovell 1989, 1992; Oliveira et al. 1987b; Telles 1994).

In response, Edward Telles (1994) has raised questions about the polarized perspective of the São Paulo school of sociology and the quantitative studies developed since the 1970s. Relying on complex analyses of statistical data, Telles contends that "industrialization reduces, maintains, and even increases racial inequality in Brazil, *depending on the level of occupational structure analyzed*" (1994, 42, emphasis mine). The novelty of this approach lies in the degree of refinement in the relation between race and class. In effect, what Telles suggests is that the relevance of race tends to increase in proportion to the specialization of the remunerated

---

different disciplines over the discrepancies between a person's self-declared "color" and the supposedly "objective" one ascribed by an interviewer (compare Sansone 1992; N. V. Silva 1994).

activities. In other words, in Brazil racism tends to increase with level of wages. As I see it, this is an interesting clue for qualitative ethnographic studies inclined to confront the complex and contradictory symbols and values of class, distinction, and mutability in diverse social situations.

Practical Reason and Symbolic Reason

The logic of practical reason views race as a "social problem," but we must also consider values that have imbued Brazilian race relations with moral meaning.[7] The dominant ideology still seems to assume a "meeting of three races" that complement each other, "whitening" as a corollary of this "meeting," and "integration of differences through miscegenation" (Da Matta 1988). In Brazilian social consciousness, this peculiar morality, which developed in the 1930s, supports a controversial paradox. The interpretation that miscegenation has served as an indicator of the absence of discrimination and racial inequality in Brazil highlights the different cultural terrain in which racism has developed. Contrary to exclusion guided by symbolic purism, we have intense manipulation of the racial mix (Nogueira 1954; Ramos 1954). Instead of legal segregation, Brazil created a discriminatory integration: whites on top and "blacks" at the base of the social hierarchy, and a subtle gradation of colors—tabulated in official censuses as *pardo* ("brown")—which favors ideological whitening (Da Matta 1987, 1991 [1987]).

Although being "black" remains associated with slavery, filth, and danger, even those who call themselves "pure whites" sample the rituals considered to be of "mixed-black" origin: eating habits, music, jokes and games, and religious and celebratory spaces. These rituals, transformed into symbols of nationality (Fry 1975), develop in multiple and complex spaces, giving rise to manipulation of racial identity because they mask the condition of "color" as a strong criterion of social selection and, therefore, of the construction of differences, both positive and negative.

Although there are many qualitative ethnographic studies of these rituals, studies of the "mixed-black" population's participation in the world of work are still rare. Those that do exist confront the subtleties of gener-

---

7. Nelson do Valle Silva and Deborah Roditi (1988 [1986]), using new models of statistical treatment of qualitative data related to "occupational mobility" and "social stratification," conclude that "no clear benefit in the sphere of distribution of relative opportunities of life for the different social strata flows *automatically* from economic growth" (114). Although development facilitates social ascent by creating opportunities through structural change, it definitely does not constitute a remedy for racial inequality.

ation, class, and gender associated with the etiquette of race relations in
Bahia (Agier 1990a, 1990b; Guimarães and Agier 1990; Guimarães 1993;
Sansone 1992; P. C. Silva 1993; Figueiredo 1994). These themes also appear in a more implicit form in studies of domestic workers or of professional activities related to the arts or sports. Thus, the relational
dimension of different occupational paths remains linked to anachronistic parameters of social subordination. At most, these studies refer to
mythical times that, as Patricia Birman (1990) suggests, tend to construct
homologies between *senzala* (slave quarters) and maid's quarters, between "black" women and slaves, between employer and slave owner.
These generalizations are transformed into discourse that universalizes
models of subordination, reinforcing even more stereotypical perceptions of "individual dramas" and "fragmented identities" in the "nonwhite" population (Hasenbalg 1979). Thus, the lack of academic
curiosity about the meanings of racial condition in contemporary feminine and masculine career trajectories—whether ascendant or not—functions as an invisible barrier to the liberation of the very object of those
studies.

Career Trajectories and Narratives

In 1992, when I initiated research on occupational careers by race and
gender, my proposal was to compare the *narratives*—obtained through
lengthy interviews—of sixty-six people, who at the time of the field
study held positions in eleven job categories in the urban labor market of
Rio considered relevant according to the statistical map of occupational
classification. This map, constructed and analyzed by Neuma Aguiar and
Nelson do Valle Silva (1994 [1992]), was my initial point of orientation.
However, as an anthropologist, it was necessary for me to deconstruct
that statistical arrangement and to transform racism toward Brazilian
women from a "social problem" (Lenoir 1990)—with all its moral implications—into the object of study. First, I asked:

• How can we study racial differences in values and representations,
  based on the interviewees' interpretations of these differences?
• How and through whom does "color" operate as a principle of social
  selection (Martinez-Alier 1973)?

As part of this deconstruction, I selected narratives of people who
classified themselves as "nonwhites" and who held superior positions in

the occupational hierarchy, and complementarily, of people who classi-fied themselves as "white" although they were situated at the base of the hierarchy or in intermediate positions. From this perspective, the vari-ables of gender and age played a dependent—but not irrelevant—role. To render the comparisons plausible, I considered equivalencies in the con-ditions of the gender and age variables, combining them with education and family structure. Instead of comparing career paths based on posi-tions "naturally" attributed to "nonwhite" and "white" people, I sought to subvert the "natural order of things" and select several people from whose narratives I could discuss the questions formulated at the opening of this chapter, to examine not only the directions but also the meanings of dislocations within the occupational hierarchy.

Why do I analyze narratives? Rather than being a tool capable of pro-ducing the Truth about the past, narrative is, as Renato Rosaldo (1989) suggests, "a form of social analysis" and "a cognitive instrument." Tak-ing up the perspective of the philosopher of history Louis Mink, Rosaldo recalls that "narrative analysis places essentially discrete factors within larger sets of relationships, rather than isolating them as separate vari-ables." In this way, the central preoccupation is that "social analysis should attempt to reveal not historical laws but an understanding of what happened in a specific place, at a particular time, and under certain circumstances" (Rosaldo 1989, 130–31). Gestures are described in detail in the field notebook—most of all, those of employees at the moment of racial self-identification (Goffman 1970).[8] Likewise the interviews were carefully transcribed to register the [INAUDIBLE] moments and [LAUGHS] as well as the vernacular peculiarities used during the inter-view, because the way people express themselves—the narrative style—can furnish innumerable clues as to how they reconstruct their own images (Essed 1991; Etter-Lewis 1991).

Comparing Career Trajectories

By comparing the selected career paths, it is possible to observe similari-ties and differences among those groups holding socially valued posi-

8. Having selected trajectories for comparison, I returned to some interviewees, this time un-armed (that is, without tape recorder or questionnaire). Attenuating the "symbolic violence" of communication in interview situations demands a knowledge of power relationships objectified through the sum of linguistic and social capital that enters into the interviewee-interviewer rela-tionship. For this reason, Pierre Bourdieu (1993) approaches this relationship as part and parcel of the construction of the very object of research.

tions or positions perceived as privileged (Lenoir 1990). This means not only positions earning a high income but also the symbolic capital arising from one's position in the professional hierarchy and the way racial designations are employed and operate with greater or lesser intensity toward this capital in terms of "condition of class and position of class."[9] With this theoretical perspective and considering the moment in the career trajectories captured in the interviews, as well as the effects of those trajectories over time, I focus in this chapter on the narratives of four women: Jacirema, Severiana, Amélia, and Marta.

The Interviews: A Brief Profile

Jacirema was 37 years old when she granted a long interview in December 1994 at her workplace, a large and well-decorated accounting office in a commercial building in Copacabana.[10] The day of the interview, Jacirema—who classified herself as "black" and commented in a sarcastic tone, "White is what I am not!"—dressed in a classic linen suit (skirt and blazer) and a silk blouse. She had been an "accounting technician" when the opportunity arose to "set up the office" in 1982. She immediately hired a secretary and an office boy. That year she also enrolled in a school of accounting sciences (*Ciênciás Contàbeis*), and in 1986 she earned a degree. In 1991 she (unofficially) married a "black guy" with two daughters. She had no children of her own, so she considered her "14-year-old stepdaughter," who lived with the couple, as a "sort of adoption."

Severiana is an "accounting technician" who completed high school. She was interviewed in August 1993 at her workplace—a large nongovernmental organization (the Center for Social and Economic Assistance, or CASE) located in the neighborhood of Catete. She worked as an "assistant in the personnel department." Although Severiana was born in 1954, in a lapse of memory she said she was 31 instead of 39. The interview took place during her lunch hour in a "more private" room of a woman who worked in another department. Severiana had been married for ten years but had now been separated for two. Her son was 8 years old and her daughter was 2. Severiana, who declared herself "white," fre-

---

9. Empirical sociology understands "class" as resulting from a combination of income and occupation. In the research reported in this chapter, class not only is a matter of "social structure" but also of symbolic systems and mechanisms. These vary diachronically and synchronically, involving lifestyles (consumption as a means of communication), as well as the combination of different types of capital (educational, linguistic, social, and cultural) and of the strategic use of the possibilities of reconverting one type of capital to another (Bourdieu 1966).

10. The names of women interviewed and the locations of the interviews are fictitious.

quently expressed discomfort with the financial insecurity related to working a double shift. And after the interview, feeling legitimated, she expressed appreciation "for being selected."

Amélia was 39 at the time of the interview in February 1994 and a "senior administrator" in a branch of a large, national banking institution in downtown Rio de Janeiro. After several telephone contacts and much difficulty in her managing to "find the time," the interview finally took place at the bank in the late afternoon, after a forty-minute wait because Amélia was still busy. She was extremely receptive and agreed to be interviewed because of intermediation by a mutual friend—who classified her as "more or less mulatta."[11] Amélia, however, in describing her relationship with her colleagues, declared herself "black." She had been "officially" married for three years to a "black" man, a manager at an important multinational banking institution and the father of her only child, a girl now 15 years old. After beginning a course in business administration in 1990, Amélia was "obliged" to quit college "for lack of time" because of her administrative duties and also to be closer to her daughter.

Marta, 49 years old and "white," worked as principal of a public elementary school in Ipanema at the time of the interview in July 1993. She insisted on a very concise interview of little more than an hour; she spoke in a pausing and chronologically unified style, consistently developing a central idea. Marta held bachelor's and master's degrees in pedagogy and was attending graduate school in psychology. She had returned to work in elementary education in 1988 after more than ten years in business activities. She and her husband had separated in 1987; at the time of the interview, her daughter was 17 and her son was 15.

Synchronies and Diachronies

In a synchronic perspective (that is, considering their career trajectories at the moment captured in the interviews), Jacirema, Severiana, Amélia,

11. Interviewees were located through mutual friends, who were asked to find individuals who did not hold militant views on race or gender. Additionally, I asked the intermediaries to identify the potential subject's occupational category, position in the workplace (employee, self-employed, employer, and so forth), and, finally, "color" or "race." The discrepancies in racial designation by the intermediary and the interviewee is part of the landscape of moral, ethical, and aesthetic values attributed to appearance that will be discussed at another time. Given these considerations, race and color terms and the categories to which these refer are placed in quotation marks. I did this to emphasize that what is written in this chapter is the result of a dialogue among different and often conflicting visions of the world *and does not attempt to name primordial principles or biological essences.*

and Marta held quite distinct positions in the occupational hierarchy. Jacirema was experiencing an ascent that she herself described: as of the 1980s, she made "a radical change, you know?! I went from being a secretary to owning the business! I had to go forward and *not fall.*" Severiana found herself in a phase of stagnation, even decline, which she interpreted as resulting from her separation: "From '80 to '90, I was more or less stable because until then I lived with my husband, but now we are separated and he is unemployed." In these circumstances and despite low wages, she said she was satisfied. "CASE," she explained, "is one of the best jobs I've had so far, you know? Because I have medical insurance, you know? They give me . . . it's . . . day care, right?" As a senior manager, Amélia was in a phase of ascent in the occupational hierarchy, yet she offered a negative assessment of her professional activity: "The banker today is really a salesman of luxury, isn't he? The difference between me and the street vendor is that I am better off—he's on the street and I'm here in the air conditioning. But like him, I have to sell." However, in cautiously examining the system "in a large bank," Amélia emphasized her upward mobility in a positive assessment of her path in the institution: "I've grown professionally. . . . I became more independent, more secure."

As we shall see, from a diachronic viewpoint the first three trajectories are homologous, up to a point. The "white" interviewee, Marta, stands out in this comparative context more for her differences from the "black" interviewees than for the similarities in their paths.

Jacirema: From Maid to Small-Business Owner

Jacirema, the "black professional," entered the job market in 1967 at the age of 12 as a housekeeper who "did full service." At that time she had not completed elementary school, and she stopped her studies completely. From ages 12 to 15, she recalled, "I made the rounds of five houses." Her mother, from whom she had been separated for many years, also worked in a "family home." Jacirema explained her employment circuit of those three years as the result of a strategic decision: "I was looking for a house where I could study. I found that when I came to the S. family's house, and there I began to type and went back to night school."

Jacirema worked for the S. family for five years and completed elementary school and a secondary technical course in accounting. She did not reproduce her mother's trajectory, thanks to her strategy of choosing to acquire academic capital. However, it was precisely the experience of growing up in her mother's line of work—"she raised me on the job"—that furnished the instruments and the means to culturally calculate the relationships of exchange that were possible with her employers, who "granted the privilege" of studying. The relationship of patronage no doubt was asymmetrical, with rules that Jacirema dominated in practice. She worked "like a beast of burden," yet in the end "nothing was lost," because a close friend of her employer hired Jacirema to work in the accounting office that eventually became her own.

Severiana: From Maid to Personnel Department Assistant

Severiana began working in "family house" as a nanny when she was around "12 or 13 years old" at the suggestion of her own father ("a groundskeeper" who "earned very little"). She had an older sister (also a domestic worker) and two younger brothers. Her mother had no wage-earning activity. Severiana worked "other times in family houses" but said, "What I wanted was to study, right? Not to work, you know? It was not at all what I wanted, to work, you know? But I had no choice ..." At 13 she started elementary school at night and, like Jacirema, completed a secondary technical course in accounting. In 1975 she left the "family house," worked in various companies, and experienced several periods of unemployment.

She was an operator in a silk-screen factory, then a receptionist, a secretary, and an office assistant before going to work at CASE, where she was an assistant in the personnel department. In recounting her trajectory, Severiana—unlike Jacirema—allowed the negative value that she ascribed to her experience as a maid to surface. Referring to that job in an ambiguous way, she said:

> Right . . . . this is how I remember it—the companies I worked at, you know? First, *when I left the family house*—in '75 this was my first job . . . (I'm, well . . . getting it mixed up) . . . *My first job, you know? In '75 I worked in a factory*, you know? Silk screen. You know what that is, don't you?

The key expression in Severiana's narrative is the lack of opportunity. At CASE, for example, she felt she "deserved" to be in a "better situation" and attributed her stagnation in the same job to a "lack of opportunity" because, she said, "They don't value you here."

Amélia: From Domestic Jobs to Senior Manager

Amélia had her first paid job at the age of 14 as a "packer in a noodle factory." Two hours into the interview, she remembered that she had worked before at age 11 (in 1966), doing household chores at the home of the principal of the school where she studied in exchange for payment for her secondary studies. Amélia further recalled that up to that age, before and after school she went to the cleaners where her mother "worked ironing clothes" and where they "ate from the lunchbox together." At age 11 she began staying home with her 14-year-old brother, who had returned from boarding school and "went to work at a construction site" as a "servant." At this juncture, Amélia's mother had no means to continue paying for her daughter's school and "negotiated" with the principal for the girl to continue her studies. So, like Jacirema and Severiana, Amélia had worked as a maid, a phase that lasted for about four years, during which time she finished school. In Amélia's case, though, it was her mother's strategy to exchange domestic work for educational capital that enabled Amélia to complete her basic education. During secondary school, she was employed at an interior design shop (as an office worker). At age 22, through a "selection" exam, she entered a real estate credit company that was bought by the banking network where she would later work and make her career. Amélia was a receptionist, teller, treasurer's assistant, treasurer, assistant sales manager, and senior manager, temporarily "substituting for the executive manager of the agency." A peculiarity in her path is that her mother went to high school with her: "My mother left the cleaners and faced high school with me," then "took the nursing course," and eventually retired as a nurse.

Marta: From Entrepreneur to Principal of a Public Elementary School

Marta's occupational trajectory was in an evident state of decline, captured at the moment of the interview and identified by her return to the school system. This return took place following some experiences as a businesswoman and an administrator. In the first experience, she related, "I had an enormous firm, about thirty employees, an enormous shop floor, all of which was built over ten years in clothing manufacture . . . that ended in 1985." In 1986 she had "a small business, that is, I was self-employed, but it wasn't a registered company or anything . . . just a sewing shop, you know? And it didn't work out." Finally in 1987, she worked as a "production manager in a furniture factory."

"In 1988," Marta continued, "I returned to teaching. I took the exam and then requested *readmission* to a certification that I had left in the municipality, and I returned to teaching with two certifications." Shortly afterward, Marta left the teaching position to become the principal "elected by the group" (of parents and teachers). In addition to a reduction of income and the consequent household budget cuts, the impact of these changes signified a "fall" in her "standard of living" and that of her children, whom she transferred from an excellent private school to a public school, "the best that it was possible to find." It bears noting that Marta's father was an "industrialist" and her mother a "public functionary" in the second echelon of the Ministry of Agriculture.

Marta perceived her process of dislocation in the hierarchy of positions more as a loss of status than as a radical shift in her class condition, to the extent that the capital she had acquired—not only financial, but particularly in specialized knowledge in the industrial and commercial branches of feminine fashion—could not be reconverted to another area of production (predominantly masculine), as evidenced by her negative experience as a production manager in the upholstered furniture industry. Finally, the lack of "autonomy" as a principal in the public school system together with the "deficiencies" of the system itself were interpreted as negatives that led Marta (with a master's in pedagogy) to return to the university to pursue an advanced degree in psychology with the goal of having her own clinic: "I'm going to school, I'm working toward a degree specializing in clinical psychology. Then what I would like to do is begin a clinical practice for children with learning disabilities and, who knows, open my own clinic."

Appearance and "Good" Appearance

What are the factors of success or failure in career trajectories? The comparison of trajectories invites discussion of several recurrent themes in the Brazilian sociological literature, such as patronage, "whitening," construction of ethnic or racial identity, and the role of the notion of "good" appearance. The career paths examined here of the college-educated women who declared themselves "black" reveal a rupture in the pattern of entering the labor market and retaining jobs. In the competition for work, education is relevant only when supportive social relationships also play a role in social ascent. Thus, in the narratives of Jacirema and Amélia, the relationships with mothers, uncles, grandparents, husbands, or the circle of patronage-based personal contacts surface—just as they are absent in the narratives of Severiana and Marta.

In the case of Jacirema and less explicitly of Amélia, the factors of success appear to be located on three planes. First, there are relationships of patronage, operating in the domestic or private sphere (help from employers or a friend of an employer, or from the school principal), which tend to disguise racism. Thus, early on these women were inculcated in the rules of patronage relationships.[12] Second, there are strategies (Jacirema's decision to work only in a "family house" where the employers let her complete her studies and, having achieved this goal, not to have children, and Amélia's mother's initial negotiation to exchange her daughter's domestic service for education). Finally, the type of linkage that is constructed between the market for academic degrees and the positions obtained in the workplace seems relevant. This linkage is formed in a contradictory way, as shown by the career paths of Amélia and Jacirema. In Jacirema's case, she has a college-level accounting degree (which today is more available to "nonwhite" women), but the senior manager of a branch bank does not have a college degree.[13]

Jacirema became a small-business owner in the mid-1980s with the help of a woman friend of her employers. Having no patron or boss, her professional visibility depended on the network of clients to whom she provided accounting services. Jacirema reconstructed her racial identity by recalling ideological conflicts with her mother, who aspired for her daughter "at most, that I become a nurse" and that she not marry, "much less to a big, 'black' handsome boy like my companion, eh? [LAUGHS]." In her occupational trajectory, she experienced more ex-

12. The statistical data indicate a significant majority of "black" and "brown" women occupying subordinate positions in the urban labor market, particularly in domestic service. At the other end of the occupational hierarchy, "black" and "brown" women are absolutely underrepresented. In my research, when describing their relationships with patrons, the "black-mestizo" maids made no comment about the place they occupy in the employment hierarchy or their racial condition. Instead, they interpreted those relationships in terms of greater or lesser hierarchical proximity mediated (and measured) by such moral values as friendliness, understanding, and honesty. Claudia B. Rezende (1995) addressed this in her research; and, as I see it, the silence about racial condition relates to the naturalizing of domestic employment, always female and reified through the homology of "black" woman and slave, of maid's quarters and slave quarters (compare Birman 1990). On the other hand, in reconstructing their own trajectories in the labor market, ex-maids Jacirema and Amélia revealed this naturalization.

13. Two questions should be raised, even though for lack of space they cannot be addressed here. First is the question of patronage relationships (Da Matta 1987), which are essential in establishing the initial context in which a person's occupational trajectory unfolds. Second is the relative importance of networks of ascription (Granovetter 1974) and the value attributed to race in regard to obtaining certain jobs, titles, and positions in the work hierarchy.

plicit racism when she changed her professional status and her class position. In these circumstances, discrimination did not operate through clients of her accounting office (most of them "old, white women"), but rather through lower-level workers, mainly in places that offer services to the public or when she opened her office door to attend a salesman:

> It's always, "Is the manager here, please? The owner?" No black is ever the owner of anything! When I say, "I am . . . !" "Ah! Oh . . . OK . . ." Then he gets so disconcerted that by the time he comes to his senses I've already sent him out the door—"Thanks, but I'm not interested [LAUGHS]."

Something similar happened with Amélia, but discrimination came less through the clients of the branch bank she managed than through the employees under her. The conflicts depicted in the two narratives led me to raise the hypothesis that for the social group of origin (especially the family) and for subordinate groups (in the workplace or directly related to it) each woman simultaneously "whitened" and "darkened," due to opposing forces created by upward mobility.[14]

Factors that explain Marta's loss of professional status or the stagnation in Severiana's position appear to dislocate them in a direction different from the other two women. In Marta's case, the emphasis falls on the combination between work and family and the different representations of gender relations: "The idea is that the man supports the family, so he needs more [a higher salary] because behind this working man is a family he has to support. The woman—it's assumed that she is supported by a family." In both narratives, marital separation assumes a role of supreme importance, which does not happen in the reconstructions of Jacirema and Amélia—the former is single and childless, living with a "companion" who is separated and with one of his two daughters; the latter receives alimony from her ex-husband and lives with her mother and daughter.

14. N. V. Silva (1994) attributes discrepancies between interviewers' racial classification of subjects and interviewees' self-identification to "socioeconomic characteristics" and not to "fluidity between the color categories that are used" (67). In short, after quantitative evaluation of what the author calls "the whitening effect" based on data from a survey conducted in São Paulo in 1986, he concludes that if money "whitens," the lack of it "darkens" (78). My observation is that the manipulation of color by interviewee and interviewer is a relevant index of power relations among racial groups and social classes; this power depends on accumulated capital (other than socioeconomic). The same individual can "whiten" for his or her group of origin (families or childhood friends, for example) and "darken" through the paradoxes and opposing forces created in upward mobility.

The relationship between accumulated resources (especially educational) and the cultural qualities needed by "black" candidates to achieve prized jobs—as well as to keep such jobs once the initial hurdles are overcome—seems to engender multiple identities. Strategically pursued, the multiple identity is not the ambivalent, exotic, whitened persona frequently portrayed in assimilationist literature. According to the narratives of the "black" women interviewed, if their teachers underestimated the women's abilities during basic schooling, once they overcame the initial educational barriers, their "bosses" demanded that they be more articulate, aggressive, and even better qualified (as Amélia emphasized several times). And they had to accomplish all this without appearing threatening, especially in performing the duties of administration, management, or supervision. For this reason, "whitening" in speech, posture, gestures, dress, cultivation of particular tastes—as a means of erasing traces of origin—can be translated less as linear and hegemonic and more as a method of establishing limits, by means of "irreproachable behavior," to the redoubled demands placed on them. Additionally, these women limited their relationships with subordinates. I observed *in loco* the behavior of an employee of Amélia, a "white" male of Portuguese nationality, who after interrupting her more than once to ask the same question and obtain the same response, gruffly threw the paper on the manager's table. She did not hesitate in commenting:

> It's nothing, it's no use. You have to get used to it! I'm in charge, aren't I? See, the relationship with employees in supervisory positions, it's a complicated thing, isn't it? It's difficult because you're in charge of fifteen people and before you know it you're in charge of . . . fifty-six people . . . which is the number of people in this branch. It gets very difficult to please people, you know? Because you have to treat them in a different way . . . and sometimes there's whispering, there's envy—you know how it goes—because I have this position, you know? And *because I'm black, having gotten where I've gotten by my own merits*—I don't get involved with anyone at the bank—not to speak of. . . . They gave me the job, and I went to work. . . . It's complicated. . . . *Lots of people don't accept me as the boss . . . precisely because I'm a woman and I'm black.*

In my research, this is not the only case in which the "whitening" of public behavioral style is accompanied by the affirmation of multiple identities, among them the "black" identity. In other words, social mobility "blackens" as much as it "whitens," depending on the *field* of professional activity, on the position occupied, on the kinds of capital (economic, cultural, political, and so forth) one has inherited, acquired, and reconverted, and on the combination of these as moral qualities—both positive and negative—attributed to "appearance" or phenotypic features.

The trajectories of Jacirema and Amélia, or better still, the way they narrated and recounted their work experiences, render a set of beliefs, expectations, and knowledge of rules and norms of behavior that orient strategic decisions about how to cope with racism in everyday life. This is especially apparent when access to highly valued jobs is the nucleus of calculation. Included in that calculation is the problematic of institutionalized racism based on moral judgments linked to appearance (and "good" appearance)—a problematic that is almost always difficult to describe, though deeply rooted—which contributes to self-analysis like that undertaken by Jacirema and Amélia.[15] As successful women, they elaborate a sense of "self" that appears in the symbolic space of racially legitimated aesthetics connected to the importance of appearance.

Jacirema described situations in which she experienced employment discrimination. In her early searches for a job, she encountered postings that required typing skills, basic education, and "good appearance." When a job interviewer asked about her previous work experience, she would reply that she had been employed as a domestic worker. However well-groomed she appeared, the work history as a maid cut short the job interview. Jacirema changed tactics, acquired a second official work card not signed by her former domestic employers. When she used that approach at an interview for a laboratory position, the prospective employer told Jacirema that she was over-qualified.

With regard to "color," the incident that most stood out in her experience took place soon after she opened her accounting office. She arrived at a bank to make deposits for fifty clients and was treated rudely by a bank teller. Jacirema asked to speak to the manager, who ordered the teller to attend her. "She didn't think much of me," Jacirema recalled. "She didn't like my looks, no doubt." From that day on, however, she

---

15. The differences in the accounts involve the narrative styles of the interviewees. Jacirema's narrative is predominantly segmented and dialogic, and a droll tone prevails that borders on irony, especially when she recounts "little stories" of racism. Amélia has a predominantly unified, chronologically ordered style. Dialogic style appears in the moments in which, to reconstruct her racial identity, she refers to situations involving her ex-husband, a "black" marketing manager for a multinational banking institution. For a classification of narrative styles, I used Etter-Lewis 1991.

was greeted as a businesswoman at the bank: "How are you, Dr. Jacirema? Good morning, Dr. Jacirema!"

Severiana and Marta expressed themselves with regard to appearance and racial condition by explicitly articulating what for Jacirema and Amélia is as difficult to describe as it is deep-rooted. Severiana felt that although discrimination against "blacks" and "browns" had diminished, "people pay a lot of attention to appearance. . . . It counts for a lot, doesn't it?" She could not recall incidents of racism in her own experience but had heard others speak of it. She told of a friend who worked in the back offices of a bank: "She never had access to the public, you know? She didn't say anything, but she knew it was because she was dark-skinned." Severiana considered knowledge and performance, not "color," as appropriate criteria for advancement in the workplace, but she reiterated her belief that "appearance" had as much to do with discrimination as "color" itself. "I can't change my appearance. It's very important to everyone, all they talk about is appearance, appearance, appearance."

Marta categorized racial discrimination in the labor market as "a fact." She cited an equation in which being attractive and being white equaled getting the "best jobs." Like Severiana, she also expressed the view that ideally people would be judged in the workplace "by their capacity . . . by what they produce, you know, and not by their appearance."

Polysemy: From the Modern "Market of Good Appearance" to "Townhouses and Shanties"

"Whitening" is still perceived as a synthesis and mitigation of Brazilian racial-political tensions. Yet the production of "good" appearance among "mixed-black" women, as a surety for obtaining work and competing successfully to keep valued positions, can contradict that synthesis and indicate a polysemy. Jacirema, dressed in silk and linen, her hair arranged carefully in a discreet "afro" style, sought to produce an image that matched the activities of "assisting individuals and companies" of a largely "white" clientele. Likewise Amélia, as a manager in a large branch bank, dressed discretely and wore her hair in a "naturally" curly style. Both constructed a "black" identity as they talked about their careers.

Ângela Figueiredo, in one of the only contemporary studies of "the market of good appearance," examines some of its aspects in relation to hair. She calls attention to the historical perception of "kinky" or "coarse" hair as synonymous with "ugly" and as the feature "that most bothers some whites about the physical aspect of blacks" (1994, 35). The author approaches the meanings of inculcating "blacks" themselves with this pattern—which I contend is not only aesthetic but largely moral—when she points out two important issues for analyzing the polysemy of "good appearance": "The private meaning is most closely related to autonomy, to personal taste. This area is more sensitive to the discourse of negritude and black beauty proffered by black movements. In the public sense, it is more related to work and mainly to looking for work, in the first contact with a company, where being black signifies more of a barrier in the mechanisms of selection" (1994, 35).

The public and private meanings of "good" appearance, when associated with what I called effects of trajectory, lead us to reevaluate the relation between "whitening" and social ascent. The widely disseminated idea that "money whitens" can be accompanied by a "darkening" slowly produced by the paradoxes and opposing forces created during the upward movement, as demonstrated in the narratives of Amélia and Jacirema.

If we return to Gilberto Freyre's *Sobrados e Mucambos* (1936), for example, we see how the link between "good" appearance and social ascent or "whitening" has been a theme inscribed in the history of Brazilian ideas and culture that Freyre translated into academic language.[16] In his evaluation, "good" appearance was produced through "adaptations" of items of clothing by "mulattos," who were rising socially mainly at the end of the nineteenth century. These adaptations—from the hat to the shoes and extending to the accessories, fabrics, styles of clothing, and fashions in haircuts and beards—aimed to overcome the "disproportions" of the "body" of "blacks" and their mixed descendants, favoring the social ascent of the latter (Freyre 1936, chap. 11).

Freyre, in discussing the aesthetic conventions of painters and sculptors, underscored the "extra-European" or "extra-Greco-Roman" meaning of these conventions, but without actually deeming them "African." Aleijadinho—a "mulatto El Greco"—is for Freyre the defining case in the use of these "extra-European" conventions. Comparing Aleijadinho's nose to the noses of the "white dominators of the colonies," Freyre observes that Aleijadinho's "deformation, almost a caricature," is

16. The work of historian Carlo Ginzburg (1993 [1976]) is the basis for my theoretical approach in which I look back in time to see how certain ideas were formed and disseminated by social classes. I refer to Freyre's *Sobrados e Mucambos*, written in the 1930s when Brazilian social classes were becoming culturally distinct as well as economically distant, even in geographical terms. Not by chance, urbanization and industrialization intensified during this period.

"the major point of *somatic* or *plastic* contrast between the *oppressed* and the *oppressors* in Brazil" (Freyre 1936, 979, emphasis mine). Nevertheless, although the meaning of the "deformation" is "extra-European," it is not clearly African but "only marginally *African*. Characteristically Brazilian, that is, *mestizo* or *culturally plural*" (Freyre 1936, 980, emphasis mine). Similarly, the author insists, the "blond or target type of woman" had suffered the impact of miscegenation. As early as the nineteenth century, the "sweet mulatta or the coy brunette" appeared frequently in the verses and novels of the educated as well as in popular song (Freyre 1936, 981).

The production of discourses and behaviors in terms of the moral and aesthetic qualities of appearance are not new. What perhaps is new is the production of "good" appearance combined with the production of "black" identity, not only in contexts of politicizing identity, such as in the "black" movement but also, as Figueiredo (1994) reminds us, in work situations associated with "progress and modernity." In these contexts, the "coy" and the "sweet" of the "mulatta" or the "brunette" tend to have less effect. When submitted to the new modes of competing for social and symbolic space, educated "mixed-black" women learn that those attributes may have value toward certain ends but are insufficient for attaining and keeping more advantageous positions in certain segments of the job market.[17] On the contrary, following Telles (1994), it is precisely in performing more specialized activities that these women experience the explicit force of exclusion based on racism.

To conclude, while *boa aparência* is frequently characterized in the sociological literature as a perverse symbol of the ideology (or myth) of racial democracy and as a reinforcement of the idea of social "whitening," the concept of *boa aparência* in fact follows a more paradoxical, nonlinear route. The discourses of the four women we interviewed reveal a logic underlying social classification that tells us less about "whitening" as a corollary of racial democracy than about the heterogeneous means by which racial biases operate, particularly in the workplace.

In Gilberto Freyre's (1936) descriptions, we have seen that at the end of the nineteenth century, aristocrats elected to link certain "moral" qualities with certain phenotypical characteristics that were embedded in

17. In carnival (and the innumerable paid activities connected to it), the archetypal image of the Brazilian mulatta has greater value. Constituting almost an ethnic, female, seasonal sector of the Brazilian labor market, carnival, along with miscegenation, is a focus of domestic and foreign diffusion of markedly characteristic aspects of the national identity. As Lilia M. Schwarcz emphasizes, this mixed-race representation is transformed from "negative to exotic and modified from the scientific into a spectacle" (1993, 249).

the notion of *boa aparência*. However, in the contemporary experiences portrayed in this essay, this linkage has taken a different direction. In effect, it became necessary to accentuate or invent social distances that are not just about the aesthetic qualities that defined the aristocrats' worldview, but about degrees of social exclusion, with "color" and *boa aparência* as the mediating principles. *Boa aparência* has become a semantic trick meant to minimize the weight of race (but not necessarily to "whiten") precisely where selective rules are most severe for people of color: the workplace.

REFERENCES

Adorno, S. 1991a. Violência urbana, justiça criminal, e organização social do crime (Urban violence, criminal justice, and social organization of crime). *Revista Crítica de Ciências Sociais* (Centro de Estudos Sociais, Coimbra) 33 (October): 145–56.

———. 1991b. O sistema penitenciário no Brasil: Problemas e desafios (The penitenciary system in Brazil: Problems and challenges). *Revista USP* (São Paulo) 9 (March–May): 65–78.

———. 1994. Crime, justiça penal, e igualdade jurídica: Os crimes que se contam no tribunal do júri. (Crime, criminal justice, and judicial equality: Crimes reported in jury tribunals). *Revista USP* (São Paulo) 21 (March–May): 133–51.

———. 1995. Criminal violence in modern Brazilian society. In *Social changes, crime, and police,* ed. L. Shelley and J. Vigh. Chur, Switzerland: Harwood Academic Publishers.

———. 1996. Racismo, criminalidade violenta, e justiça penal: Réus brancos e negros em perspectiva comparativa. *Estudos Históricos* (Rio de Janeiro) 9, no. 18: 282–300.

———. n.d. Black criminality on the defendants' bench: Discrimination and inequality in access to criminal justice. NEV-USP Research Project in accord with the Instituto da Mulher Negra/Geledés. São Paulo, Mimeographed.

Adorno, S., and E. Bordini. 1989. Reincidência e reincidentes penitenciários em São Paulo, 1974–1985 (Recidivism and repeat offenders in São Paulo, 1974–1985). *Revista Brasileira de Ciências Sociais* (Associação Nacional de Pós-Graduação e Pesquisa em Ciência Sociais [ANPOCS], São Paulo) 9, no. 3 (February): 70–94.

Agier, M. 1990a. Espaço urbano, família, e status social: O novo operariado baiano nos seus bairros (Urban space, family, and social status: The new Bahian workers in their neighborhoods). *Cadernos* CRH 13:39–62.

———. 1990b. Lógica da diferenciação social: Notas sobre as trajetórias profissionais do novo operiado baiano (The logic of social differentiation: Notes on the professional trajectories of the new Bahian working class). *Cadernos* CRH 12:97–109.

———. 1992. Etnopolítica: A dinâmica do espaço afro-baiano. *Estudos Afro-Asiáticos* (Rio de Janeiro) 22:99–115.

Aguiar, N. 1994. *Rio de Janeiro plural: Um guia para políticas sociais por gênero e raça.* Rio de Janeiro: Editorial Rosa dos Ventos/IUPERJ.

Aguiar, N., and N. Silva. 1994 [1992]. Categorias ocupacionais por sexo e cor no Rio de Janeiro. Mimeographed.

Althauser, R., and M. Wigler. 1972. Standardization and component analysis. *Sociological Methods and Research* 1:97–135.

Alvarez, S. 1990. *Engendering democracy in Brazil: Women's movements in politics.* Princeton: Princeton University Press.

Anderson, B. 1991. *Imagined communities: Reflections on the origin and spread of nationalism.* London: Verso.

Andrews, G. R. 1986. Black and white workers: São Paulo, Brazil, 1888–1928. *Hispanic American Historial Review* 68, no. 3.

———. 1991. *Blacks and whites in São Paulo, 1888–1988.* Madison: University of Wisconsin Press.

———. 1992a. Desigualdade racial no Brasil e nos Estados Unidos: Uma comparação estatística (Racial inequality in Brazil and the United States: A statistical comparison). *Estudos Afro-Asiáticos* (Rio de Janeiro) 22:47–83.

———. 1992b. Black political protest in São Paulo, 1888–1988. *Journal of Latin American Studies* 24:147–71.

Antunes, R. C. 1991. *O que é sindicalismo.* São Paulo: Brasiliense.

Anyon, J. 1990. Interseções de gênero e classe: Acomodação e resistência de mulheres e meninas às ideologias de papéis sexuais. *Cadernos de Pesquisa* (São Paulo) 73 (May): 13–25.

Apple, M. W. 1989. *Educação e poder.* Porto Alegre: Artes Médicas.

Azevedo, C. C. M. 1987. *Onda negra, medo branco: O negro no imaginário das elites no século XIX* (Black wave, white fear: The black in the consciousness of elites in the 19th century). Rio de Janeiro: Paz e Terra.

Azevedo, J. S. G. 1975. Industrialização e incentivos fiscais na Bahia: Uma tentativa de interpretação histórica (Industrialization and fiscal incentives in Bahia: An attempt at historical interpretation). Ph.D. diss., Federal University of Bahia, Salvador.

Azevedo, T. 1953. *As elites de cor: Um estudo de ascensão social.* São Paulo: Companhia Editora Nacional.

———. 1955. As elites de cor, um estudo de ascensão social. São Paulo: Editorial Nacional.

———. 1956. Classes e grupos sociais de prestígio (Classes and social groups of prestige). In *Cultura e situação racial no Brasil.* Rio de Janeiro: Civilização Brasileira.

———. 1966. *Cultura e situação racial no Brasil.* Rio de Janeiro: Civilização Brasileira.

Bairros, L. 1987. Pecados no paraíso racial: O negro na força de trabalho na Bahia, 1950–1980 (Sins in racial paradise: Blacks in the labor force in Bahia 1950–1980). Master's thesis, University Federal of Bahia, Salvador.

———. 1988. Pecados no paraíso racial. In *Escravidão e invenção da liberdade,* ed. J. Reis. São Paulo: Editorial Brasiliense.

———. 1991. Mulher negra: O espaço da subordinação (Black woman: The space of subordination). In *Desigualdade racial no Brasil contemporâneo,* ed. P. A. Lovell, 177–193. Belo Horizonte: CEDEPLAR/UFMG.

Bairros, L., V. Barreto, and N. A. Castro. 1992. Negros e brancos num mercado de trabalho em mudança (Blacks and whites in a changing labor market). *Ciências sociais hoje.* Rio de Janeiro: Associação Nacional de Pós-Graduação e Pesquisa em Ciência Sociais (ANPOCS).

Bairros, L., N. A. Castro, and V. Barreto. 1990. Vivendo em sobressalto: Composiçâo étnica e dinâmica conjuntural do mercado de trabalho. In the VII Encontro Nacional de Estudos Populacionais, *ABEP Annals* (Belo Horizonte) 2:21–50.

Bairros, L., et al. 1993. Vivendo em sobressalto: Composiçâo étnica e dinâmica conjuntural do mercado de trabalho. *Revista Força de Trabalho* 10, no. 1: 13–21.

Balandier, G. 1976. *Antropo-lógicas.* São Paulo: Cultrix/University of São Paulo.

Barbosa, W. do N., and J. Rufino dos Santos. 1994. *Atrás do muro da noite: Dinâmica das culturas afro-brasileiras.* Brasília: Ministério da Cultura/Fundação Cultural Palmares.

Barreira, I. A. 1993. Ideologia e gênero na política: estratégia de identificação em torno de uma experiência. *DADOS Revista de Ciências Sociais* 36: 441–68.

Barros, R. P., and L. Fox. 1990. Female-headed households, poverty, and the welfare of children in urban Brazil. Rio de Janeiro, IPEA. Mimeographed.

Barros, R. P., and R. Mendonça. 1996. Diferenças entre discriminação racial e por gênero e o desenho de políticas anti-discriminatórias. *Estudos Feministas* 4, no. 1: 189.

Barros R. P., R. Mendonça, and T. Velazco. 1996. *O papel da cor no processo de estratificação social brasileiro.* Rio de Janeiro: IPEA.

Barry, M. F., and J. W. Blassingame. 1982. *Long memory: The black experience in America.* New York: Oxford University Press.

Bastide, R. 1978. *The African religions of Brazil.* Baltimore: John Hopkins Press.

Bastide, R., and F. Fernandes. 1959. *Brancos e negros em São Paulo* (Whites and blacks in São Paulo). São Paulo: Nacional.

Benevides, M. V. 1983. *Violência, povo e polícia (Violência urbana no noticiário de imprensa)* [Violence, the people, and police (Urban violence reported in print news media)]. São Paulo: Brasiliense.

BENFAM/DHS. 1991. *Pesquisa sobre saúde familiar no nordeste.* Brasil: BENFAM/DHS.

Bento, M. A. 1988. Racismo no trabalho: Algumas experiências práticas. *São Paulo em Perspectiva* (Revista da Fundação SEADE, São Paulo) 2, no. 2 (April–June).

———. 1992. Resgatando minha bisavó: Discriminação no trabalho e resistência na voz de trabalhadores negros. Master's thesis, Pontifícia Universidade Católica, São Paulo.

Bergman, B. 1971. The effects on white incomes of discrimination in employment. *Journal of Political Economy* 79:294–313.

Berquó, E. 1988. Demografia da desigualdade: Algumas considerações sobre os negros no Brasil. VI Encontro Nacional de Estudos Populacionais, *ABEP Annals* (Belo Horizonte) 3.

———. 1989. A esterilização feminina no Brasil hoje. In *Quando a paciente é mulher.* Brasília: Conselho Nacional dos Direitos da Mulher.

———. 1991. Como se casam negros e brancos no Brasil. In *Desigualdade racial no Brasil contemporâneo,* ed. P. A. Lovell. Belo Horizonte: CEDEPLAR/UFMG.

———. 1993a. Brasil, um caso exemplar (Anticoncepção e parto cirúrgicos) à espera de uma ação exemplar. *Estudos Feministas* (Rio de Janeiro) 1, no. 2.

———.1993b. A saúde reproductiva das mulheres negras e a dinâmica demográgica da população negra no Brasil. Paper presented at the National Seminar on Policies and Reproductive Rights of Black Women, August, Itapecerica da Serra, Brazil.

Berquó, E., and L. F. de Alencastro. 1992. A emergência do voto negro. *Novos Estudos CEBRAP* (São Paulo) 43 (June): 77–88.

Berquó, E., A. Bercovich, and E. M. Garcia. 1986. Estudo da dinâmica demográfica da população negra no Brasil (Campinas: Nepo/Unicamp). *Textos Nepo,* no. 9.

Berriel, M. M. A. 1989. A identidade fragmentada: As muitas maneiras de ser negro. Ph.D. diss., University of São Paulo, São Paulo.

Bilac, E. 1978. Famílias de trabalhadores: Estratégias de sobrevivência. *Coleção Ensaio e Memória 9.* São Paulo: Símbolo.

Birman, P. 1990. Beleza negra. *Estudos Afro-Asiáticos* (Rio de Janeiro) 18, no. 5: 12.

Blau, P., and O. D. Duncan. 1967. *The American occupational structure.* New York: John Wiley.

Blinder, A. 1973. Wage discrimination: Reduced form and structural estimates. *Journal of Human Resources* 7:436–55.

Bobbio, N. 1986. *Dicionário de política.* Brasília: Universidade de Brasília Press.

———. 1988. *Liberalismo e democracia* (Liberalism and democracy). São Paulo: Brasiliense.

Boletim Estatístico. 1996. Os números da cor. *Boletim estatístico sobre a situação socio-econômica dos grupos de cor no Brasil e em suas regiões.* Rio de Janeiro: Centro de Estudos Afro-Asiàticos, no. 4 (October).

Bongaarts, J. 1987. The projection of family composition over the life course using the family status life table. In *Family Demography,* ed. J. Bongaarts et al. Oxford: Clarendon.

Borges Pereira, J. B. 1982. Aspectos do comportamento político do negro em São Paulo. *Ciência e Cultura* 34, no. 10.

Boshi, R., and L. Valladares. 1982. Movimentos associativos de camadas populares urbanas: Análise comparativa de seis casos. In *Movimentos coletivos no Brasil urbano,* ed. R. Boshi. Rio de Janeiro: Zahar.

Bourdieu, P. 1966. Condition de classe et position de classe. *Archives Européenes de Sociologie* 7:201–23.

———. 1989. *O poder simbólico.* Lisbon: Difel.

———. 1993. *La misére du monde.* Paris: Editorial Seuil.

Bowser, Benjamin, ed. 1995. *Racism and anti-racism in world perspective.* Thousand Oaks, Calif.: Sage.

Braga, O. M. 1952. *Bibliografia de Joaquim Nabuco.* Instituto Nacional do Livro: Coleção B.1: Bibliografia VIII, Rio de Janeiro.

Brazil Election Factbook. 1966. Institute for Comparative Study of Political Systems (U.S.), Supplement no. 2.

Bretas, M. L. 1991. O crime na historiografia brasileira: Uma revisão na pesquisa recente (Crime in Brazilian historiography: A revision in recent research). *Boletim Informativo e Bibliográfico de Ciências Sociais* (Associação Nacional de Pós-Graduação e Pesquisa em Ciências Sociais [ANPOCS], Rio de Janeiro) 32: 49–61.

Bruschini, C. 1989. Tendências da forca de trabalho feminina brasileira nos anos setenta e oitenta: Algumas comparações regionais. Texto da Fundação Carlos Chagas, no. 1/89.

Caldeira, T. P. 1991. Direitos humanos ou "privilégios de bandidos"? *Novos Estudos* (CEBRAP, São Paulo) 30 (July): 162–74.

Campos Coelho, E. 1978. *A ecologia do crime* (The ecology of crime). Rio de Janeiro: Comissão Nacional Justiça e Paz/Educam.

———. 1980. Sobre sociólogos, pobreza, e crime (Of sociologists, poverty, and crime). *Dados* (Revista de Ciências Sociais, IUPERJ, Rio de Janeiro) 23, no. 1: 377–83.

Candido, A. 1951. The Brazilian family. In *Portrait of a half continent,* ed. T. L. Smith. New York: Dryden Press.

Cardia, N. 1994. Direitos humanos: Ausência de cidadania e exclusão moral. In *Princípios de Justiça e Paz.* São Paulo: Arquidiocese de São Paulo/Comissão de Justiça e Paz.

Cardoso, F. H. 1962 [1971]. *Capitalismo e escravidão no Brasil meridional.* São Paulo: Difusão Européia do Livro (Difusão Européia do Livro, DIFEL).

———. 1978. Partidos e deputados em São Paulo (O voto e a representacao politica). In *Os partidos e as Eleições no Brasil.* Rio de Janeiro: Paz e Terra.

———. 1991. Democracia e desigualdades sociais. *Revista Crítica de Ciências Sociais* (Centro de Estudos Sociais, Coimbra) 32 (June): 23–27.

Cardoso, R. C. 1983. Movimentos sociais urbanos: Balanço crítico. In *Sociedade e Política no Brasil Pós-1964,* ed. B. Sorj and M. H. de Almeida. São Paulo: Brasiliense.

Carneiro, S. 1995a. Defining black feminism. In *Connecting across cultures and continents.* New York: UNIFEM.

———. 1995b. Gênero, raça, e ascensão social. *Estudos Feministas* 3, no. 1: 544–52.

———. 1996. O mito da democracia racial. In *Brasil e África do Sul: Uma comparação,* ed. B. Lamounier. São Paulo: IDESP.

Carneiro, S., and T. Santos. 1985. *Mulher negra.* São Paulo: Nobel/CESF.

Carvalho, E. 1985. Identidade e projecto político: Notas para a construção teórica do conceito de antropologia. In *Identidade: Teoria e pesquisa,* ed. A. Z. Bassit. São Paulo: EDUC [Série Cadernos PUC, no. 20].

Carvalho, J. M., and C. Wood. l988. *The demography of inequality in Brazil.* Cambridge: University of Cambridge Press.

Castro, M. G. 1991. Mulheres chefes de famílias, racismo, códigos de idade e pobreza no Brasil (Bahia e São Paulo). In *Desigualdade racial no Brasil contemporâneo,* ed. P. A. Lovell. Belo Horizonte: CEDEPLAR/UFMG.

Castro, M. M. P., et al. 1993. *Quando a vida não tem valor: Assassinato de crianças e adolescentes no Estado de São Paulo.* Relatório de Pesquisa, convênio FCBIA-SP/NEV-USP. São Paulo, Mimeographed.

Castro, N. A. 1985. O emprego não-agrícola no estado da Bahia. 1950–1980: Algumas considerações a partir dos censos econômicos (Nonagricultural employment in the state of Bahia 1950–1980: Some considerations from the economic census). *Força de trabalho e emprego* 1, no. 3: 12–22.

———. 1988. Novo operariado, novas condições de trabalho, e novos modos de vida nas fronteiras do moderno capitalismo industrial brasileiro (New working class, new labor conditions, and new ways of life on the frontiers of Brazilian modern industrial capitalism). VII Encontro Nacional de Estudos Populacionais, *ABEP Annals* (Belo Horizonte) 2.

———. 1993. Mercado de trabalho, mobilidade social, e diferenciação racial. *Revista Força de Trabalho e Emprego* 10, no. 1: 43–54.

———. 1994. Inequalities in a racial paradise: Labor opportunities among blacks and whites in Bahia, Brazil. *SPURS* 35 (Spring).

Castro, N. A., and A. S. Guimarães. 1993. Desigualdades raciais no mercado de trabalho. *Estudos Afro-Asiáticos* (Rio de Janeiro) 24 (July 1993): 23–60.

Castro, N. A., and V. Sá Barreto. 1992. Os negros que dão certo: Mercado de trabalho, mobilidade, e desigualdades raciais. Paper presented at the XVI Associação Nacional de Pós-Graduação e Pesquisa em Ciência Sociais National Meeting, 15–18 October, Caxambu, Brazil.

Cavalcanti, M. L. 1990. A temática racial no carnaval carioca: Algumas reflexões. *Estudos Afro-Asiáticos* (Rio de Janeiro) 18: 27–44.

CEBRAP. 1992. *Pesquisa sobre saúde reprodutiva da população negra.* Brasil: CEBRAP.

Chaia, M. W. 1988. Negro: Entre o trabalho forçado e o trabalho restrito. *São Paulo em Perspectiva* (Revista da Fundação SEADE, São Paulo) 2, no. 2 (April–June).

———. 1989. Os negros e a discriminação racial no mercado de trabalho (Blacks and racial discrimination in the labor market). In *Mercado de trabalho na grande São Paulo* (Labor market of Greater São Paulo: Research of employment and unemployment). São Paulo: Pesquisa de Emprego e Desemprego/SEAD-DIEESE.

Comer, J. P. 1985. Black violence and public police. In *American violence and public police*, ed. L. A. Curtis. New Haven: Yale University.

Contins, M., and L. C. Santana. 1996. O movimento negro e a questão da ação afirmativa. *Estudos Feministas* (IFCS/UFRJ-PPCIS/UERJ) 4, no. 1: 220.

Corrêa, M. 1982. As ilusões da liberdade. A escola Nina Rodrigues e a Antropologia no Brasil. Ph.D. diss., FFLCH/Universidade São Paulo.

———. 1983. *Morte em família* (Death in the family). Rio de Janeiro: Graal.

Costa, E. V. 1982. *Da senzala à colônia*, 2d ed. São Paulo.

Costa, I., R. Slenes, and S. Swartz. 1987. A família escrava em Lorena (1801). *Estudos Econômicos* (IPE/USP) 17, no. 2.

Costa, T. C. N. A. 1974. O princípio classificatório "cor," sua complexidade e implicações para um estudo censitário. *Revista Brasileira de Geografia* (Rio de Janeiro) 36, no. 3: 91–103.

———. 1987. A classificação de "cor" na pesquisa do IBGE: Notas para uma discussão. *Cadernos de Pesquisa* [Número especial sobre raça negra e educação] (São Paulo) 63 (November): 14–16.

Covin, D. 1990. Afrocentricity in o movimento negro unificado. *Journal of Black Studies* 21:126–44.

Cross Jr., W. 1991. *Shades of black: Diversity in African-American identity.* Philadelphia: Temple University Press.

Cunha, M. C. da. 1985. *Negros estrangeiros: Os escravos libertos e sua volta à África.* São Paulo: Brasiliense.

Cunha, O. M. G. da. 1991. Corações rastafari: Lazer, política, e religião em Salvador. Master's thesis, National Museum, Universidade Federal do Rio de Janeiro, Rio de Janeiro.

Curtis, L. A. 1985. *American violence and public police.* New Haven: Yale University Press.

D'Araujo, M. C. n.d. O PTB na Cidade do Rio de Janeiro—1945–1955. *Revista de Estudios Políticos* (Centro de Estudios Constitucionales, Madrid, Spain): 192.

Da Matta, R. 1979. *Carnavais, malandros, e heróis: Para uma sociologia do dilema brasileiro* (Carnivals, rogues, and heroes: Toward a sociology of the Brazilian dilemma). Rio de Janeiro: Zahar.

———. 1982. As raízes da violência no Brasil. In *A violência brasileira.* São Paulo: Brasiliense.

———. 1985. *A Casa e a rua (House and street).* São Paulo: Brasiliense.

———. 1987. *A casa e a rua: Espaco, cidadania, mulher, e morte no Brasil.* Rio de Janeiro: Editorial Guanabara.

———. 1991 [1987]. Digressão: A fábula das três raças ou o problema do racismo à brasileira. In *Relativizando: Uma introdução á antropologia social.* Rio de Janeiro: Editorial Rocco.

———. 1995. For an anthropology of the Brazilian tradition or "a virtude está no meio." In *The Brazilian puzzle,* ed. D. J. Hess and R. A. DaMatta. New York: Columbia University Press.

Damasceno, C., S. Giacomini, and M. Santos. 1988. Catálogo de entidades do movimento negro no Brasil. *Comunicações* do ISER 5: 1–17.

Datafolha. 1995. *300 anos de Zumbi: Os Brasileiros e o preconceito de cor.* São Paulo: Datafolha.

Davis, A. 1981. *Women, race, and class.* New York: Random House.

Davis, D. R., and W. H. Moore. 1997. Ethnicity matters: Transnational ethnic alliances and foreign policy behavior. *International Studies Quarterly* 41:174.

Davis, F. J. 1991. *Who is black? One nation's definition.* University Park: Pennsylvania State University Press.

Degler, C. 1971. *Neither black nor white: Slavery and race relations in Brazil and the United States.* New York: Macmillan.

de la Fuente, Alejandro. 1995. Raça e desigualdade em Cuba (1899–1981). *Estudos Afro-Asiáticos* 27 (April): 7–43.

de Souza, A. 1971. Raça e política no Brasil urbano. *Revista de Administração de Empresas* (Rio de Janeiro) 11, no. 4: 61–70.

Dias, J. L. 1991. Legislação eleitoral e padrões de competição politico-partidário. In *Sistema eleitoral brasileiro: Teoria e pratica.* Rio de Janeiro: Rio Fundo Editora.

do Patrocínio, J. G. de T. 1887. *Gazeta da Tarde.* 5 May.

Encontro Estadual de Mulheres Negras. 1993. *Final Document of III Encontro Estadual de Mulheres Negras* [Third State Encounter of Black Women], São Paulo.

Enzensberger, H. M. 1967. *Politique et crime* (Politics and crime). Paris: Gallimard.

Enguita, M. F. 1989. *A face oculta da escola: Educação e trabalho no capitalismo.* Porto Alegre: Artes Médicas.

Epstein, B. S. 1981. Patterns of sentencing and their implementation in Philadelphia city and country, 1795–1829. Ph.D. diss., University of Pennsylvania.

Escobar, A., and S. E. Alvarez. 1992. *The making of social movements in Latin America: Identity, strategy, and democracy.* Boulder, Colo.: Westview.

Essed, P. 1991. *Understanding everyday racism.* London: Sage Publications.

Etter-Lewis, G. 1991. Black women's life stories: Reclaiming self in narrative texts. In *Women's words: The feminist practice of oral history,* ed. S. Gluck and D. Patai. New York: Chapman and Hall.

Ewald, F. 1993. *Foucault: A norma e o direito* (Foucault: The norm and the law). Lisbon: Vega (Communications and Linguistics Collection no. 7).

Eyerman, R., and A. Jamison. 1991. *Social movements: A cognitive approach.* University Park: Pennsylvania State University Press.

Faria, J. E. 1989. *Direito e justiça. A função social do judiciário* (Law and justice: The social workings of the judiciary). São Paulo: Ática.

———. 1991. Justiça e conflito: Os juízes em face dos novos movimentos sociais (Justice and conflict: Judges faced with the new social movements). *Revista dos Tribunais* (São Paulo).

Fausto, B. 1984. *Crime e cotidiano: A criminalidade em São Paulo (1880–1924)* [Crime and daily life: Criminality in São Paulo (1880–1924)]. São Paulo: Brasiliense.

Fernandes, F. 1968. Mobilidade social e relações raciais: O drama do negro e do mulato numa sociedade em mudança. *Cadernos Brasileiros* (Rio de Janeiro) 10, no. 47: 51–67. [Reprinted in 1972 as O *negro no mundo dos brancos.*]

———. 1969. *The negro in Brazilian society.* New York: Columbia University Press.

———. 1971. *The negro in Brazilian society.* New York: Atheneum.

———. 1972. *O negro no mundo dos brancos.* São Paulo: Difusão Europeia do Livro.

———. 1974 [1965]. *A integração do negro na sociedade de classes.* 2 vols. São Paulo: Editorial Ática.

———. 1978. *A integração do negro na sociedade de classes.* 3d ed., 2 vols. São Paulo: Ática.

———. 1979. The negro in Brazilian society: Twenty-five years later. In *Brazil: Anthropological perspectives,* ed. M. Margolis and W. Carter. New York: Columbia University Press.

———. 1986. Mercado de trabalho na Bahia: Um diagnóstico (Labor market in Bahia: A diagnostic). *Força de trabalho e emprego* 1, no. 7: 19–34.

Figueiredo, A. 1994. O Mercado da boa aparência: As cabelereiras negras (The market of good appearance: Black hairdressers). *Análise e Dados* (Bahia) 3, no. 4: 33–36.

Fletcher, P. R., and S. C. Ribeiro. 1987. O ensino de primeiro grau no Brasil de hoje. Brasília: IPEA. Mimeographed.

Folha de São Paulo. 1996. 5 November, sec. 1, pp. 1–5.

Fontaine, P.-M., ed. 1985. *Race, class, and power in Brazil.* Los Angeles: UCLA Center for Afro-American Studies.

Foucault, M. 1980. *La verdad y las formas jurídicas* (The truth and juridical forms). Barcelona: Gedisa.

Freyre, G. 1933. *Casa grande e senzala.* Rio de Janeiro: Schmidt.

———. 1936. *Sebrados e mucambos.* (English: *The mansions and the shanties: The making of modern Brazil.* Westport, Conn.: Greenwood Press, 1963).

———. 1963. *Casa grande e Senzala: Formação da família brasileira sob o regime de economia patriarcal.* 12th ed. Brasília, Brazil: Editora Universidade de Brasília.

Fry, P. 1975. Soul food, e feijoada. *Ensaios de Opinião* 4:45–47.

———. 1991. Politicamente correto num lugar, incorreto noutro: Relações raciais no Brasil, nos Estados Unidos, em Moçambique e no Zimbábue (Politically correct in one place, incorrect in another: Race relations in Brazil, in the United States, in Mozambique, and in Zimbabwe). *Estudos Afro-Asiáticos* (Rio de Janeiro) 21:167–77.

———. 1996. Color and the rule of law in Brazil. Paper presented at conference on The Rule of Law and the Underprivileged in Latin America, 16 November, University of Notre Dame, Notre Dame, Indiana.

Garcia Tamburo, E. M. 1987. Mortalidade infantil da população negra Brasileira, *Texto NEPN* (UNICAMP, Campinas) 1, no. 1.

Ginzburg, Carlo. 1993. *O queijo e os vermes: O cotidiano e as idéias de um moleiro perseguido pela Inquisição.* São Paulo: Editorial Schwarcz.

Giroux, H. 1983. *Pedagogia radical: Subsídios.* São Paulo: Cortez; Autores Asociados.

Glèlè-Ahanhanzo, Maurice (Special Rapporteur on Contemporary Forms of Racism, Racial Discrimination, Xenophobia and Related Intolerance). 1995. Implementation of the programme of action for the third decade to combat racism and racial discrimination. Commission on Human Rights, United Nations Economic and Social Council, 23 January, New York.

Goffman, E. 1961. *Asylums: Essays on the social situation of mental patients and other inmates.* (Brazilian: *Manicômios, prisões e conventos.* São Paulo: Perspectiva, 1974).

———. 1970. *Ritual de la interacción.* Buenos Aires: Editorial Tiempo Contemporáneo.

Goldani, A. M. 1989. Women's transitions: The intersection of female life course, family, and demographic transition in twentieth-century Brazil. Ph.D. diss., University of Texas at Austin.

———. 1990. Diferenças raciais no processo de formação da família no Brasil. *Estudos Afro-Asiáticos* (Rio de Janeiro) 19 (December).

———. 1991. Trajetórias de vida familiar das mulheres brasileiras: Variações por coorte no século XX. In *História e população: Estudos sobre a América Latina,* ed. S. O. Nadalin, M. L. Marcílio, and A. P. Balhana. São Paulo: ABEP/IUSSP/CELADE.

Gomes, O. C. 1957. *Manuel Vitorino Pereira: Médico e cirurgião.* Rio de Janeiro: Livraría Agir.

Gonzalez, L. 1982. O movimento negro na última década. In *Lugar de Negro,* ed. Gonzalez and Hasenbalg, 9–66. Rio de Janeiro: Marco Zero.

———. 1985. The unified black movement: A new stage in black political mobilization. In *Race, class, and power in Brazil,* ed. P.-M. Fontaine, 120–34. Los Angeles: CAAS.

Gordon, L. 1976. *Woman's body, woman's right: Birth control in America.* New York: Penguin.

Graham, H. D., and T. R. Gurr. 1969. *The history of violence in America.* New York: Bantam.

Granovetter, M. S. 1974. *Getting a job: A study of contacts and careers.* Cambridge: Harvard University Press.

Guillaumin, C. 1992. Race et nature. In *Sexe, race, et pratique du pouvoir: L'idée de nature.* Paris: Côtefemmes éditions.

Guimarães, A. S. 1988. Factory regime and class formation: The petrochemical workers in Brazil. Ph.D. diss., University of Wisconsin, Madison.

———. 1993. Operários e mobilidade social na Bahia: Análise de uma trajetória individual (Workers and social mobility in Bahia: Analysis of an individual trajectory). *Revista Brasileira de Ciências Sociais* (ANPOCS, São Paulo) 22:81–97.

———. 1995. Racism and anti-racism in Brazil: A postmodern perspective. In *Racism and anti-racism in world perspective,* ed. B. P. Bowser. Thousand Oaks, Calif.: Sage.

———. 1996. A desigualdade que anula a desigualdade: Notas sobre a ação afirmativa no Brasil. Paper presented to the International Conference on Multiculturalismo e Racismo: O Papel da Ação Afirmativa nos Estados Democráticos Contemporâneos, 2–4 July, Ministério da Justiça (Ministry of Justice) do Brasil, Brasília.

———. Forthcoming. Cor, classes, e status nos estudos de Pierson, Azevedo, e Harris na Bahia, 1940–1960. In *Raça, ciência, e sociedade no Brasil,* ed. M. C. Maio and R. Santos. Fiocrus/Centro Cultural Banco do Brasil.

Guimarães, A. S., and M. Agier. 1990. Identidades em conflito: Técnicos e peões na petroquímica da Bahia (Identities in conflict: Technicians and peons in the petrochemical industry of Bahia). *Revista Brasileira de Ciências Sociais* (ANPOCS, São Paulo) 13:51–68.

Gurr, T. R. 1977. Crime trends in modern democracies since 1945. *International Annals of Criminology* 16.

Hahner, J. E. 1981. *A mulher brasileira e suas lutas sociais, 1850–1937.* São Paulo: Brasiliense.

Haller, A. O., and A. Portes. 1973. Status attainment process. *Sociology of Education* 46:51–91.

Hanchard, M. G. 1994. *Orpheus and power: The "Movimento Negro" in Rio de Janeiro and São Paulo, Brazil.* Princeton: Princeton University Press.

Harris, M. 1952. Race relations in Minas Velhas, a community in the mountain region of Brazil. In *Race and class in rural Brazil,* ed. C. Wagley. Paris: UNESCO.

———. 1964a. *Patterns of race in the Americas.* New York: Walter.

———. 1964b. Racial identity in Brazil. *Luso-Brazilian Review* 1:21–28.

Harris, M., et al. 1993. Who are the whites? Imposed categories and the racial demography in Brazil. *Social Forces* 72, no. 2: 451–62.

Hasenbalg, C. 1979. *Discriminação e desigualdades sociais no Brasil* (Discrimination and racial inequalities in Brazil). Rio de Janeiro: Graal.

———. 1983. 1976: As desigualdades raciais revisitadas. In *Movimentos sociais urbanos, minorias étnicas, e outros estudos,* ed. L. A. Machado da Silva et al. Brasília: ANPOCS.

———. 1985. Race and socioeconomic inequalities in Brazil. In *Race, class, and power in Brazil,* ed. P.-M. Fontaine. Los Angeles: UCLA Center for Afro-American Studies.

———. 1990. Notas sobre a pesquisa das desigualdades raciais e bibliografia selecionada. Seminário Internacional sobre Desigualdade Racial no Brasil Contemporaneo. Belo Horizonte. Mimeographed.

———. 1991. O negro na indústria: Proletarização tardia e desigual (Blacks in industry: delayed and unequal proletarianization). Paper presented to the fifteenth annual conference of the Associação Nacional de Pós-Graduação e Pesquisa em Ciência Sociais (ANPOCS), Working Group on Labor Process and Social Claims, 15–18 October, Caxambu, Brazil.

———. 1992a. A pesquisa sobre migrações, urbanização, relações raciais, e pobreza no Brasil: 1970/1990. In *Temas e problemas da pesquisa em ciências sociais,* ed. S. Miceli. São Paulo: Sumaré.

———. 1992b. O negro na indústria: Proletarização tardia e desigual. *Ciências Sociais Hoje 1992* (ANPOCS, Rio de Janeiro): 13–31.

Hasenbalg, C., and N. V. Silva. 1988. *Estrutura social, mobilidade e raça.* São Paulo/Rio de Janeiro: Vértice/IUPERJ.

REFERENCES
261

———. 1990. Raça e oportunidades educacionais. *Estudos Afro-Asiáticos* (Rio de Janeiro) 18:73–89.

———. 1991. Raça e oportunidades sociais no Brasil. In *Desigualdade racial no Brasil contemporâneo,* ed. P. A. Lovell. Belo Horizonte: CEDEPLAR/UFMG.

———. 1992. *Relações raciais no Brasil contemporâneo.* Rio de Janeiro: Rio Fundo Editora, IUPERJ.

———. 1993. Notas sobre desigualdade racial e política no Brasil. *Estudos Afro-Asiaticos* 25:141–59.

———. 1996. Racial inequalities in Brazil and throughout Latin America: Timid responses to disguised racism. In *Constructing democracy: Human rights, citizenship, and society in Latin America.* Boulder: Westview Press.

Hasenbalg, C., N. V. Silva, and L. C. Barcelos. 1989. Notas sobre miscigenação racial no Brasil. *Estudos Afro-Asiáticos* (Rio de Janeiro) 16.

Hellwig, D., ed. 1992. *African American Reflections on Brazil's Racial Paradise.* Philadelphia: Temple University Press.

Henriques, M. H. T., and N. V. Silva. 1989. *Adolescents of today, parents of tomorrow: Brazil.* Washington, D.C.: The Alan Guttmacher Institute.

Heringer, R. 1995. Introduction to the analysis of racism. In *Racism and anti-racism in world perspective,* ed. B. P. Bowser. Thousand Oaks, Calif.: Sage.

———. 1996. Ação afirmativa (1). *Jornal do Brasil* (July 1).

Hess, J., and R. A. Da Matta, eds. 1995. *The Brazilian puzzle.* New York: Columbia University Press.

Hodge, R., and P. Hodge. 1965. Occupation assimilation as a competitive process. *American Journal of Sociology* 71:249–64.

Holanda, S. B. 1995. Raízes do Brasil. São Paulo: Companhia das Letras.

Iam, H. M., and A. Thornton. 1975. Decomposition of differences. *Sociological Methods and Research* 3:341–52.

Ianni, O. 1972. *Raças e classes sociais no Brasil* (Races and social classes in Brazil). Rio de Janeiro: Civilizaçao Brasileira.

———. 1978. *Escravidão e racismo* (Slavery and racism). São Paulo: Hucitec.

———. 1988. *Escravidão e racismo.* 2d ed. São Paulo: Hucitec.

IBGE (Instituto Brasileiro de Geografia e Estatística). 1950. *Censo demográfico 1940* (Demographic census for 1940). Vol. 2. Rio de Janeiro: IBGE.

———. 1950. *Censo demográfico 1940 (Demographic census for 1940).* Vol. 2. Rio de Janeiro: IBGE.

———. 1956. *Censo demográfico 1950 (Demographic census for 1950).* Vol. 1. Rio de Janeiro: IBGE.

———. n.d. *Censo demográfico 1960 (Demographic census for 1960).* Vol. 1. Rio de Janeiro: IBGE.

———. 1973. *Censo demográfico 1970 (Demographic census for 1970).* Vol. 1. Rio de Janeiro: IBGE.

———. 1980. *Censo demográfico.* Rio de Janeiro: IBGE.

———. 1991. *Censo demográfico.* Rio de Janeiro: IBGE.

———. 1983. *Censo demográfico 1980 (Demographic census for 1980).* Vol. 1, tomo 4. Rio de Janeiro: IBGE.

———. 1982. *Censo demográfico de São Paulo 1980 (Demographic census of São Paulo 1980).* Rio de Janeiro: Fundação Instituto Brasileiro de Geografia e Estatística.

————. 1990. *Estatísticas históricas do Brasil: Séries Econômicas 1980 (Demographic census of São Paulo 1980).* Rio de Janeiro: Fundação Instituto Brasileiro de Geografia e Estatística.

————. 1992. *Anuário estatístico do Brasil 1992.* Rio de Janeiro: IBGE.

————. 1994. *Mapa do mercado de trabalho no Brasil,* no. 1. Rio de Janeiro: IBGE.

Jaguaribe, H. 1986. *Brasil 2000.* Rio de Janeiro: Paz e Terra.

————. 1989. *Alternativas do Brasil* (Alternatives of Brazil). Rio de Janeiro: José Olympio.

Jaguaribe, H., et al. 1990. *Brasil, reforma ou caos* (Brazil, reform or chaos). Rio de Janeiro: Paz e Terra.

Januário, M., et al. *Analfabetismo, raça e gênero.* São Paulo, 1993.

Jatobá, J. 1990. A família na força de trabalho: Brasil metropolitano: 1978–1986. VII Encontro Nacional de Estudos Populacionais, *ABEP Annals* (Belo Horizonte) 2:147–76.

Jencks, C., et al. 1973. *Inequality.* New York: Basic Books.

Johnston, H., E. Laraña, and J. Gusfield. 1994. *New social movements: From ideology to identity.* Philadelphia: Temple University Press.

Jornal do Brasil. 1991. Arco-íris (3 September); Negros querem sua cor assumida no censo 91 (24 September); and Betinho pede por negros ao falar ao censo (16 October).

Kennedy, J. 1986. Political liberalization, black consciousness, and recent Afro-Brazilian literature. *Phylon* 47:199–208.

Klandermans, B., and S. Tarrow. 1988. Mobilization into social movements: Synthesizing European and American approaches. In *International social movements research. Vol. 1. From structure to action: Comparing social movement research across cultures,* ed. B. Klandermans, H. Kriesi, and S. Tarrow. London: Jai Press.

Kuntz, W. F., II. 1978. Criminal sentencing in three nineteenth-century cities: A social history of punishment in New York, Boston, and Philadelphia, 1830–1880. Ph.D. diss., Harvard University.

Lamounier, B. 1976. Educação. *Cadernos do CEBRAP* (São Paulo) 15:14–22.

————. 1978. Comportamento eleitoral em São Paulo: Passado e presente. In *Os partidos e as eleições Brasil.* 2d. ed. Rio de Janeiro: Paz e Terra.

Lamounier, B., and R. Meneguello. 1986. *Partidos políticos e consolidação democrática: O caso brasileiro.* São Paulo: Brasiliense.

Lane, R. 1979. *Violent death in the city: Suicide, accident, and murder in nineteenth-century Philadelphia.* Cambridge: Harvard University Press.

————. 1986. *Roots of violence in Black Philadelphia, 1860–1900.* Cambridge: Harvard University Press.

Larangeira, S., ed. 1990. *Classes e movimentos sociais na América Latina.* São Paulo: Hucitec.

Lebrun, G. 1987. O Brasil de Florestan Fernandes. In *O saber militante: Ensaios sobre Florestan Fernandes,* ed. A. D'Incao. Rio de Janeiro: Paz e Terra; São Paulo: Editora da UNESP.

Leers, B. 1987. Filosofia, moral, ética, família, e sociedade no Brasil (1964–1984). In *Menor e sociedade brasileira,* ed. I. Ribeiro and M. L. Barroso. Seminários Especiais, Centro João 23. Rio de Janeiro: Edicões Loyola.

Lenoir, Remi. 1990. Objet sociologique et problème social: Iniciation à la practique sociologique. In *Iniciation à la practique sociologique,* ed. Champagne et al. Paris: Dunod.

Lima, R. K. 1989. Cultura jurídica e práticas policiais: A tradição inquisitorial (Juridical culture and police practices: The inquisitional tradition). *Revista Brasileira de Ciências Sociais* (ANPOCS, São Paulo) 10, no. 4: 65–84.

———. 1990. Constituição, direitos humanos e processo penal inquisitorial: Quem cala, consente? (Constitution, human rights, and inquisitional criminal process). *Dados* (Revista de Ciências Sociais, Rio de Janeiro) 33, no. 3: 471–88.

———. 1994. *A polícia da cidade do Rio de Janeiro: Seus dilemas e paradoxos.* (Police of the city of Rio de Janeiro: Their dilemmas and paradoxes). Rio de Janeiro: Polícia Militar do Estado do Rio de Janeiro.

Lopes, J. R. L. 1989. A função política do poder judiciário (The political function of the judicial branch). In *Direito e justiça: A função social do judiciário* (Law and justice: The social function of the judiciary), ed. J. E. Faria. São Paulo: Ática.

Lovell, P. 1987. The myth of racial equality: A study of race and mortality in Northeast Brazil. *Latinamericanist* (University of Florida) 22, no. 2.

———. 1989. Racial inequality and the Brazilian labor market. Ph.D. diss., University of Florida, Gainesville.

———. 1992. *The Economics of Race, Class, and Gender in Brazil.* Mimeographed.

———. 1993. Raça, classe, gênero, e discriminação salarial no Brasil. *Estudos Afro-Asiáticos* 22:85–98.

Macedo, C. 1977. *A reprodução da desigualdade.* São Paulo: Hucitec.

Machado de Castro, M. M. 1993. Raça e comportamento político. *Dados* 36, no. 3: 469–91.

Maggie, Y. 1989a. *Catálogo: Centenário da abolição.* Rio de Janeiro: Federal University of Rio de Janeiro.

———. 1989b. Cor, hierarquia, e sistema de classificação: A diferença fora do lugar. In *Catálogo: Centenário de abolição.* Rio de Janeiro: Universidade Federal do Rio de Janeiro/Núcleo da Cor.

———. 1991. *A ilusão do concreto: Análise do sistema de classificação racial no Brasil.* Rio de Janeiro: Universidade Federal do Rio de Janeiro. (Tese para concurso de professor titular.)

———. 1996. "Aqueles a quem foi negada a cor do dia": As categorias cor e raça na cultura Brasileira. *Raça, Ciência e Sociedade.* Rio de Janeiro: Editora Fiocruz.

Maggie, Y., and K. S. Mello. 1988. O que se cala quando se fala do negro in Brasil. Rio de Janeiro. Mimeographed.

Maio, M. C. 1993. Negros e judeus no Rio de Janeiro: Um ensaio de movimento pelos direitos civis. *Estudos Afro-Asiáticos* 25:161–88.

Mare, R. 1980. Social background and school continuation decisions. *Journal of the American Statistical Association* 75:195–305.

Martinez-Alier, V. 1973. Cor como símbolo de classificação social. *Revista de História* (Universidade de São Paulo) 96 (October–December): 453–72.

Martins, J. de S. 1984. *A militarização da questão agrária* (The militarization of the agrarian issue). Petrópolis: Vozes.

Martins, S. da S. 1996. Ação afirmativa e desigualdade racial no Brasil. *Estudos Feministas* (IFCS/UFRJ-PPCIS/UERJ) 4, no. 1: 206.

Marx, A. W. 1998. *Making race and nations: A comparison of South Africa, the United States, and Brazil.* New York: Cambridge University Press.

Masters, S. 1975. *Black-white income differentials.* New York: Seminar.

Maués, M. A. 1991, Da "branca senhora" ao "negro herói": A trajetória de um discurso racial. *Estudos Afro-Asiáticos* 25:161–88.

Mello, C. A. B. de. 1993. *Conteúdo jurídico do princípio da igualdade.* São Paulo: Malheiros.

Melo, C., and R. C. F. Coelho, eds. *Educação e Discriminação dos negros.* Belo Horizonte: Instituto de Recursos Humanos João Pinheiro.

Metcalf, A. 1990. A família escrava no Brasil colonial: Um estudo de caso em São Paulo. *História e população: Estudos sobre a América Latina,* ed. S. O. Nadalin, M. L. Marcílio, and A. P. Balhana. São Paulo: ABEP/IUSSP/CELADE.

Ministério do Trabalho, Ministério da Justiça, e Organização Internacional do Trabalho [Ministry of Labor, Ministry of Justice, and the International Labour Organisation]. 1996. Encontro Tripartite sobre Implementação de Políticas Voltadas à Diversidade. Relatório, São Paulo (24–25 October): 71–78.

Mitchell, M. 1977. Racial consciousness and the political attitudes and behavior of blacks in São Paulo. Ph.D. diss., Indiana University.

Monteiro, H. 1991. O ressurgimento do movimento negro no Rio de Janeiro na década de 70. Master's thesis, Universidade Federal do Rio de Janeiro, Rio de Janeiro.

Morales, A. 1988. O afoxé Filhos de Gandhi pede paz. In *Escravidão e invenção da liberdade: Estudos sobre o negro no Brasil,* ed. J. Reis. São Paulo: Brasiliense.

———. 1991. Blocos negros em Salvador: Reelaboração cultural e símbolos de baianidade. *Caderno do CRH,* Supplement: 72–92.

Morell, M. G. G. 1994. Anticoncepção em São Paulo em 1986: Prevalência e características. In *A fecundidade da mulher paulista* (Informe Demográfico, no. 25). São Paulo: Fundação SEADE.

Morris, T. 1989. *Crime and criminal justice since 1945.* London: Institute of Contemporary British History; Basil Blackwell.

Motta, A., and R. C. dos Santos. 1994. Questão racial e política: Experiências em políticas públicas. São Paulo: CEBRAP.

Moura, C. 1980. Organizações negras. In *São Paulo: O povo em movimento,* ed. P. Singer and V. Brant. São Paulo: CEBRAP.

———. 1983. Brasil: As raízes do protesto negro. São Paulo: Global.

Müller, R. G. 1988. Identidade e cidadania: O teatro experimental do negro. *Dionysos* 28:11–52.

Munanga, K. 1986. *Negritude: Usos e sentidos.* São Paulo: Atica.

Nascimento, M. E. 1989. A estratégia da desigualdade: O movimento negro dos anos 70. Master's thesis, Pontifícia Universidade Católica, São Paulo.

Negrão, E. V. 1987. A discriminação racial em livros didáticos e infanto-juvenis. In Rosemberg and Pinto, *Cadernos de Pesquisa* 63 (November): 86–87. São Paulo: Fundação Carlos Chagas.

———. 1987b. História e histórias da literatura infantil brasileira. São Paulo: Fundação Carlos Chagas. Mimeographed.

Negrão, E. V., and T. Amado. 1989. A imagem da mulher no livro didático: Estado da arte. *Textos* (Fundação Carlos Chagas, São Paulo) 2.

Neumann, F. 1964. *The democratic and the authoritarian state: Essays in political and legal theory.* New York: The Free Press of Glencoe.

Neves, M. 1996. Estado democrático de direito e discriminação positiva: Um desafio para o Brasil. Paper presented to the International Conference on Multiculturalismo e racismo: O papel da ação afirmativa nos estados democráticos contemporâneos, 2–4 July, Ministério da Justiça (Ministry of Justice) do Brasil, Brasília.

Nobles, M. 1995. "Responding with good sense": The politics of race and censuses in contemporary Brazil. Ph.D. dissertation, Yale University.

Nogueira, O. 1955. *Tanto preto quanto branco: Estudos de relações raciais*. São Paulo: T. A. Queiroz.

———. 1995 (1954). Preconceito racial de marca e preconceito racial de origem (Racial prejudice of feature and racial prejudice of origin). *Annals of the 31st International Congress of Americanists* 1, São Paulo.

O Alfinete. 1918. Na terra do preconceito. 22 September, p. i. Cited in Andrews 1991, 139.

O'Donnell, G. 1984. Democracia en la Argentina: Micro e macro (Democracy in Argentina: Micro and macro). In *Proceso, crisis, y la transición democrática* (Trial, crisis, and the democratic transition), ed. O. Oszlak. Buenos Aires: Centro Editorial de América Latina.

———. 1986. *Contrapontos: Autoritarismo e democratização* (Counterpoints: Authoritarianism and democratization). São Paulo: Vértice.

———. 1987. *Reflexões sobre os estados burocrático-militares* (Reflections on bureaucratic-military states). São Paulo: Vértice; Editora Revista dos Tribunais.

Oliveira, C. 1991. O negro e o poder: Os negros candidatos a vereador, em 1988. *Caderno CRH Suplemento.* Salvador: Factor.

Oliviera, I. M. 1994. *Preconceitos e autoconceito: Identidade e interação na sala de aula.* São Paulo: Papirus.

Oliveira, L., R. M. Porcaro, and T. C. Araújo. 1983. *O lugar do negro na força de trabalho.* Rio de Janeiro: IBGE.

———. 1987a. Repensando o lugar da mulher negra (Rethinking the place of the black woman). *Estudos Afro-Asiáticos* (Rio de Janeiro) 13:87–109.

———. 1987b. Efeitos da crise no mercado de trabalho urbano e reprodução da desigualdade racial (Effects of the crisis in the urban labor market and reproduction of racial inequalities). *Estudos Afro-Asiáticos* (Rio de Janeiro) 14:98–107.

Oliveira e Oliveira, E. 1974. O mulato, um obstáculo epistemológico. *Argumento* (Rio de Janeiro) 1, no. 3 (January): 65–73.

Os números da cor. 1996. *Boletim estatístico sobre a situação sócio-econômica dos grupos de cor no Brasil e em suas regiões* (Rio de Janeiro: Centro de Estudos Afro-Asiáticos) 4 (October).

Pacheco, M. de P. T. 1987. A questão da cor nas relações de um grupo baixa renda. *Estudos Afro-Asiáticos* (Rio de Janeiro) 14:85–97.

Page, J. A. 1995. *The Brazilians.* New York: Addison Wesley.

Paixão, A. L. 1982. A organização policial numa área metropolitana (The police organization in a metropolitan area). *Dados* (Revista de Ciências Sociais, Rio de Janeiro) 25, no. 1: 63–85.

———. 1983. Crime e criminosos em Belo Horizonte 1932–1978 (Crime and criminals in Belo Horizonte 1932–1978. In *Crime, violência, e poder* (Crime, violence, and power), ed. P. S. Pinheiro. São Paulo: Brasiliense.

———. 1986. Políticas públicas de controle do crime e estatísticas oficiais de criminalidade: Notas preliminares (Public policies of crime control and official crime statistics: Preliminary notes). Belo Horizonte. Mimeographed.

———. 1988. Crime, controle social, e consolidação da democracia (Crime, social control, and consolidation of democracy). In *A democracia no Brasil: Dilemas e perspectivas* (Democracy in Brazil: Dilemmas and perspectives), ed. F. W. Reis and G. O'Donnell. São Paulo: Vértice; Editora Revista dos Tribunais.

Pastore, J. 1979. *Desigualdade e Mobilidade Social no Brasil.* São Paulo: EDUSP.

Paulston, R. 1993. Mapping ways of seeing in educational studies. *La Educación* 114:1–18.

Pereira, J. B. B. 1967. *Cor, mobilidade, e profissão: O negro e o rádio de São Paulo* (Color, mobility, and profession: Blacks and radio in São Paulo). São Paulo: Pioneira.

———. 1982. Aspectos do comportamento político do negros em São Paulo. *Ciencia e Cultura* 34:1286–94.

Petchesky, R. 1990. *Abortion and women's choice: The state, sexuality, and reproductive freedom.* 2d ed. Boston: Northeastern University Press.

Phillips, A. 1993. *Democracy and difference.* University Park: Pennsylvania State University Press.

Pierson, D. 1942 [1974]. *Negroes in Brazil: A study in race contact.* Carbondale: University of Illinois Press.

———. 1951. *Cruz das Almas: A Brazilian village.* Washington: Smithsonian Institute.

———. 1955. Race relations in Portuguese America. In *Race relations in world perspective,* ed. A. Lind. Honolulu: University of Hawaii Press.

———. 1967. *Negros in Brazil: A study of race contact in Bahia.* Chicago: University of Chicago Press.

Pinheiro, P. S. 1982. Polícia e crise política: O caso das Polícias Militares (Police and political crisis: The case of the military police forces). In P. S. Pinheiro et al., *A violência brasileira* (Brazilian violence). São Paulo: Brasiliense.

———. 1984. *Escritos indignados* (Indignant writings). São Paulo: Brasiliense.

———. 1991. Autoritarismo e transição. *Revista USP* (São Paulo) 9 (March–May): 45–56.

Pinto, R. 1990. Movimento negro e etnicidade. *Estudos Afro-Asiáticos* (Rio de Janeiro) 19: 109–24.

———. 1993. *O movimento negro em São Paulo: Luta e identidade.* Master's thesis, Universidade de São Paulo.

———. n.d. *Problemas subjacentes ao processo de coleta da cor da população brasileira.* São Paulo: Fundação Carlos Chagas. Mimeographed.

Piven, F. F., and R. A. Cloward. 1979. *Poor people's movement.* New York: Vintage Books.

Piza, E. 1990. Da cozinha para o mundo: Uma nova personagem feminina negra na literatura juvenil. Pontifícia Universidade Católica, São Paulo. Mimeographed.

Porcaro, R. M. 1988. Desigualdade racial e segmentação do mercado de trabalho (Racial inequality and segmentation of the labor market). *Estudos Afro-Asiáticos* 15:171–207.

Porcaro, R., and Araújo, T. C. N. 1988. Mudanças na divisão social do trabalho e (re)produção da desigualdade racial. *São Paulo em Perspectiva* (Revista da Fundação SEADE, São Paulo) 2, no. 2 (April/June).

Portes, A., and K. Wilson. 1976. Black-white differences in educational attainment. *American Sociological Review* 41:414–31.

Prandi, R. 1996. Raça e voto na eleição presidencial de 1994, *Estudos Afro-Asiáticos* (Rio de Janeiro) 30 (December): 75.

Queiroz, R. de. 1968. Carta aberta ao ministro Jarbas Passarinho. *Diário de Notícias* (Salvador) 10–11 November, 4.

Queiroz, S. R. R. 1977. *Escravidão negra em São Paulo: Um estudo das tensões provocados pelo escravismo no século XIX.* Rio de Janeiro.

Rabinow, P., ed. 1984. *The Foucault reader: An introduction to Foucault's thought.* London: Penguin.

Rama, G. W. 1989. Estrutura social e educação: Presença de raças e grupos sociais na escola. Cadernos de Pesquisa (São Paulo) 69 (May): 3–96.

Randall, V. 1982. *Women and politics.* New York: St. Martin's Press.

Rawls, J. 1971. *A theory of justice.* Cambridge: Harvard University Press.

Reichmann, R. 1995. Women organize to fight gender discrimination. *NACLA Report on the Americas* 28, no. 6 (May/June): 40–41.

———. 1995. Brazil's denial of race. *NACLA Report on the Americas* 28, no. 6 (May/June): 35–45.

———. 1997. Equality and difference: Identity politics in Brazil. Working Paper No. 16. Chicano/Latino Research Center, University of California at Santa Cruz.

———. Forthcoming. *Difference and equality: Identity politics in Brazil.* Oxford: Berg Publishers.

Ramos, G. 1954. O problema do negro na sociedade Brasileira. *Cadernos de Nosso Tempo* 2:207–15.

Reis, F. W., and G. O'Donnell, eds. 1988. *A democracia no Brasil: Dilemas e perspectivas* (Democracy in Brazil: Dilemmas and perspectives). São Paulo: Vértice/Editora Revista dos Tribunais.

Reis, J. J., and Silva, E. 1989. *Negociação e conflito.* São Paulo: Companhia das Letras.

Reiss Jr., A. J., 1974. Discretionary justice. In *Handbook of criminology,* ed. D. Glaser. Chicago: Rand-McNally.

———. 1976. Settling the frontiers of a pioneer in American criminology: Henry McKay. In *Delinquency, crime, and society,* ed. J. F. Short Jr. Chicago: University of Chicago Press.

Report to the UN Commission on Human Rights. 1996.

Rex, J. 1988. *Raça e Etnia* (Race and ethnicity). Lisbon: Editorial Estampa.

Rezende, C. B. 1995. Empregadas domésticas e seus patrões: Amizade com desigualdade social e racial. Paper presented to the nineteenth annual meeting of the Associação Nacional de Pós-Graduação e Pesquisa em Ciência Sociais (ANPOCS).

Ribeiro, C. A. C., Jr. 1993. Cor e criminalidade: Estudo e análise da Justiça no Rio de Janeiro. Master's thesis, IFCH/UFRJ, Rio de Janeiro.

Ribeiro, F. R. 1996. Diversity and assimilation in Brazil. In *Now that we are free: Coloured communities in a democratic South Africa,* ed. W. James, D. Caliguire, and K. Cullinan. Boulder, Colo.: Lynne Rienner.

Rios, A. M. L. 1990. Família negra no pós-abolição (Paraíba do Sul, 1889–1920). VII Encontro Nacional de Estudos Populacionais, *ABEP Annals* (Belo Horizonte) 2:211–40.

Risério, A. 1981. *Carnaval Ijexá: Notas sobre afoxés e blocos no novo carnaval afrobaiano.* Salvador: Corrupio.

Robert, P. H., et al. 1994. *Les comptes du crime: Les délinquances en France et leurs mesurs.* Paris: L'Harmattan.

Rocha, E. A. 1991. Processo de trabalho e desgaste operário: Um estudo de caso (Labor process and worker expense: A case study). Ph.D. diss., Federal University of Bahia, Salvador.

Rodrigues, A. M. 1984. *Samba negro, espoliação branca.* São Paulo: Hucitec.

Rodriguez, G., and J. N. Hobcraft. 1980. Illustrative analysis: Life table analysis of birth intervals in Colombia. *Scientific Reports: World Fertility Survey (WFS)* 16 (May).

Rodriguez, R. N. 1945. *Os Africanos no Brasil,* 3d ed. São Paulo: Companhia Editôra Nacional.

Roland, E. 1996. Women's health needs in underserved communities. Paper presented to the 336th session of the Salzburg Seminar, Meeting the Health Needs of Underserved Communities, April, sponsored by the Kellogg Foundation.

Roosevelt, T. 1914. *Outlook* 106, 21 February, 409–11. Quoted in D. Hellwig, ed., *African American reflections on Brazil's racial Paradise,* 31–33. Philadelphia: Temple University Press, 1992.

Rosaldo, R. 1989. *Culture and truth: The remaking of social analysis.* Boston: Beacon Press.

Rosemberg, F. 1987. Instrução, rendimento, discriminação racial e de gênero. *Revista de Estudos Pedagógicos* (Brasília) 68, no. 159 (May–August): 324–55.

———. 1990. Segregação espacial na escola paulista. *Estudos Afro-Asiáticos* (Rio de Janeiro) 19:97–107.

———. 1991. Raça e educação inicial. *Cadernos de Pesquisa* (São Paulo) 77:25–34.

Rosemberg, F., and R. P. Pinto, eds. 1987. Raça negra e educação. *Cadernos de Pesquisa* 63 (November). Fundação Carlos Chagas, São Paulo.

Rosemberg, F., R. P. Pinto, and E. V. Negrão. 1986. A situação educacional de negros (pretos e pardos). Research report, Department of Educational Research, Fundação Carlos Chagas, São Paulo.

Rufino dos Santos, J. 1988. IPCN e Cacique de Ramos: Dois exemplos de movimento negro no Rio de Janeiro. *Comunicações do ISER* 28:5–20.

Sá Barreto, V. 1992. Blacks who do well: Labor market, mobility, and racial inequalities. Paper presented to the sixteenth annual meeting of the Associação Nacional de Pós-Graduação e Pesquisa em Ciência Sociais (ANPOCS), 15–18 October, Caxambu, Brazil.

———. 1993. Cor tem lugar: A estrutura ocupacional na RMS. *Revista Força de Trabalho* 10, no. 1: 61–65.

Sahlins, M. 1979. *Cultura e razão prática.* Rio de Janeiro: Zahar.

Samara, E. M. 1988. A família negra no Brasil: Escravos e libertos. VI Encontro Nacional de Estudos Populacionais, *ABEP Annals* (Belo Horizonte) 3:39–58.

———. 1989. *As mulheres, o poder e a família: São Paulo, Século XIX.* São Paulo: Editora Marco Zero e Secretaria de Estado e Cultura de São Paulo.

Sandoval, S. 1991. Los mecanismos de discriminación racial en el mercado de trabajo en el caso del Brasil urbano (Mechanisms of racial discrimination in the labor market in the case of urban Brazil). *Estudos Sociológicos* 9, no. 25: 35–60.

Sansone, L. 1992. Cor, classe, e modernidade em duas áreas da Bahia: Algumas primeiras impressões (Color, class, and modernity in two areas of Bahia: Some first impressions). *Estudos Afro-Asiáticos* (Rio de Janeiro) 23:143–73.

———. 1993. Pai preto, filho negro: Trabalho, cor, e diferenças de geração. *Estudos Afro-Asiáticos* 25:73–98.

Santos, B. De S. 1995. *Toward a new common sense: Law, science, and politics in the paradigmatic transition.* New York: Routledge.

Santos, G. G. 1992. Partidos políticos e etnia negra. Master's thesis, Pontifíca Universidade Católica, São Paulo.

Santos, M. 1991. 13 de maio, 20 de novembro: Uma descrição da construção de símbolos raciais e nacionais. Master's thesis, Universidade Federal do Rio de Janeiro, Rio de Janeiro.

Santos, P. R. dos. 1986. *Instituições Afro-Brasileiras*. Rio de Janeiro: Centro de Estudos Afro-Asiaticos.

Santos, W. G. 1981. Reflexões sobre a questão do liberalismo: Um argumento provisório (Reflections on the issue of liberalism: A conditional argument). In *Direito, cidadania e participação* (The law, citizenship, and participation), ed. B. Lamounier et al. São Paulo: T. A. Queiroz.

Schwarcz, L. M. 1987. *Retrato em branco e negro: Jornais, escravos, e cidadãos em São Paulo no final do século XIX* (Portrait in black and white: Newspapers, slaves, and citizens in São Paulo at the end of the nineteenth century). São Paulo: Companhia das Letras.

———. 1993. *O espetáculo das raças: Cientistas, instituições e questão racial no Brasil, 1870–1930*. São Paulo: Campanhia das Letras.

Schwartzman, S., H. M. B. Homeny, and V. M. R. Costa. 1984. *Tempos de Capanema*. São Paulo: EDUSP; Rio de Janeiro: Paz e Terra.

SEADE. 1992. *Pesquisa de condição de vida na Região Metropolitana de São Paulo*. São Paulo: SEADE.

Seiferth, G. 1989. A estratégia do branqueamento. *Ciência Hoje* 5, no. 25: 54–61.

———. 1991. Os paradoxos da miscigenção: Observação sobre o tema imigração e raça no Brasil. *Estudos Afro-Asiáticos* (Rio de Janeiro) 20:165–85.

Sellin, T. 1928. The negro criminal: A statistical note. *Annals of the American Academy of Political and Social Science* 140:52–64.

Serva, M. P. 1923. *A virilisação da raça*. São Paulo: Companhia Melhoramentos de São Paulo.

Sewell, S., and R. Hauser. 1972. Causes and consequences of higher education: Models of the status attainment process. *American Journal of Agricultural Economics* 54:851–61.

———. 1975. *Education, occupation, and earnings: Achievement in the early career*. New York: Academic.

Shaw, C. R., and D. H. McKay. 1931. Social factors in juvenile delinquency: A study of the community, the family, and the gang in relation to delinquent behavior. In *Report of the Causes of Crime* 2, no. 3, produced by the National Commission on Law Observance and Enforcement. Washington, D. C.: Government Printing Office.

Silberman, C. 1978. *Criminal justice, criminal violence*. New York: Random House.

Silva, A. 1992. Los Angeles ou Zululândia. *Jornal do Brasil* (25 October): 29.

Silva, A. C. 1988. O estereótipo e o preconceito em relação ao negro no livro de comunicação e expressão de primeiro grau, nível um. Master's thesis, Federal University of Bahia.

Silva, J. C. 1988. Histórias de lutas negras: Memórias do surgimento do movimento negro na Bahia. In *Escravidão e invenção da liberdade*, ed. J. Reis. São Paulo: Editorial Brasiliense.

Silva, L. A., and A. Ziccardi. 1983. Notas para uma discussão sobre os movimentos sociais urbanos. In *Movimentos sociais urbanos, minorias étnicas e outros estudos*. Brasília: ANPOCS.

Silva, M. B. N. 1984. *Sistema de casamento no Brasil colonial*. São Paulo: Editora da Universidade de São Paulo.

Silva, N. V. 1973. Posição social das ocus. Mimeographed.

———. 1978. White-nonwhite income differentials: Brazil. Ph.D. diss., University of Michigan, Ann Arbor.

———. 1980a. O preço da cor: Diferenças raciais na distribuição da renda no Brasil (The price of color: Racial differences in income distribution in Brazil). *Pesquisa e Planejamento Econômico* 10:21–44.

———. 1980b. O viés das variáveis omitidas e o viés da crítica. *Pesquisa e Planejamento Económico* 10:1007–12.

———. 1985. Updating the cost of not being white in Brazil. In *Race, Class, and Power in Brasil,* ed. P.-M. Fontaine. Los Angeles: UCLA Center for Afro-American Studies.

———. 1992a. A sociedade. In *Sociedade, estado, e partidos na atualidade brasileira,* ed. H. Jaguaribe. Rio de Janeiro: Paz e Terra.

———. 1992b. Distância social o casamento inter-racial no Brasil. In *Relações raciais no Brasil contemporâneo,* ed. C. A. Hasenbalg and N. V. Silva. Rio de Janeiro: Rio Fundo Editora, IUPERJ.

———. 1994. Uma nota sobre "raça social" no Brasil. *Estudos Afro-Asiáticos* (Rio de Janeiro) 26:67–80.

———. 1996. Morenidade: modo de usar. *Estudos Afro-Asiáticos* 30 (December): 91.

Silva, N. V., and C. Hasenbalg. 1992. Família, cor, e acesso à escola no Brasil. *Relatórios de pesquisa e desenvolvimento* (Rio de Janeiro: LNCC/CNPq): 15.

———. 1992. *Relações racias no Brasil contemporâneo.* Rio de Janeiro: Rio Fundo Editora.

Silva, N. V., and D. Roditi. 1988. Et plus ça change…tendências históricas da fluidez social no Brasil. In *Estructura Social, Mobilidade, e Raça,* ed. C. Hasenbalg and N. V. Silva. Rio de Janeiro: Editorial Vértice/IUPERJ.

Silva, P. C. 1993. Negros à luz dos fornos: Representações do trabalho e da cor entre metalúrgicos da moderna indústria bahiana (Blacks in the light of the furnaces: Representations of work and color among metalworkers of modern Bahian industry). Master's thesis, Federal University of Bahia, Salvador.

Silva Jr., H. 1996. Adivinhe quem veio para o jantar. *PT Notícias* 13 (26 August): 4.

Simon, W., et al. 1976. Continuity in delinquency research. In *Delinquency, crime, and society,* ed. J. F. Short Jr. Chicago: University of Chicago Press.

Singer, P. 1996. Pobreza e desigualdade social: Perfil e opções políticas. In *Brasil e África do Sul: Uma comparação,* ed. B. Lamounier. São Paulo: IDESP.

Skidmore, T. E. 1974. *Black into white: Race and nationality in Brazilian thought.* New York: Oxford University Press. (Brazilian: *Preto no branco: raça e nacionalidade no pensamento brasileiro.* Rio de Janeiro: Paz e Terra, 1976).

———. 1991. Fato e mito: Descobrindo um problema racial no Brasil (Fact and myth: Discovering a racial problem in Brazil). *Cadernos de Pesquisa* (São Paulo: Fundação Carlos Chagas) 79:5–16.

———. 1992. Fact and myth: Discovering a racial problem in Brazil. Working Paper #173 (April), Kellogg Institute, University of Notre Dame, Notre Dame, Indiana.

Slenes, R. 1987. Padrões de casamento e estabilidade familiar numa comunidade escrava (Campinas, Século XIX). *Estudos Economicos* (Universidade de São Paulo) 17, no. 2.

———. 1988. Lares negros, olhares brancos: Histórias da família escrava no século XIX. *Revista Brasileira de História* (São Paulo) 8, no. 16: 189–203.

Sniderman, P., and Piazza, T. 1993. *The scar of race.* Cambridge: Belknap Press/Harvard University.

Soares, G., and N. V. Silva. 1987. Urbanization, race, and class in Brazilian politics. *Latin American Research Review* 22, no. 2: 155–76.

Souza-Lobo, E. 1991. O gênero da representação: Movimento de mulheres e representação política no Brasil (1980–1990). *Revista Brasileira de Ciencias Sociais* 17:8–14.

State of São Paulo. 1993. *Contagem de crianças e adolescentes em situação de rua na Cidade de São Paulo.* São Paulo: Secretaria da Criança, Familia e Bem-Estar Social.

Stepan, A., ed. 1988. *Democratizando o Brasil* (Democratizing Brazil). Rio de Janeiro: Paz e Terra.

Stepan, N. L. 1991. *The hour of eugenics: Race, gender, and nation in Latin America.* Ithaca: Cornell University Press.

Stolcke, V. 1982. A família que não é sagrada (Sistemas de trabalho e estrutura familiar: O caso das fazendas de café em São Paulo). In *Colcha de Retalhos: Estudos sobre a família no Brasil.* São Paulo: Editora Brasiliense.

———. 1991. Sexo está para gênero assim como raça esta para etnicidade? *Estudos Afro-Asiáticos* (Rio de Janeiro) 20:101–20.

Stolzenberg, R. 1973. Occupational differences in wage discrimination against black men. Ph.D. diss., University of Michigan, Ann Arbor.

———. 1975. Occupations, labor markets, and the process of wage attainment. *American Sociological Review* 40(5): 645–65.

Tabak, F. 1987. *Perfil da vereadora brasileira.* Rio de Janeiro: Pontifícia Universidade Católica do Rio de Janeiro.

Tabak, F., and M. Toscano. 1982. *Mulher e política.* Rio de Janeiro: Paz e Terra.

Telles, E. E. 1995. Who are the Morenas? *Social Forces* 73, no. 4: 1609–11.

———. 1994. Industrialização e desigualdade racial no emprego: O exemplo Brasileiro. *Estudos Afro-Asiáticos* 26:21–51.

———. 1996. Início no Brasil e fim no EUA? *Estudos Feministas* (IFCS/UFRJ–PPCIS/UERJ) 4, no. 1: 194.

Thurow, L. 1967. The occupational distribution of the returns to educational experience for whites and negros. *Proceedings of the Social Statistics Section of the American Statistical Association.* Washington: American Statistical Association.

Troyano, A. A., et al. 1985. A necessidade de uma nova conceituação de emprego: A pesquisa Fundação SEADE/DIEESE (The need for a new concept of employment and unemployment: The research of Fundação SEADE/Dieese). *São Paulo em Perspectiva* (Revista da Fundação SEADE, São Paulo) 1, no. 10: 2–6.

Turner, J. M. 1985. Brown into black: Changing racial attitudes of Afro-Brazilian university students. In *Race, class, and power in Brazil,* ed. P.-M. Fontaine. Los Angeles: UCLA Center for Afro-American Studies.

Vachet, A. 1970. *L'ideologie liberale: L'individu et sa propriété* (Liberal ideology: The individual and his/her property). Paris: Anthropos.

Valente, A. L. 1986. *Política e relações raciais: Os negros e as eleições paulistas de 1982.* São Paulo: FFLCH/USP.

Valle, A. 1987. *Partidos políticos.* Rio de Janeiro: Partido Liberal.

Velho, O. 1984. As bruxas soltas e o fantasma do funcionalismo. *Dados* 28, no. 3.

Vianna, F. J. de Oliveira. 1934. *Raça e assimilação.* São Paulo: Companhia Editora Nacional.

Vieira, R. M. 1995. Black resistance in Brazil: A matter of necessity. In *Racism and anti-racism in world perspective*, ed. B. P. Bowser. Thousand Oaks, Calif.: Sage.

———. 1995. Brazil. In *No longer invisible: Afro-Latin Americans today.* London: Minority Rights Publications.

Wagley, C. 1952. *Race and class in rural Brazil.* New York: Columbia University Press.

Weiner, N. A., and M. Wolfgang. 1985. The extent and character of violent crime in America. In *American violence and public policy: An update of the National Commission on the Causes and Prevention of Violence,* ed. L. A. Curtis. New Haven: Yale University Press.

Williams, P. 1995. *The rooster's egg.* Cambridge: Harvard University Press.

Wilson, W. J. 1989. The underclass: Issues, perspectives, and public policy. *Annals of the American Academy of Political and Social Science* 501 (January).

Winant, H. 1992. Rethinking race in Brazil. *Journal of Latin American Studies* 24:173–92.

———. 1994. *Racial conditions: Politics, theory, comparisons.* Minneapolis: University of Minnesota Press.

Wolfgang, M. E. 1972. *Delinquency in a birth cohort.* Chicago: University of Chicago Press.

Wolfgang, M. E., et al. 1976. Seriousness of crime and police of juvenile justice. In *Delinquency, crime, and society,* ed. J. F. Short Jr. Chicago: University of Chicago Press.

Wood, C. H. 1991. Categorias censitárias e classificações subjetivas de raça no Brasil. In *Desigualdade Racial no Brasil Contemporâneo,* ed. P. A. Lovell. Belo Horizonte: CEDEPLAR/UFMG.

Wood, C. H., and J. A. M. de Carvalho. 1988. *The demography of inequality in Brazil.* Cambridge: Cambridge University Press.

Wood, C. H., and P. Lovell. 1986. Racial inequality and child mortality in Brazil. University of Florida. Mimeographed.

World Bank. 1993. *World development report 1993—Investing in health: World development indicators.* Washington, D.C.: The World Bank.

Wright, K. N. 1987. *The great American crime myth.* New York: Praeger.

Zaluar, A. 1985. *A máquina e a revolta: As organizações populares e o significado da pobreza* (The machine and revolt: Popular organizations and the meaning of poverty). São Paulo: Brasiliense.

———. 1986. Democracia também serve para os pobres? (Does democracy also serve the poor?). *Presença. Revista de Cultura e Política* (Rio de Janeiro) 7:40–43.

———. 1989b. A polícia e a comunidade: Paradoxos da (in)convivência [Police and the community: Paradoxes of (non)coexistence]. *Presença. Política e Cultura* (Rio de Janeiro) 13 (May): 144–53.

———. 1991. Brasil na transição: Cidadãos não vão ao paraíso. *São Paulo em Perspectiva* (Fundação SEADE, São Paulo) 5, no. 1: 19–25.

———. 1993. Urban violence, citizenship, and public policies. *International Journal of Urban and Regional Research* (Oxford/Cambridge) 17, no. 1: 55–66.

ABOUT THE AUTHORS

Sérgio Adorno holds a doctorate in sociology from the University of São Paulo, where he is associate professor of sociology and co-director of the Center for the Study of Violence. Dr. Adorno is also executive secretary of the Brazilian National Association of Graduate Research in the Social Sciences (ANPOCS) and ex-president of the Brazilian Sociology Association (1991–95). He has written and published widely on human rights and the judiciary in Brazil.

Luiz Claudio Barcelos is completing a doctorate in sociology at the University of Pittsburgh. He holds a master's degree in sociology from the University Institute for Research of Rio de Janeiro (Instituto Universitário de Pesquisas do Rio de Janeiro, IUPERJ). Mr. Barcelos has edited a catalogue of Brazilian scholarship on race relations.

Maria Aparecida Silva Bento is a human relations professional and is completing a doctorate in social psychology at the Catholic University of São Paulo. Ms. Bento coordinates research and labor-union education programs at the Center for the Study of Labor Relations and Inequality (CEERT) in São Paulo.

Elza Berquó, demographer, received her doctorate in biostatistics from Columbia University and is coordinator of the Center for Population Studies, State University of Campinas. Dr. Berquó is Brazil's leading analyst of demographic patterns among the African Brazilian population. She is also a senior researcher with the São Paulo social science research institute, CEBRAP, and has published extensively on demographic transitions in Brazil.

Sueli Carneiro is a master's candidate in philosophy at the University of São Paulo. She is founder and vice president of the Geledés Black Women's Institute and coordinates Geledés' SOS Racism program. Ms. Carneiro serves on various editorial boards and is an advisor to the Brazilian Institute for Defense of Citizenship in São Paulo.

Nadya Araújo Castro holds a doctorate from the National Autonomous University of Mexico and is currently a researcher at the São Paulo social science research institute CEBRAP. She is emeritus professor of sociology, Federal University of Bahia. Dr. Castro specializes in the sociology of labor relations in industrial economies undergoing structural transformation.

Caetana Maria Damasceno received a doctorate in social anthropology from the National Museum of the Federal University of Rio de Janeiro. She is currently adjunct professor in the Department of Letters and Social Sciences, Rural Federal University of Rio de Janeiro. Since the 1980s, she has investigated race relations and published articles on this topic from an interdisciplinary perspective. Dr. Damasceno has held research affiliations with several institutions, including the Center for Afro-Asian Studies and Cândido Mendes University. She also works with nongovernmental organizations, evaluating race-based social movements and racism in Brazil.

Ana Maria Goldani holds a doctorate in demography from the University of Texas at Austin. She is professor of sociology and researcher at the Center of Population Studies (NEPO) and the Center of Gender Studies (PAGU), both at the State University of Campinas (UNICAMP). Dr. Goldani specializes in demographic transitions of the family and women's roles in contemporary Brazil.

Antonio Sérgio Alfredo Guimarães holds a doctorate from the University of Wisconsin, Madison, and is professor of sociology, University of São Paulo. Dr. Guimarães specializes in the study of race relations in Brazil, focusing on racism and the construction of racial and national identities.

Carlos Hasenbalg holds a doctorate in sociology from the University of California, Berkeley, and is vice-director of the Center for Afro-Asian

Studies and professor of sociology at the University Institute for Research of Rio de Janeiro (Instituto Universitário de Pesquisas do Rio de Janeiro, IUPERJ). Dr. Hasenbalg has published widely on racial inequality in Brazil.

Cloves Luiz Pereira Oliveira received a master's degree in sociology, with a specialization in Latin American Studies, from the University of Pittsburgh. He is professor of Political Science at the State University of Feira de Santana-Bahia (UEFS) and at the Universidade Faculdades Salvador (UNIFACS). He is also a researcher in the Bahian Program on Color (UFBa/Fundação Ford), where he works on projects on political participation and political-electoral recruitment in Brazil. His areas of interest include electoral behavior, race relations and politics, and government and public policy.

Edith Piza received her doctorate in social psychology from the Catholic University of São Paulo. A specialist on gender, race, and age issues, Dr. Piza is currently postdoctoral visiting researcher at the Psychology Institute, University of São Paulo.

Rebecca Reichmann holds a doctorate in education from Harvard University. She is the co-author of two books and has published numerous articles on race and gender in Brazil and women in development. From 1988 to 1995, Dr. Reichmann lived in Rio de Janeiro, during which time she was a Ford Foundation program officer. From 1995 to 1997, she was a visiting scholar at the Center for Iberian and Latin American Studies, University of California, San Diego, and she is currently vice president of Programs of the San Diego Foundation.

Edna Roland is a psychologist and president of Fala Preta Black Women's Organization in São Paulo. Ms. Roland was a visiting fellow at the Harvard Center for Population and Development Studies in 1998, is a board member of the Brazilian nongovernmental Commission on Citizenship and Reproduction, and is a member of the International Consulting and Working Group of the Comparative Human Relations Initiative, sponsored by the Southern Education Foundation. A cofounder of the Geledés Black Women's Institute, Ms. Roland was coordinator of its Health Program for nine years.

Fúlvia Rosemberg holds a doctorate in psychology from the University of Paris. She is professor of social psychology, Catholic University of

São Paulo, and senior researcher, Carlos Chagas Foundation. Dr. Rosemberg serves as editor of the education journal *Revista Cadernos de Pesquisa*, and she has published widely on child development and gender and race relations.

Nelson do Valle Silva holds a doctorate in sociology from the University of Michigan. He is currently professor at the University Institute for Research of Rio de Janeiro (Instituto Universitário de Pesquisas do Rio de Janeiro, IUPERJ) and senior researcher at the National Laboratory of Scientific Computation (LNCC). Dr. Silva has published widely on demographic trends and racial stratification in Brazilian society.

INDEX

abolitionists, 18 n. 25
Adorno, Sérgio, 31, 153 n. 8
affirmative action
  black movement on, 147–48
  Brazilian efforts for, 20, 35, 144 n. 4
  civil rights and, 148
  color denominations and, 148–50
  debate over, 143–50
  implementation problems of, 148–49
  legality of, 145–47
  racial democracy myth and, 143–45, 149
  reasons for Brazilian opposition to, 31–32, 151
  in United States, 145–46
AFL-CIO (American Federation of Labor and Congress of Industrial Organizations), 120
Afoxé Filhos de Gandhi, 161
Agier, Michel, 163, 230
Aguiar, Neuma, 234
Alencastro, Luis Felipe de, 27, 164
Alvarez, Sonia E., 16 n. 23, 165 n. 19
American Federation of Labor and Congress of Industrial Organizations (AFL-CIO), 120
Anderson, Benedict, 39
Antunes, Ricardo, 119
Araújo, T. C. N., 110, 112
arrastões, 6
assimilationist hypothesis, 67–68, 69

attorneys, 133–34, 133 n. 10, 133–34 n. 11, 136
Azevedo, C. C. M., 40 n. 6
Azevedo, Thales de, 24, 25, 107, 231 n. 4

Bairros, L., 112
Barbosa, W. do N., 221
Barcelos, Luiz Claudio, 10, 27, 32
Barreto, Sá, 173
Barros, Ricardo Paes de, 26, 26 n. 38
Bastide, Roger, 3, 157, 231 n. 4
Bento, Maria Aparecida Silva, 30–31
Bercovich, A., 50–51
Bergman, B., 80
Berquó, Elza
  on black movement, 27
  on color attributions, 50–51
  on culture of sterilization, 33–34, 201
  on ethnic vote, 164
  on population policy, 197
  statistics and, 26 n. 39
Berriel, M. M. A., 156
Birman, Patricia, 234
Birth Control Federation of America, 196
black Americans, 2–3, 2–3 n. 4. See also United States
Black Experimental Theater (Teatro Experimental do Negro) (TEN), 158–59, 161

black movement, 14–20, 27
  on affirmative action, 147–48
  black women's movement and, 224, 226
  as component of contemporary racial
    mobilization, 159 n. 7
  criticism of educational system, 54
  electoral process and, 32
  familial reactions to, 11
  history of, 14–16
  influence on social science research,
    112
  racial democracy myth and, 221
  strategies of, 163
  transnational organization of, 17–20,
    18 n. 25, 23 n. 33, 35
  women's movement and, 220–21, 224–27
  See also names of specific organizations
blacks. See negros
"black soul," 159–60, 161
black women's movement, 224–27
Black Women's Reproductive Health
  research project, 211
Blau, P., 75
Bloco Afro Ilê Aiyê, 160, 161–62
boa aparência, 34, 230, 241–46, 248–49
Bobbio, Norberto, 112
Bogaarts, John, 187, 187 n. 5
Boshi, R., 158 n. 5
Bourdieu, P., 235 n. 8
brancos, definition of, 2 n. 3, 84 n. 4. See also
  whites
brancos da Bahia, 97
brancos da terra, 97
Brandão, Zaia, 53
Brazilian Black Front (Frente Negra
  Brasileira) (FNB), 14, 15, 158
Brazilian Center for Analysis and Planning
  (Centro Brasileiro de Análise e
  Planejamento) (CEBRAP), 211
Brazilian Communist Party (Partido
  Comunista Brasileiro) (PCB), 14
Brazilian Declaration of the Rights of Man
  and the Citizen (1789), 123
Brazilian Democratic Movement Party
  (Partido do Movimento Democrático
  Brasileiro) (PMDB), 15
Brazilian Institute of Geography and
  Statistics (Instituto Brasileiro de
  Geografia e Estatística) (IBGE), 29 n. 43,
  110, 231

Brazilian Popular Party (Partido Popular
  Brasileiro) (PPB), 17
Brazilian Workers' Party (Partido de
  Trabalhadores Brasileiros), 14
bribery, in criminal justice system, 133
Brizola, Leonel, 15, 15 n. 20, 165 n. 18

caboclos, definition of, 41
cafusos, definition of, 41 n. 8
Campaign to Enforce the International
  Labour Organisation (ILO) Convention
  111, 19, 120
capitalist development, equality and, 124,
  233 n. 7
Cardoso, Fernando Henrique
  anti-racial discrimination programs of, 19,
    23 n. 33, 120–21
  on democracy, 165 n. 19
  on diversity, 21–22
  National Human Rights Plan and, 13 n. 17
  racial identification of, 8
  São Paulo school and, 25, 231 n. 4
  speech at conference on Diversity,
    Multiculturalism, and Affirmative
    Action, 20
  on sterilization, 204 n. 5
Cardoso, Ruth, 21
Carlos Chagas Foundation, 54
Carneiro, Sueli
  on Cardoso administration, 20
  on color terminology, 8, 8 n. 11
  on feminist movement, 34
  on race versus class, 112
  on racism and equal legal rights,
    198
Carnival, 4, 162 n. 14, 248 n. 17
Carvalho, Alberto Magno, 26
Carvalho, Edgar, 117
Carvalho, J. A. M. de, 9
Carville, James, 17 n. 24
Castro, Nadya Araújo, 30, 84 n. 3, 173,
  174 n. 7
Catholic Church, 205 n. 5
CEBRAP (Centro Brasileiro de Análise e
  Planejamento) (Brazilian Center for
  Analysis and Planning), 211
CEERT (Centro de Estudos das Relações do
  Trabalho e Desigualdades) (Center for
  the Study of Labor Relations and
  Inequality), 16, 19, 119–20, 120 n. 3

censuses
    color classification in, 37–38, 39, 40–42,
        229 n. 3 (*see also* color denominations)
    color data collection in, 40, 40 n. 7, 42–44,
        110
    head of household self-identification in, 49,
        49 n. 12
    hetero-identification in, 37, 43–44
    interviewers and, 42–43, 44
    methodology for, 42, 50
    nationalities in, 39–40
    1982, 49
    1950, 41–42
    1940, 41
    1990, 110
    1991, 47
    1970, 74
    1920, 41
    pardos in, 40–41
    United Nations' guidelines for, 42
    See also PNAD (Pesquisa Nacional por
        Amostragem de Domicílios)
Center for the Study of Labor Relations and
    Inequality (Centro de Estudos das
    Relações do Trabalho e Desigualdades)
    (CEERT), 16, 19, 119–20, 120 n. 3
Central Única dos Trabalhadores (Central
    Union of Workers) (CUT), 16, 19, 21,
    120
Centro Brasileiro de Análise e Planejamento
    (Brazilian Center for Analysis and
    Planning) (CEBRAP), 211
Centro de Cultura e Arte Negra, 160
Centro de Estudos Afro-Asiáticos, 160
Centro de Estudos das Relações do Trabalho
    e Desigualdades (Center for the Study of
    Labor Relations and Inequality)
    (CEERT), 16, 19, 119–20, 120 n. 3
CGT (Confederação Geral de Trabalhadores)
    (General Confederation of Workers), 17,
    120
Chaia, M. W., 112
children
    color studies of, 50–51, 51 n. 13
    mortality of, 26
    racial bias among, 48
citizenship rights
    black women's, 227
    emergent, 157, 157 n. 3
    obstacles to full, 125–26

Civil Code, 180
Civil Police, 130 n. 7
civil rights, affirmative action and, 148
civil rights movement, in United States, 160
claros, 97
class
    definition of, 236 n. 9
    electoral process and, 172–73, 174
    versus race, 23, 24, 25, 25 n. 36, 26, 29–30,
        112
    social movements and, 157
    See also socioeconomic level
Cloward, R. A., 175
color denominations
    affirmative action and, 148–50
    classifications for, 8–9, 10, 37–38, 50–51,
        107, 200 n. 2, 228, 229 n. 3
    contraception and, 211
    definition of, 83 n. 1
    electoral process and, 170, 171
    in labor market, 96–100
    literature on, 38
    purpose of, 29
    racial democracy myths and, 7–10
    revisions of classifications for, 45
    terminology for, 2 n. 3, 8, 8 n. 11, 11 n. 15,
        38, 47
    See also censuses: color classification in;
        phenotypes; race; *names of specific color
        groups*
Comissão Nacional contra o Racismo
    (National Commission Against Racism),
    120
Commission of Human Rights' Program of
    Action to Combat Racial
    Discrimination, 19–20
communist parties, 14, 171 n. 5
Confederação Geral de Trabalhadores
    (General Confederation of Workers)
    (CGT), 17, 120
Constitution (1988), 146, 193, 198, 219, 221
constitutional law, on racial discrimination,
    140, 198
Contins, Márcia, 147–48
contraception, 203 n. 4
    color and, 211
    educational level and use of, 208, 210–11,
        214–15
    race and, 207–11
    See also reproductive rights; sterilization

Convention 111 (ILO), 19, 120
Coordenadoria do Negro (Municipal
     Department of Black Coordination),
     16
COR da Bahia program, 28 n. 42
Corrêa, M., 128 n. 3
corruption, in criminal justice system, 133
Costa, Emilia Viotti da, 111
Costa, Tereza Cristina Araújo, 42, 43, 45
Council for the Participation and
     Development of the Black Community,
     15 n. 21
crime, potential criminals and, 127
criminal justice system
     acquittal in, 134, 135
     capitalist development and, 124
     confessions in, 132–33
     conviction rates in, 135–36
     corruption in, 133
     costs in, 134
     defendants' rights in, 126, 130–31
     in democracy, 128
     ethnicity and, 126–28
     government promotion of inequality in,
          125
     internationalized crime and, 127
     judges in, 135, 135 n. 13
     methodology for study of, 129–30
     negros' access to, 128, 131–36
     nulla poena sine lege in, 130
     "probable cause" in, 141 n. 2
     procedures in, 130–31, 130 n. 8, 131 n. 9
     public defenders in, 133–34, 133 n. 10,
          136
     racial inequality and, 31–32
     reasons for inequality in, 124
     structure of, 126
     trial outcome in, 135–36
     university-educated criminals and,
          125
     whitening and, 129–30
     whites in, 132–33
     witness presentation in, 134–35, 137
Cross, W., Jr., 48–49, 118
"crowding hypothesis," 80, 81–82
culture of sterilization. See sterilization
Cunha, Manuela Carneiro da, 117, 163
CUT (Central Única dos Trabalhadores)
     (Central Union of Workers), 16, 19, 21,
     120

Damasceno, Caetana Maria, 34, 159 n. 8
Da Matta, Roberto
     on racial conflicts, 5 n. 6, 9–10
     on racial democracy myth, 4, 4 n. 5, 24
     on whitening, 5
Datafolha survey, 5, 8, 11 n. 15, 21
Davis, Angela, 195–96
Davis, D. R., 23 n. 33
Debret, Jean-Baptiste, 4
decomposition technique, 71–72
defamation, 143
Degler, Carl, 25 n. 36
democracy, 128, 165 n. 19. See also racial
     democracy myth
Democratic Workers Party (Partido
     Democrático Trabalhista) (PDT), 14–15,
     171 n. 5
Departamento Intersindical de Estudos
     Sócio-econômicos (State Intersindical
     Department for Socioeconomic Studies)
     (DIEESE), 84 n. 2
Diários Associados, 144
DIEESE (Departamento Intersindical de
     Estudos Sócio-econômicos) (State
     Intersindical Department for
     Socioeconomic Studies), 84 n. 2
difference, 1–2 n. 2, 4, 33, 46
discrimination. See racial discrimination
Diversity, Multiculturalism, and Affirmative
     Action conference, 20
diversity, organizations and, 20, 21–23,
     23 n. 33, 120–21
divorce, 180, 188
Duncan, O. D., 75

"economic-threat hypothesis," 80, 81–82
education
     contraceptive use and level of, 208, 210–11,
          214–15
     familial background and, 74–76, 74 n. 4,
          81
     gap in, 74–75
     labor market and, 90, 92, 93, 95–96, 99–100
     morenos and, 100, 173
     mulatos and, 100
     negros and, 74–75, 92, 173
     pardos and, 30, 54, 55, 57, 60, 63–64, 65
     of political candidates, 168, 173
     pretos and, 30, 54, 55, 57, 60, 63–64, 65, 90,
          100

research on race and, 21–22, 53–54, 63–64, 74
statistics on, 54–55, 60
sterilization and, 210–11
use of contraception and level of, 208, 210–11, 214–15
whites and, 54–55, 57, 61, 63–64, 73, 75, 100, 197
women and, 90, 92, 100, 192
See also overeducation, in labor market; university education
educational system
access to, 57–60, 63–64
black movement criticism of, 54
financial return for schooling in, 70
as form of racism, 21, 29–30
performance inequalities in, 55–57
return to, 75, 81
school drop-out rates in, 61
student advancement through, 54, 58, 60–64, 73, 232
truancy in, 65
elderly, 193
electoral process
black candidates in, 27 n. 40, 32, 164, 168–69, 173–74, 175, 176
candidacy class affiliations in, 172–73, 174
candidacy failures in, 168–69
candidate educational level and, 168, 173
candidate numbers in, 171–72, 171 n. 4
candidate occupations and, 170 n. 3, 172 n. 6, 173–74, 175
candidate profiles in, 176, 177
coalitions in, 171 n. 4
mobilization in, 32
procedures and regulations for, 169 n. 2, 170–72, 171 n. 4
race in, 17, 170, 171, 173–75
research methodology for study of, 169–70
voting patterns in, 164, 175
whites in, 174
women candidates in, 168–69, 172–73, 176, 176 n. 8
elites
Africanness and, 8
color-identification system and, 10
whitening and (see also whitening; whites)
employment mobility, discrimination in. See labor market; workplace

Erundina, Luisa, 16, 17
Estudos Afro-Asiáticos, 12–13
Estudos Feministas, 149
ethnicity, 46–47, 126–28. See also race
eugenics policy, 33, 201–4
experience, income and returns to, 76, 78, 79, 79 n. 5, 81

families
background and education in, 74–76, 74 n. 4, 81
black movement and, 11
careers and, 243
demographic profile of, 182–83
effect of slavery on, 180–81
female-headed, 180, 182–83, 191
instability of black, 181
marriage and, 184 n. 1, 185 n. 3, 187, 191
slavery impact on, 180–81
See also women: life patterns of
Family Status Life Table, 187, 187 n. 5, 190
Feminist Encounters, 219
feminists, 33, 34, 149, 204, 219. See also women's movement
Fernandes, Florestan
affirmative action and, 144 n. 4
on incomplete family, 181
on racial democracy myth, 111, 231, 231 nn. 4 and 5
on racial mobilization, 157
on racial stratification, 24–25
fertility rates, 199, 200–201, 211
Figueiredo, Ângela, 163 n. 16, 246–47, 248
First National Encounter of Black Organizations, 221
First National Encounter of Black Women, 224, 225
Fletcher, Philip R., 57
FNB (Frente Negra Brasileira) (Brazilian Black Front), 14, 15, 158
Fontaine, P.-M., 163–64
Força Sindical, 16–17, 120
forward-survival estimates, 50
France, 135 n. 12
Frazier, E. Franklin, 2–3
French, on racial democracy myth, 3
Frente Negra Brasileira (Brazilian Black Front) (FNB), 14, 15, 158

Freyre, Gilberto
    on *boa aparência*, 248–49
    influence of, 6 n. 6, 24, 40, 181
    on miscegenation, 8, 197, 230, 247–48
    on whitening, 7–8, 247 n. 16
Fry, P., 13, 13 n. 17
Fundação Sistema Estadual de Análise de
    Dados (State Foundation for Data
    Analysis) (SEADE), 45–46, 84 n. 2

Garcia, E. M., 50–51
Geledés Black Women's Institute, 16, 20,
    140
gender
    career performance and, 104–5, 243
    difference and, 1 n. 2
    discrimination and, 157 n. 3
    discrimination as human rights violations,
        19
    income and, 105–6
    labor market and, 88–89, 88–89 n. 9, 101,
        107
    political candidacies and, 168–69
    quotas and, 21
    racial discrimination and, 143
    racial identities and, 32–33
    self-identification and, 50
    workplace discrimination and, 30
    See also women
General Confederation of Workers
    (Confederação Geral de Trabalhadores)
    (CGT), 17, 120
Giacomini, S., 159 n. 8
Ginzberg, Carlo, 247 n. 16
Glèlè-Ahanhanzo, Maurice, 8, 35
Goldani, Ana Maria, 32–33
Grupo de Trabalho André Rebouças, 160
Grupo Evolução, 160
Grupo Negro, 160
Guillaumin, Colette, 153
Guimarães, Antonio Sérgio Alfredo, 30,
    31–32, 84 n. 3

Hanchard, M. G., 163
Harris, Marvin, 9, 38, 231 n. 4
Hasenbalg, Carlos
    on color and children, 50
    on labor market discrimination, 68, 85,
        85 n. 6
    on labor market segregation, 25

on race versus class, 26, 29–30, 112
    on racial mobilization, 164
health, of women, 33, 211. *See also*
    contraception; reproductive rights;
    sterilization
hetero-identification
    in censuses, 43–44
    definition of, 37
    See also identification, self-
hiring. *See* labor market: recruitment
Hirschman, Albert, 39
Hodge, P., 77
Hodge, R., 77
Holanda, Sérgio Buarque de, 113 n. 2
human-capital discrimination, 73–76
human rights violations, race and gender
    discrimination as, 19. *See also* National
    Human Rights Plan (Plano Nacional dos
    Direitos Humanos); United Nations
    Commission on Human Rights
Hutchison, W. H., 231 n. 4

Ianni, Otávio, 25, 111, 231 n. 4
IBGE (Instituto Brasileiro de Geografia e
    Estatística) (Brazilian Institute of
    Geography and Statistics), 29 n. 43, 110,
    231
identification, self-, 8, 9
    in censuses, 42–43, 47
    definition of, 37
    by head of household, 49, 49 n. 12
    men versus women, 50
    as mestizos, 39, 47, 150
    as *morenos*, 9, 10, 51
    as *negros*, 149, 150
    as *pardos*, 9, 39, 150
    in PNAD, 231–32 n. 6
    whitening and, 113
    See also hetero-identification; racial
        democracy myth
identity
    African and Brazilian national, 8, 233
    boa aparência and (*see boa aparência*)
    color and (*see* color denominations)
    development stages of, 48–49
    difference and, 1–2 n. 2, 33, 46
    negro, 161–64, 162 n. 14
    race and, 7 n. 8, 112, 142
    resistance and, 112
    See also gender

IFCS (Institute of Philosophy and Social Sciences), 28 n. 42
illiteracy rates, whites versus blacks, 54–55, 197
ILO (International Labour Organisation), 19, 22, 120
income
  analysis of discrimination in, 78–81, 233
  data and model for study of, 70–73
  gaps in, 76
  gender and, 105–6
  hypotheses for racial discrepencies in, 67–68, 69, 77, 80, 81
  in labor market, 105–6, 110, 115, 116
  models for, 72, 74, 75, 78
  occupation and, 77, 78
  reference population for, 67 n. 1
  regional differences in, 71–72
  returns to experience and, 76, 78, 79, 79 n. 5, 81
  See also "income of" under specific color groups
income-determination model, 70–71
index of dissimilarity, 96–97, 96–97 n. 15
Institute of Philosophy and Social Sciences (IFCS), 28 n. 42
Instituto Brasileiro de Geografia e Estatística (Brazilian Institute of Geography and Statistics) (IBGE), 29 n. 43, 110, 231
Instituto de Pesquisa das Culturas Negras, 160
The Integration of the Negro in a Class Society (Fernandes), 24–25
Inter-American Trade Union Conference for Racial Equality, 19
Inter-American Union Institute on Racial Equality, 120
Interministerial Working Group to Develop Policies Valuing the Black Population, 19
International Labour Organisation (ILO), 19, 22, 120
intra-occupational earning functions, 78

James, E. R., 3 n. 4
Jobim, Nelson, 121
job titles, 115
Jornal do Brasil, 144
judicial system, capitalist development and, 124. See also criminal justice system
juries, 131 n. 9

Klandermans, B., 155, 156

labor federations, 19, 21, 22
labor market
  age at entry into, 89–90
  black versus white niches in, 34, 85 n. 6
  black versus white occupations in, 86, 88
  career perfomance in, 78, 102–5, 232, 233–34
  case studies of, 238–41
  case study methodology for, 236–37, 237 n. 11, 245 n. 15
  color classifications in, 96–100
  education and, 90, 92, 93, 95–96, 99–100
  foreigners in industrial, 85 n. 6
  gender and, 88–89, 88–89 n. 9, 101, 107 (see also women: labor market and)
  Hasenbalg on, 25, 68, 85, 85 n. 6
  hierarchy in, 93, 95, 242 n. 12
  human-capital discrimination in, 73–76
  income in (see income: in labor market)
  occupational and wage discrimination in, 76–80
  occupational segmentation in, 77, 95–96
  overeducation and, 100–102
  patronage-based career trajectories in, 242–43, 242 n. 12
  promotions in, 102–3, 117
  recruitment in, 92–93, 99, 105–6, 116
  slavery impact on, 111
  state-owned versus private companies and, 92–93, 102–4, 106, 107
  sterilization and, 203
  studies of discrimination in, 30–31, 69, 83
  types of racial discrimination in, 25, 68, 73, 73 n. 3, 85, 85 n. 6, 106
  urban, 86
  whitening in, 86, 247
  women in, 92–93, 104–5, 106, 108, 192
  See also boa aparência; "labor market and" under specific color groups; workplace
Law 7716, 140, 141, 143, 198, 221
Law 9263, 204 n. 5
left-wing political parties, 14, 171, 171 n. 5
Lei do Ventre Livre (Law of the Free Womb), 37 n. 1
life expectancy, 188, 190. See also mortality rates
Lima, R. K., 130, 134–35

Lopes, Juarez Brandão, 19 n. 28, 26 n. 39
Lovell, P., 69

Machado de Castro, Monica Mata, 27,
    27 n. 40
machismo, 223
Maggie, Yvonne, 46
Maio, M. C., 164
Malaysia, 39
Maluf, Paulo, 17, 17 n. 24
The Mansions and the Shanties (Sobrados e
    Mucambos) (Freyre), 230, 247–48,
    247 n. 16
Mare, R., 63 n. 4
marriage, 184 n. 1, 185 n. 3, 191
Martins, Sérgio da Silva, 146–47, 149
Marxism, race and, 157
Maués, M. A., 163
McKay, D. H., 127
Mello, Celso Antônio Bandeira de, 146
Mendonça, Rosane Silva Pinto, 26 n. 38
mestizos
    de Queiroz on, 145
    self-identification as, 39, 47, 150
migration hypothesis, 9, 10
Military Police, 130 n. 7
Ministry of Foreign Affairs, 20, 22
Ministry of Health, 200 n. 2
Ministry of Justice, 20, 22
Ministry of Labor, 22, 26
Mink, Louis, 235
miscegenation, 3
    Freyre on, 8, 197, 230, 247–48
    Rufino dos Santos on, 222
    scientific racism and, 7 n. 9
    support for, 7
Mitchell, M., 158 n. 6
MNU (Movimento Negro Unificado)
    (United Black Movement), 160–61,
    163, 220
Mohamed, Leda, 44
Monteiro, H., 163
Montoro, Franco, 15, 15 n. 21, 165 n. 18
Moore, W. H., 23 n. 33
morenos
    definition of, 2 n. 3, 92 n. 11
    education and, 100, 173
    in electoral process, 173, 175
    income of, 105
    labor market and, 92, 93, 96

    occupations of, 174
    self-identification as, 9, 10, 51
    whitening and, 5
mortality rates, 26, 188, 190, 197, 200 n. 2
motherhood
    single, 180, 182–83, 184, 191
    timing of, 185–87, 190–91
Moura, C., 159
Movimento Negro Unificado Contra a
    Discriminação Racial, 160–61
Movimento Negro Unificado (Unified Black
    Movement), 15
Movimento Negro Unificado (United Black
    Movement) (MNU), 160–61, 163,
    220
Movimento Unificado Contra a
    Discriminação Racial, 160–61
mulatos
    Carnival and, 248 n. 17
    definition of, 2 n. 3, 92 n. 11
    education of, 100
    labor market and, 92, 93, 96, 97
"mulatto escape hatch" hypothesis, 68, 69, 81
Müller, R. G., 159
Municipal Department of Black
    Coordination (Coordenadoria do
    Negro), 16

Nabuco, Joaquim, 18 n. 25
Nascimento, Abdias do, 15 n. 20, 144 n. 4,
    158
National Commission Against Racism
    (Comissão Nacional contra o Racismo),
    120
National Commission of Blacks, 16
National Household Survey. *See* PNAD
    (Pesquisa Nacional por Amostragem de
    Domicílios) (National Household
    Survey)
National Human Rights Plan. *See* Plano
    Nacional dos Direitos Humanos
    (National Human Rights Plan)
nationality, race and, 39–40
negão, as derogatory term, 141
Négritude Movement, 158
negros
    access to criminal justice system by, 128,
    131–36
    affirmative action and, 148–49
    conviction rates of, 135–36

crime and, 124, 127, 129
definition of, 2 n. 3, 38 n. 4, 45–46, 84 n. 4, 110 n. 1, 197
educational gap and, 74–75
education and, 92, 173
in electoral process, 32, 164, 168–69, 173–74, 175, 176
family instability of, 181
income of, 67, 69, 110, 115, 116
income study model for, 70–73
labor market and (*see* labor market)
mortality rates of, 188, 197, 200 n. 2
occupational achievement and, 78
versus *pardo* category, 46
political construction of, 11–13
public policy and, 21
resistance and, 117–18 (*see also* black movement)
self-identification as, 149, 150
slurs against, 141
unemployment of, 86 n. 7
NEINB (Nucleus for Interdisciplinary Studies on Black Brazilians), 28 n. 42
Neves, Marcelo, 146
Nobles, Melissa, 4, 11–12, 29 n. 43
Nogueira, Oracy, 107, 231, 231 n. 4
"nonwhite," definition of, 229 n. 1
Núcleo da Cor, 28 n. 42
Nucleus for Interdisciplinary Studies on Black Brazilians (NEINB), 28 n. 42
nulla poena sine lege, 130

O Alfinete, 14
occupations
achievement and, 78, 80, 102, 103
black versus white, 86, 88
classification map of, 234
discrimination in labor market and, 76–80
income and, 77, 78 (*see also* income)
of *morenos,* 174
of political candidates, 170 n. 3, 172 n. 6, 173–74, 175
segmentation of, 77, 95–96
whites and, 86, 88, 88 n. 8, 174
women and, 172 n. 6
Oliveira, Clóves Luiz Pereira, 32
Oliveira, Ivone Martins de, 48
Olodum, 16
opportunistic political parties, 171
overeducation, in labor market, 100–102

Pacheco, M. de P. T., 43 n. 9, 47
Page, Joseph, 4
Paim, Paulo, 18 n. 26
PAISM (Programa de Assistência Integral de Saúde da Mulher) (Program of Integral Assistance to Women's Health), 33, 204
Palmares, Zumbi de, 18
pardos
in censuses, 40–41
definition of, 2 n. 3, 41, 48
education of, 30, 54, 55, 57, 60, 63–64, 65
female-headed families, 182
income of, 67, 69
income study model for, 70–73
labor market and, 34
versus *negro* category, 46
occupational achievement and, 78
in 1984 PNAD study, 185 n. 4
political activity of, 12–13, 13 n. 16
versus *preto* category, 30 n. 44
reproductive rights of, 199
self-identification as, 9, 39, 150
social conditions of, 182
parental background effect, 74–76, 74 n. 4, 81
parenthood, 184, 185. *See also* motherhood: timing of
Partido Comunista Brasileiro (Brazilian Communist Party) (PCB), 14
Partido Democrático Trabalhista (Democratic Workers Party) (PDT), 14–15, 171 n. 5
Partido de Trabalhadores Brasileiros (Brazilian Workers' Party), 14
Partido dos Movimento Democrático Brasileiro (Brazilian Democratic Movement Party) (PMDB), 15
Partido do Trabalhadores (Workers' Party) (PT), 16, 17, 21, 171 n. 5
Partido Popular Brasileiro (Brazilian Popular Party) (PPB), 17
Partido Socialista Brasileiro (Social Progressive Party), 14
Passarinho, Jarbas, 144
Patrocínio, José do, 7
patronage-based career trajectories, in labor market, 242–43, 242 n. 12
Paulston, R., 161 n. 11
PCB (Partido Comunista Brasileiro) (Brazilian Communist Party), 14

PDT (Partido Democrático Trabalhista) (Democratic Workers Party), 14–15, 171 n. 5

PED (Pesquisa de Emprego e Desemprego) (Research on Employment and Unemployment), 84 n. 2

Pesquisa Nacional por Amostragem de Domicílios. *See* PNAD (Pesquisa Nacional por Amostragem de Domicílios) (National Household Survey)

Petchesky, Rosalind, 203–4, 205

phenotypes, 48, 83 n. 1, 107, 108. *See also* race

Phillips, Anne, 1–2 n. 2

Piazza, T., 151

Pierson, Donald, 24, 25, 153 n. 9, 231 n. 4

Pinto, L. A. Costa, 231 n. 4

Pinto, Regina, 46, 158, 158 n. 6, 159, 159 n. 7

Pitta, Celso, 17, 17 n. 24, 27 n. 40

Piven, F. F., 175

Piza, Edith, 29

Plano Nacional dos Direitos Humanos (National Human Rights Plan), 13, 13 n. 17, 19, 20–21, 121, 146

PMDB (Partido do Movimento Democrático Brasileiro) (Brazilian Democratic Movement Party), 15

PNAD (Pesquisa Nacional por Amostragem de Domicílios) (National Household Survey)
  1988, 67, 70–82
  1984, 184, 185 n. 4
  1986, 204, 207
  1982, 55, 60
  1990, 197, 199
  1976, 8 n. 11, 26, 30, 38 n. 5, 69, 231 n. 6

police
  abuses of, 131, 137
  classification of discrimination crimes by, 142–43
  types of, 130 n. 7

political parties, 170–72, 171 n. 5. *See also names of specific parties*

Population Council, 201

Porcaro, R., 110, 112

Portes, A., 73

PPB (Partido Popular Brasileiro) (Brazilian Popular Party), 17

Prandi, Reginaldo, 12–13, 13 n. 16, 27, 27 n. 40

premarital pregnancies, 186–87

pretos
  definition of, 2 n. 3, 41, 48, 92 n. 11
  education of, 30, 54, 55, 57, 60, 63–64, 65, 90, 100
  female-headed families, 182
  income of, 5, 105
  labor market and, 34, 92, 93, 96, 97, 98–99, 106, 107
  overeducation of, 101
  parenthood and, 185
  political activity of, 12–13, 13 n. 16
  promotions of, 103
  reproductive rights of, 199
  self-identification as, 51, 150
  social conditions of, 182
  workplace discrimination against, 88

Principles and Recommendations for National Population Censuses 1959 (United Nations), 42

Programa de Assistência Integral de Saúde da Mulher (Program of Integral Assistance to Women's Health) (PAISM), 33, 204

PT (Partido dos Trabalhadores) (Workers' Party), 16, 17, 21, 171 n. 5

public defenders, in criminal justice system, 133–34, 133 n. 10, 136

Public Ministry, 131

Queiroz, Raquel de, 144–45, 144 n. 4, 149

Queiroz, Sueli Robles de, 111

quotas, gender and, 21

race
  Brazilian scholarship on, 23–28
  versus class, 23, 24, 25, 25 n. 36, 26, 29–30, 112, 157
  contraceptive use and, 207–11
  definition of, 83 n. 1, 155 n. 1
  discrimination as human rights violations, 19
  effect on education, 21–22, 53–54, 63–64, 74 (*see also* educational system)
  electoral process analysis by, 17, 170, 171, 173–75
  future research needs on, 27–28
  identity and, 7 n. 8, 112, 142 (*see also* identification, self-)
  Marxism and, 157

nationality and, 39–40 (*see also* racial democracy myth)
new concepts of, 152–53
practical reason theory of, 233
public policy and, 20–21
social mobility and, 67
social science research literature on, 111–12
statistics on, 26, 26 n. 39, 51
sterilization and, 202 n. 3
as taboo, 221
of trial judges, 135 n. 13
See also color denominations; ethnicity; phenotypes
racial democracy myth, 2–7
affirmative action and, 143–45, 149
black Americans on, 2–3, 2–3 n. 4
black movement and, 221
Brazilians on, 4–7, 111
campaign against, 10, 11
color denominations and, 7–10
Da Matta on, 4, 4 n. 5, 24
denunciations of, 14
Fernandes on, 111, 231, 231 nn. 4 and 5
French on, 3
identity markers and, 142
impact of, 230
literature on, 1, 1 n. 1, 230
reproductive rights and, 196, 197
São Paulo school and, 231
tolerance of, 125, 144–45
See also Freyre, Gilberto; miscegenation
racial discrimination
case studies of, 139–40
constitutional law on, 140, 198
explanation for, 68
hypotheses about, 143
legal definition of, 140–42
police classification of crimes of, 142–43
programs against, 19–23, 23 n. 33, 120–21 (*see also* affirmative action)
status-based discrimination versus, 153
surveys on, 5, 8, 11 n. 15
See also Law 7716
racial mobilization
actors in, 32, 157
challenges to, 157–58
citizenship issues in, 164–65
contemporary, 159–61, 159 n. 7
early twentieth-century, 158–59, 161

identity and cultural issues in, 161–64
ideological issues in, 164–65
press role in, 158, 161 n. 13
theoretical background for, 156–58
racism
in color criteria usage, 45
definition of, 140–42
economic development and, 233 n. 7
educational system as form of, 21, 29–30
equal legal rights and, 198
public sensitivity to, 28–29
scientific, 7, 7 n. 9, 152
segregationist, 140–41
types of, 141
verbalization of, 142–43
workplace (*see* workplace)
Rama, Germán W., 49, 50
Ramos, Guerreiros, 231, 231 n. 4
Randall, V., 168–69
Record of Criminal Occurrence, 130, 130 nn. 5, 7, and 8
Regional Electoral Tribunal of Bahia (Tribunal Regional Eleitoral da Bahia) (TRE), 169–70
Reichmann, Rebecca, 201
relative ages, 185 n. 2
reparations, for slavery, 18, 18 n. 26
reproductive rights
fertility rate, 199, 200–201, 211
of *pardos,* 199
population growth, 198–200
population policy, 197–98, 204
of *pretos,* 199
racial democracy myth and, 196, 197
in United States, 195–96, 205
See also contraception; sterilization
Research on Employment and Unemployment (Pesquisa de Emprego e Desemprego) (PED), 84 n. 2
resistance, definition of, 112, 117–18
Rezende, Claudia B., 242 n. 12
Ribeiro, Darcy, 15 n. 20
Ribeiro, Sérgio Costa, 57
Rocha, Elisa Amélia, 84 n. 3
Roditi, Deborah, 233 n. 7
Roland, Edna, 33
Roosevelt, Theodore, 2
Rosald, Renato, 235
Rosemberg, Fúlvia, 29, 112
Rufino dos Santos, Joel, 221–22

salaries, in labor market. *See* income
Salvador Metropolitan Region, 84
Sandoval, S., 89
Sanger, Margaret, 196
Sansone, Livio, 5, 9
Santana, Luiz Carlos, 147–48
Santos, Jocélio Teles dos, 144 n. 5
Santos, M., 159 n. 8
Santos, T., 112
São Paulo school, 24–25, 25 n. 36, 231, 231 n. 4, 232
school drop-out rates, 61
Schwarcz, Lilia M., 37 n. 1, 248 n. 17
scientific racism, 7, 7 n. 9, 152
SEADE (Fundação Sistema Estadual de Análise de Dados) (State Foundation for Data Analysis), 45–46, 84 n. 2
Seiferth, G., 45
self-identification. *See* identification, self-
Sellin, T., 127
Serva, M. P., 40 n. 6
Shaw, C. R., 127
Silva, Benedita da, 6, 6 n. 7, 17, 27 n. 40, 144 n. 4
Silva, Hédio, Jr., 17
Silva, J. C., 163
Silva, José da, 14–15 n. 19
Silva, Nelson do Valle
    on black political participation, 27 n. 40
    on discrimination, 68
    on economic development and racism, 233 n. 7
    occupational classification map of, 234
    on race versus class, 26, 29–30, 30 n. 44
    on racial mobilization, 164
    on self-identification, 9, 43, 50
single motherhood, 180, 182–83, 184, 191
Skidmore, T. E., 7, 18 n. 25, 40
slavery
    impact on family life, 180–81
    impact on labor market, 111
    reparations for, 18, 18 n. 26
Sniderman, P., 151
Soares, Sebastião, 163
Sobrados e Mucambos (*The Mansions and the Shanties*) (Freyre), 230, 247–48, 247 n. 16
socialismo moreno, 15
social mobility, race and, 67
Social Progressive Party (Partido Socialista Brasileiro), 14

Sociedade de Intercâmbio Brasil-Africa, 160
socioeconomic level
    of candidates in electoral process, 174
    educational achievement and, 54, 58
    educational advancement and, 60–61
    occupational achievement and, 80
    whitening and, 9, 25, 38
    whites and adversity in, 86 n. 7
    See also income
Souza, Amaury de, 27 n. 40
Souza, Herbert de, 10
Souza, Vicente de, 21
Souza-Lobo, E., 157, 157 n. 3
Special Agency in the Fight Against Racism, 120
State Foundation for Data Analysis (Fundação Sistema Estadual de Análise de Dados) (SEADE), 45–46, 84 n. 2
State Intersindical Department for Socioeconomic Studies (Departamento Intersindical de Estudos Sócio-econômicos) (DIEESE), 84 n. 2
statistics
    on class, 29–30
    conviction rates of *negros,* 135–36
    crime, 126, 126 n. 1
    on education, 54–55, 60
    fertility rates, 199, 200–201, 211
    forward-survival estimates, 50
    illiteracy rates, 54–55, 197
    methodology for, 63, 63 n. 4
    mortality rates, 26, 188, 190, 197, 200 n. 2
    on race, 26, 26 n. 39, 51
    school drop-out rates, 61
    See also Instituto Brasileiro de Geografia e Estatística (Brazilian Institute of Geography and Statistics) (IBGE); SEADE (Fundação Sistema Estadual de Análise de Dados) (State Foundation for Data Analysis)
sterilization
    Caesarian sections and, 201–2
    Cardoso on, 204 n. 5
    education and, 210–11
    labor market and, 203
    race and, 202 n. 3
    racial differences in, 208
    racial makeup and, 211–14
    tubal ligations, 33–34, 212, 212 n. 2
    in United States, 196

women and culture of, 33–34
See also contraception; reproductive rights
Stinson, L. H., 2 n. 4
Stolzenberg, R., 77, 80

Tanto preto quanto branco: Estudos de relações raciais (Nogueira), 231 n. 4
Tarrow, S., 155, 156
Teatro Experimental do Negro (Black Experimental Theater) (TEN), 158–59, 161
technicians, definition of, 95 n. 14
Telles, Edward, 149, 232–33
TEN (Teatro Experimental do Negro) (Black Experimental Theater), 158–59, 161
Tiriríca, 28
transnational organization, black movement and, 17–20, 18 n. 25, 23 n. 33, 35
TRE (Tribunal Regional Eleitoral da Bahia) (Regional Electoral Tribunal of Bahia), 169–70
tubal ligations, 33–34, 212, 212 n. 2

unemployment, 84 n. 2, 86 n. 7
UNESCO (United Nations Economic and Social Council)
   antiracism programs of, 152
   Commission of Human Rights' Program of Action to Combat Racial Discrimination, 19–20
   São Paulo school and, 24–25
Unified Black Movement (Movimento Negro Unificado), 15
unions, 14–15, 19, 119–20
United Black Black Movement (Movimento Negro Unificado) (MNU), 160–61, 163, 220
United Nations, 19, 42
United Nations Commission on Human Rights, 22, 23 n. 34
United Nations Economic and Social Council. *See* UNESCO (United Nations Economic and Social Council)
United Nations Nondiscrimination Convention, 19
United States
   affirmative action in, 145–46
   black Americans in, 2–3, 2–3 n. 4
   blacks' educational achievement in, 73
   blacks versus whites in, 124, 125

influence on Brazil, 23 n. 33, 160
reproductive rights in, 195–96, 205
returns to schooling in, 75
United States Information Agency (USIA), 23 n. 33
university education
   criminal justice system and, 125
   electoral process and, 173
   whites versus blacks, 55, 57
USIA (United States Information Agency), 23 n. 33

Valladares, L., 158 n. 5
Valle, A., 171
Velho, Otávio, 4, 4 n. 5
Vianna, Oliveira, 7
Vitorino, Manoel, 18 n. 25

wages. *See* income
Wagley, Charles, 231 n. 4
whitening
   black movement and, 221
   career performance and, 107, 243 n. 14, 244
   criminal justice system and, 129–30
   economic status and, 9, 25, 38
   elites and, 5–6
   Freyre on, 7–8, 247 n. 16
   immigration and, 40
   in labor market, 86, 247
   1991 census and, 47
   scientific racism and, 7, 7 n. 9
   self-identification and, 113
   Silva on, 243 n. 14
   See also censuses; color denominations; *types of color classifications*
whites
   affirmative action and, 151
   in criminal justice system, 132–33
   definition of, 2 n. 3
   education of, 54–55, 57, 61, 63–64, 73, 75, 100, 197
   in electoral process, 174
   income of, 67, 69, 86 n. 7, 105
   income study model for, 70–73
   labor market and, 69, 92, 96, 97–98, 107
   life expectancy of, 188
   occupational achievement and, 78, 102, 103

occupations and, 86, 88, 88 n. 8, 174
workplace discrimination against blacks by,
  121
Williams, Patricia, 33
Wilson, K., 73
Winant, H., 27 n. 41
women
  culture of sterilization and, 33–34
  divorce and, 180, 188
  education of, 90, 92, 100, 192
  in electoral process, 168–69, 172–73,
    176, 176 n. 8
  health of, 33, 211
  ideal family model and, 180
  impact of slavery on, 180–81
  income of, 105
  labor market and, 92–93, 104–5, 106, 108,
    192
  life patterns of, 183–84, 191–92
  motherhood and, 184–87, 190–91 (see also
    single motherhood)
  objectification of white, 222, 223
  occupations and, 172 n. 6
  overeducation of, 101–2
  racial discrimination crimes against, 143
  racial identities of, 32–33
  relationship to black men, 34, 222, 224
  rights of, 165 n. 18, 227
  self-identification and, 50
  as wives, 188, 190, 192
  See also families; feminists; gender;
    reproductive rights; women's movement
Women, Race, and Class (Davis), 195–96

women's movement
  background of, 218–19
  black movement and, 220–21
  black women's movement and, 224, 226
  future of, 219–20
  gains of, 219
  See also feminists
Women's Police Stations, 219
Wood, C. H., 9, 26, 50, 51 n. 13
Workers' Party (Partido dos Trabalhadores)
  (PT), 16, 17, 21, 171 n. 5
Working Group on the Elimination of
  Occupational and Employment
  Discrimination, 19, 26, 120–21
workplace
  discrimination in, 30–31, 88, 121
  employment mobility and discrimination
    in, 115–17
  gender discrimination and, 30
  on-the-job discrimination in, 114–15
  organizing strategies against discrimination
    in, 118–21
  recruitment discrimination in, 114–15
  study methodology for discrimination in,
    112–13
  See also labor market

Xavier, Arnaldo, 223

"yellow" classification, 43, 45, 55 n. 2, 70,
  229 n. 1

Zimmerman, Ben, 231 n. 4